SELECTED WORKS OF MODERN CHINESE LEARNING

COTTON INDUSTRY AND TRADE IN CHINA

H. D. Fong

商務印書館
SINCE1897 The Commercial Press

2014 • BEIJING

First Edition 2014

ISBN 978-7-100-08958-6

Published by
The Commercial Press
36 Wangfujing Road, Beijing 100710, China
www.cp.com.cn

H. D. Fong

(1903—1985)

Editorial Note

One hundred years ago, Zhang Zhidong tried to advocate Chinese learning by saying: "The course of a nation, be it bright or gloomy, the pool of talents, be it large or small, are about governance on the surface, and about learning at the root." At that time, the imperialist powers cast menacing eyes on our country, and the domestic situation was deteriorating. The quick infiltration of Western learning made the long-standing Chinese tradition come under heavy challenge. In those days, Chinese learning and Western learning stood side by side. Literature, history and philosophy split up, while many new branches of learning such as economics, politics and sociology were flourishing, which made many Chinese dazed. However, there appeared a vital and vigorous learning climate out of the confusing situation. It was at this critical moment that modern Chinese scholarship made the transition—by exchanging views, basing on profound contemplation and even with confrontation of idea and clash of views, the scholarship made continuous progress, bringing up a large number of persons of academic distinction and creating numerous innovative works. Changes in scholarship and in general modes of thinking made transition in all aspects of the society possible, thus laying a solid foundation for revitalizing China.

It's over a century since the journey of modern Chinese learning started, during which various schools of thought stood in great numbers, causing heated discussions. The journey sees schools of thought as well as relevant arguments rising and falling, waxing and waning instantly, leaving complicated puzzles to followers. By studying and reviewing the selected works, one may gain new insights into that journey; and it is the editor's sincere hope that readers would ponder over the future by recalling the past. That's why we have compiled "Selected Works of Modern Chinese Learning". The effort includes masterpieces of celebrated scholars from diverse fields of study and different schools of thought. By tracing back to the source and searching for the basis of modern Chinese learning, we wish to present the dynamics between thought and time.

The series of "Selected Works of Modern Chinese Learning" includes works (both in Chinese and in foreign languages) of scholars from China—mainland, Hong Kong, Macau, and Taiwan—and from overseas. These works are mostly on humanities and cover all fields of subjects, such as literary theory, linguistics, history, philosophy, politics, economics, jurisprudence, sociology, to name a few.

It has been a long-cherished wish of the Commercial Press to compile a series of "Selected Works of Modern Chinese Learning". Since its foundation in 1897, the Commercial Press has been privileged to have published numerous pioneering works and masterpieces of modern Chinese learning under the motto of "promoting education and enlightening people". The press has participated in and witnessed the establishment and development of modern Chinese learning. The series of "Selected Works of Modern Chinese Learning" is fruit of an effort to relay the editorial legacy and the cultural propositions of our senior generations. This series, sponsored by National Publication Foundation, would not be possible if there were no careful planning of the press itself. Neither would it be possible without extensive collaboration among talents of the academic circle. It is our deeply cherished hope that titles of this series will keep their place on the bookshelves even after a long time. Moreover, we wish that this series and "Chinese Translations of World Classics" will become double jade in Chinese publishing history as well as in the history of the Commercial Press itself. With such great aspirations in mind, fearing that it is beyond our ability to realize them, we cordially invite both scholars and readers to extend your assistance.

Editorial Department of the Commercial Press

December 2010

CONTENTS FOR VOLUME I

A LIST OF ILLUSTRATIONS

Page

A LIST OF TABLES

Page

Page

PREFACE

The rapid spread of industrialization in China since the World War, and the manifold effects which it gives rise, have been a subject of considerable interest among the Chinese and foreign economists and social reformers. A good deal of prophesizing, on the basis of the Western experience, has already issued forth from the press at home and abroad, and the consensus of opinion seems to have been that China, endowed with a wealth of human and natural resources, holds the brightest prospect for immediate industrialization. Such an industrialization, it is hoped, will, on the one hand, relieve the pressure of over-population and raise the general standard of living in China, and, on the other, absorb the world's surplus production. While much prophesizing has proceeded along this line of reasoning, little information of a scientific character is as yet available on the extent and effects of China's industrialization. Realizing the importance and the need for more concrete data on the subject. The *Nankai University Committee on Social and Economic Research,* now the *Nankai Institute of Economics,* decided in 1929 to make a field survey of the industrialization in China for some sample district. Tientsin, as one of the leading industrial and commercial centres, constitutes a region by itself for the purpose. It is chosen in preference to other industrial and commercial centres because of the *Institute's* location in Tientsin and of the facilities it offered.

The *Institute* began its work for field investigation, as well as the compilation of data papers, on the first of June, 1929. The first data paper on *The extent and effects of industrialization in China* was published in 1929, and revised under the new title *China's industrialization, a statistical summary* in 1931. In the latter year another data paper on the *Industrialization and labor in Hopei* was issued under the auspice of the *Conference on People's Livelihood* in Shanghai. The field investigation, chiefly on the two types of industries in Tientsin, the handicraft industry representing the old economic order and the factory industry the new one, is turned over to my charge. Thus far three reports on the handicraft industries in Tientsin have been issued, namely, *Tientsin carpet industry, Hosiery knitting in Tientsin,* and *Rayon and cotton weaving in Tientsin.* Among the factory industries the samples chosen include the cotton manufacturing and the flour milling. The report on the flour milling is still in the course of preparation, while that on the cotton manufacturing is embodied in the present report on the *Cotton industry and trade in China.*

In this connection, it remains to be explained that the scope for the present report is not confined to Tientsin, but extended to the country at large. The widening of the scope is based on several considerations. In the first place, cotton industry, unlike the handicraft industries, is more localized. While Tientsin is one of the few favored spots for the industry, Shanghai is by far the largest centre. A study of the industry in Tientsin without reference to Shanghai and other centres gives obviously an incomplete picture. Secondly, cotton industry, the largest factory industry of China to-day, has not yet been treated satisfactorily. As shown in the bibliography to the present report, most of the information now available on the subject are either too brief or too specialized. Of the former may be mentioned *China's cotton industry* by D. K. Lieu and *Cotton industry of Japan and China* by Arnold Pearse; of the latter may be mentioned *A study of the standard of living of working families in Shanghai* by Simon Yang, *Report of the Cotton Mission* by the British Economic Mission to the Far East, and *Marketing of cotton in Hopei Province* by T. S. Chu. Besides, much information may be found, in Chinese and foreign languages, in scattered sources,—in periodicals such as the *Chinese Economic Journal, Foreign Trade Guide, Social Monthly* (Shanghai), and *China Weekly Review*, and in treatises such as the *East India Company Trading to China* by H. B. Morse, and the *Annual Reports* on labor disputes, wages and hours of work by the Shanghai Bureau of Social Affairs. With these considerations in mind, I have decided to broaden the scope of my investigation on the cotton industry, which is well indicated by the title for the present report.

I wish to take this opportunity of acknowledging my indebtedness to all those who have helped one way or the other towards the completion of this study. Although two of the six mills in Tientsin have failed to comply with the *Institute's* request for investigation, the other four mills have offered us necessary facilities in a very cordial spirit. The managers and staff members, in particular, have placed us under deep obligation with their much needed assistance in hunting up accounts and records, which, in Chinese mills, are seldom preserved for any length of time. The initiative and resourcefulness of my investigators, Messrs. H. C. Wang, Y. C. Hang, S. S. Li, Y. Y. Chuan, Z. W. Wang, C. Wang and T. L. Shang, have contributed a great deal towards the completion of the study, in making necessary connections and in collecting the field data. The tedious process of computation and tabulation of the data is left to Messrs. Y. T. Hu, C. T. Lin and Wellington Lee, while Messrs. T. S. Yen and Y. C. Hu have helped to design and trace the various charts under the able direction of Mr. Tayeh Wu. Professors S. L. Yao and C. C. Lien, of the

Accounting Department of the *School of Commerce*, have freely given their knowledge on the analysis of the financial statements of the Tientsin mills. Mr. W. L. Holland, Acting Research Secretary of the *Institute of Pacific Relations*, has kindly read over the manuscript, and has made several important suggestions. Dr. J. B. Condliffe, for a long time the Research Secretary of the *Institute of Pacific Relations* and now member of the *Economic and Financial Section* of the *League of Nations* and Professor James T. Shotwell of the *Columbia University*, erstwhile chairman of the International Research Committee of the *Institute of Pacific Relations*, have helped considerably in promoting the general interest in the *Tientsin industrialization project*, and in securing for it a generous grant from the *Institute of Pacific Relations*. Dr. Franklin L. Ho, above all others, has a large share in the suggestion of the project, as well as in the completion of it. As the Director of the Institute, he has assigned to himself many of the administrative and other duties which would have interfered with my investigation and research. His deep interest in the whole project, and his invaluable advice during the various stages in the progress of the present study, have all along been the chief source of my inspiration.

H. D. Fong

Nankai Institute of Economics
Nankai University, Tientsin
July, 1932.

Standards of weights and measures vary all over the country, despite the new *Law of Weights and Measures* of Feb. 16, 1929 officially adopting the metric system. For our purpose we may note only those commonly recognized units referred to in this study (For details see Chinese Maritime Customs: *Tables of Equivalent Weights and Measures*, Shanghai, 1931).

Chinese weights and measures

Length:—			
10 Ts'un	= 1 Ch'ih	= 0.32 metre	= 1.045 feet
1,800 Ch'ih	= 1 Li	= 576 metres	= 0.358 mile
Area:—			
10 Fên	= 1 Mow	= 6.144 ares	= 0.1518 acre
Money weights:—			
10 Li	= 1 Fên (candareen)		
10 Fên	= 1 Ch'ien (mace)		
10 Ch'ien	= 1 Liang (tael)	= 37.301 grammes	= 575.6 grains
16 Liang	= 1 Chin (catty)	= 569.816 grammes	= 1.316 lbs. avdp.

Treaty or Haikwan weights

10 Li	= 1 Fên		
10 Fên	= 1 Ch'ien		
10 Ch'ien	= 1 Liang	= 37.7994 grammes	= 583.3 grains
16 Liang	= 1 Chin (catty)	= 604.79 grammes	= 1.33 lbs. avdp.
100 Chin	= 1 Tan (picul)	= 60.479 kilogrammes	= 133.33 lbs. avdp.

The currencies in China are most confusing, and we need to note only those commonly recognized units referred to in this study (For details see Kann's *Currencies of China*, Shanghai, 1926).

Taels in China

Name	Fineness in pure silver	Fineness in sycee silver	Weight in grammes	Weight in grains
Haikwan tael	1.000		37.80	583.3
Kuping tael	.923	.987	37.24	574.6
Sycee tael	.935	1.000		
Shanghai tael	.917	.980	36.61	564.9

A yuan or dollar, with a nominal fineness of 0.9, weighs 72 candareen in Kuping taels (see money weights referred to above), i.e. 26.86 grammes or 414.4 grains; it has a nominal silver content of 24.17 grammes or 373 grains. Theoretically speaking, a Haikwan tael, with 583.3 grains of silver, is worth 1.56 Chinese dollars.

Recently, a customs gold unit is adopted which is equivalent to 40 cents U. S. currency. One gold dollar is worth 2.5 gold units, and one pound sterling is worth 12.1664 gold units.

Cotton Industry and Trade in China

CHAPTER I. HISTORY AND LOCALIZATION

History

Cotton spinning and weaving is one of the earliest industries in China. According to the ancient proverb, should one woman fail to spin and weave, the nation at large might have to suffer from the lack of clothing.[1] In old classics we find cotton mentioned as having been used in the manufacture of cloth and given as tribute to the Middle Kingdom as early as between 2197 and 2205 B. C. It has been manufactured into cloth ever since that time and has always been widely used in the fifth century.[2] It is not correct to state, as Mr. Lieu did in his "China's Cotton Industry", that the "cotton plant was first introduced into China from India during the Tang Dynasty (618-907 A.D.), at the same time that Buddhism was introduced."[3]

As a modern industry, however, cotton spinning and weaving had a recent origin. The opening up of China to foreign commerce, after the first Opium War of 1840, introduced the machine-spun yarn in large quantities from England and other European nations, and in considerable degree replaced the hand-spun yarn.[4] As shown in Table 1 the quantity of cotton yarn and thread imported into China increased from the small figure of 33,507 piculs in 1867 to the huge total of 2,748,644 piculs in 1899, an increase of 82 times in the course of 33 years. This total, moreover, is the highest ever attained throughout the whole period, for after 1899 the amount of cotton yarn and thread imported remained stationary, and since 1913 has shown a considerable decline. In 1913 the amount imported reached 2,702,851 piculs, but in 1930 it was reduced to 169,620 piculs, approximately seven percent of the total for 1913. The decline in the quantity of cotton yarn and thread imported, however, does not indicate a similar decline in the consumption of machine spun yarn, but helps to explain the substitution of the imported yarn by the homespun yarn produced by the newly introduced machine spinning industry. That this is the case can be shown very clearly by the rapid increase of raw cotton import since the outbreak of the World War. Whereas in 1913 China's import of raw cotton amounted only to 134,735 piculs, it was rapidly raised to 407,644 piculs in 1916, 678,297 piculs in 1920, 1,780,618 piculs in 1922,

1. 一女不織或爲之寒
2. Fung, D. K.: Cotton culture, in *Chinese Social and Political Science Review*, October, 1916, pp. 97-8.
3. Lieu's assertion is based on a Chinese treatise by Hsu She-yen, entitled *Outline of Chinese Industrial Development*. See Lieu, *China's Cotton Industry*, Shanghai, 1929.
4. cf. *Infra*, Chapter IX. Machine spun yarn was first imported from England in 1821.

Table 1. Net import of raw cotton, cotton Yarn and thread into China, 1867-1930 (1913=100)

Year	Raw Cotton		Cotton Yarn & Thread		Year	Raw Cotton		Cotton Yarn & Thread	
	Piculs	Index	Piculs	Index		Piculs	Index	Piculs	Index
1867	335,976	249.36	33,507	1.24	1899	278,366	206.60	2,748,644	101.69
1868	305,886	227.01	54,212	2.01	1900	134,750	100.01	1,490,732	55.15
1869	193,648	143.73	131,525	4.87	1901	254,855	189.15	2,276,309	84.22
1870	225,414	167.30	52,083	1.93	1902	248,566	184.49	2,452,864	90.75
1871	340,778	252.92	69,816	2.58	1903	59,494	44.16	2,744,974	101.56
1872	207,144	153.74	49,809	1.84	1904	60,057	44.57	2,289,842	84.72
1873	201,045	149.22	67,833	2.51	1905	90,590	67.23	2,569,644	95.07
1874	11,811	8.77	68,819	2.55	1906	45,357	33.66	2,551,027	94.38
1875	169,676	125.93	91,403	3.38	1907	116,307	86.32	2,281,657	84.42
1876	236,918	175.84	112,908	4.18	1908	99,022	73.49	1,831,624	67.77
1877	154,892	114.96	116,163	4.30	1909	114,389	84.90	2,419,404	89.51
1878	106,027	78.69	108,360	4.01	1910	205,915	152.83	2,298,012	85.02
1879	175,534	130.28	137,889	5.10	1911	39,171	29.07	1,877,166	69.45
1880	87,486	64.93	151,519	5.61	1912	279,192	207.22	2,312,528	85.56
1881	137,869	102.33	172,482	6.38	1913	134,735	100.00	2,702,851	100.00
1882	178,478	132.47	184,940	6.84	1914	126,488	93.88	2,559,443	94.69
1883	211,306	156.83	228,006	8.44	1915	364,390	270.45	2,700,592	99.92
1884	187,105	138.87	261,458	9.67	1916	407,644	302.55	2,486,004	91.98
1885	131,404	97.53	387,820	14.35	1917	300,128	222.75	2,102,335	77.78
1886	94,382	70.05	384,582	14.23	1918	190,110	141.70	1,152,881	42.65
1887	173,728	128.94	593,728	21.97	1919	239,003	177.39	1,432,553	53.00
1888	156,579	116.21	684,959	25.34	1920	678,297	503.43	1,345,101	49.77
1889	113,545	84.27	679,728	25.15	1921	1,682,526	1,248.77	1,296,640	47.97
1890	149,562	111.00	1,083,405	40.08	1922	1,780,618	1,321.57	1,242,038	45.95
1891	110,618	82.10	1,212,921	44.88	1923	1,614,371	1,198.18	787,649	29.14
1892	106,635	79.14	1,305,572	48.30	1924	1,219,284	904.95	587,058	21.72
1893	53,419	39.65	983,399	36.38	1925	1,807,450	1,341.49	656,132	24.27
1894	43,103	31.99	1,161,694	42.98	1926	2,745,017	2,037.35	460,230	17.03
1895	44,711	33.18	1,134,110	41.96	1927	2,415,482	1,792.76	304,272	11.26
1896	99,129	73.57	1,624,806	60.11	1928	1,916,140	1,422.15	294,125	10.88
1897	160,256	118.94	1,573,116	58.20	1929	2,514,786	1,866.47	241,819	8.95
1898	229,005	169.97	1,962,537	72.61	1930	3,456,494	2,565.40	169,620	6.28

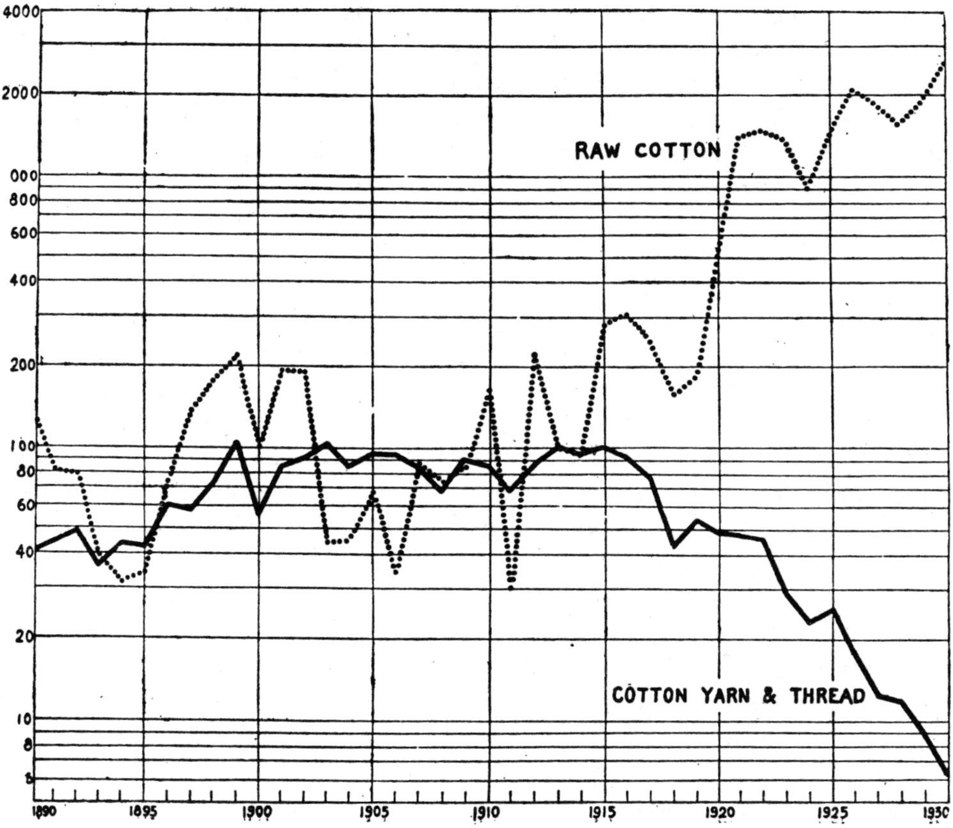

Fig. 1. China's import of raw cotton compared with import of cotton yarn and thread, 1867-1930 (1913=100) (Logarithmic) (*See* Table 1)

2,745,017 piculs in 1926, and 3,456,494 piculs in 1930, the figure for the last year being the highest ever reached since 1967 (Fig. 1).

About ten years before China reached the highest total in her import of cotton yarn and thread, that is, around 1890, the new industry of cotton spinning by power machinery was introduced. Li Hung-chang, the most far-sighted statesman of the Manchu Dynasty, was the first one to organize a mill called the Machine Weaving Mill in Shanghai, in 1888, under the Chinese name of Yang-pu-chu (洋布局). Two years later another cotton factory, the New Spinning and Weaving Mill, was also organized in the same locality, under the Chinese name of Fang-chih-hsin-chu (紡織新局). The building for the Machine Weaving Mill was destroyed by fire in 1891, before the arrival of the machinery. As the Manchu House was unwilling to appropriate more funds for its reconstruction, Li asked Shen Hsuan-hwai (盛宣懷), then Inspector General of the Maritime Customs in Tientsin, to raise private capital for the purpose. At that time the organization of corporations on the basis of share capital was an innovation, and cotton spinning and weaving with modern machinery was another. Consequently, public response was slow towards the new enterprise, and only one third of the authorized capital of 800,000 taels was subscribed. With much perserverance and resourcefulness Shen raised enough money to operate the factory under the name of Hua Shen (華盛) Cotton Mill, with 65,000 spindles and 600 power looms. The Machine Weaving Mill or Yang-pu-chu was therefore the first modern cotton mill in China.[5] It was reorganized several times under the various names of Yu Hsin (又新), Chih Cheng (集成), and is now known as the San Hsin (三新) Cotton Mill. During the Chinese Revolution in 1912 the Mill was registered with the Government of Hongkong as a British mill, as Shen, being a Manchu official, feared the effects of Manchu downfall upon his property. Like the Machine Weaving Mill the New Spinning and Weaving Mill or Fang-chih-hsin-chu was later on reorganized as the Fu Tai (復泰) Cotton Mill, but failed under semi-government ownership. It was then turned over to one of the large shareholders, Mr. Nieh Chung-fu (聶仲甫), and was called the Heng Feng (恆豐) Cotton Mill.[6]

Chang Chih-tung (張之洞), another far-sighted Viceroy of the Manchu Dynasty, organized the Wuchang (武昌) Weaving Mill in 1891 and the Wuchang Spinning Mill in 1894. Both mills, like those in Shanghai, were financed by the government, setting an example for the business men to follow. In 1895 another mill, Ta Shun (大純), was organized in Shanghai. In the same year Yeh Ch'in (業成) was organized in Wusih, and Kwang Hsin (廣新) in Changchow. Meantime, the conclusion of the Treaty of Shimonoseki with Japan, after the Sino-Japanese War of 1894, gave the foreigners the right to establish factories in treaty ports, —a right which was immediately exercised in Shanghai. The British started the Ewo (怡和) Mill in 1895, and the Lao Kung Mow (老公茂) Mill in 1896; the Germans the Jui Chi (瑞記) Mill in 1896; and the Americans the Hung Yuan (鴻源) Mill in 1897. Although some of these foreign owned mills were later transferred to owners of other nationalities,[7] yet their rise must be attributed to the conclusion of the Treaty of Shimonoseki. The Japanese people, who were responsible for the grant of the privilege of establishing factories on the Chinese soil, were not the first to exercise it. Instead, they adopted the policy of purchasing Chinese owned mills. In 1902 both Ta Shun and San Tai (三泰) were transferred from Chinese

5. Kiangsu Industrial Bureau, *The Cotton Spinning and Weaving Industry of Kiangsu*, Commercial Press, Shanghai, 1920, p. 1.
6. *Ibid*, pp. 39-40.
7. Including the transfer of Lao Kung Mow from the British to the Japanese, that of Hung Yuan from the American first to the British and then to the Japanese, that of Jui Chi from the German first to the British and then to the Chinese.

to Japanese ownership, under the new names of Shanghai No. 1 and Shanghai No. 2 respectively.

The conclusion of the Treaty of Shimonoseki in 1895, which introduced many foreign owned mills in Shanghai, gave an impetus to the further organization of Chinese owned mills, not only in Shanghai, but also in the interior. In 1896 San Tai and Yu Yuan (裕源) were organized in Shanghai, Su Lun (蘇倫) in Soochow, and Tung I Kung (通益公) in Hangchow. Three years later Tung Hui Kung (通惠公) was organized in Hsiaoshan (蕭山), and No. 1 of a series of mills under the name of Ta Sheng (大生) was organized in Nantung. After 1899, however, the construction of new mills came to a stop, and was not resumed until 1905, caused partly by the inadequate supply of raw cotton and factory labor, and partly by the lack of credit and transport facilities.

In 1905 the conclusion of Russo-Japanese War presented a prospect for renewed economic activity in the Far East. By that time China had already recovered from the aftermath of the Boxer Uprising in 1900. Up to 1899 there were seventeen mills in China, including 13 mills in Kiangsu (9 in Shanghai, 1 in Wusih, Changchow, Nantung and Soochow respectively), 2 mills in Hupeh (Wuchang), and 2 mills in Chekiang (1 in Hangchow and 1 in Hsiaoshan); but from 1905 to 1913 13 more mills were organized, including 11 mills in Kiangsu (6 in Shanghai, 1 in Wusih, Nantung, Kiangyin, Changshu and Taits'ang respectively), 1 mill in Chekiang (Ningpo) and 1 mill in Honan (Anyang). During these two periods, namely, 1890-1904 and 1905-1913, there was a marked change in the nationality of foreign owned mills. Whereas during the first period 2 British owned mills, 1 German owned mill and 1 American owned mill were established, during the second 2 Japanese owned mills and 1 British owned mill were established. In other words, while the other nationals began to disappear in the establishment of new mills on Chinese soil, the Japanese people commenced to assume an active role. It was also during this period that two Chinese owned mills, Ta Shun and San Tai in Shanghai, were purchased by the Japanese.

With the declaration of World War in 1914, a new era was introduced into the cotton industry of China. The stoppage of foreign supply, and consequently of foreign competition, opened a lucrative field for profit-making to the native manufacturers. To the foreign manufacturers, especially the Japanese, other advantages offer further attractions. In China, low wages and long hours of work, as well as a plentiful supply of raw cotton, help to reduce the cost of production, in addition to which is the exemption from tariff charges. Besides, spinning for direct sale in China saves the expense of transport, and dispenses with the middleman's commission. Indeed, from 1914 to 1925 new mills were erected year after year while old ones were planning for an expansion. During this period a leading part was taken by the Chinese themselves, but the Japanese capitalists played a substantial role. The Japanese owned mills were mostly grouped into large combines with strong financial backing, while the Chinese owned mills, with few exceptions, were independent units poorly financed. During this period 87 mills were organized, of which 53 were owned by the Chinese, 33 by the Japanese, and 1 by the British. Whereas the 53 Chinese mills had a total of 1,768,500 spindles or an average spindleage of 33,368 per mill, the 33 Japanese owned mills had a total of 1,239,156 spindles, or an average spindleage of 37,550 per mill. Again, while 33 Japanese owned mills belonged to 17 companies, 53 Chinese owned mills belonged to 40 companies. Among the Japanese owned mills 4 companies had 2 or more mills each, owning respectively 13 (Naigai Wata 內外), 3 (Japan-China 日華), 2 (Dai Nippon 大康) and 2 mills (Tung Shing 同興). Among the Chinese owned mills 6 companies had 2 or more mills each, owning respectively 5 (Shen Hsin 申新), 4 (Hua Hsin 華新), 3 (Pao Cheng 寶成), 3 (Wing On 永安), 2 (Ta Sheng 大生) and 2 mills (P'u I 溥益). Three of the Chinese owned mills, however, were transferred to Japanese ownship, while one of the Japanese owned mills was transferred to Chinese ownership.[8]

During the third period in the development of China's cotton industry, from 1914 to 1925, the sudden and rapid rise of Japanese owned mills demands further explanation. During this period 33 Japanese owned mills were established, namely, 2 in 1914, 3 in 1917, 2 in 1918, 1 in 1919 and 1920 respectively, 5 in 1921, 8 in 1922, 4 in 1923 and 1924 respectively, and 3 in 1925. Out of these 33 mills, as many as 24 were established after 1920, in a period of only five years. This is due chiefly to the tariff revision of 1918, which became effective on August, 1919. In that revision differences between coarse and fine cotton yarns were recognized, as were differences between coarse and fine cotton piece goods. The revision provided, for instance, a specific duty per picul of Hk. Tls. 1.28 for counts up to and including 17, Hk. Tls. 1.38 for counts 18 to 23, Hk. Tls. 1.90 for counts 24 to 35, Hk. Tls. 2.18 for counts 36 to 45, and an *ad valorem* duty of five percent for counts above 45. The Japanese importers, realising the higher duty that the present revision imposed upon the finer counts of yarn and the potentiality of a further raise that future revisions might create, immediately seized the opportunity to establish more mills in China, so as to dispense with the payment of tariff entirely. This step was wisely taken from the viewpoint of Japanese importers, as could be

8. The Chinese mills included Hua Feng (華豐) with 37,120 spindles, Pao Cheng No. 1 and Pao Cheng No. 2 with 68,432 and 68,432 spindles respectively. The Japanese mill referred to Lung Mow, (隆茂) with 10,432 spindles.

seen from the tariff revisions in 1922, 1928 and 1930, each of which provided a higher schedule of duties on cotton yarn than the preceding tariff.

Counts of cotton yarn	Tariff per picul 1918 Hk. Tls.	1922 Hk. Tls.	1928 Hk. Tls.	1930 G.U.*
17 or below	1.28	2.00	3.00	5.30
18 - 23	1.38	2.20	3.30	5.80
24 - 35	1.90	3.00	4.50	7.90
36 - 45	2.18	3.40	5.10	8.90
Above 45	5%	5%	7½%	7½%

* 1 gold unit is equivalent to 40 cents gold (American currency).

After 1925, China's cotton industry entered into another period of inactivity. The May 30th incident in 1925, which was responsible for most of the 38 strikes during the year, strengthened the workers' demands and ushered in an era of labor unrest in Shanghai mills, especially those of Japanese ownership. The strikes in Shanghai mills. which increased from 2 in 1924 to 38 in 1925, rose still further to 78 in 1926, and dropped only to 55 in 1927. Consequently, only a few new mills were organized, namely, 1 Chinese owned mill in 1926 and 1927 respectively, 1 Japanese owned mill in 1928, 2 Chinese owned mills in 1929, and 5 Chinese owned mills in 1930. On the other hand, many of the old mills, mostly of Chinese ownership, were reorganized, rented or sold. Whereas in 1927 only 1 mill was sold, 4 mills rented, and 2 mills reorganized, in 1928 as many as 8 mills were sold, 7 mills rented, and 1 mill reorganized.[9] Labor trouble, of course, is not the only factor for the reorganization, sale or renting of these mills. During these years from 1926 to 1930 civil strife inflicted untold distress upon China's industrial development. The interruption in the means of transport, as well as the increase in the burden of taxation, crippled almost every industry in China. Meantime, the purchasing power of the nation was considerably reduced in face of a rising cost of living. In Tientsin, the workers' cost of living rose from 100 in 1926 to 108.59 in 1927, 113.29 in 1928, 116.28 in 1929, and 119.02 in 1930; while in Peiping it rose from 100 in 1927 to 101.6 in 1928, 106.5 in 1929 and 109.6 in 1930. In Shanghai where the rise in the workers' cost of living is not so rapid as that in Tientsin until 1930, it rose from 100 in 1926 to 106.7 in 1927, 107.9 in 1929 and 121.8 in 1930, with a slight fall to 102.5 in 1928.[10]

9. In 1928 the Japanese bought 3 Chinese owned mills (Pao Cheng Nos. 1 & 2 and Hua Feng) and 1 British owned mill (Lao Kung Mow); while the Chinese bought 1 German owned mill from the British (Jui Chi or Oriental 東方). In 1929 the Japanese bought 1 Chinese owned mill (Tokwa No. 1 東華第一). For further details, see *Infra*, Vol. II, Appendix II.

10. *Quarterly Journal of Economics and Statistics*, March, 1932, pp. 188-91.

Table 2. Cotton spindles and looms in China classified by nationality of ownership, 1890-1930

	Spindles								Looms							
	Chinese		Japanese		British		Total		Chinese		Japanese		British		Total	
Year	No.	1913=100	No.	1913=100	No.	1913=100	No.	1913=100	No.	1913=100	No.	1913=100	No.	1913=100	No.	1913=100
1890	114,712	17.60					114,712	11.67	1,612	34.79					1,612	17.17
1891	204.712	31.41					204,712	20.83	1,612	34.79					1,612	17.17
1892	204,712	31.41					204,712	20.83	1,612	34.79					1,612	17.17
1893	204,712	31.41					204,712	20.83	1,612	34.79					1,612	17.17
1894	204,712	31.41					204,712	20.83	2,267	48.93					2,267	24.15
1895	221,744	34.03	22,432	9.61	72,312	74.02	316,488	32.20	2,267	48.93	664	18.73	896	74.05	3,827	40.76
1896	324,116	49.74	123,480	52.89	72,312	74.02	519,908	52.90	3,713	80.14	3,046	100.00	896	74.05	7,655	81.53
1897	324.116	49.74	149,608	64.09	72,312	74.02	546,036	55.56	3,713	80.14	3,546	100.00	896	74.05	8,155	86.86
1898	324,116	49.74	149,608	64.09	72,312	74.02	546,036	55.56	3,713	80.14	3,546	100.00	896	74.05	8,155	86.86
1899	416,056	63.84	149,608	64.09	72,312	74.02	637,976	64.91	4,433	95.68	3,546	100.00	896	74.05	8,875	94.53
1900	416,056	63.84	149,608	64.09	72,312	74.02	637,976	64.91	4,433	95.68	3,546	100.00	896	74.05	8,875	94.53
1901	416,056	63.84	149,608	64.09	72,312	74.02	637,976	64.91	4,433	95.68	3,546	100.00	896	74.05	8,875	94.53
1902	416,056	63.84	149,608	64.09	72,312	74.02	637,976	64.91	4,433	95.68	3,546	100.00	896	74.05	8,875	94.53
1903	416,056	63.84	149,608	64.09	72,312	74.02	637,976	64.91	4,433	95.68	3,546	100.00	896	74.05	8,875	94.53
1904	416,056	63.84	149,608	64.09	72,312	74.02	637,976	64.91	4,433	95.68	3,546	100.00	896	74.05	8,875	94.53
1905	484,136	74.29	149,608	64.09	72,312	74.02	706,056	71.84	4,433	95.68	3,546	100.00	896	74.05	8,875	94.53
1906	507,336	77.85	149,608	64.09	72,312	74.02	729,256	74.20	4,433	95.68	3,546	100.00	896	74.05	8,875	94.53
1907	596,084	91.47	149,608	64.09	97,688	100.00	843,380	85.81	4,633	100.00	3,546	100.00	1,210	100.00	9,389	100.00
1908	622,676	95.55	149,608	64.09	97,688	100.00	869,972	88.52	4,633	100.00	3,546	100.00	1,210	100.00	9,389	100.00
1909	651,676	100.00	149,608	64.09	97,688	100.00	898,972	91.47	4,633	100.00	3,546	100.00	1,210	100.00	9,389	100.00
1910	651,676	100.00	172,648	73.95	97,688	100.00	922,012	93.81	4,633	100.00	3,546	100.00	1,210	100.00	9,389	100.00
1911	651,676	100.00	172,648	73.95	97,688	100.00	922,012	93.81	4,633	100.00	3,546	100.00	1,210	100.00	9,389	100.00
1912	651,676	100.00	172,648	73.95	97,688	100.00	922,012	93.81	4,633	100.00	3,546	100.00	1,210	100.00	9,389	100.00
1913	651,676	100.00	233,448	100.00	97,688	100.00	982,812	100.00	4,633	100.00	3,546	100.00	1,210	100.00	9,389	100.00
1914	687,967	105.57	307,048	131.53	153,320	156.95	1,148,332	116.84	4,633	100.00	3,546	100.00	1,900	157.02	10,079	107.35
1915	687,964	105.57	307,048	131.53	153,320	156.95	1,148,332	116.84	4,633	100.00	3,546	100.00	1,900	157.02	10,079	107.35
1916	817,660	125.47	307,048	131.53	153,320	156.95	1,278,028	130.04	5,983	129.14	3,546	100.00	1,900	157.02	11,429	121.73
1917	837,628	128.53	397,448	170.25	153,320	156.95	1,388,396	141.27	6,065	130.91	3,546	100.00	1,900	157.02	11,511	122.60
1918	1,025,772	157.41	423,576	181.44	153,320	156.95	1,602,668	163.07	7,985	172.35	4,346	122.56	1,900	157.02	14,231	151.57
1919	1,173,012	181.00	455,640	195.18	153,320	156.95	1,781,972	181.31	9,495	204.94	4,346	122.56	1,900	157.02	15,741	167.65
1920	1,358,552	208.47	540,752	231.64	153,320	156.95	2,052,624	208.85	9,695	209.26	5,398	152.23	1,900	157.02	16,993	180.99
1921	1,749,468	268.46	902,960	386.79	153,320	156.95	2,805,748	285.48	11,309	244.10	7,453	210.18	1,900	157.02	20,662	220.07
1922	2,061,770	316.38	1,268,344	543.31	153,320	156.95	3,483,434	354.44	13,310	287.29	8,453	238.38	1,900	157.02	23,672	252.12
1923	2,191,120	336.23	1,404,848	601.78	153,320	156.95	3,749,288	381.49	15,465	333.80	8,453	238.38	1,900	157.02	25,818	274.98
1924	2,205,684	388.46	1,553,120	665.30	153,320	156.95	3,912,124	398.05	15,965	344.59	11,367	320.56	1,900	157.02	29,232	311.34
1925	2,256,624	346.28	1,636,156	700.87	153,320	156.95	4,046,100	411.69	16,005	345.46	11,367	320.56	1,900	157.02	29,272	311.77
1926	2,277,104	349.42	1,636,156	700.87	153,320	156.95	4,066,580	413.77	16,005	345.46	11,367	320.56	1,900	157.02	29,272	311.77
1927	2,287,152	350.96	1,636,156	700.87	153,320	156.95	4,076,626	414.79	16,005	345.46	11,367	320.56	1,900	157.02	29,272	311.77
1928	2,287,152	350.96	1,674,844	717.44	153,320	156.95	4,115,316	418.73	16,005	345.46	11,367	320.56	1,900	157.02	29,272	311.77
1929	2,304,592	353.64	1,674,844	717.44	153,320	156.95	4,132,756	420.50	16,005	345.46	11,367	320.56	1,900	157.02	29,272	311.77
1930	2,395,792	367.64	1,674,844	717.44	153,320	156.95	4,223,956	429.78	16,005	345.46	11,367	320.56	1,900	157.02	29,272	311.77

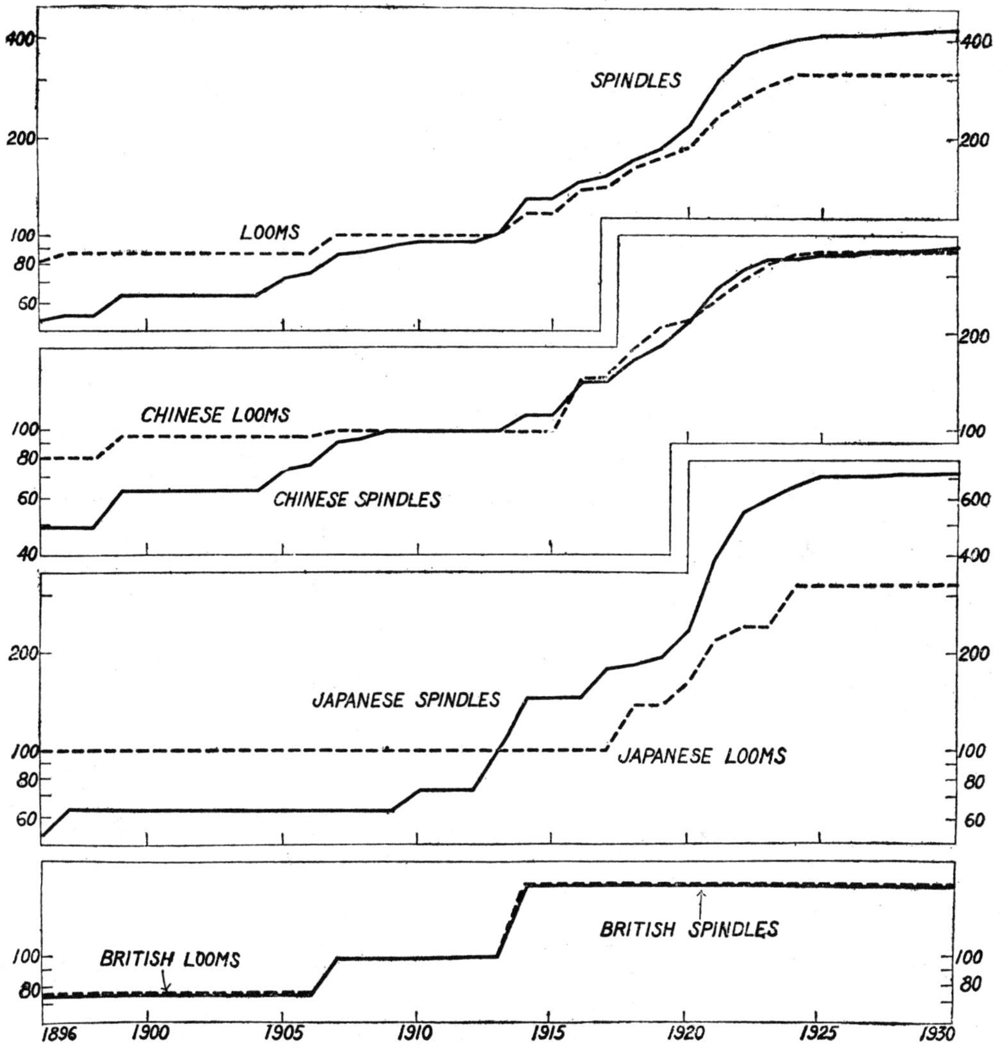

Fig. 2. Growth of spindles and looms in China according to nationality of ownership, 1896-1930 (1913=100) (Logarithmic) (*See* Table 2)

In Table 2 the cotton mills in China in 1930 are classified by the year of establishment, under four different periods, namely, 1890-1904, 1905-1913, 1914-1925, and 1926-1930. Of the 127 mills and 4,223,956 spindles in China in 1930, 17 mills (13.39%) with 637,976 spindles (15.11%) were organized in the first period; 13 mills (10.24%) with 344,836 spindles (8.17%) in the second period; 87 mills (68.50%) with 3,063,288 spindles (72.52%) in the third period; and 10 mills (7.87%) with 177,856 spindles (4.20%) in the fourth period. The third period, extending from 1914 to 1925, is therefore the most important, which witnesses the establishment

Table 3. Estimates on the number of cotton spindles in China, 1889-1930

Year	Lee, B.T.[11]	C.W. Wang[12]	Hsin Wen[13] Pao	Chu, S.F.[14]	D.K. Lieu;[15] Y.T. Yeh	Chinese Economic Bulletin[16]	C.C.M.A.[17]	Probable estimate No.	Probable estimate %	Spindles in Table 2 No.	Spindles in Table 2 %
1889				65,520							
1890				100,912						114,712	2.72
1891		65,000			65,000			65,000	1.54	204,712	4.85
1894	65,000			190,912							
1895				400,590						316,488	7.50
1896	429,609	417,000		440,090	417,000			429,609	10.17	519,908	12.31
1897				515,952				515,952	12.21	546,036	12.93
1899										637,976	15.11
1900				573,352							
1902	509,934	565,000			565,252			509,934	12.07		
1903						1,009,000					
1905										706,056	16.72
1906	640,924			638,152				640,924	15.17	729,256	17.27
1907	755,936			700,608				755,936	17.90	843,380	19.97
1908	784,106			754,828				784,106	18.56	869,972	20.60
1909	821,313			786,828				821,313	19.44	898,972	21.29
1910	824,103							824,103	19.51	922,012	21.84
1911	904,246	831,000		806,828	831,106			904,246	21.41		
1912	885,127							885,127	20.95		
1913	964,032		1,000,000	836,828				964,032	22.82	982,812	23.28
1914	1,023,895		1,050,000	855,196				1,023,895	24.24	1,148,332	27.20
1915	1,090,206		1,000,000	976,620				1,090,206	25.81		
1916	1,121,251	1,145,000	1,250,000	1,228,152	1,145,136			1,121,251	26.55	1,278,028	30.27
1917	1,222,233		1,300,000	1,280,672				1,222,233	28.94	1,388,396	32.88
1918	1,248,591	1,478,000	1,480,000	1,456,012	1,478,926			1,456,012	34.47	1,602,668	37.95
1919			1,530,000	2,366,722				2,366,722	56.03	1,781,972	42.19
1920		1,650,000	1,400,000	3,110,546	1,650,641			3,110,546	73.64	2,052,624	48.60
1921			1,800,000	3,191,546		1,650,000		3,191,546	75.56	2,805,748	66.43
1922			2,344,000	3,266,546	2,452,728	1,888,000		3,266,546	77.33	3,483,434	82.47
1923						2,953,000				3,749,288	88.77
1924					3,537,405	3,381,000	3,645,126	3,645,126	86.30	3,957,124	93.69
1925					3,533,918	3,350,000	3,603,838	3,603,838	85.32	4,046,100	95.80
1926										4,066,580	96.28
1927						3,529,130	3,674,690	3,674,690	87.00	4,076,628	96.52
1928							3,850,016	3,850,016	91.15	4,115,316	97.44
1929										4,132,756	97.84
1930					3,699,000		4,223,956	4,223,956	100.00	4,223,956	100.00

11. Pearse, *Cotton Industry of Japan and China*, 1929, p. 154.
12. *Shanghai Chamber of Commerce Journal*, March, 1922.
13. *Journal of Agriculture and Commerce*, Dec. 15, 1923.
14. *China Cotton Journal*, Jan. 1923, pp. 2-3.
15. *China's Cotton Industry*, p. 5; *Foreign Trade Guide*, Jan. 1931.
16. May 18, 1929.
17. *Annual lists for* ***1924, 1925, 1927, 1928 and 1930***, by Chinese Cotton Millowners' Association, Shanghai.

of 68.50% of the mills with 72.52% of the spindles. In respect of looms, it is also during the third period that the highest percentage, namely, 67.92%, is installed, with 30.32% for the first period but 1.76% for the second.

The interpretation of Table 2, however, is subject to criticism. In classifying the mills, spindles and looms according to the year of establishment, it must be borne in mind that the year of expansion is not taken into account. A mill, for instance, was established in 1919 with 30,000 spindles, but in 1926 another 10,000 spindles were installed. In Table 2 where only the year of establishment is taken into account, the year 1919 is credited with 40,000 spindles, whereas actually only 30,000 spindles were installed during that year. In view of the absence of statistics on the expansion of cotton mills in China, Table 3 is compiled as a check to Table 2. In Table 3 I have assembled the available estimates on the number of spindles in China, from 1890 to 1930. A comparison of Tables 2 and 3 shows that the number of spindles during the first and second period is approximately similar, but during the third and fourth periods there is a difference of about ten percent. This difference can be explained by a further analysis of Table 3. According to that Table, there were 3,850,016 spindles in 1928, but 4,223,956 spindles in 1930. In other words,

	Spindles (in percentage)	
Period	Table 2	Table 3
1890-1904	12.21	15.11
1905-1913	10.61	8.17
1914-1925	62.50	72.52
1926-1930	14.68	4.20
Total	100.00	100.00

373,940 spindles or 8.85% were installed in the course of three years, mostly in those mills which were established during the third period. But according to Table 2 there was an increase of only 108,640 spindles or 2.54% from 1928 to 1930. This discrepancy arises from the fact that Table 3 includes a large number of spindles that were newly installed in 1930, which in Table 2 are distributed to the earlier years according to the practice of classifying the newly installed spindles by the year of the mill's establishment, not by the year of the installation of new spindles. Table 3, which is more fragmentary in character, gives nevertheless a truer picture of the development of China's cotton industry.

In Tables 4a and 4b the cotton mill statistics in China are given for the period from 1924 to 1930, in absolute as well as in relative terms. These statistics are compiled by the Chinese Cotton Millowners' Association in Shanghai, and as pointed out in the chapter on Industrial Organization, are in many respects unsatisfactory. I have, however, revised the statistics for 1930 whenever necessary, so as to give a truer picture of the conditions in the industry. Table 4a shows that from 1925 to 1930 the mills have increased from 125 to 127, the spindles from 3,603,838 to 4,223,956, the laborers from 209,959 to 252,031,

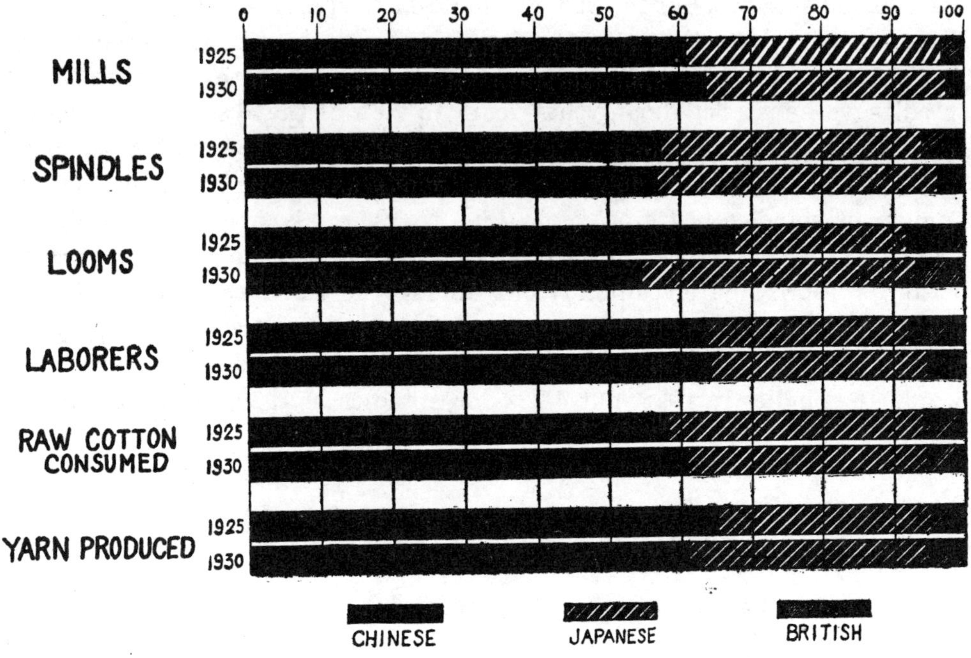

Fig. 3. Distribution of cotton mill statistics in China according to nationality of ownership, 1925 and 1930 (in percentages) (*See* Table 4b)

the raw cotton consumed from 6,776,847 piculs to 8,750,019, and the yarn spun from 1,798,038 bales to 2,445,177; but the looms have decreased during the same period from 30,024 to 29,272. The decrease in the number of looms is, however, nominal, as actually the *operating* looms have increased from 25,934 in 1925 to 28,522 in 1930. In Table 4b the percentage distribution of the cotton mill statistics in China during 1925 and 1930 is given in respect of the nationality of ownership. Little change, except in the larger proportion of looms for the Japanese, has occurred during the interval (Fig. 3). Roughly speaking, the Chinese claim about 60, the Japanese 35, and the British 5 percent of the cotton industry in China.

Table 4a. Cotton mill statistics in China classified by nationality of ownership, 1924-1930

Item	1924 (5th list)				1925 (6th list)				1927 (7th list)				1928 (8th list)				1930 (9th revised list)			
	Chinese	Japanese	British	Total	Chinese	Japanese	British	Total	Chinese	Japanese	British	Total	Chinese	Japanese	British	Total	Chinese	Japanese	British	Total
No. Mills	73	41	5	119	76	45	4	125	73	42	4	119	73	44	3	120	81	43	3	127
Capital & Surplus																				
Taels	47,619,000	11,670,000	14,001,670	73,290,670	40,520,750	6,670,000	13,201,760	60,392,510	46,923,540	38,447,000	13,201,760	98,572,300	35,678,551	33,482,000	9,000,000	78,160,551				
Yen		288,945,000		288,945,000		172,705,000		172,705,000		328,195,700		328,195,700		290,047,707		290,047,707				
Dollars	73,307,800			73,307,800	72,642,245			72,642,245	71,051,692			71,051,692	72,898,712			72,898,712	126,908,222	148,919,916	12,500,000	288,328,138
Dollars (Fengtien currency)					4,600,000			4,600,000	4,600,000			4,600,000	6,500,000			6,500,000				
Spindles	2,176,146	1,218,544	250,516	3,645,206	2,066,214	1,332,304	205,320	3,603,838	2,099,058	1,370,312	205,320	3,674,690	2,181,880	1,514,816	153,320	3,850,016	2,395,792	1,674,844	153,320	4,223,956
Operating	1,812,366	923,728	250,516	2,986,610	1,897,682	1,326,920	205,320	3,429,922	2,084,058	1,369,584	205,320	3,658,962	2,127,440	1,514,816	153,320	3,795,576	2,215,072	1,647,644	153,320	4,016,036
Spinning	1,779,318	923,728	250,516	2,953,562					2,018,588	1,291,952	205,320	3,515,860	2,059,088	1,397,272	153,320	3,609,680	2,146,152	1,462,160	153,320	3,761,632
Doubling	33,048			33,048					65,470	77,632		143,102	68,352	117,544		185,896	68,920	185,484		254,404
Not yet operating	363,780	294,816		658,596	168,532	5,384		173,916	15,000	728		15,728	54,440			54,440	180,720	27,200		207,920
Spinning	348,676	294,816		643,492					15,000	728		15,728	54,440			54,440	180,720	27,200		207,920
Doubling	15,104			15,104																
Looms	13,689	5,925	2,863	22,477	20,171	7,505	2,348	30,024	13,459	13,981	2,348	29,788	16,783	10,896	1,900	29,579	16,005	11,367	1,900	29,272
Operating	9,481	3,929	2,863	16,273	16,381	7,205	2,348	25,934	12,109	9,625	2,348	24,082	13,117	10,801	1,900	25,818	15,255	11,367	1,900	28,522
Not yet operating	4,208	1,996		6,204	3,790	300		4,090	1,350	4,356		5,706	3,666	95		3,761	750			750
Motive power	56,747	16,600		73,347	68,646	69,100		137,746	77,936	51,207		129,143	86,279	54,098		140,377	91,629	63,829		155,457
K. W.	30,107	16,600		46,707	52,041	69,100		121,141	58,556	48,072		106,628	61,431	51,323		112,754	68,363	58,211		126,574
H. P.	35,520			35,520	22,140			22,140	25,840	4,180		30,020	33,130	3,700		36,830	31,021	7,490		38,511
Workers	131,063	45,628	19,000	195,691	133,771	59,688	16,500	209,959	138,613	79,427	16,500	234,540	156,298	72,321	13,000	241,619	161,949	77,082	13,000	252,031
Cotton consumed (piculs)	2,457,976	1,644,675	458,000	4,560,651	3,941,272	2,445,575	390,000	6,776,847	4,504,586	2,785,441	390,000	7,680,027	4,946,495	2,927,527	300,000	8,174,022	5,320,692	2,976,000	453,327	8,750,019
Yarn spun (bales)	1,019,718	422,250	31,800	1,473,768	1,169,770	543,718	84,550	1,798,038	1,261,548	690,759	150,522	2,102,829	1,377,788	695,656	129,522	2,202,966	1,500,248	825,407	129,522	2,455,177
Cloth woven (pieces)					3,320,767	680,000		4,000,767	4,259,666	4,739,704		8,999,370	6,900,038	7,758,750		14,658,788	6,625,544	8,153,994		14,779,538

Note: The 1928 and 1930 lists are the original lists issued by the Chinese Cotton Millowners' Association; the 1924, 1925 and 1927 lists are given in the following references:—

1924: *Chinese Economic Bulletin*, Supplement No. 24; *Shanghai Chamber of Commerce Journal*, November, 1924 (in Chinese)

1925: *Chinese Economic Monthly*, February, 1926; *Chinese Weekly Economic Bulletin*, Dec. 12, 19, 1925 (in Chinese)

1927: *Chinese Economic Journal*, April, 1928; *Semi-Monthly Economic Journal*, January, 1928 (in Chinese)

The lists as reproduced in the above references contain many errors, but as each list is reproduced in two references, the one serves as a check for the other. Besides, even the original lists are not always correct, especially in regard to the totals.

Table 4b. Cotton mill statistics in China classified by nationality of ownership, 1924-1930 (In percentages)

Item	1924				1925				1927				1928				1930			
	Chinese	Japanese	British	Total	Chinese	Japanese	British	Total	Chinese	Japanese	British	Total	Chinese	Japanese	British	Total	Chinese	Japanese	British	Total
No. mills	61.34	34.45	4.20	100	60.80	36.00	3.20	100	61.35	35.29	3.36	100	60.83	36.67	2.50	100	63.78	33.86	2.36	100
Spindles	59.70	33.43	6.87	100	57.33	36.97	5.70	100	57.12	37.29	5.59	100	56.67	39.35	3.98	100	56.72	39.65	3.63	100
Operating	60.68	30.93	8.39	100	55.32	38.69	5.99	100	56.96	37.43	5.61	100	56.05	39.91	4.04	100	55.16	41.03	3.81	100
Spinning	60.24	31.28	8.48	100					57.41	36.75	5.84	100	57.04	38.71	4.25	100	50.05	38.87	11.08	100
Doubling	100.00			100					45.75	54.25		100	36.77	63.23		100	27.09	72.91		100
Not yet operating	55.24	44.76		100	96.90	3.10		100	95.37	4.63		100								
Spinning	54.18	45.82		100					95.37	4.63		100	100.00			100	86.92	13.08		100
Doubling	100.00			100																
Looms	60.90	26.36	12.74	100	67.18	25.00	7.82	100	45.18	46.94	7.88	100	56.74	36.84	6.42	100	54.68	38.83	6.49	100
Operating	58.26	24.14	17.59	100	63.17	27.78	9.05	100	50.28	39.97	9.75	100	50.81	41.83	7.36	100	53.49	39.86	6.65	100
Not yet operating	67.83	32.17		100	92.67	7.33		100	23.66	76.34		100	97.47	2.53		100	100.00			100
Motive power	77.37	22.63		100	49.84	50.16		100	60.35	39.65		100	61.46	38.54		100	58.94	41.06		100
K. W.	64.46	35.54		100	42.96	57.04		100	54.92	45.08		100	54.38	45.52		100	54.01	45.99		100
H. P.	100.00			100	100.00			100	86.08	13.92		100	89.95	10.05		100	80.55	19.45		100
Workers	66.97	23.32	9.71	100	63.71	28.43	7.86	100	59.10	33.87	7.03	100	64.69	29.93	5.38	100	64.25	30.58	5.16	100
Cotton Consumed	53.90	36.06	10.04	100	58.16	36.09	5.75	100	58.65	36.27	5.08	100	60.51	35.82	3.67	100	60.81	34.01	5.18	100
Yarn spun	69.19	28.65	2.16	100	65.06	30.24	4.70	100	59.99	32.85	7.16	100	62.54	31.58	5.88	100	61.11	33.62	5.27	100
Cloth woven					83.00	17.00		100	47.33	52.67		100	47.07	52.93		100	44.83	55.17		100

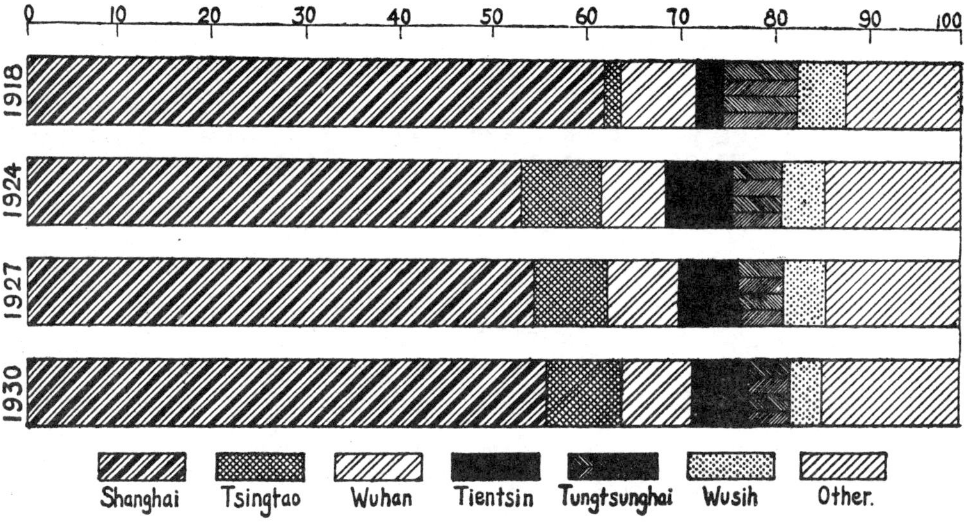

Fig. 4. Distribution of cotton spindles in China by cities, 1918-1930 (in percentages) (*See* Table 5b)

Localization

Cotton centres:—The cotton industry in China is a highly localized business. As shown in Tables 5a and 5b, the province of Kiangsu is comparable to Lancashire in respect of localization. In 1918 this province claimed as much as 80.32% of the total spindleage in China, and even after other provinces have begun to develop their own mills, Kiangsu's share in China's cotton industry does not tend to decrease. Briefly, its percentage since 1924 has been as follows: 66.11 in 1924, 66.30 in 1927, and 66.42 in 1930. Hupeh, with 7.80% of China's total spindleage in 1918, used to rank after Kiangsu. As its percentage since 1918 has remained rather stationary, being 6.69 in 1924, 7.82 in 1927, and 7.33 in 1930, its position as the second cotton spinning province is now relegated to Shantung. The latter, with only 1.73% of China's total spindleage in 1918, increased its share to 8.58% in 1930. Hopei, the fourth cotton spinning province, had only 2.60% of China's total spindleage in 1918, but 7.26% in 1930. Liaoning, with 3.38% of China's total spindleage in 1930, ranks as the fifth province, while Chekiang, the third province in 1918, is now reduced to the sixth place. Chekiang, with 4.79% of China's total spindleage in 1918, claimed only 1.45% in 1930. In Table 5b the spindles in China from 1918 to 1930 are further distributed by cities (Fig. 4). This table shows that six cities claim about 85 percent of the total spindles in China. In 1930 the percentage is 55.79 for Shanghai, 7.88 from Tsingtao, 7.33 for Wuhan, 5.70 for Tientsin, 4.42 for Tungtsunghai, and 3.36 for Wusih—a

Table 5a. Geographical distribution of spindles in China's cotton industry, 1918-1930

Province or City	1918 Operating	1918 Not yet operating	1924 Operating	1924 Not yet operating	1925 Operating	1925 Not yet operating	1927 Operating	1927 Not yet operating	1928 Operating	1928 Not yet operating	1930 Operating	1930 Not yet operating
Kiangsu	927,238	70,000	1,974,398	378,644	2,333,602	33,832	2,425,950	728	2,510,736	29,440	2,667,650	107,120
Shanghai	713,658	50,000	1,581,290	316,104	1,914,294	8,432	1,985,678	728	2,071,560	28,800	2,240,634	30,000*
Wusih	59,192		136,680	8,800	138,800	10,400	150,800		150,800		134,800[23]	107,120
Tungtsunghai	91,380	20,000	153,620	29,000	171,960	11,000	176,924		176,924	640	177,564	30,000*
Other	63,008		102,808	24,740	108,548	4,000	112,548		111,452[20]		114,652	
Soochow	22,568		22,568		22,568		22,568		22,568		28,168	
Changchow			29,800	9,740	35,540	4,000	39,540		35,804[20]		33,404[21]	
Kiangyin	15,000		15,000		15,000		15,000		15,000		15,000	
Ch'angshu	12,740		12,740		12,740		12,740		12,740		12,740	
Taichang	12,700		22,700		22,700		22,700		25,340		25,340	
Jukao				15,000								
Hupeh	90,000	30,000	199,816	48,080	277,472	9,000	286,216		290,152		294,470	29,600
Wuhan	90,000	30,000	199,816	48,080	277,472	9,000	286,216		290,152		294,470	9,600
Shasi												20,000
Hopei	30,000	25,000	253,396	58,472	229,348[22]	58,440	285,356		289,756		291,756	
Tientsin	30,000	25,000	207,580	46,072	179,200	46,040	222,808		226,808		228,808	
Other			45,816	12,400	50,148	12,400	62,548		62,948		62,948	
Tangshan			24,000		24,300		24,300		24,700		24,700	
Shihchiachuang			20,736		24,768		24,768		24,768		24,768	
Paoti			1,080	12,400	1,080	12,400	13,480		13,480		13,480	
Shantung	20,000	10,000	276,000	73,000	294,188	384	307,916		323,780		344,468	27,200
Tsingtao	20,000		250,000	73,000	268,188	384	281,916		297,780		316,468	27,200
Tsinan		10,000	26,000		26,000		26,000		26,000		28,000	
Liaoning			96,360	20,000	94,392[19]		95,544		125,544		135,764	
Mukden			20,000		21,368		21,368		21,368		21,368	
Dairen			20,000	20,000	17,664[19]		18,816		18,816		19,836	
Liaoyang			31,360		31,360		31,360		31,360		31,360	
Chingchow			25,000		24,000[19]		24,000		54,000		63,200	
Chekiang	55,260		46,120	3,640	46,120	3,640	57,760		58,120		58,120	
Ningpo	23,200		23,200		23,200		23,200		23,200		23,200	
Hangchow	20,060[18]		12,000		12,000		20,000		20,360		20,360	
Hsiaoshan	12,000[24]		10,920	3,640	10,920	3,640	14,560		14,560		14,560	
Hunan		40,000	30,000	10,000	40,000		40,000		40,000		40,000	
Changsha		40,000	30,000	10,000	40,000		40,000		40,000		40,000	
Shansi				12,800	9,600	9,240	19,640		19,648		39,648	14,000
Yutsu				12,800	9,600	3,200	13,600		13,600		33,600	
Hsinkiang						6,040	6,040		6,048		6,048	14,000
Anhwei			15,200		15,200		15,200		15,200		15,200	
Wuhu			15,200		15,200		15,200		15,200		15,200	
Kiangsi				15,360		15,360	15,360		15,360	10,000	20,480	
Kiukiang				15,360		15,360	15,360		15,360	10,000	20,480	
Honan	32,000		95,240	23,600	90,000	29,020	110,020		107,280		107,280	
Anyang	32,000		28,000	10,000	28,000	10,000	29,000		29,000		29,000	
Chenchow			41,840[25]		34,560	17,280	51,840		53,000		53,000	
Wuchih			5,400	1,600	5,040	1,740	6,780		2,800[26]		2,880	
Chihhsien			10,000	12,000	22,400		22,400		22,400		22,400	
Sinkiang											1,200	
Dihhua											1,200	
Shensi				15,000		15,000		15,000*		15,000*		
Weipei				15,000		15,000		15,000*		15,000*		
Total	1,154,498	175,000	2,986,530	658,596	3,429,922	173,916	3,658,962	728	3,795,576	39,440	4,016,036	177,920
								15,000*		15,000*		30,000*

*Not operating or suspended.

18. Tung I Kung, which under the name of Ting Hsin had 20,060 spindles in 1918, had only 12,000 spindles in 1924. 19. The reduction of spindles in Liaoning from 96,360 in 1924 to 94,392 in 1925 was caused by the reduction of spindles in Dairen and Chingchow. 20. The reduction of spindles in Changchow from 39,540 in 1927 to 35,804 in 1928 was caused by the reduction of spindles in Shen Hsin No. 6 from 18,200 in 1927 to 14,264 in 1928. Meantime, the spindles in Tung Cheng increased by 200. 21. The spindles for Kwang Hsin which amounted to 5,600 in 1928, were reduced to 3,200 in 1930 under the new name of Fu Ta.. 22. The reductfon was chiefly caused by the fact that whereas in 1924 Yu Yuan mill reported a total operating spindles of 70,000, in 1925, the operating spindles were reduced to 39,800, with 40,200 spindles not operating. 23. The reduction of spindles from 150,800 in 1928 to 134,800 in 1930 was caused by the suspension of 30,000 spindles. 24. The increase of spindles from 10,920 to 12,000 is evidently an error, as can be seen from the data for the following year. 25. 17,280 spindles are not operating, as can be seen from the data for the following year. 26. The spindles for Cheng Shing mill were reduced from 6,780 in 1927 to 2,880 in 1928.

Table 5b. Geographical distribution of operating spindles in China's cotton industry, 1918-1930 (in percentages)

Province or city	1918	1924	1925	1927	1928	1930
Kiangsu	80.32	66.11	67.94	66.30	66.15	66.42
Shanghai	61.82	52.95	55.68	54.27	54.58	55.79
Wusih	5.13	4.58	4.06	4.12	3.97	3.36
Tungtsunghai	7.92	5.14	5.03	4.84	4.66	4.42
Other	5.45	3.44	3.17	3.07	2.94	2.85
Hupeh	7.80	6.69	8.12	7.82	7.64	7.33
Wuhan	7.80	6.69	8.12	7.82	7.64	7.33
Hopei	2.60	8.48	6.71	7.80	7.64	7.26
Tientsin	2.60	6.95	5.24	6.09	5.98	5.70
Other		1.53	1.47	1.71	1.66	1.56
Shantung	1.73	9.24	8.60	8.42	8.53	8.58
Tsingtao	1.73	8.37	7.84	7.70	7.85	7.88
Other		0.87	0.76	0.72	0.68	0.70
Liaoning		3.23	2.76	2.61	3.31	3.38
Chekiang	4.79	1.54	1.35	1.58	1.53	1.45
Hunan		1.00	1.17	1.09	1.05	1.00
Shansi			0.28	0.54	0.52	0.99
Anhwei		0.52	0.44	0.42	0.40	0.38
Kiangsi				0.42	0.40	0.51
Honan	2.76	3.19	2.63	3.00	2.83	2.67
Sinkiang						0.03
Total	100.00	100.00	100.00	100.00	100.00	100.00

total of 84.48 percent for the six cities. Because of the special importance that these six cities occupy in China's cotton industry, detailed statistics are compiled for each of the cities in Appendix III.

Factors for localization:—The localization of China's cotton industry in the six cities, especially Shanghai, is the outcome of several factors. These six cities, including Shanghai, Wusih, Tungtsunghai, Tsingtao, Wuhan and Tientsin, are located in the centres of cotton production. The four provinces in which the six cities are located are responsible for a maximum annual output of 90.7% and a minimum annual output of 66.6% of China's cotton crop from 1918 to 1929. In 1929 these four provinces claim 83% of the total cotton crop in China. Kiangsu leads with 32.3%, after which follow Hupeh with 22%, Shantung with 17.3%, and Hopei with 11.4%. For the period 1918 to 1929 these four provinces produce, on the average, an annual cotton crop of 70,500,000 piculs, or 78.2%, which is distributed as follows: 28,523,000 piculs or 31.6% for Kiangsu, 17,894,000 piculs or 19.9% for Hupeh, 14,660,000 piculs or 16.3% for Shantung, and 9,423,000 piculs or 10.4% for Hopei. Besides, some of these six cities are also centres of cotton import. During the period 1912 to 1929, Shanghai and Kiaochow import as much as 18,431,000 piculs or 90% of China's total cotton import from foreign countries, while exporting only 4,633,000 piculs or 13% of China's total cotton export to foreign countries.

Besides the abundance of raw cotton, the availability of coal and electric power constitutes the second factor in the localization of China's cotton industry. Hopei and Shantung, in which the cotton centres of Tientsin and Tsingtao are located, are coal producing provinces. These two provinces produce from the minimum of 28.2% of China's total coal output in 1927 to the maximum of 34.9% in 1924. Kiangsu and Hupeh are not coal producing provinces, but the cotton centres there, Shanghai and Hankow, are large coal importing centres. During the period 1912 to 1929 Shanghai claims 46.5% of China's total coal import, whereas Hankow claims 5.9%.[27] In respect of electric power Kiangsu is also unsurpassed by other provinces. According to a field survey of the electric plants by Mr. C. S. Chang, Kiangsu possesses 149 of the 499 plants in China, with 259,285 kilowatts or 42.2% of the total power capacity (614,860 K. W.). In Shanghai, for instance, is located the largest power plant in China, namely, the Shanghai Power Company, formerly the Electricity Department of the Shanghai Municipal Council, which possesses a total power capacity of 161,000 kilowatts.[28] The latter lets out power to industrial plants, especially to the cotton mills. In July, 1925 when the Department cut off its electric supply on account of the May incident, it was estimated that 450,000 spindles, or 64.7% of the total spindles in Chinese owned mills (696,000), had to suspend operation.[29] In August, 1931, the President of the Company stated that "when it is realized that there are over 60 cotton mills supplied by the Shanghai Power Company, these mills having a capacity of over 2,000,000 spindles and 17,000 looms employing over 130,000 operatives, and that this represents more than half the total spindles installed in China, it will be understood the tremendous part that electricity has had in the development (of Shanghai)".[30]

A third factor in the localization of China's cotton industry is facility of transport. No one of the six cotton centres except Tungtsunghai is not crossed by some of the important railways in China. Shanghai, the chief cotton centre of China, is crossed by two lines, namely, Shanghai-Nanking (1908) and Shanghai-Hankow-Ningpo (1908). The former passes through Wusih, another cotton centre, on the way from Shanghai to Nanking. Tsingtao, the second cotton centre, is the terminus for the Kiao-Tsi Railway (1904). Hankow is crossed by the Peiping-Hankow line (1905) as well as by the Hupeh-Hunan line (1918), while Tientsin

27. *Special Report of the Geological Survey of China* (General Statement on the Mining Industry), No. 2 (1918-25), Table II; No. 3 (1925-28), Table I.
28. *Statistical Monthly*, September, 1929.
29. *Shanghai Chamber of Commerce Journal*, July, 1925.
30. P. S. Hopkins, President of Shanghai Power Company: World's cheapest electricity supplied by Shanghai Power Company, in *China Press*, Aug. 29, 1931.

is crossed by the Peiping-Mukden (1903) and Tientsin-Pukow (1912) lines. These seven lines, it may be noted, have a total length of 4,894 kilometres, which is 32% of the total railway length in China (15,300 kilmetres).[31] Again, for three of the four provinces in which the cotton centres are located, the average number of kilometres of railway per 1,000 square miles is several times higher than that for the country at large. Such average, which is 6.53 kilometres for China as a whole, is 18.30 for Shantung, 18.13 for Kiangsu, 16.66 for Hopei (Chihli) and 5.08 for Hupeh.[32]

In addition to the railways, the cotton centres are surrounded by large navigable rivers. Shanghai is the gateway to the Yangtze Valley, along which are located Wusih on the southern bank and Tungtsunghai on the northern bank; while Wuhan is its central basin. Tientsin is the concentration centre for five noted rivers in Hopei, namely, Peiho, Yungtingho, Tats'ingho, Hsutoho and Yunho, which flow from all parts of the province to meet there under the general name Haiho. Tsingtao, finally, is located on the eastern side of the Kiaochow Bay. Shanghai, Tsingtao, and Tientsin are closely connected by coastal steamers, while Shanghai, Tungtsunghai, Wusih and Wuhan are similarly connected by inland steamers. During the period 1912 to 1929 34.4% of the vessels were registered for inland water steam navigation at the two ports of Shanghai and Hankow. In 1928, 1,099 vessels or 38.4% were so registered, including 734 vessels or 25.6% for Shanghai and 365 vessels or 12.8% for Hankow.

A fourth factor in the localization of China's cotton industry is the presence of a great market. The four provinces in which the cotton centres are located have a population of 125,977,632 which is 26 percent of China's total population (485,163,386), with an area of 261,965 square miles which is 5.5 percent of China's total area (4,786,915 square miles). These four provinces, in other words, have a population density of 481 per square mile. Kiangsu leads with a population density as high as 801 per square mile, —the highest in all China. Shantung, with a density of 466 per square mile, is third; while Hopei, with a density of 450 per square mile, is fourth. Hupeh, with a population density of 341, ranks as ninth. Because of the relatively adequate means of transport that these four provinces possess, the output of the cotton centres reaches the population not only in their own provinces, but also in the neighbouring provinces whose density of population is equally high. Chekiang, Honan, Anhwei, Hunan and Kiangsi have a population density of 508, 426, 361, 356 and 335 re-

31. *Statistics of Railways for* 1924, published by the Ministry of Communications, Part I, Table I; Part II, Table C.
32. *Ibid*, Part II, Table D.

spectively. These five provinces have a population of 131,483,151, which is 27 percent of China's total population, and an area of 340,999 square miles, which is 7.1 percent of China's total area. These five provinces, in other words, have a population density of 386 per square mile.[33]

A fifth factor is the presence of commercial and financial facilities. Four of the six cotton centres are treaty ports, namely, Shanghai, Tientsin, Hankow and Tsingtao (located in the treaty port of Kiaochow). These four ports occupied in 1929 50.07% of China's whole trade, 67.93% of China's direct foreign trade, and 78.51% of China's transit trade. In these ports are to be found many of the largest exporters and importers, whose function in China's cotton industry is to import raw cotton from India and the United States, and meantime to export native cotton yarn and piece goods to the interior as well as abroad, especially to the Strait Settlements. In these ports, the largest financial institutions, such as banks, exchanges, insurance agencies etc., are to be found. Here capital is more abundant, and can be readily obtained at a rate of interest which is decidedly lower than that in the interior. Here fire insurance for the mills can be underwritten by some of the largest agencies at a more reasonable rate of commission. In Shanghai, future trading in cotton and cotton yarn is provided for by the Chinese Cotton Goods Exchange for hedging or speculative purposes. In all these ports, imported cotton, whether from the interior or from other ports, is now carefully inspected by the Cotton Testing House of the Bureau for the Inspection and Testing of Commercial Commodities of the Ministry of Industries, at the payment of a reasonable fee. Adulteration is thus being prevented, and a better quality of cotton is thereby assured to the spinners.

A final factor in the localization of China's cotton industry is the early development of mills. In these six centres, especially Shanghai, the first mills were built. During the first period of China's cotton industry, 13 of the 17 mills were built in four of the six centres, namely, 9 in Shanghai, 2 in Wuhan, and 1 in Wusih and Tungtsunghai respectively. Following this early development 8 of the 13 mills during the second period from 1905 to 1913, 69 of the 87 mills during the third period from 1914 to 1925, and 4 of the 10 mills during the fourth period from 1926 to 1930, were built in these centres. Shanghai, in particular, has maintained its key position in China's cotton industry ever since the establishment of the first two mills in 1890. Today, it is the largest cotton centre in China, and will be for many years to come.

33. Chen, C. M.: A study in China's population statistics, in *Statistical Monthly*, June, 1930.

CHAPTER II. RAW COTTON: I

Production

Factors in cotton culture:—Geographically, the region of cotton culture in China lies between 20° to 40° northern latitude, but east of 110° eastern longitude. The northern limit of cultivation at present follows the course of the Yellow River (the middle part of the Yellow River is located at about 40° N.), which compares favorably with the northern boundary of cotton culture in the United States, namely, 37° N. This difference in the northern boundary for cotton culture is due to the coincidence of the rainfall with summer temperature in North China. The western boundary is roughly limited to 110° E., for west of that meridian the elevation rises above the altitude at which cotton can be profitably cultivated.

Cotton culture, in other words, is limited by three factors, namely, temperature, rainfull and altitude. It is well known to cotton growers that the temperature must be fairly constant during the growing season, a period of six or seven months, at 60° F. or above. In the northern region of the Basin of the Yellow River the isotherm of 60° F. runs northwestward diagonally from 40° N. to 45° N. during the month of May, and the growing season can be maintained as late as October in which month the isotherm 59° F. coincides with the upper course of the Yellow River, the northern limit of the cotton region. In that region the mean temperature is 75° for June, 78° for July and August, and 68° for September, while in the northern cotton limit of the United States it reaches 75° for June, 78° for July, 77° for August, 70° for September, and 60° for October. Hence we may conclude that since in the northern portion of the cotton belt in China the growing season is short, the early varieties are most suitable. The central cotton region in China lies in the Basin of the Yangtze River, where we find a mean isotherm of 57° in April, 60° in May, 78° in June, 82° in July, 80° in August, 74° in September, 64° in October, and 56° in November,—a growing period of about eight months. The southern region of cotton culture, which lies in the Basin of the Sikiang River, has a growing period of nine to ten months, as the mean isotherm here is 60° in March, 68° in April, 75° in May, 82° in June, July and August, 78° in September, 71° in October, 60° in November and 53° in December.

The second factor for cotton culture is rainfall. Along the northern limit of the cotton region the precipitation is in general deficient, but on account of the fertility of the soil in the Basin of the Yellow River, consisting of loess in most regions, cotton cultivation has been fairly successful. The valleys of the Yangtze River and of the Sikiang River are also fertile, with sufficient rainfall. Here the annual rainfall decreases from the south to the north, namely, 79 inches in Pakhoi (21° 29′ N.), 42.7 inches in Amoy (24° 27′ N.), 40.4 inches in Zikawei (31° 12′ N.),

27.3 inches in Tsingtao (36° 4′ N.) and 27 inches in Peiping (39° 57′ N.). It also decreases from the coast to the interior, as shown by the records in the Yangtze Valley, namely, 41 inches in Chinkiang (Long. 119° 30′), 40.8 inches in Wuhu (Long. 118° 22′), 53 inches in Kiukiang (Long. 115° 48′), 51.5 inches in Hankow (Long. 114° 20′), 42.3 inches in Ichang (Long. 111° 19′) and 39.2 inches in Chungking (Long. 104° 11′).

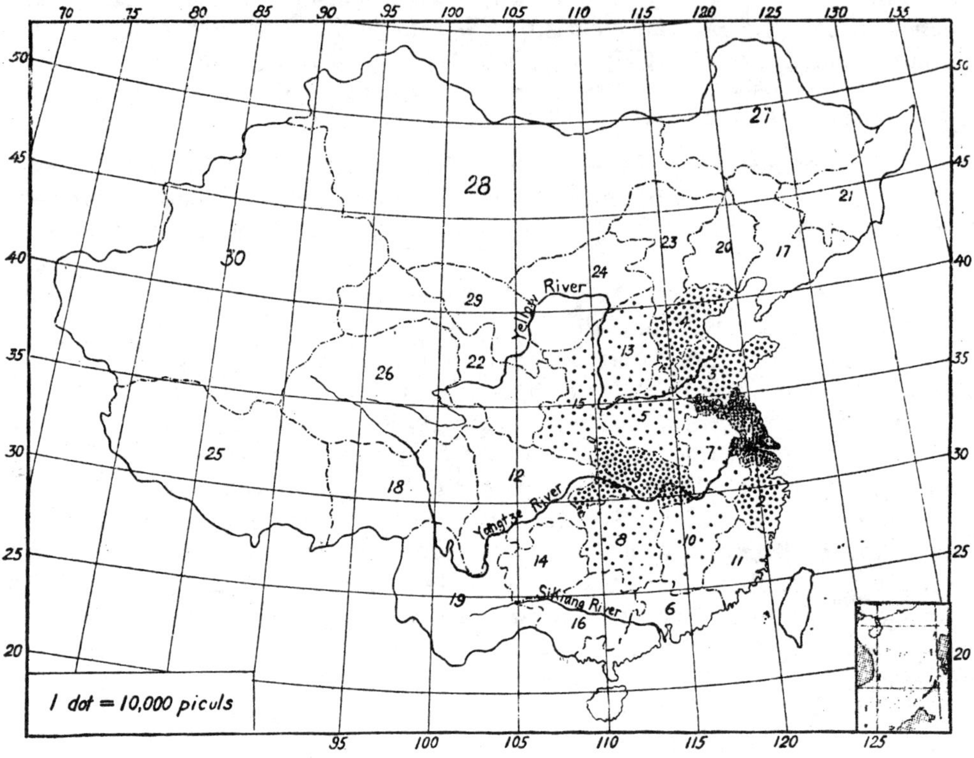

Fig. 5. Map of cotton production in China, annual average, 1925-1929 (*See* Table 6a) The provinces are numbered according to the density of population. The density per square mile is 401 or above for 1-5, 301-400 for 6-11, 201-300 for 12, 101-200 for 13-17, 51-100 for 18-20, 50 or below for 21-30. The density for China as a whole is 101 per square mile. After *Statistical Monthly*, July, 1930.

1. Kiangsu	11. Fukien	21. Kirin
2. Chekiang	12. Szechuen	22. Kansu
3. Shantung	13. Shansi	23. Chahar
4. Hopei	14. Kweichow	24. Suiyuan
5. Honan	15. Shensi	25. Tibet
6. Kwangtung	16. Kwangsi	26. Kokonor
7. Anhwei	17. Liaoning	27. Heilungkiang
8. Hunan	18. Sikong	28. Mongolia
9. Hupeh	19. Yunnan	29. Ninghsia
10. Kiangsi	20. Jehol	30. Sinkiang

The third factor for cotton culture is altitude, which must not exceed the limit of 1,600 feet for the profitable cultivation of cotton. Along the basins of the Yellow River and of the Pei-ho which form the northern region of cotton culture, along the basins of the Sikiang and of the Mingkiang which mark off the southern portion, the altitude ranges from sea level to 600 feet. North of the middle portion of the Yellow River, i.e. the northern limit of the cotton region, the altitude ranges from 3,000 to 6,000 feet, and west of 110 E. Long. we meet with the same condition, except that in some places it rises to 9,000 feet, the beginning of the mountain range of Tibet, where we find the maximum altitude of 16,000 feet, the roof of the World.[1]

Area and crop:—Among the three regions of cotton cultivation in China, two thirds of Chinese cotton are grown in the central region, and another third in the northern region, while the southern region, because of the competition of silk and tea, grows little cotton that enters into domestic or foreign trade. The cotton region, in other words, is confined chiefly to that portion of China lying between 28° to 40° in the northern latitude. In the central region, along the Basin of the Yangtze River, there are six provinces producing 4,816,000 piculs of lint cotton during the season 1929-1930, or 68.5 percent of the total production, the other 2,211,000 piculs or 31.5 percent being produced by another five provinces in the northern region, along the Basin of the Yellow River. In terms of area of cultivation, 24,741,000 *mow* or 75.1 percent of the total area belong to the central region, and 8,212,000 *mow* or 24.9 percent belong to the northern region. The yield per *mow*, therefore, is higher for the northern (26.9 catties per *mow*) than that for the southern region (15.5 catties per *mow*), due mainly to the fact that in northern region more "foreign cotton" with greater yield is grown.[2]

Of the 31.5 percent of cotton produced in the northern region during the season 1929-1930, Shantung contributed 1,213,000 piculs or 17.3 percent; Hopei 801,000 piculs or 11.4 percent; and the other three provinces, namely, Honan, Shansi and Shensi, 197,000 piculs or 2.8 percent. In Shantung cotton is grown in three sections, namely, eastern section with Pin hsien (濱縣) (along the Yellow River) as the centre, western section with Linch'ing (臨清) (along the Grand Canal) as the centre, and southern section with Tsao hsien (曹縣) as the centre. Among these sections the western section is the most important, followed by the eastern and southern sections. The Chinese cotton, known as small cotton, is more popular than the American cotton known as large cotton. The former has

1. Fung, H.K.: Cotton Culture, in *Chinese Social and Political Science Review*, Oct., 1916, pp. 97-105.
2. *Statistics of Cotton Production in China*, 1929, published by the Chinese Cotton Millowners' Association, Shanghai, 1930.

several varieties called white cotton, purple cotton, long staple, short staple, green stalk etc., while the latter is chiefly of the Trice type. In Hopei cotton is grown in three sections, namely, Hsi-ho (西河) in the west, Tung-ho or Yü-ho (御河) in the east, Tung-pei-ho (東北河) in the northeast of the province, of which the first is the most important and the last the least important. In these sections Chinese and American cottons are grown, and are generally named after the place of production. In the Hsi-ho section cocoon cotton is the principal variety, in addition to which there are purple cotton and large cotton,—a deteriorated variety of the American cotton. The American cotton is of the Trice type, grown in all of the three sections, especially in the Tung-pei-ho section.[3] In Honan American cotton is also grown, chiefly in Shen hsien, (陝縣) Lingpao (靈寶), Mengtsin (孟津) and Hsinhsiang (新鄉), and is generally known as the Lingpao or "German cotton"—German in the sense of high grade. Chinese cotton has several varieties including white, purple, cocoon, long staple etc. In Shensi cotton cultivation is confined to the valley of Wei River, (渭水), where American cotton of the Trice variety has been so successfully cultivated in recent years that its Chinese name, Shensi cotton, commands the best price in the market. Chinese cotton, however, is little grown here. In Shansi cotton cultivation is carried on in the Hotung district (河東道), where three varieties of cotton are grown, namely, native, Shensi and American. The last variety is of three types, namely, Lonestar, Trice and Acala.

Of the 68.5 percent of cotton produced in the central region during the season 1929-1930, Kiangsu contributed 2,277,000 piculs or 32.4 percent; Hupeh 1,548,000 piculs or 22 percent; Chekiang 408,000 piculs or 5.8 percent; Hunan 394,000 piculs or 5.6 percent; and the other two provinces, Kiangsi and Anhwei, 189,000 piculs or 2.7 percent. In this region, there are two principal cotton producing sections, namely, Kiangche (Kiangsu and Chekiang) and Lianghu (Hupeh and Hunan). In Kiangsu cotton cultivation is confined to the two sides of the Yangtze River, the northern side including Nantung, Haimen and Tsungming and the southern side including Kiangyin, Changshu, Taich'ang, Chiating, Paoshan, Shanghai and Fengyi (奉賢). In both sections, Chinese cotton only is grown, and is often named after the place of production. Kiangyinsha, the best grade, is produced near Kiangyin. Shanghai or Taich'ang cotton is also well known, being consumed largely by the Shanghai mills, but its grade is rather low. Tungchow cotton, which is grown in Nantung and vicinity, has until recently been accepted as the basis cotton for spot and future trading. In Chekiang the growth of cotton is a recent development, for it is essentially a silk province. Here cotton cultivation is centred in

3. Chu, T.S. and Chin T.: *Marketing of Cotton in Hopei Province*, 1929, Peiping, pp. 3-5.

Yuyao and vicinity, for which reason Chekiang cotton generally goes under the popular term "Yuyao cotton." Hupeh, the second largest cotton province in China, centers its cotton cultivation along the two rivers, the Han River and the Yangtze River. Three varieties of Chinese cotton, namely, iron seed, white seed and green seed, are grown, although American cotton, due to increasing demand for long staple, has become rather popular recently among the farmers. Chiahsiang (家鄉) cotton from Hsinchow (新洲), a Chinese variety, is considered the best. In Hunan cotton cultivation is carried on around the Tungting Lake, with Chinese cotton predominating. Kiangsi and Anhwei, like Hunan, are tea producing provinces and grow little cotton.[4]

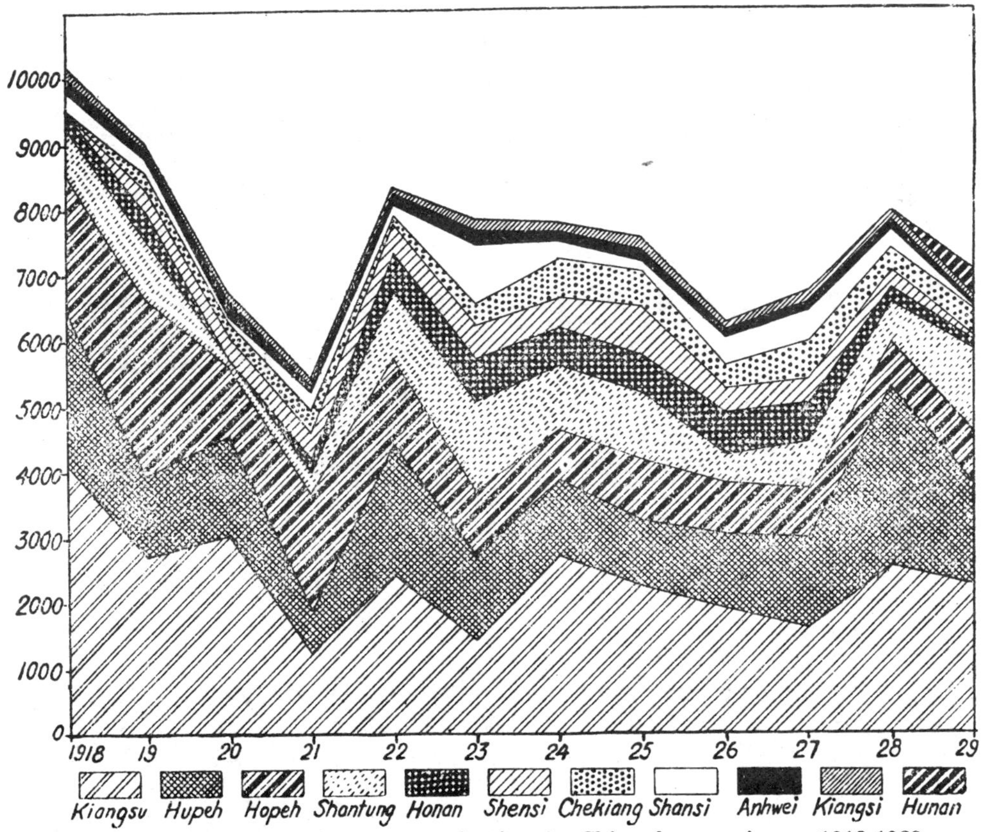

Fig. 6. Distribution of cotton production in China by provinces, 1918-1929 (in thousand piculs) (*See* Table 6a)

Crop yield:—In Table 6 the cotton production of China from 1918 to 1930 is given for eleven provinces, in terms of area as well as of crop. In Table 7, which is derived from Table 6, the crop yield per *mow* is given. An examination of these two tables reveals important facts in regard to

4. *Statistics of Cotton Production in China*; *Foreign Trade Guide*, Jan., 1931.

Table 6a. Cotton Production in China, 1918-1930, by Provinces

(Area in 1,000 mow and crop in 1,000 piculs)

Season	Hopeh		Shantung		Shansi		Honan		Shensi		Kiangsu		Chekiang		Anhwei		Kiangsi		Hupeh		Hunan		Liaoning		China	
	Area	Crop	Area	Crop	Area	Crop	Area	Crop	Area	Crop	Area	Crop	Area	Crop	Area	Crop	Area	Crop	Area	Crop	Area	Crop	Area	Crop	Area	Crop
1918-19		2,099		721		304		268				4,129				243		131		2,325						10,221
1919-20	6,397	2,684	3,218	894	486	202	1,418	428		355	19,278	2,763		265	763	126		105	1,478	1,207					33,038	9,028
1920-21	4,391	1,022	428	126	615	65			1,284	294	12,475	3,022	1,270	251	1,196	292	390	98	6,270	1,580					28,327	6,750
1921-22	4,710	1,819	2,333	295	695	249	856	219	2,406	430	11,813	1,284	1,199	309	1,099	164	257	45	2,849	615					28,216	5,429
1922-23	4,352	1,295	3,535	1,005	839	164	3,047	555	1,867	477	9,606	2,447	1,096	98	1,148	155	362	85	7,613	2,030					33,465	8,310
1923-24	3,631	945	3,677	1,388	876	931	2,693	668	1,642	462	8,165	1,489	1,181	330	1,151	190	690	172	5,848	1,272					29,554	7,145
1924-25	3,068	799	2,984	937	613	162	2,677	572	1,642	468	7,761	2,769	1,867	676	1,036	153	690	154	6,433	1,119					28,772	7,809
1925-26	2,895	958	3,099	996	755	162	2,986	545	1,316	772	7,815	2,242	1,773	506	841	176	714	170	5,927	1,007					28,121	7,534
1926-27	2,433	814	3,285	518	1,407	381	2,881	557	1,447	371	8,129	1,921	1,731	327	434	126	542	116	5,061	1,112					27,350	6,244
1927-28	2,491	771	3,173	710	1,299	502	2,817	590	1,443	358	7,329	1,638	1,734	529	437	130	597	144	6,292	1,351					27,610	6,722
1928-29	2,103	653	3,317	620	949	289	1,567	214	1,283	265	8,824	2,542	1,731	346	469	146	577	124	9,824	2,728					30,644	7,930
1929-30	2,567	801	4,239	1,213	313	40	908	123	185	34	9,511	2,277	1,660	408	466	82	304	107	11,410	1,548	1,390	394			32,955	7,027
*1929-30	2,950	835	6,544	2,171	275	63	2,680	567	1,209	135	8,625	1,085	1,852	473	491	96	286	73	11,466	3,062	1,215	251			37,593	8,810
*1930-31	2,953	844	7,335	2,155	273	82	2,506	579	1,822	379	7,656	569	1,981	520	463	43	31	5	6,930	1,060	1,088	45	1,145	180	34,183	6,461

* The figures for the two years 1929-30 and 1930-31 are estimated by the *Chinese Cotton Statistics Bureau*, and differ from the returns of the *Chinese Cotton Millowners' Association* for some provinces in 1929-30, especially Shantung, Honan, Shensi, Kiangsu, and Hupeh.

Table 6b. Cotton Production in China, 1918-1930, by Provinces

(in percentage)

Season	Hopeh		Shantung		Shensi		Honan		Shensi		Kiangsu		Chekiang		Anhwei		Kiangsi		Hupeh		Hunan		Liaoning		China	
	Area	Crop	Area	Crop	Area	Crop	Area	Crop	Area	Crop	Area	Crop	Area	Crop	Area	Crop	Area	Crop	Area	Crop	Area	Crop	Area	Crop	Area	Crop
1918-19		20.5		7.1		3.0		2.6				40.4				2.4		1.3		22.7						100
1919-20	19.4	29.7	9.7	9.9	1.5	2.2	4.3	4.7		3.9	58.3	30.7		2.9	2.3	1.4		1.2	4.5	13.4					100	100
1920-21	15.5	15.1	1.5	1.9	2.2	1.0			4.5	4.4	44.1	44.7	4.5	3.7	4.2	4.3	1.4	1.5	22.1	23.4					100	100
1921-22	16.7	33.5	8.3	5.4	2.5	4.6	3.0	4.0	8.5	7.9	41.9	23.8	4.2	5.7	3.9	3.0	0.9	0.8	10.1	11.3					100	100
1922-23	13.0	15.6	10.6	12.1	2.5	2.0	9.1	6.7	5.6	5.7	28.7	29.4	3.3	1.2	3.4	1.9	1.1	1.0	22.7	24.4					100	100
1923-24	12.3	13.2	12.4	19.4	3.0	3.2	9.1	9.3	5.6	6.5	27.6	20.9	4.0	4.6	3.9	2.7	2.3	2.4	19.8	17.8					100	100
1924-25	10.7	10.2	10.4	12.0	2.1	2.1	9.3	7.3	5.7	6.0	26.9	35.4	6.5	8.7	3.6	2.0	2.4	2.0	22.4	14.3					100	100
1925-26	10.3	12.7	11.0	13.2	2.7	2.2	10.6	7.2	4.7	10.2	27.8	29.8	6.3	6.7	3.0	2.3	2.5	2.3	21.1	13.4					100	100
1926-27	8.9	13.0	12.0	8.3	5.1	6.1	10.5	8.9	5.3	5.9	29.8	30.9	6.3	5.2	1.6	2.0	2.0	1.9	18.5	17.8					100	100
1927-28	9.0	11.5	11.5	10.6	4.7	7.5	10.2	8.8	5.2	5.3	26.5	24.3	6.3	7.9	1.6	1.9	2.2	2.1	22.8	20.1					100	100
1928-29	6.9	8.2	10.8	7.8	3.1	3.6	5.1	2.7	4.2	3.3	28.8	32.2	5.6	4.4	1.5	1.8	1.9	1.6	32.1	34.4					100	100
1929-30	7.8	11.4	12.9	17.3	0.9	0.6	2.8	1.8	0.6	0.5	28.9	32.3	5.0	5.8	1.4	1.2	0.9	1.5	34.6	22.0	4.2	5.6			100	100
*1929-30	7.9	9.5	17.4	24.6	0.7	0.7	7.1	6.4	3.2	1.5	22.9	12.3	4.9	5.4	1.3	1.1	0.8	0.8	30.5	34.8	3.2	2.8			100	100
*1930-31	8.6	13.1	21.5	33.3	0.8	1.3	7.3	9.0	5.3	5.8	22.4	8.8	5.8	8.0	1.4	0.7	0.1	0.1	20.3	16.4	3.2	0.7	3.3	2.8	100	100

China's cotton production. In the first place, China's cotton production, in terms of area or of crop, has actually shown a decline since **1918 (Fig. 6)**. This decline, as explained in a later paragraph, is partly due to the defective method in collecting statistics, but largely due to the recurrence of war, famine, and insect pests. Civil war, in particular, frequently gives rise to the interruption in the means of communication and the consequent increase in the cost of transport. However, the decline in cotton production would have been greater but for the presence of favorable factors. The great demand for raw cotton, a result of the rapid growth in China's spinning industry during the War; the opening up of new lands for cotton cultivation, especially in Kiangsu and Hupeh; the long harvesting season for cotton which frees it from the risk of complete crop failure; the capacity of cotton plant to endure the drought;—all these factors are responsible for the smaller decline in China's cotton production as compared with that of rice. In the second place, the cotton yield per *mow* has also tended towards a decline. An examination of Table 7 shows that cotton yield per *mow* has decreased from 27.3 catties in 1919-1920 to 21.3 in 1929-30. During the intervening years it has fluctuated within these two limits. Among the different provinces, the cotton yield per *mow* in a given year varies as much as one to two hundred percent. During 1919-20, for instance, it is 42.0 catties for Hopei, but 14.3 catties for Kiangsu. During 1929-30 Kiangsi has a yield of 35.2 catties per *mow*, while Shansi has one of 12.8 catties. Generally, the yield per *mow* is larger for the northern than for the central provinces. During the eleven years from 1919-1929 the highest yield per *mow* occurs in the northern provinces, namely, 58.7 piculs for Shensi in 1925-6, 42.0 for Hopei in 1919-20, 41.6 for Shansi in 1919-20, and 37.7 for Shantung in 1923-4, while the lowest yield per *mow* occurs in the central provinces, namely, 8.9 piculs for Chekiang in 1922-23 and 10.9 for Kiangsu in 1921-2.[5]

Table 7. Cotton yield in China, 1919-1929

(catties per mow)

	1919	1920	1921	1922	1923	1924	1925	1926	1927	1928	1929
Hopei	42.0	23.3	38.6	29.8	26.0	26.0	33.1	33.5	31.0	31.1	31.2
Shantung	27.8	29.4	12.6	28.4	37.7	31.4	32.1	15.8	22.4	18.7	28.6
Shansi	41.6	10.6	35.8	19.5	26.4	26.4	21.5	27.1	38.6	30.5	12.8
Honan	30.2		25.6	18.2	24.8	21.4	18.3	19.3	20.9	13.7	13.5
Shensi		22.9	17.9	25.5	28.1	28.5	58.7	25.6	24.8	20.7	18.4
Kiangsu	14.3	24.2	10.9	25.5	18.2	35.7	28.7	23.6	22.4	28.3	23.9
Chekiang		19.8	25.8	8.9	27.9	36.2	28.5	18.9	30.5	20.0	24.6
Anhwei	16.5	24.4	14.9	13.5	16.5	14.8	20.9	29.0	29.7	31.1	17.6
Kiangsi		24.6	17.5	23.5	24.9	22.3	23.8	21.4	24.1	21.5	35.2
Hupeh		25.2	21.6	26.7	21.8	17.4	17.0	22.0	21.5	27.8	13.6
Hunan											28.3
China	27.3	23.8	19.2	24.8	24.2	27.1	26.8	22.8	24.3	25.9	21.3

5. Statistics of Cotton Production in China, *op. cit.*

Improvement:—Because of the great decline in China's cotton production, attempts at improvement have been made along three directions, namely, technique, seed, and area. The planting of better seed under improved method in a larger area will undoubtedly raise the quality as well as the quantity of Chinese cotton. Both public and private bodies have helped towards the promotion of this type of work, although the results achieved are still inconsiderable. The passing of favorable legislation for cotton cultivation would have been a great help but for the lack of enforcement. The laws on the encouragement of cotton cultivation promulgated in April, 1914, as well as those on the purchase and distribution of American seed promulgated in 1918, were all laid aside. The Bureau for the Rehabilitation of Cotton Cultivation established in 1919, as well as the four cotton experiment stations established at Chingting (Hopei), Nantung, Wuchang in 1915 and at Peiping in 1918, have suspended to function for many years, except that the Nantung station is now re-organized as the Kiangsu Provincial Cotton Experiment Station, with branch stations at Nanwei and Choupu. The provincial governments, such as Kiangsu, Chekiang, Shansi, Shantung, Honan, and Hunan, have also established cotton experiment stations at different producing centres, with varying degrees of success. In an attempt to improve China's cotton production, Mr. H. Jopson, American expert, was invited to China in 1915, and later on American seeds were purchased for distribution. In 1929 the Social Affairs Bureau of the Greater City of Shanghai also established a cotton experiment station in Pootung, which succeeded in increasing the yield to a minimum of 60 catties and a maximum of 100 catties per *mow*.[6] Besides public efforts, private bodies have helped along similar lines. Since the Revolution in 1912, Chang Chieh, a strong advocate of the "iron and cotton policy" during his tenure of office as the Minister of Agriculture and Commerce in 1914, helped to organize directly or indirectly more than forty companies for the opening up of salt lands to cotton cultivation in the northern part of Kiangsu province, with a total capital investment of almost $30,000,000; but many of them failed on account of bad planning, insufficient capital, poor management, and limited conservancy work.[7] The Cotton Improvement Society, organized by Mr. H. Y. Moh, was the first to introduce American seed for trial cultivation, and helped a great deal in cotton improvement and research. In 1919 the Chinese Cotton Millowners' Association organized the Cotton Improvement Committee, which established cotton experiment stations in Paoshan, Nanking, etc. In 1920 the work of the Committee was enlarged, with an annual appropriation of $35,000 subscribed by the various Chinese

6. Shanghai Commercial and Savings Bank, Commodity series, No. 2, *Cotton*, 1931, p. 131.
7. Reclamation and Salt Manufacturing Companies in Northern Kiaugsu, in *Chinese Economic Monthly*, Nov., 1924.

mills. The Nanking station was made the headquarter, with branches in different provinces. In 1922 both the Society and the Committe were amalgamated with the Department of Agriculture of the Southeastern University. The latter has done good work in cotton improvement, including the establishment of about ten experiment stations, with a total area of 3,000 *mow*, in the four provinces of Kiangsu, Hupeh, Honan, and Hopei; the invitation of two American experts, O.F. Cook in 1919 and J. B. Griffing in 1920, for technical advice on the introduction of American cotton into China; research on the extermination of insect pests; the distribution of improved seeds to the farmers; the organization of summer schools for cotton education; lecture tours and cotton exhibitions, etc. In 1927, however, the Department went over to the National Central University, and has had little new development since then. Another university, the University of Nanking, has also done good work in cotton improvement since 1919.[8]

Anti-adulteration:—Partly due to the short-sighted policy of the cotton farmers and merchants, and partly due to the lack of organization among the cotton exporters and millowners, adulteration has for many years become a common characteristic of Chinese cotton production. The practice adopted is to adulterate cotton with water in several different ways. The farmer may splash water on the ground first, and then cover it with newly ginned cotton for a night or so in order to absorb sufficient moisture. Another method is to spread water upon each layer of lint cotton, and then pack all these layers together into a bale. A third method, which is more injurious to cotton, is to pound it with a thong, so as to break apart the wax layer on the fibre and thus to facilitate the absorption of moisture. Lately, it is reported that even a mechanical splasher has been invented in order to perpetuate the abuse. The adulteration of cotton with moisture, however, is not the only evil, for different kinds of foreign matter have been employed for the same purpose, including broken seeds or seed cotton, sand or mud, waste cotton or cotton of an inferior grade, gypsum powder etc. At other times the cotton farmer or merchant simply hides the foreign matter somewhere in the bale. Naturally, such adulteration produces disastrous effect not only upon the cotton itself, but also upon the machinery with which it is spun into yarn. Wet cotton is hard to store, as it is easily subject to deterioration or fire. It may be spotted or loses its lustre. Furthermore, it can hardly mix well with American or Indian cotton possessing a standard moisture content, and is hard to separate from the foreign matter contained. The speed of machinery is slowed down, and the cost for power is thus enhanced. In some mills where the machinery for preparatory processes such as opening, carding, drawing etc. is limited in number, the spinning machinery is held up from

8. *Foreign Trade Guide*, January, 1931.

work because of insufficiency in the supply of roving stock. Certain parts of the machinery are easily worn out, requiring further delay for repair. The quantity of cotton waste is also increased. At times when wet cotton is adulterated with foreign matter, all these difficulties of a technical nature are intensified. Some attempt against adulteration, therefore, is inevitable. The commonest solution is the testing of cotton, which, although confined to a few places, has had a history of three decades in China. In such cases the standard moisture content is generally fixed at 11 or 12 percent, which is considerably higher than the so-called "regain" prevalent in foreign countries, namely, 7.83 percent. The latter is agreed to be the natural percentage, as cotton under normal circumstance is not wholly dry.[9]

In Shanghai the first attempt against cotton adulteration was made by foreign exporters and millowners, who in May, 1901 secured the permission from the Chinese officials to establish 38 testing houses. But because of the farmers' opposition to these houses in February of the following year, Chinese cotton merchants succeeded in persuading the local officials to establish their own testing house, the Shanghai Cotton Testing House, in September. The foreign testing houses, meantime, were closed down in October. When the Revolution broke out in 1912 the House suspended work, and was not restored until 1913. At that time it was considerably handicapped for lack of funds, and almost ceased to function. In 1914 the cotton mills in Japan, which used a good deal of Chinese cotton, had to take steps themselves in order to prevent the excess moisture, by establishing their own testing houses through the Japanese Cotton Millowners' Association in each of the four Japanese ports, namely, Yokohama, Kobe, Moji, and Nagasaki. The requirement was rather strict; consequently, the return of Chinese cotton exported to Japan became a constant nuisance to the Japanese exporters in Shanghai. The latter thus united in 1916 to establish a new testing house, to which foreign merchants of other nationalities also joined in 1917. But poor management and predominance of the Japanese interests resulted in the close-down of the house in March, 1919. On the third of March, 1921 the Chinese and foreign millowners and foreign exporters united to establish the Shanghai Cotton Anti-Adulteration Association, which in June started the Shanghai Cotton Testing House.[10] The Chinese millowners, however, withdrew from the Association soon afterwards, leaving the latter in control of the situation until November 1, 1928, when the National Cotton Testing Bureau was established in Shanghai by the former Ministry of Agriculture and Mining. Opposition against the Bureau was very strong among the cotton merchants, as it attempted to test all kinds of cotton. Consequently, it was

9. *Ibid*, April 1, 1930; *China Cotton Journal*, Vol. VI, No. 2, pp. 23-26.
10. *Foreign Trade Guide*, April 1, 1930; Jan. 1, 1931.

turned over to the Shanghai Bureau of Inspection and Testing for Commercial Commodities, on the ground that export cotton, which alone was tested at that time, was more a commercial commodity than an agricultural product.[11] The Bureau was formally opened on March 1, 1929, but started cotton testing on the first of April, 1929. According to its revised regulations dated June 17th, 1929, the testing of export cotton from the port of Shanghai is compulsory, but that of the cotton consumed by the cotton mills or transacted among the cotton merchants within Shanghai or vicinity is voluntary, upon the application of the mills or merchants. In order to encourage the testing of non-export cotton the testing fee is fixed at six cents per picul for export cotton but three cents per picul for non-export cotton. The standard moisture content is set at 12 percent, and the maximum moisture content for certification at 15 percent. Cotton containing more than 15 percent of moisture or adulterated with foreign matter is not certified or allowed to pass through the Customs. In respect of samples, for press packed bales four bales are opened out of every 100 bales and four tubes of samples not exceeding two pounds each are taken for test. Testing is completed within two days after the date of collection of samples, with the exception of Sundays and other holidays, and certificates issued by the Bureau are valid only within one month after the date of issue. Merchants desiring retesting may apply to the Bureau within three days after completion of the first testing, but only one retesting is granted, for which no charge is made. Finally, cotton certified by the Bureau of Inspection and Testing for Commercial Commodities of the Ministry at other ports, but to be exported from the port of Shanghai within one month after certification by the respective Bureau, is subject to retesting but free of charge.[12] On September 20, 1929 the Shanghai Bureau took over the old testing house in Ningpo, which was made a branch of the Bureau. A little later in January, 1930, the Bureau's plan to reduce the moisture percentage for all kinds of cotton within five years was approved by the Ministry. This plan, which was also passed at the National Inspection and Testing Conference held at Nanking from the 11th to the 15th of Feburary, 1930,[13] applied to the three provinces of Kiangsu, Chekiang and Anhwei, where the branches for the Bureau would be established in Nantung and Wuhu in addition to the branch in Ningpo. The maximum moisture percentage is to be reduced to 14 from 1930 to 13 from 1931, and finally to 12 from 1932. The scope of testing is to be confined to export cotton from April 1, 1929, but to cotton consumed by

11. *Textile News*, Nos. 552-3, 555-6, 559.
12. A complete set of regulations in English may be found in Pearse, *Cotton Industry of Japan and China*, 1929, pp. 195-6; for that in Chinese see Cotton, *op. cit.*, pp. 170-4.
13. *Foreign Trade Guide*, Jan. 1, 1931.

the mills in Shanghai from Feb. 1, 1930. From Shanghai the testing of mill consumed cotton is to extend to Ningpo, Nantung, Wusih and Wuhu from July 1, 1930. The final step in this respect is to extend cotton testing to the producing regions by means of propaganda on the one hand, and of registration of cotton gins on the other. This work is to commence with the year 1930 for the principal producing regions in the two provinces of Kiangsu and Chekiang, and is to be gradually extended to Anhwei and the less important regions in Kiangsu and Chekiang.[14]

In Hankow the moisture percentage varies with the harvest conditions, being 15 to 17 percent in bad year, but 13½ percent in good year. In 1924 the Chinese Cotton Exporters' Association, with the cooperation of the foreign exporters, especially the Japanese, proposed to test the cotton in Hankow, but failed on account of the strong opposition of cotton merchants and farmers. But on the first of May, 1929, cotton testing was started with the formal opening of the Hankow Bureau for the Inspection and Testing of Commercial Commodities, with similar regulations like those for the Shanghai Bureau, although opposition from the cotton merchants were at first strong. These merchants claimed that Hankow cotton was mostly exported to Shanghai, where it would have to go through the process of retesting, as the Hankow Bureau, unlike the Shanghai Bureau, required the testing of moisture only, not of staple, color and grade.[15] The Hankow Bureau, however, has functioned successfully, and since September 26, 1929, has started a new testing branch in Shasi.[16]

In Tientsin the moisture percentage of cotton did not go any lower than that in Shanghai or Hankow, being 15 to 20 percent. In August, 1911 the Tientsin General Chamber of Commerce, composed of Europeans and Americans, secured the cooperation of the Japanese merchants to organize in May of the following year the Cotton Anti-Adulteration Association of Tientsin, which had on its Board of Directors two Europeans and Americans, two Japanese and two Chinese. The Association worked together with the Customs, through which the testing was performed by the Cotton Testing House. It was provided that beginning with Nov. 1, 1912 no cotton with higher than 12% of moisture could be allowed to pass through the Native Customs and that the testing fee should be seven cents per bale of 100 to 120 catties, five cents per bale of 60 to 100 catties, and three cents per bale of below 60 catties. It was also provided that in case of difficulty the Customs might restrict the scope of testing like the Shanghai Cotton Testing House, namely, to export cotton instead of to all kinds of cotton. Retesting was allowed within forty-eight hours after testing, with additional charge provided that the result remained the

14. *Ibid*, April 1, 1930.
15. *Textile News*, No. 610.
16. *Foreign Trade Guide*, Jan. 1, 1931.

same as that for the first testing. In 1915 the former Ministry of Agriculture and Commerce was informed by the American consul that cotton exported from Tientsin to the United States should be inspected in respect of insect infection. At this occasion the Ministry ordered the Commissioner of Foreign Affairs in Chihli (now Hopei) to negotiate with the foreign merchants to turn over the Cotton Testing House to the Chinese authorities, but failed on account of the recurrence of civil war. In September, 1928 the Ministry of Industries, formerly the Ministry of Industry, Commerce and Labor, again sent a representative to negotiate with the foreign merchants for the return of the Cotton Testing House to Chinese control. The foreign merchants were indifferent at first, but through repeated representations, the Association replied the Ministry in April, 1929, to the effect that the decision rested with the Chief Inspector of Customs. The latter was given in favor of the Chinese authorities, at the order of the Ministry of Finance, and the right of cotton testing in Tientsin was restored to the Chinese. In August, 1929 the Tientsin Bureau of Inspection and Testing for Commercial Commodities was formally inauguarated. A month later, the testing of cotton was commenced by the Bureau, under similar regulations that prevailed in other Bureaus.[17] The moisture percentage, however, remained at 12%, and testing was applied to all kinds of cotton that passed through the Native Customs, instead of to export cotton only.

In Tsingtao the export of cotton, chiefly from Tsinan, constitutes also a large item. The testing of cotton was begun in April, 1913, by the provincial government, but failed on account of the opposition from cotton merchants. A little later the cotton exporters in Tsingtao were compelled for trade reasons to organize a new Cotton Testing House, which unfortunately had no power of compulsion, but depended upon the voluntary application of the exporters for testing. In July, 1929 the Tsingtao Bureau of Inspection and Testing for Commercial Commodities was established, and immediate steps were taken to organize a testing house in Tsinan, which had similar regulations for cotton testing like those in force elsewhere.[18]

Standardization:—Generally, two types of cotton are now grown in China, namely, American and Chinese. Neither type, however, possesses a uniform system of classification that can be applied all over the country. In fact, Chinese grown cotton, whether native or foreign, is commonly identified with the place of production, which may be a district or a province. Shensi cotton, referring to the cotton grown in the province of Shensi, has now been applied even to the long staple cotton grown in Hankow. The great diversity of cotton standards that now prevails on the

17. *Tientsin Cotton*, a Monthly published by the Cotton Testing House, Tientsin Bureau of Testing and Inspection for Commercial Commodities, June to July, 1930.
18. *Foreign Trade Guide*, Jan. 1, 1931.

market is an intolerable curse to the trade. It is further complicated by the practice of adulteration on the part of cotton farmers and merchants. Not only is the cotton produced in one district different from that produced in another, but diversity of standards also exists among the cotton produced in the same district. Disputes, therefore, often arise between buyers and sellers over the perennial issue of cotton grading. On the one hand, the farmers are discouraged when they fail to have their grades recognized in a market flooded with many others, while on the other hand, the buyers complain of the difficulty in getting the right kind of cotton. The cotton mills are constantly confronted with the problem of having to use different grades of cotton in spinning the same count of yarn. The exporters, too, have to collect a large lot from an extended territory than is needed elsewhere in order to sort out the proper grade for foreign demand. Under such circumstance it would have been impossible to improve the cotton culture in China, for an improved variety is soon reduced to a deteriorated one by lack of encouragement. In Shanghai where future trading in raw cotton is carried on in the Chinese Cotton Goods Exchange the need for uniform cotton standards is an imperative one, but the solution for it is not wholly satisfactory. The Exchange has a Cotton Grading Committee composed of ten experts and appointed from time to time by the Board of Managers since its establishment in 1922. The 28th list of cotton grades, which was fixed by the Committee on Oct. 14, 1928, included such cottons as were commonly delivered on the Exchange's contract. The Hankow long staple cotton was chosen as the standard, with Chenchow long staple, Taich'ang black seed, Changshu black seed, and Changyin cotton as substitutes. Besides, there were two superior and two inferior grades that could be delivered as alternatives. Among the superior grades one tael was added for every picul of Tungchow cotton, and one fourth of a tael for every picul of Taich'ang white seed; among the inferior grades one fourth of a tael was deducted from every picul of Shanghai or Shanghai steam-pressed cotton.[19] The list is unsatisfactory, as it covers a small portion of Chinese cotton, changes frequently, and fails to prescribe the essential qualities of cotton. Any cotton that is not found on the Exchange's list has to be graded by the Committee separately when tendered for delivery, thus involving delay and expense. Recently, the Bureau of Inspection and Testing for Commercial Commodities in Shanghai has commenced to tackle with the problem of cotton classification in a more scientific manner. Ever since the organization of the Bureau's Cotton Testing House in April, 1929, from every lot of samples collected in the course of the Bureau's administrative work with cotton testing, a small sample of four or five ounces has been kept, reaching at present a total of about 3,000 samples. These samples, composed chiefly of Kiangsu

19. Chen. T. C.: *A Proposal for the Classification of Tientsin Cotton*, 1930, p. 9.

cotton, serve as the basis for the scientific determination of staple and grade. As may be seen from Table 8, the Bureau has already made a preliminary test of 18 varieties of native cotton, with regard to staple, fineness, twist and tensile strength. For the future it plans to send own investigators to the cotton producing regions for sample selection, as the samples that come within the reach of the Bureau

Table 8. Results of testing for 18 kinds of Chinese cotton, 1930*

Name of cotton	Staple		Fineness		Twist		Tensile strength	
	Rank	Inch	Rank	Inch	Rank	No. per inch	Rank	Gram
Linpao, Honan	1	31/32	1	.000844437	4	93.9229	15	4.2300
Chenchow, Honan	2	7/8	3	.000870354	6	91.2234	16	3.8630
Shantung	3	27/32	15	.000980557	11	68.9899	17	3.6965
Changshu, Kiangsu	4	13/16	13	.000971997	9	71.7065	14	5.4930
Tungchow, Kiangsu	5	25/32	16	.001023922	10	70.0130	13	5.7300
Tsungming, Kiangsu	6	25/32	10	.000935877	12	68.8390	2	8.2797
Hankow, Hupeh	7	25/32	7	.000914096	1	117.8833	11	5.7900
Changyin, Kiangsu	8	3/4	6	.000911608	14	68.3788	3	8.0750
Shensi	9	3/4	4	.000879995	5	93.2830	12	5.9900
Shasi, Hupeh	10	3/4	5	.000897239	2	109.6384	7	6.6766
Pingchow, Shantung	11	3/4	9	.000931660	7	75.2868	18	2.5700
Tientsin, Hopeh	12	3/4	11	.000960864	8	74.4310	10	5.9330
Yuyao, Chekiang	13	3/4	17	.001048392	15	57.8068	4	7.7416
Taich'ang, Kiangsu	14	3/4	12	.000961452	17	55.3670	1	8.4500
Yencheng, Kiangsu	15	3/4	8	.000919948	3	95.9705	9	5.9633
Kiukiang, Kiangsi	16	23/32	14	.000975893	18	51.4522	5	7.1950
Shanghai, Kiangsu	17	23/32	18	.001066100	16	55.4165	8	6.0096
Anch'ing, Anhwei	18	23/32	2	.000865533	13	68.4741	6	7.1830

* By the Cotton Testing House, Shanghai Bureau of Inspection and Testing for Commercial Commodities, Ministry of Industries. In *Foreign Trade Guide*, June 1, 1930.

at present are partly adulterated by the cotton merchants, and partly rendered unfit for testing by machine pressing. Secondly, it plans to build a new testing house that may meet with the scientific requirement for such purpose, especially in respect of light. In the third place, the Bureau plans to organize a Chinese Cotton Classification Committee. The Committee, which is to be composed of leading cotton merchants and experts, will proceed with the work of establishing uniform standards for Chinese cotton, on the basis of the Bureau's present research. Such standards may be classified into three groups, namely, American upland cotton, Chinese white seed short staple, and Chinese black seed long staple. For the American upland cotton which has been extensively cultivated in North China, such as Weinan in Shensi and Linpao in Honan, the official cotton standards of the United States for grades and colors of American upland cotton may be adopted, while for the Chinese cotton the color of the seed as well as the length of staple may be taken as the basis for classification. White seed cotton is generally stiff, with short staple, of which Yuyao, Hofei (合肥), Hankow short staple, Shanghai, and Kiangyin white seed are examples. Black seed cotton is generally soft, with long staple, of which Tungchow Chicken-foot and Shiaokan (孝感) long staple are examples.[20] In Tientsin the Bureau of Inspection and Testing for Commercial Commodities has also proposed to classify the cotton produced in the region around Tientsin, which generally goes under the name "Tientsin cotton" in the trade. According to the proposal Tientsin cotton is to be divided into eight groups, namely, Hsi-ho, Yü-ho, brown, Tung-pei-ho, American seed, Shansi, red and coarse. Each group is again divided into one to six grades, on the basis of staple, color, bloom and degree of adulteration. All these grades of cotton, however, must not have a moisture content of more than twelve percent, and must not be adulterated with more than five percent of cotton seed or seed cotton or more than one percent of sand, or any amount of brick, gypsum etc.[21]

Consumption

The demand for raw cotton in China comes from three sources, namely, export, mill consumption and stock, and native spinning and padding; while its supply comes from two sources, namely, home production and import. Import and export statistics are furnished by the annual returns of the Chinese Maritime Customs, while statistics on home production are compiled by the Chinese Cotton Millowners' Association. Mill consumption and mill stock, as estimated by the International Cotton Federation, is based on the actual returns by the Chinese Cotton Millowners' Association in Shanghai. Cotton consumed for padding and native spinning is not recorded, but the Association has estimated it at 15 percent of the total home production. Table 9, which sums up the above statistics, shows the supply of and demand for raw cotton in China from 1919 to 1929. Although for some years such as 1923, 1925 and 1926 the supply barely meets with the demand, but for other years such as 1922, 1924, 1927 and 1928, the demand exceeds the supply. The excess would have been greater but for the fact that the estimate for mill consumption and stock as well as that for padding and native spinning were rather conservative. The accuracy of the import and export statistics cannot be denied; so the excess lies chiefly in the under-estimate for home production. Such under-estimate has been openly admitted by the Chinese Cotton Millowners' Association by which the statistics have been collected and compiled since 1918. The Association's estimate, in the first place, covered only ten provinces up to 1928, after which another province, Hunan, was added. It failed to include many other provinces equally suitable for

20. *Foreign Trade Guide*, Aug. 1, 1930.
21. Chen, *op. cit.*

cotton cultivation, such as Szechuen, Sinkiang, Kwangsi, Yunnan, Kweichow, and Liaoning. Kwangsi, for instance, organized a Provincial Bureau for the Promotion of Cotton Cultivation in 1919. The cotton produced in Sinkiang or Chinese Turkestan is well known, amounting to two to three hundred thousand piculs per year; it is largely exported to Russia via Siberia. In Liaoning the Japanese have promoted cotton cultivation to a large extent. Around the region of Liaoyang the annual production is estimated at four to five hundred thousand piculs. Besides, even for the provinces included, the statistics are by no means complete, as the Association is handicapped not only by the limited finance and lack of trained investigators, but also by the recurrence of war and famine, the constant interruption of communication, the farmers' fear for taxation, and the absence of a uniform system of weights.[22]

Table 9. Supply of and demand for raw cotton in China, 1919-1929

(in 1,000 piculs)

Year	Supply: Import[24]	Supply: Production[23]	Supply: Total	Demand: Export[24]	Demand: Mill Consumption[25]	Demand: Mill Stock[25]	Demand: Padding & Native Spinning[26]	Demand: Total
1919	239	10,221	10,460	1,072	?	?	1,533	?
1920	678	9,028	9,706	376	?	?	1,354	?
1921	1,683	6,750	8,433	609	?	?	1,013	?
1922	1,781	5,429	7,210	842	5,621	1,193	814	8,470
1923	1,614	8,310	9,924	975	6,034	1,065	1,247	9,321
1924	1,219	7,145	8,364	1,080	5,891	750	1,072	8,793
1925	1,807	7,809	9,616	801	6,038	1,076	1,171	9,086
1926	2,745	7,534	10,279	879	6,581	1,196	1,130	9,786
1927	2,415	6,244	8,659	1,447	7,200	960	937	10,544
1928	1,916	6,722	8,638	1,112	7,560	1,189	1,008	10,869
1929	2,515	7,748	10,263	944	7,338	?	1,162	?

Import and export

Early history:—China's import of cotton during the early period came chiefly from India, in the so-called 'country ships' of the East India Company. According to the *Chronicles* of the Company, the *Catherine* was despatched from Surat in April, 1704 to Pulo Condore and Amoy, with 1,116 piculs of raw cotton. The latter 'being only sent on trial, was to be sold at Malacca, provided nine Dollars per pecul could be obtained for it'. The cotton, however, was not disposed at Malacca, but carried to Amoy. As the Amoy merchants were at that year first organized into a

22. Statistics of Cotton Production in China, *op. cit.*, pp. 15-20.
23. *Ibid*, p. 16.
24. Chinese Maritime Customs: *Foreign Trade of China.*
25. Pearse, *op. cit.*, p. 193.
26. Estimated at 15% of total production by the Chinese Cotton Millowners' Association, in *Statistics of Cotton Production in China*, p. 18.

close corporation,—the precursor of the Cohong of Canton, and as the supercargoes of five English ships were competing one against the other, the prices were keenly debated, the advantage being all on the side of the Chinese. For the *Catherine's* cotton, Tls. 7.00 was asked; the buyers first offered Tls. 4.50, then Tls. 5.20, and finally Tls. 5.50, which was accepted.[27]

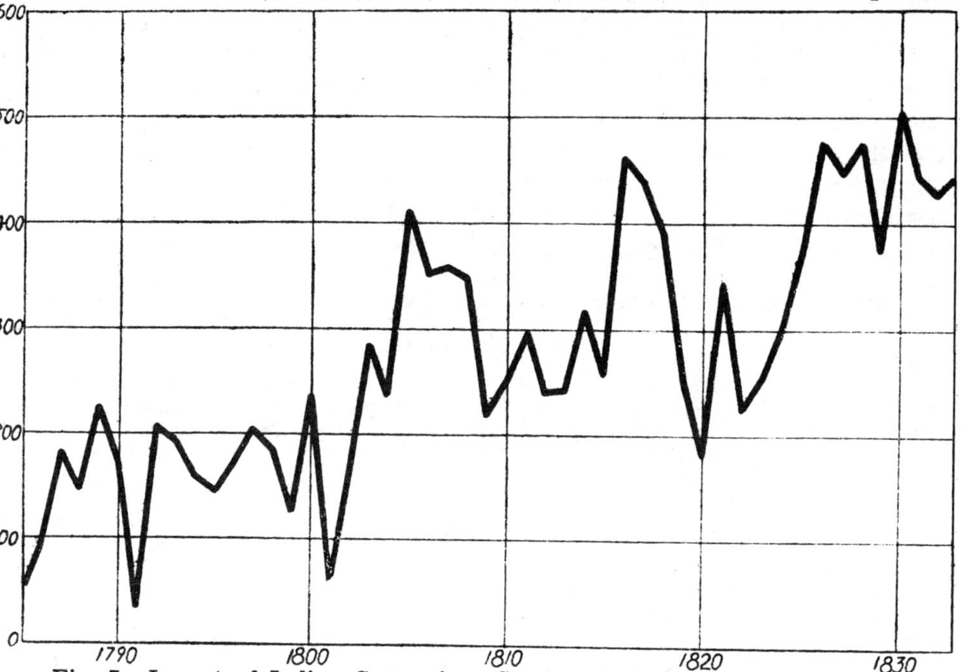

Fig. 7. Import of Indian Cotton into Canton, 1785-1833 (in 1,000 piculs)
(*See* Table 10)

The Amoy shipment of 1704 was incidental, and 32 years again elapsed before another import of 605 piculs, at a price of Tls. 8.50 per picul, was recorded in 1735. Then followed an intermittent import of 250 bales containing 125 candys or 737 piculs in 1739, 870 piculs in 1742, and 1,859 piculs in 1759, the last being carried by Dutch ships. Since then no import had been recorded until 1768, in which year a great increase took place. Altogether 21,996 piculs were imported by ships under different flags in that year, namely, 20,939 piculs by English ships, 954 piculs by Dutch ships, and 103 piculs by French ships. After 1768 several other imports were recorded rather closely, including 12,201 piculs in 1769, 37,429 piculs in 1771, 28,679 piculs in 1772, 814 piculs in 1773, and 45,862 piculs in 1774. An interval of ten years again passed before the import was resumed, without any interruption, for the rest of the period for which the *Chronicles* were kept, that is, up to 1833. In 1784 the Com-

27. Morse, H. B.: *The Chronicles of the East India Company Trading to China*, 1635-1834, 5 vols., 1926-1929, I: 130, 132.

Table 10. Import of Indian cotton into Canton by vessels of different flags, 1785-1833

Year	Company Piculs	Company Value	English Country or private Piculs	English Country or private Value	Total Piculs	Total Value	American Piculs	American Value	Other Piculs	Other Value	Grand Total Piculs	Grand Total Value
1785	17,389		28,690		46,079				2,413		48,492	
6	28,120		65,130		93,250				322		93,572	
7	82,150	T 103,670	101,161		183,311				4,000		187,311	
8	61,632		84,168		145,800		545				146,345	
9	65,426		143,952		209,378		17,411				226,789	
1790	45,823	131,744	124,558		170,381		1,432		411		172,224	
1	16,529		15,505		32,034				273		32,307	
2	43,138		152,884		196,022		4,926		7,836		208,784	
3	30,780		149,430		180,210		9,363		4,600		194,173	
4	17,994		133,687		151,681		4,964		2,209		158,854	
5	4,929	61,597	130,363		135,292		10,412				145,704	
6	44,955		118,668		163,,623		1,500		6,431		171,554	
7	77,445		127,287		204,732				709		205,441	
8	39,483		144,756		184,239				1,014		185,253	
9	63,709		64,122		127,831	T 1,700,000					127,831	
1800	90,764	396,422	147,222		237,986						237,986	
1	38,571	169,485	15,619		54,190		1,873				56,063	
2	49,287		112,151		161,438						161,438	
3	69,228		214,959		284,187		383				284,570	
4	59,751		170,200		229,951		2,417				232,368	
5	96,102		310,392		406,494		7,714				414,208	
6	92,986	412,971	261,883		354,869						354,869	
7	93,327	422,983	265,151		358,478		2,210				360,688	
8	127,179	634,126	218,903		346,082		2,198				348,280	
9	51,647	234,194	146,184		197,831		22,006				219,837	
1810	107,039	555,636	143,527		250,566		1,905				252,471	
1	139,440	736,064	146,110		285,550		9,442				294,992	
2	144,881	1,161,046	95,130		240,011		268				240,279	
3	132,815	977,584	110,415		243,230						243,230	
4	91,177	705,400	225,845		317,022						317,022	
5	126,711	1,529,464	129,606		256,317		320		520		257,157	
6	130,163	1,007,984	333,704		463,867						463,867	
7	83,530	$1,629,550	354,867	$6,346,600	438,397	$7,976,150					438,397	$7,976,150
8	68,808	1,347,586	323,842	5,534,916	392,650	6,882,502					392,650	6,882,502
9	95,772	1,643,143	138,174	2,361,583	233,946	4,004,726	19,149	$ 359,044			253,095	4,363,770
1820	84,627	1,341,150	97,785	1,898,781	182,412	3,239,931	120	?			182,532	3,239,931
1	146,990	1,896,725	194,641	3,113,942	341,631	5,010,667	3,516	42,192			345,147	5,052,859
2	50,344	689,059	175,322	2,295,939	225,666	2,984,998	888	9,876			226,554	2,994,874
3	118,050	1,803,398	137,013	2,283,550	255,063	4,086,948		19,260			255,063	4,106,208
4	106,254	1,842,536	194,591	3,378,315	300,845	5,220,851	1,575	31,500			302,420	5,252,351
5	102,881	1,951,914	270,286	4,275,826	373,167	6,227,740	195	3,802			373,362	6,231,542
6	133,042	2,061,771	342,735	5,153,561	475,777	7,215,332	1,020	14,280			476,797	7,229,612
7	176,206	2,307,216	270,538	3,480,083	446,744	5,787,299	1,307	16,991			448,051	5,804,290
8	148,855	1,836,613	326,530	3,767,340	475,385	5,603,953					475,385	5,603,953
9	119,648	1,744,340	256,313	7,335,760	375,961	5,080,100					375,961	5,080,100
1830	147,240	1,832,197	351,409	3,796,288	498,649	5,628,485	3,271	39,252			501,920	5,667,737
1	91,862	1,088,308	351,206	3,842,935	443,068	4,931,243	170	1,890			443,238	4,933,133
2	102,546	1,426,693	324,942	4,048,132	427,488	5,474,825					427,488	5,474,825
3	116,247	1,842,332	326,393	4,884,407	442,640	6,726,739					442,640	6,726,739
1817-1833	1,892,902	28,284,531	4,436,587	63,797,958	6,329,489	92,082,489	31,211	538,087			6,360,700	92,620,576
1785-1833	4,173,472		9,067,949		13,241,421		132,500		30,738		13,404,659	
1785-1833	31.13%		67.65%		98.78%		0.99%		0.23%		100%	

pany's cotton import from India amounted to Tls. 40,362, while the first American ship, the *Empress of China,* carried 316 piculs valued at Tls. 3,160.[28] The import of Indian cotton after 1785 shows a very rapid increase, reaching as high as 93,572 piculs in 1786, and 187,311 piculs in 1787. Since 1787 the import tended to increase on the whole. The annual average for the ten year period from 1791-1800 amounted to 166,788.7 piculs, that from 1801-1810 to 268,479.2 piculs, that from 1811-1820 to 308,322.1 piculs, and that from 1821-1830 to 378,066 piculs (Fig. 7). For the period covered (1785-1833) the total import of raw cotton amounted to 13,404,659 piculs, giving an average annual import of 273,564.4 piculs. The import was mostly carried from India to China in English vessels, only 163,238 piculs or 1.22% being carried by vessels under other flags, especially under American flag. Of the 6,329,489 piculs carried by English vessels, 4,173,472 piculs or 31.13% were carried by the company ships, while 9,067,949 piculs or 67.65% were carried by the country ships.[29]

The import of Indian cotton must have been a highly profitable trade. Available statistics for the six years including 1768, 1774, 1792, 1795, 1796 and 1800 show a rate of profit ranging from the lowest of 27% for 1800 to the highest of 113.8% for 1774. Such fluctuating rate of profit, however, can hardly be explained in terms of ordinary economic operations. In 1795 and 1796, for instance, two lots of raw cotton were sold at about the same price in the Canton market, namely, Tls. 12.70 and Tls. 12.50 per picul respectively, but the rate of profit was 38.4% for 1795 but 105.3% for 1796. Unusual circumstances, of which we may suggest the uncertanity of cotton crop and the probability of a disorganized cotton market in India, must have been at work to account for the great fluctuation in profit.[30]

Year	Piculs		Prime cost			Realized Value	Profit	Selling price (Tls. per picul)
1768		Rup.	125,790	(₮72,891)	Tls.	97,225	33.4%	9.0
1774		,,	12,841		,,	8,982	113.8%	
1792	5,881	,,	123,077		,,	67,627	67.5%	11.5
1795	4,929	,,	133,538		,,	61,597	38.4%	12.7
1796	5,589	,,	103,968		,,	69,858	105.3%	12.5
1800					,,	396,422	27.0%	

The above fluctuation in the rate of profit was repeated in a more detailed statement of two transactions for 1804. In that year, one lot of cotton costing Tls. 96,289 realized a profit of Tls. 93,136 or 96.7%, while

28. *Ibid,* I: 238, 265, 283, 292; II: 94, 95; V: 139, 145, 155, 170, 176, 191.
29. *Ibid,* II: 111, 119, 135, 136, 152, 173, 179, 180, 184, 193, 205, 256, 265, 266, 278, 294, 311, 322, 323, 347, 348, 357, 358, 389, 401, 416; III: 2, 26, 27, 54, 55, 76, 77, 100, 101, 130, 131, 157, 158, 174, 175, 189, 190, 205, 206, 226, 228, 243, 308, 328, 331, 344, 347, 365, 383; IV: 4, 20, 53, 67, 71, 84, 89, 99, 103, 118,123, 139, 145, 158, 162, 181, 185, 195, 223, 248, 253, 271, 325, 339, 343, 369.
30. *Ibid,* II: 192,265, 266,347; V: 134, 189.

another lot costing Tls. 276,574 realized a profit of only Tls. 77,182 or 27.9%.[31]

From Bengal:	Tls.	Tls.
Cost at Calcutta Sª Rup. 241,406	80,469	
Estimate of freight, £4,120	12,360	
Charges at Madras, Pag. 3,090	3,460	96,289
Sold 13,152 piculs at Tls. 14.50	190,698	
Deduct unloading charges	1,273	189,425
Gain on transaction		93,136
From Bombay:	B'y Rup.	Tls.
3,457,214 lb @ 784 per candy are 4,410 candy @ 150 Rupees, computed cost to commanders, B'y Rup.	670,282	
Screwing and other charges	44,097	
Freight, 2,416 tons	72,481	
Insurance at 3 per cent	21,431	
Interest, 4 months @ ¾ per mensem	21,431	
B'y Rup.	829,722 =	276,574
Out-turn 3,388,070 lb=25,410 picul @ Tls. 14.00	355,740	
Deduct unloading charges	1,984	353,756
Gain on transaction		77,182

Development Since 1867:—The statistics on raw cotton import from 1833 to 1867 are not available, but in comparing the figures between these two years the change during the period could not have been very great, the raw cotton import being 442,640 piculs for 1833 but 335,976 piculs for 1867. An export, meantime, was developing, which amounted to 29,391 piculs in 1867. In other words, there was in 1867 an unfavorable balance of 306,585 piculs for China's foreign trade in raw cotton. The unfavorable balance, as shown in Table 11a, continued, with the exception of 1874, for a period of 21 years, up to 1887. After the latter year China exported more cotton than she imported, and thus acquired, with the exception of 1899, a favorable balance during a period of 32 years from 1888 to 1919. In 1919 China had an export of 1,072,040 piculs and an import of 239,003 piculs, with a favorable balance of 833,037 piculs. After 1919, however, another period of unfavorable balance was ushered in, which reached the climax in 1930. In the latter year, China imported 3,456,494 piculs but exported 825,545 piculs, with an unfavorable balance reaching as high as 2,630,949 piculs. China's foreign trade in raw cotton from 1867 to 1930 can, therefore, be divided into three periods, namely, the period of unfavorable balance from 1867 to 1887, the period of favorable balance from 1888 to 1919, and the period of unfavorable balance from 1920 to 1930

31. *Ibid*, II: 419-20.

Table 11a. China's foreign trade in raw cotton, 1867-1930
(+)=favorable balance, (—)=unfavorable balance

Year	Piucls Import	Export	Balance	Hk. Tls. Import	Export	Balance
1867	335,976	29,391	— 306,585	5,162,937	458,424	— 4,704,513
8	305,886	38,141	— 267,745	4,295,349	587,821	— 3,707,528
9	193,648	69,274	— 124,374	2,807,505	1,039,067	— 1,768,438
1870	225,414	22,356	— 203,058	3,291,761	335,335	— 2,956,426
1	340,778	10,764	— 330,014	3,962,894	129,350	— 3,833,544
2	207,144	5,981	— 201,163	2,324,692	71,752	— 2,252,940
3	201,045	25,349	— 175,696	2,133,407	228,774	— 1,904,633
4	11,811	94,183	+ 82,372	109,638	847,907	— 738,269
5	169,676	31,610	— 138,066	1,494,478	322,569	— 1,171,909
6	236,918	42,976	— 193,942	2,251,417	393,508	— 1,857,909
7	154,892	33,216	— 121,676	1,463,554	329,781	— 1,133,773
8	106,027	23,311	— 82,716	970,495	236,817	— 733,678
9	175,534	12,362	— 163,172	1,553,693	123,248	— 1,430,445
1880	87,486	18,077	— 69,409	903,822	180,071	— 723,751
1	137,869	22,908	— 114,961	1,487,162	228,076	— 1,259,086
2	178,478	41,690	— 136,788	1,916,734	404,405	— 1,512,329
3	211,306	22,074	— 189,232	2,100,300	241,026	— 1,859,274
4	187,105	53,572	— 133,533	1,784,451	614,701	— 1,169,750
5	131,404	61,850	— 69,554	1,298,007	717,489	— 580,518
6	94,382	47,572	— 46,810	825,624	523,380	— 302,244
7	173,728	69,227	— 104,501	1,433,203	677,660	— 755,543
8	156,579	202,546	+ 45,967	1,512,651	2,228,284	+ 715,633
9	113,545	504,420	+ 390,875	1,213,349	5,044,806	+ 3,831,457
1890	149,562	298,887	+ 149,325	1,577,018	2,989,274	+ 1,412,256
1	110,618	355,584	+ 244,966	1,195,262	3,841,129	+ 2,645,867
2	106,635	508,843	+ 402,208	1,157,001	5,089,361	+ 3,932,360
3	53,419	576,155	+ 522,736	660,707	6,166,182	+ 5,505,475
4	43,103	747,231	+ 704,128	556,203	7,361,343	+ 6,805,140
5	44,711	896,096	+ 851,385	568,917	11,202,661	+ 10,633,744
6	99,129	418,102	+ 318,973	1,307,975	5,017,899	+ 3,709,924
7	160,256	493,139	+ 332,883	2,260,191	7,393,456	+ 5,132,265
8	229,005	273,739	+ 44,734	2,839,730	3,151,161	+ 311,431
9	278,366	229,220	— 49,146	3,475,780	2,980,373	— 495,407
1900	134,750	711,882	+ 577,132	1,832,966	9,860,969	+ 8,028,003
1	254,855	290,865	+ 37,010	3,868,252	4,705,606	+ 837,354
2	248,566	774,536	+ 525,970	3,857,507	13,161,051	+ 9,303,544
3	59,494	759,521	+ 700,027	933,602	13,294,614	+ 12,361,012
4	60,057	1,228,588	+1,168,531	1,013,068	24,811,595	+ 23,798,527
5	90,590	789,273	+ 698,683	1,540,334	12,029,326	+ 10,488,992
6	45,357	769,542	+ 724,185	728,105	11,631,138	+ 10,903,033
7	116,307	988,055	+ 871,748	1,704,765	16,959,737	+ 15,254,972
8	99,022	613,509	+ 514,487	1,744,406	10,345,205	+ 8,600,799
9	114,389	633,687	+ 519,298	2,000,915	14,452,021	+ 12,451,106
1910	205,915	1,247,304	+1,041,389	4,463,995	28,141,234	+ 23,677,239
1	39,171	877,744	+ 838,068	905,738	21,404,115	+ 20,498,377
2	279,192	805,711	+ 526,519	6,179,852	17,021,093	+ 10,841,241
3	134,735	738,812	+ 604,077	3,017,318	16,235,604	+ 13,218,286
4	126,488	659,704	+ 533,216	2,872,118	12,339,549	+ 9,467,431
5	364,390	725,955	+ 361,565	6,651,841	13,700,496	+ 7,048,655
6	407,644	851,037	+ 443,393	8,068,790	17,091,073	+ 9,022,283
7	300,128	832,463	+ 532,335	6,406,224	20,035,862	+ 13,629,638
8	190,110	1,292,094	+1,101,984	6,070,517	37,887,337	+ 31,816,820
9	239,003	1,072,040	+ 833,037	6,499,073	30,253,447	+ 23,754,374
1920	678,297	376,230	— 302,067	17,993,170	9,224,512	— 8,768,658
1	1,682,526	609,481	—1,073,045	35,866,856	16,483,234	— 19,383,622
2	1,780,618	842,010	— 938,608	41,956,187	22,861,434	— 19,094,753
3	1,614,371	974,574	— 639,797	53,816,201	32,605,771	— 21,210,430
4	1,219,284	1,080,019	— 139,265	48,817,558	40,420,414	— 8,397,144
5	1,807,450	800,786	—1,006,664	69,965,177	29,844,467	— 40,120,710
6	2,745,017	878,512	—1,866,505	93,750,540	29,399,381	— 64,351,159
7	2,415,482	1,446,950	— 968,532	79,812,653	47,306,699	— 32,505,954
8	1,916,140	1,111,558	— 804,582	67,981,417	34,158,765	— 33,822,652
9	2,514,786	943,786	—1,571,000	91,123,857	29,603,791	— 61,520,066
1930	3,456,494	825,545	—2,630,949	132,265,669	26,499,307	—105,766,362

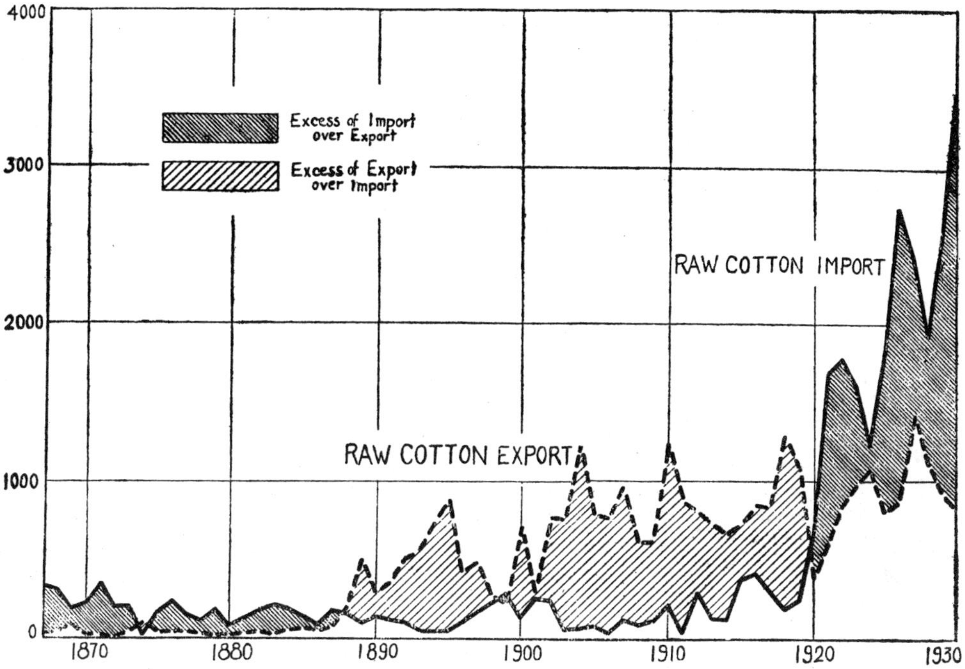

Fig. 8. China's cotton import and export, 1867-1930 (in 1,000 piculs) (*See* Table 11a)

(Fig. 8). The transition from the second to the third period is at least due to two sets of factors, namely, the recurrence of civil war and the growth in China's cotton industry. The first factor is responsible for the reduction or stationary status in China's cotton production, while the second one gives rise to a greater demand for raw cotton in China.

An examination of Table 11b leads to further significant conclusions. During the period under study, namely, from 1867 to 1930, China had a total import of 30,752,063 piculs and a total export of 32,831,619 piculs, with a favorable balance of 2,079,556 piculs. Of the total import of 30,752,063 piculs during the period of 64 years, the ten year period from 1921 to 1930 claimed 21,152,168 piculs or 68.78%. On the other hand, of the total export of 32,831,619 piculs during the same period, the twenty-five year period from 1906 to 1930 claimed 21,997,108 piculs or 67%. The export, therefore, was more evenly distributed than the import. Indeed, the five year period from 1926 to 1930 claimed as much as 13,047,919 piculs or 42.43% of the total import. A second significant conclusion to be drawn from Table 11b is the relatively lower price paid for the cotton exported from China. During the whole period from 1867 to 1930 the total import of 30,752,063 piculs of foreign cotton was valued at Hk. Tls. 865,604,848, giving an average price of Hk. Tls. 28.14 per picul, while the total export of 32,831,619 piculs of Chinese cotton during the same period was valued at Hk. Tls. 734,925,937, giving an average price of Hk. Tls. 22.44 per picul. As is generally expected, this discrepancy in the price paid for Chinese and foreign cotton proves indirectly the lower quality of the former.

Table 11b. China's foreign trade in raw cotton, 1867-1930

	Import		Export		Import		Export	
Period	Piculs	%	Piculs	%	Hk. Tls.	%	Hk. Tls.	%
1867-1870	1,060,924	3.45	159,162	0.48	15,557,552	1.80	2,420,647	0.33
1871-1875	930,454	3.02	167,887	0.51	10,025,379	1.16	1,600,352	0.22
1876-1880	760,857	2.47	129,942	0.39	7,142,981	0.83	1,263,425	0.17
1881-1885	846,162	2.75	202,094	0.62	8,586,654	0.99	2,205,697	0.30
1886-1890	687,796	2.24	1,122,652	3.42	6,561,845	0.76	11,463,404	1.56
1891-1895	358,486	1.17	3,083,909	9.40	4,138,090	0.48	33,660,676	4.58
1896-1900	901,506	2.93	2,126,082	6.48	11,716,642	1.35	28,403,858	3.87
1901-1905	713,562	2.32	3,842,783	11.70	11,212,763	1.30	68,002,192	9.25
1906-1910	580,990	1.90	4,252,097	12.94	10,642,186	1.23	81,529,335	11.09
1911-1915	943,976	3.07	3,807,926	11.60	19,626,867	2.27	80,700,857	10.98
1916-1920	1,815,182	5.90	4,423,864	13.48	45,037,774	5.20	114,492,231	15.58
1921-1925	8,104,249	26.35	4,306,870	13.12	250,421,979	28.93	142,215,320	19.35
1926-1930	13,047,919	42.43	5,206,351	15.86	464,934,136	53.70	166,967,943	22.72
Total	30,752,063	100	32,831,619	100	865,604,848	100	734,925,937	100

Origin and Destination:—China's foreign trade in raw cotton may be further examined in respect of origin and destination (Fig. 9). As shown in Table 12, during the 19 years from 1912 to 1930 China imported altogether 23,872,155 piculs of raw cotton, of which 13,128,154 piculs or 54.1 % came from British India, 5,280,291 piculs or 21.8 % from the United States, and 5,267,264 piculs or 21.7 % from Japan. As Japan is not a cotton producing country, much of China's cotton import from Japan is tran-shipped from other countries via Japan, especially India. Taking the three years 1913, 1920 and 1929 for the purpose of comparison, the share for British India declined from 59.56 % in 1913 and 60.85% in 1920 to 51.97 % in 1929, while that for the United States, which fell from 18.84 % in 1913 to 4.95 % in 1920, rose to 32.18 % in 1929. The increasing importance of American cotton is a hopeful sign, as it indirectly confirms that China is demanding a better quality of cotton for the spinning of finer counts of yarn. The share for Japan, which rose from 10.89% in 1913 to 23.53% in 1920, declined again to 14.39% in 1929.

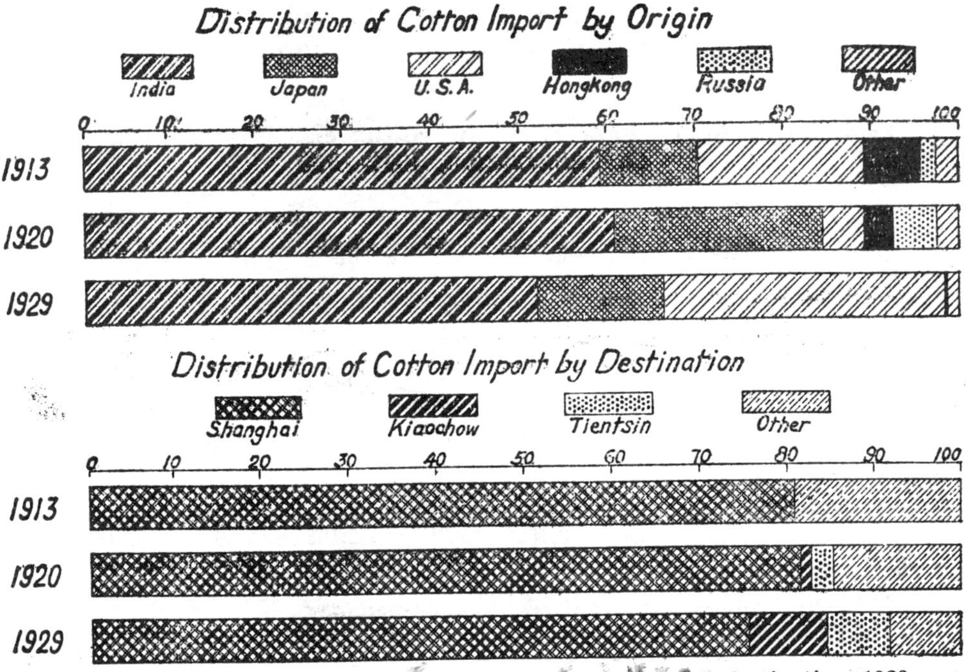

Fig. 9. Distribution of China's cotton import by origin and destination, 1929 (in percentages) (*See* Table 12)

During the period 1912-1930 more than nine-tenths of China's cotton import were absorbed by the three principal centres of China's cotton industry, namely, Shanghai, Kiaochow and Tientsin. Of the total import of 23,946,751 piculs for the 19 years from 1912 to 1930, Shanghai claimed 19,289,342 piculs or 80.6%, Kiaochow 2,108,941 piculs or 8.8%, and Tientsin 1,013,597 piculs or 4.2%. The percentage for Shanghai is rather constant, being 80.84 in 1913 and 81.31 in 1920, but in 1929 it falls slightly to 75.54. For Kiaochow the cotton import is a recent development, beginning with the first import of 206 piculs in 1915. The amount of import rose to 7,871 piculs or 1.15% in 1920 and 225,803 piculs or 8.94% in 1929. The same may be said of Tientsin. The latter imported only 5 piculs in 1912 and 1913 respectively, 7 piculs in 1914 and 24 piculs in 1915. A great increase, however, took place in 1916, when an import of 1,067 piculs of foreign cotton was recorded. Since then the amount of import has showed a considerable fluctuation, reaching 167,749 piculs in 1922, but falling again to 2,244 piculs in 1924. The highest import is that for 1929, namely, 179,156 piculs or 7.09% of China's total import. This fluctuation can be chiefly explained by the fluctuation in Tientsin's cotton import from the interior. As shown in *Appendix VIIb*, Tientsin's cotton import from the interior in 1929, 639,905 piculs, is only one half that of 1928,

1,279,082 piculs. As a consequence, the import of foreign cotton into Tientsin increased from 24,254 piculs in 1928 to 179,156 piculs in 1929.

Table 12. China's import of raw cotton classified by origin and destination, 1912-1930

	1913		1920		1929		1912-1930	
	Piculs	%	Piculs	%	Piculs	%	Piculs	%
From Foreign Countries								
British India	83,169	59.56	418,964	60.85	1,323,002	51.97	13,128,154	54.1
Japan	15,214	10.89	161,978	23.53	366,302	14.39	5,267,264	21.7
U. S. A.	26,310	18.84	34,049	4.95	819,127	32.18	5,280,291	21.8
Hongkong	9,081	6.50	22,526	3.27	4,933	0.19	277,593	1.1
Russia	2,333	1.67	34,529	5.02	—	—	51,461	0.2
Other Countries	3,540	2.54	16,450	2.38	32,125	1.26	266,214	1.1
Total	139,647	100.00	688,496	100.00	2,545,489	100.00	24,270,978	100.0
Re-export	4,912		10,199		30,703		398,823	
Net import	134,735		678,297		2,514,786		23,872,155	
Into Chinese Ports								
Shanghai	109,161	80.84	558,113	81.31	1,907,827	75.54	19,289,342	80.6
Kiaochow	—	—	7,871	1.15	225,803	8.94	2,108,941	8.8
Tientsin	5	—	15,819	2.30	179,156	7.09	1,013,597	4.2
Other Ports	25,867	19.16	104,570	15.24	212,818	8.43	1,534,871	6.4
Total	135,033	100.00	686,373	100.00	2,525,604	100.00	23,946,751	100.0
Re-export					6			
Net import	135,033		686,373		2,525,598			

In Table 13 China's export of raw cotton from 1912 to 1930 is classified in respect of origin and destination, with special reference to the three years 1913, 1920 and 1929 (Fig. 10). During this period of 19 years China's total export of raw cotton amounted to 38,280,474 piculs, of which only 16,867,011 piculs or 44.06% were exported to foreign countries, the rest being imported into other Chinese ports for home consumption. A comparison of the percentage that the export to foreign countries occupies in China's total export confirms indirectly her growing demand for raw cotton arising from the rapid development of the native cotton industry. Such percentage, which amounted to 77.71 in 1913, fell to 43.17 in 1920 and 33.92 in 1929.

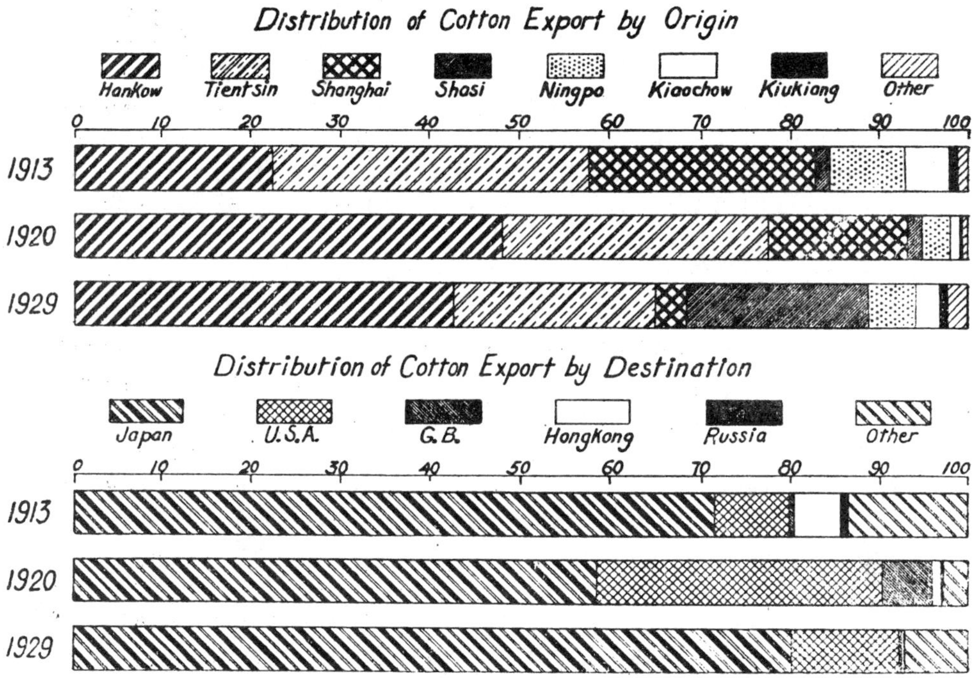

Fig. 10. Distribution of China's cotton export by origin and destination, 1929 (in percentages) (*See* Table 13)

The chief ports of China's cotton export include Hankow and Shasi on the one hand and Tientsin on the other. During the whole period from 1912 to 1930 Hankow and Shasi exported 20,349,123 piculs or 53.16%, while Tientsin exported 9,266,451 piculs or 24.21%. That these three ports should have contributed altogether more than two thirds of China's total cotton export is not unexpected, as Hankow and Shasi are located in the heart of the central producing region, while Tientsin is the collecting centre for raw cotton produced in the northern producing region. However, whereas the percentage that Hankow and Shasi occupied in China's total cotton export has shown a consistent increase from 23.94 in 1913 to 49.74 in 1920 and 62.76 in 1929, such percentage for Tientsin has shown a consistent decrease from 35.29 in 1913 to 29.67 in 1920 and 22.58 in 1929. Another difference to be noted is that while Hankow cotton is exported to Shanghai and other cotton centres along the Yangtze Valley for home consumption, Tientsin cotton is exported to foreign countries, especially to Japan and the United States, for padding, medecinal cotton, gunpowder, and mixture with other fibres. As shown in *Appendix VIIc*, of the total foreign export of 5,127,040 piculs of Tientsin cotton from 1919 to 1929, 4,194,420 piculs or 81.8% were sent to Japan, while 777,126 piculs or 15.2% were sent to the United States.

Because of the prominent part that Japan and the United States played in *Tientsin's* cotton export, 13,466,053 piculs or 79.84% of *China's* total cotton export from 1912 to 1930 were sent to Japan, while 1,934,968 piculs or 11.47% were sent to the United States. Taking the three years 1913, 1920 and 1929 for the purpose of comparison, such percentage for Japan declined from 71.37 in 1913 to 58.56 in 1920, but rose again to 80.04 in 1929; while for the United States it rose from 8.31 in 1913 to 31.80 in 1920, but declined to 12.24 in 1929.[32]

Table 13. China's export of raw cotton classified by origin and destination, 1912-1930

	1913		1920		1929		1912-1930	
	Piculs	%	Piculs	%	Piculs	%	Piculs	%
From Chinese Ports								
Hankow	213,270	22.37	419,439	48.13	1,188,143	42.70	16,346,219	42.70
Tientsin	336,384	35.29	258,568	29.67	628,300	22.58	9,266,451	24.21
Shanghai	238,802	25.05	135,999	15,60	97,121	3.49	3,914,093	10.22
Shasi	14,994	1.57	14,057	1.61	558,130	20.06	4,002,904	10.46
Ningpo	81,632	8.56	28,901	3.32	145,111	5.22	2,167,741	5.66
Kiaochow	48,275	5.06	10,752	1.23	82,037	2.95	925,215	2.42
Kiukiang	7,132	0.75	466	0.05	24,269	0.87	669,427	1.75
Other ports	12,840	1.35	3,374	0.39	59,373	2.13	988,424	2.58
Total	953,329	100.00	871,556	100.00	2,782,484	100.00	38,280,474	100.00
To Foreign countries								
Japan	527,282	71.37	220,312	58.56	755,284	80.04	13,466,053	79.84
U. S. A.	61,381	8.31	119,649	31.80	115,544	12.24	1,934,968	11.47
Great Britain	2,801	0.38	21,053	5.60	1,726	0.18	219,161	1.30
Hongkong	37,378	5.06	3,414	0.91	480	0.05	165,642	0.98
Russia	5,711	0.76	799	0.21	126	0.01	78,221	0.46
Other countries	104,259	14.11	11,003	2.92	70,626	7.48	1,002,966	5.95
Total	738,812	100.00	376,230	100.00	943,786	100.00	16,867,011	100.00
% of foreign export in China's total export		77.71		43.17		33.92		44.06

Varieties of foreign cotton and cotton bales:—The American cotton imported into China is of the Upland variety, and is used in the spinning of finer counts. The quality of it, however, varies greatly. According to the official standards of the U.S. Government, nine grades are recognized, namely, middling fair, strict good middling, good middling, strict middling, middling, strict low middling, low middling, strict good ordinary, and good ordinary. The grades preceded by the word "strict" are known as "half"

32. For detailed figures on China's foreign trade in raw cotton from 1912 and 1930, as well as similar statistics for Tientsin, see *Appendices V, VI, and VII.*

grades in trade custom, although, according to the law, these are all nine to be considered "full" grades. In the old days the American Exchanges also had "quarter" grades, for the purpose of taking care of doubtful bales, which would not come up to the nearest standard but were too good to be dropped in value all the way down to the next. There was a great fuss made about these quarter grades at one time, and they were dropped by the Exchanges and not recognized by the government.[33] In Shanghai the American cotton imported is usually of the middling or low middling grade, for the spinning of 32 or 42 counts. Lower grades possess too short staples for such purpose, and contain a good deal of foreign matter besides.

Indian cotton is named after the place of production, such as Bengal, Broach, Punjab, and Rangoon. According to quality, it is divided into seven grades, namely, super-fine, fine, very good, good, very fair, fair, and good fair. On the East India Cotton Association in Bombay, futures in Bengal, Broach and Oomra cottons are permitted. The price for Indian cotton is usually quoted in terms of rupees per Bombay candy, one Bombay candy being equivalent to seven hundred-weight or 784 lbs. But a candy elsewhere varies in weight from that in Bombay. It is equivalent to 800 lbs. in Surat, $885\,^{3}/_{4}$ lbs. in Broach, $1{,}001\,^{3}/_{7}$ lbs. in Bhownagar and Dhulia (Kathiwar), and $1{,}028\,^{4}/_{5}$ lbs. in Amreli and other places (Kathiwar).[34]

A bale of American cotton, as it comes from the gin, takes the form of an irregular rectangle about 27x54x46 inches, covered with open mesh bagging, and held together by six steel bands or "ties". The average weight per bale is supposed to be 500 pounds, but may vary from 300 to 700 pounds. Bales below 300 pounds carry a penalty as "light weight", while the very heavy bales are rare, being, for the most part, confined to those counties where a levee tax is placed upon each bale, irrespective of weight. Such a bale is called the "standard gin box", and comes from an ordinary press with a pressure of 29 pounds to the hundredweight. But as the rules of the railroads and steamship lines require that the pressure be at least 22½ pounds, shipside, guaranteed, another type of compressing reduces the bale to 28-29 inches wide, 58-59 inches long, and 18-20 inches thick. This is called "flat cotton", and it is these compressed bales which are unloaded from the steamer at Shanghai. During the war the scarcity of freight space enabled the steamship people to insist upon a greater compression, thus developing a third type of bale compressing 34 pounds to the hundredweight, instead of the usual 22½—the "high density" bale. A fourth type of bale is the "round bale", a package made by tightly rolling the cotton around a cylinder. These bales are still made, but did not meet with favor. The package was

33. Hubbard, W. H.: *Cotton and the Cotton Market*, 1925, p. 77.
34. Pearse, A. S: *The Cotton Industry of India*, 1930, pp. vii, 50

tight, but it was very difficult to get a satisfactory sample. Again, these bales, being round, would not pack as well in cars and sheds.[35]

The cotton bale made in India varies greatly in size, but the average weight is about 400 pounds. It is entirely covered with bagging and well bound with ties, which run around it spirally. It is a neat, well-protected package. The Egyptian bale, when shipped, is said to be in better condition than the bale from any other country. It weighs from 700 to 800 pounds, and is compressed to a density of about 30 pounds to a cubic foot. It is completely covered with canvas and securely bound by numerous iron bands. Egyptian bales, however, seldom come to Shanghai because of small demand.[36]

Transport:—**American** cotton is transported from the Southern ports to San Francisco, Seattle, or Los Angeles by means of railway, from which it is loaded on Pacific liners for export to Shanghai. The freight on the railway is fixed from eighty to ninety-five gold cents per hundred pounds, while the steamship freight fluctuates from thirty-five to forty-five gold cents per hundred pound. A bale of five hundred pounds will cost, therefore, approximately six to seven dollars gold for freight charges. No export duty is levied in the States, but in entering into Chinese ports foreign cotton, irrespective of origin, has to pay an import duty of 2.1 gold units (1 gold unit being equivalent to 40 cents gold) per picul, and a wharfage due (2%) and conservancy due (3%) amounting to five percent of the duty. Besides, there is an insurance cost of 3/4% to 1%, and a commission of Tls. 0.20 per bale for the importer.

Indian cotton is exported through Bombay, mostly by the Japanese merchants. For this reason it is often tran-shipped from some Japanese port. The freight per bale amounts to six rupees, while storage and reloading cost another ten rupees. Other expenses, such as tax, insurance and commission, do not differ much from those for American cotton.

Native cotton for foreign export has to pay an export duty of Hk. Tls. 1.20 per picul, and a wharfage due and conservancy due amounting to five percent of the duty. In Tientsin, most of the export cotton is sent to Japan, through Japanese liners. The exporter is usually a Japanese who receives his cotton from own agents in the interior. The freight charge is Tls. 1.50 per picul for Japanese exporter, but Tls. 2.00 for Chinese exporter.[37]

Passing through the Customs:—Passing through the Customs is a complicated procedure for the cotton merchant, and is thus delegated to a special class of agents known as the Customs brokers. These brokers, of whom there are from 160 to 170 in Shanghai, are licensed by the

35. Hubbard, *op cit.*, Chapter VIII.
36. Brown, H. B.: *Cotton*, 1927, p. 348.
37. Shanghai Commercial and Savings Bank, *op. cit.*, pp. 23-24, 27-28.

Customs and carry on business on a partnership basis. Their profit is derived from two sources, namely, the freight rebate varying from fifteen to twenty percent and the commission from the client amounting to five percent.

The import procedure may be briefly described as follows: (1) After having received the Bill of Lading, the importer fills out the 'Import Application' and the 'Import Particular' giving a description of cotton, marks, bales, gross weight, tare, net weight, and value etc. (2) The Import Application is sent to the Shipping Company, which signs it upon the payment of freight. (3) The Import Application, the Import Particular and the Bill of Lading are sent to the Customs, together with the Invoice if any. The Invoice records the original value, loading charges, freight and insurance, and serves as the basis for duty assessment. If accepted by the Customs, the Invoice is stamped with the words 'Invoice seen', which exempts the cotton from examination. (4) The Customs despatches the Import Particular to the examiner at the wharf or godown, who carries out the examination, usually in presence of the importer or his representative. After examination the Import Particular is returned to the Customs. If the Import Particular agrees with the Import Application, the Customs returns the Bill of Lading to the importer. (5) The Customs checks up the Import Application with the Import Manifest of the vessel. If no discrepancy is discovered, the duty is assessed accordingly and the Duty Memo issued to the importer. (6) At the receipt of the Duty Memo, the importer brings the Bill of Lading and the Pass to the Customs for duty payment. In case of re-export, the Pass exempts the importer from further payment of duty, and all he needs to do is to fill out the Re-export Application. (7) At the receipt of the duty, the Customs stamps the Bill of Lading, and approves the Pass if it has been compared with the Import Application, and all is found to be in order.

The export procedure may be described as follows: (1) The exporter applies for the Shipping Order from the Shipping Company and the Testing House Certificate from the Cotton Testing House of the Bureau for the Inspection and Testing of Commercial Commodities. (2) The exporter fills out the Export Application on the basis of the Shipping Order, and sends it to the Customs, together with the Shipping Order and the Cotton Testing House Certificate. (3) The Customs passes the above documents to the examiner at the wharf, who carries out the examination. (4) The Customs issues the Duty Memo if the examination is satisfactory. (5) The exporter pays duty with the Duty Memo to the Customs, through the Bank of China. (6) At the receipt of the duty the Customs' Commissioner stamps the Shipping Order and returns it to the exporter. (7) After the receipt of the Shipping Order the exporter goes to the wharf and loads his cotton on the vessel, for which a receipt is issued by the clerk.

(8) The exporter then exchanges the receipt with the Bill of Lading at the Shipping Company, and the export procedure is thus completed.

The exporter procedure, as above described, applies to cotton exported without a Pass. If native cotton has to be re-exported with a Pass, the exporter has to fill out the Re-export Application, which, together with the Pass, is sent to the Customs. The latter cancels the Pass, upon which the cotton may be loaded for re-export without further payment of duty within the period of one year. However, the cotton must have remained intact in the original packages with their original marks unchanged, in order to be entitled to the exemption. Otherwise, it has to be repacked under Customs supervision and escort. Repacking is only allowed for re-export to a foreign port, for which a special form of Pass must be used by the importer. If repacked cotton is re-exported to a native port, all re-export privileges are forfeited.

In exporting native cotton from one port to another, the export duty, the wharfage and conservancy dues are paid at the port of export, but at the port of import no further duty is levied except the wharfage and conservancy dues. However, in re-exporting foreign cotton from one port to another, the duty and the wharfage and conservancy dues are to be paid at the port of import instead of at the port of export.

If Hankow cotton is exported to Tsingtao via Shanghai, it is considered as transhipment at Shanghai. In applying for transhipment, the exporter has to fill out the Transhipment Application. The latter is effective only for a specified period, within which period neither duty nor wharfage and conservancy dues are to be paid.[38]

Financing:—Cotton imported from abroad is financed through the issuance of drafts accepted by foreign owned banks in Shanghai, as most of the importers are foreigners. The drafts may be of two kinds. In the first case, if the importer, say of Indian cotton, have a branch house in the port of original export, such as Bombay, he may cable directly to the branch for cotton purchase. After the cotton has been purchased, the branch manager prepares the shipment, secures the bill of lading and other required documents, and goes to his bank in Bombay for the acceptance of the draft drawn by him. When accepted the draft may be discounted, and the money obtained may thus be used to pay for the cotton purchased. The bank in Bombay then forwards the documents to its correspondent in Shanghai, at the time when the raw cotton is being shipped towards the same destination. Upon the arrival of the cotton in Shanghai the correspondent of the Bombay bank may have the cotton removed to a warehouse and kept under its control, properly insured, until the importer

38. *Ibid*, pp. 39-44; Chinese Maritime Customs, *Handbook of Customs Procedure in Shanghai*, 1926, Sec. 108-117, 121-125, 149-151, 160, 165, 168, 181-186.

provides funds to pay for the acceptance, at maturity or sooner. In the second case, if the importer have no branch in Bombay, he may have to resort to the letter of credit. Having purchased the cotton from some exporter in Bombay, the importer requests the local bank, through his own correspondent in Bombay, to open a credit in favor of the Bombay exporter, available by his draft drawn, say, for 60 days' sight on the correspondent bank and accompanied by certain specified shipping documents. The Bombay exporter then prepares his shipment, secures the bill of lading and other required documents, draws a draft against the designated correspondent bank in Bombay, and presents the draft to the bank for acceptance, together with the needed documents. The bank accepts the draft and thus fixes the maturity date 60 days hence. If the draft is an acceptance bill, the acceptor separates the documents from the acceptance, returns the acceptance to the exporter, and forwards the documents to the bank in Shanghai. The latter delivers the documents to the importer against such security as it deems fit, who may then unload the cotton from the ship after having gone through the Customs procedure as described in the preceding paragraph.

Traders and trading:—The import of raw cotton from foreign countries, especially from India and the United States, is handled by more than forty foreign importers, chiefly Japanese. The three Japanese firms, namely, Toyo Menkwa Kaisha (Oriental Cotton Trading Co.—an offshoot of Mitsui), Nippon Menkwa Kabushiki Kaisha (Japan Cotton Trading Company) and Gosho Kabushiki Kaisha (Gosho Merchants Co.,) which handle about 70 percent of Japan's cotton import, carry on a considerable amount of business in the import of Indian cotton. In 1928, for instance, China and Japan imported from Karachi altogether 232,809 bales, of which 117,351 bales or 50.4% were shipped by the three firms.[39] In Shanghai the millowners and importers, chiefly Japanese, are organized into the Indian Cotton Importers' Association of China, which has an agreement with three steamship lines for reduced freight, these lines being Pennisula and Oriental Steamship Navigation Co., Nippon Yusen Kaisha, and Osaka Shosen Kaisha. The rebate on cotton shipped from India to China is the same as that in force in Japan, viz., Tls. 0.30 per picul or Tls. 0.90 per bale.[40]

The foreign firms may be either importers or exporters, or both. The trade in foreign cotton is done on a forward basis, the mill placing its order with the importer two or more months before the cotton is needed in spinning. The contract is made according to sample, specify-

39. Pearse, A. S.: *The Cotton Industry of India*, p. 54.
40. Pearse, A. S.: *The Cotton Industry of Japan and China*, p. 149.

ing price and time for delivery, but a deposit with the importer is oftentimes required. The importer then places its order in foreign countries on the basis of the contract, and when the cotton arrives in Shanghai, it may be sent to the importer's godown or to that of the mill's, depending upon the terms of the contract. Payment is made against delivery, in bank checks or in 5 to 10 days' sight native bank orders, in terms of Shanghai taels.

Occasionally the importer may also buy cotton for stock, especially in a rising market. But such purchase is more or less speculative in nature, as the fluctuation in cotton prices is usually great. However, in case of loss the importer can still fall upon his commission, which is fixed at two candareens per picul.[41]

Most of the export cotton goes to Japan, especially from Tientsin. In a recent investigation by Mr. Ojima, a leading cotton merchant, it is shown that among the forty exporters in Tientsin, Japanese firms alone reach 19 in number, the nationality of the other 21 firms being as follows: 8 British, 4 German, 1 French, 1 Swiss, 1 American and 6 Chinese. Chinese exporters are engaged chiefly in the domestic trade with Shanghai and other ports.[42]

The exporter may purchase his cotton from the Chinese cotton firm or ginnery, but in case of the Japanese, it is not uncommon for them to despatch their agents to the local markets for purchase. In buying cotton from the cotton firm, the transaction is carried on through the medium of a compradore who is rewarded with a fixed commission per picul.

41. Cotton, *op. cit.*, pp. 67-71.

42. Ojima, Joji: *Tientsin Cotton*, Tientsin, 1931, pp. 225-26.

CHAPTER III. RAW COTTON: II

Marketing

In bringing raw cotton from the producer to the consumer, whether intermediate or ultimate, it has to go through three types of markets, namely, local, primary and terminal. The first two types of markets can be found practically all over the cotton regions, but the terminal markets are limited in number. Shanghai, Hankow and Tientsin are the chief terminal markets, next to which may be mentioned Chenchow, Shihchiachuang, Tsingtao and Ningpo. In this chapter an analysis of the marketing methods and organization in two of the leading cotton provinces, Kiangsu and Hopei, will be given. In these two provinces are located two of the three important terminal markets, namely, Shanghai and Tientsin.

Cotton markets and merchants in Hopei:—Among the three types of cotton markets in Hopei, we may well begin with the local market, the original market in which cotton farmers sell their products. Such market is usually established at country fairs, at which farmers, brokers, dealers and buying agents from larger markets meet to transact business. Because of their large volume of trade as well as their advantageous position, some of the local markets have developed into primary markets. Unlike the local market at which all kinds of farm products are sold, a primary market always specializes in one kind of produce. Again, in a primary market there are cotton inns which can seldom be found in a local market. These inns are frequented by large farmers who travel a long distance to sell their cotton at the primary market, as well as by buying agents of cotton merchants, exporters and mills from the terminal markets and elsewhere. The manager of such an inn, being a licensed broker, acts as the intermediary between the buyer and the seller. He serves as the public weigher when a transaction is concluded through his service, and arranges for the baling and shipment of his customers' cotton. He secures loans for his customers or lends money to them himself. Besides, it is not uncommon for him to buy future cotton on behalf of any customer whom he knows well, for which he may demand a margin deposit varying from 25 percent or more of the purchase price. The commission charged varies from 10 to 20 percent, while the expense for room and board is fixed at about 50 cents per day. At the height of the marketing season, the cotton inn is indeed the centre of activities at a primary market.

In both types of markets, whether local or primary, there are brokers and dealers, who may be buyers and sellers at the same time. The brokers, however, trade on the customer's account, while the dealers generally trade on own account. The farmer is invariably a seller, while the ginnery, which is also found in both markets, may buy or sell in the local market, but sells in the primary market. The principal function of the ginnery is twofold, namely, to do ginning work for farmers and dealers, as well as to buy seed cotton, gin it and sell it for profit. The buying agents of foreign exporters were active around 1919, but recently they have ceased to visit the primary market for several reasons. The recurrence of civil war, in the first place, interrupts the means of transport and results in frequent fluctuations in the rate of domestic exchange and freight charges. Secondly, the advantages that the foreign exporters formerly possessed over the Chinese merchants have now disappeared. The right to use a transit pass, which used to be monopolized by the foreign merchants, was granted to the Chinese merchants in 1925, thus exempting the latter from the oppressive burden of likin payment. Again, Chinese merchants have begun to study the market conditions with great care in recent years, and are actually in a better position to profit by the market changes than the foreign merchants. The cotton mills, too, have ceased to send their agents for the purchase of cotton in both markets, for fear of embezzlement as well as of risks arising from the uncertain political conditions.

Diagram I

Organization of the Local Market

Seller	1. Farmer 2. Dealer 3. Ginnery	Broker	1. Dealer 2. Ginnery 3. Cotton inn buyer 4. Manufacturer's buyer	Buyer

Diagram II

Organization of the Primary Market

Seller	1. Farmer 2. Dealer 3. Ginnery 4. Cotton inn	Cotton inn broker	1. Dealer 2. Agent of exporting companies 3. Manufacturer's buyer 4. Cotton inn buyer	Buyer

In the terminal market there are three classes of persons engaged in the cotton trade, namely, buyers, sellers, and brokers. In Tientsin, the sellers include the dealers and agents of cotton inns of different primary markets, through whom cotton is shipped from the primary markets to Tientsin for sale. Having no permanent establishment of their own in Tientsin, most of them live and transact their business in the cotton houses during the marketing season. These houses are of the same character as the cotton inns of the primary markets, but are run on a much larger scale. Their principal business is to sell cotton for the customers, although trading on own account is also resorted to. A few of the cotton houses are also engaged in warehousing business as well as in the sale of furs, wool and other commodities. In selling cotton for the customers the cotton houses have to perform a great variety of services. When the cotton arrives in Tientsin the cotton house, in co-operation with the Customs broker, secures the Customs Permit and lands the cotton either at its own warehouse or at that of the buyer's. In landing, the cotton is weighed, and its grade fixed in the presence of a weigher of the cotton house. Besides paying all the expenses thus involved, the cotton house advances loans to the customer for (1) sold cotton that has been either delivered to the buyer without payment or not yet delivered, (2) stock cotton not yet sold, (3) cotton still in transit, and (4) cotton sold on futures basis. These loans are used to finance the customer's cotton purchase in local and primary markets, in the form of drafts. The cotton house usually advances 70 to 80 percent of the market value of cotton under (1) and (2), but rarely over 50 percent of the market value of cotton under (3) and (4). In fact, the cotton house not infrequently suffers huge losses when the customer, in asking loans from the cotton house, reports a larger amount of cotton in transit than is actually the case, or fails entirely to have any cotton in transit. The interest on these loans is calculated on a monthly basis, varying from 1 to 1.2 percent. Besides landing, weighing, warehousing and financing, the cotton house arranges for the sale of the customer's cotton to the buyers, whether exporters, manufacturers or retailers. In each house are employed a number of 'runners' whose duty is to find out the market conditions and to solicit business on behalf of its customers. When a transaction is concluded, the cotton house gets a commission calculated at the rate of one and one half percent of the price, one sixth of which goes to the runner. The profit of a cotton house is derived chiefly from the commission, but for wealthy houses the interest on customers' loans is also a rich source of revenue. For still others that maintain warehouses, the warehousing fees constitute another source. Profits, furthermore, may be derived from trading operations of the house. For instance, when a customer has to return home before the disposal of his cotton, the house may buy it on own account at a reasonable price, and sells it for profit later. However, a cotton house is subject to losses, when it promises to buy from the customer at one price in the morning, but actually has to sell it at a lower one in the afternoon.

The second class of persons in the terminal market, the buyers, include the exporters, mills and retailers. The cotton mills in Tientsin are six in number, and are interested chiefly in the long staple cotton from Hopei, Shansi, Shensi, Honan and foreign countries. The retailers occupy a rather insignificant place in the terminal market, as their purchases are limited in quantity.

The middlemen, including the cotton houses and the brokers or runners, constitute the third class. The cotton houses are representatives of the sellers, and as pointed out above, some of them also trade on own account. The brokers, also known as runners, have no capital and never deal in cotton in their own names. Their function is to bring together sellers and buyers for business, on the payment of a commission which is usually one fourth of one percent of the price. Any one who is familiar with the market conditions and well known by the dealers and buyers is eligible to enter the business, for no license or special qualification is required of him in Tientsin. Since cotton houses are functioning as middlemen themselves, it may seem strange that they still need the service of a separate class of brokers. Two reasons, however, are given for this state of affair. First, as the cotton houses become virtually the selling party by dealing in cotton for the customers in their own names, they must have the broker as the third party to witness the signing of the contract. Secondly, cotton houses, handicapped by their small number of runners whose working time is limited, are not so well acquainted with the market conditions as brokers who are specialists along that line.[43]

Diagram III

Organization of the Tientsin Cotton Market

Sellers	Dealers Cotton houses Agents of cotton inns	Brokers or "Runners"	Exporting companies Cotton mills Retailers	Buyers

Spot trading in Shanghai:—Shanghai, the chief centre of cotton industry in China, is also the largest terminal market in raw cotton trade. In this market both spot and futures trading are carried on to a considerable extent, and in many respects the market in Shanghai differs from that elsewhere. Shanghai, in the first place, is the largest consuming centre in China, whether of native or of foreign cotton. Of the total amount of cotton consumed by the cotton mills in China in 1930, namely, 8,750,019 piculs, Shanghai's share amounted to 4,439,857 piculs or 50.74%. It is for this reason that the largest amount of spot trade is centred in Shanghai, between the cotton mills on the one hand, and the cotton merchants on the other. Again, in Shanghai may be found the only cotton futures market in China,—the Chinese Cotton Goods Exchange. Elsewhere futures were traded in at one time or the other, such as in Tientsin and Ningpo, and even in Shanghai there used to be another exchange, the Shanghai Stock and Produce Exchange, in which some business was done in cotton futures.

43. Chu, T. S. and Chin, T.: *Marketing of Cotton in Hopei Province*, 1929, Chapters II and III; Ojima, *op. cit.*, Chapters IV, VIII, X.

But all these markets have suspended operation in raw cotton, and in view of the supreme position that Shanghai now occupies in China's cotton trade, it is unlikely that other markets will spring up to challenge its well-established lead.

Spot trading in Shanghai offers an interesting contrast to that in Tientsin, not only in the greater variety of the traders engaged in it, but also in the larger scale of their operations. In Tientsin market it is hard to find an exact prototype of cotton dealers known as cotton *hong* or cotton *hao* in Shanghai, although dealers of another type may be found. The latter have no permanent establishment of their own in Tientsin, while the former maintain a regular office and staff in Shanghai, oftentimes with own warehouses attached. On the other hand, cotton houses which provide living accommodations and trade facilities to dealers and cotton inn agents from the primary markets are indispensable to the Tientsin market, but cannot be found in the Shanghai market. Again, as Shanghai imports annually about four fifths of the foreign cotton consumed in China, the importers there occupy a position which is beyond all possibility in Tientsin. The scale on which dealers and importers operate in Shanghai is far greater than in Tientsin. In Shanghai the cotton hao has to have a minimum capital investment of $30,000 to $50,000, while a big firm may have to provide around a million dollars for similar purpose. For the importers the capital investment is even larger. The Anderson, Clayton & Co., a branch of the noted cotton firm in the United States, must have almost unlimited resources at its command in the eyes of Chinese merchants. So also is the Jardine, Matheson & Co., with its branch offices all over the Orient, especially in China and India. In the diagram on page 60 the channels of distributing spot cotton in Shanghai are shown. The heavy arrows indicate the direction of these channels among the cotton merchants in Shanghai, while the dotted ones indicate the direction among the cotton merchants outside Shanghai who are in one way or the other connected with the Shanghai merchants.

The cotton hong is the oldest distributing institution in Shanghai. At first these hong were concentrated in Nan-shi or Southern City, for which reason Shanghai cotton is still known as Nan-shi cotton, and the street in which these hong are located is known as the Cotton Street. Later on cotton hong sprang up in Pei-shi or Northern City, and thus introduced the Pei-shi cotton into the market. In the environs of Shanghai cotton hong may also be found, but are operated on a smaller scale. Generally, the hong in Nan-shi or Pei-shi have a capital investment of from ten to thirty or forty thousand dollars each, and are owned by individual proprietors or partners. The staff is composed of a manager, an accountant, one or two runners and weighers. These hong buy cotton from the farmers in the country districts, the local markets, through the medium of brokers (鄉販).

Diagram IV Traders in Spot Cotton, Shanghai

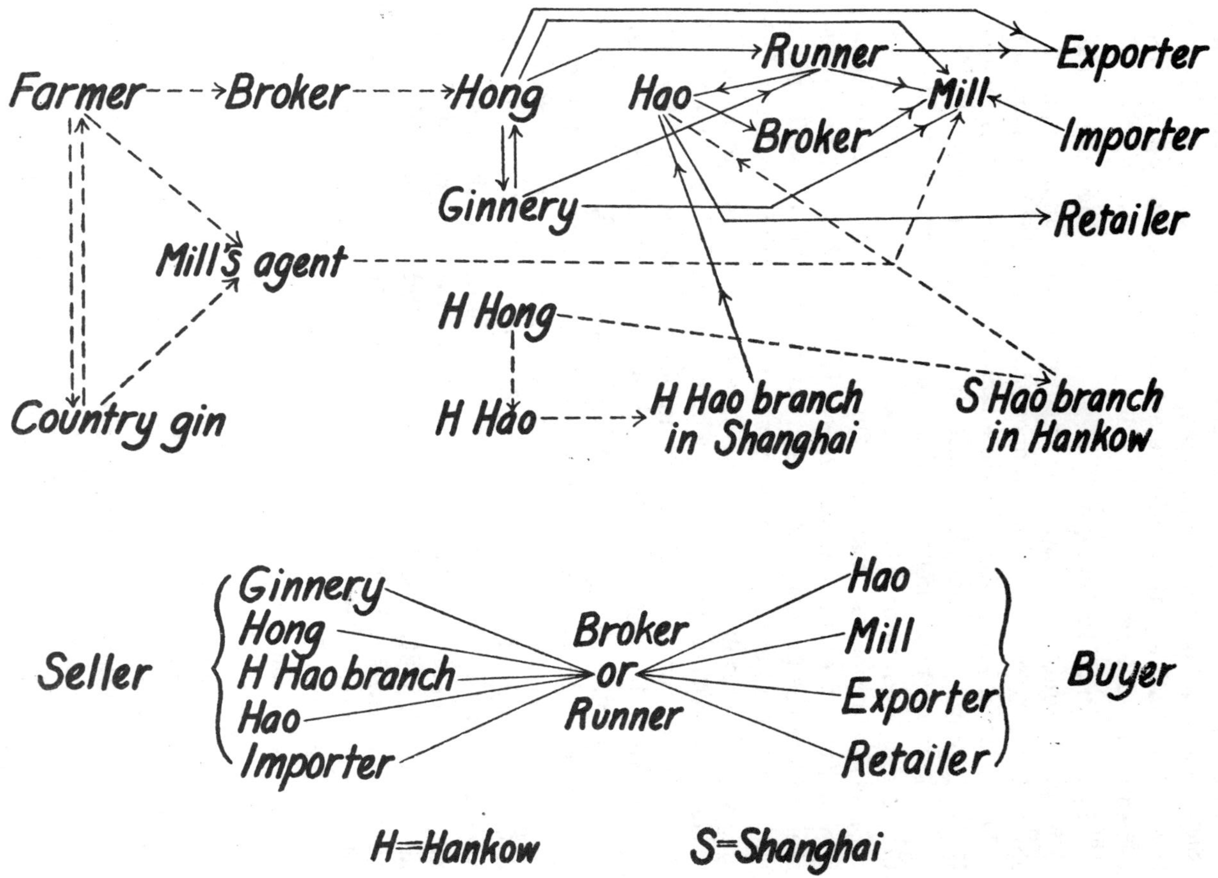

The farmer may sell the seed cotton, or have it ginned by the country gin. Such cotton is customarily brought to the hong's weigher, who determines the grade, the percentage of moisture and the weight. Szemao scale (司馬秤) is preferred, as Hwei Kwan scale (會官秤), giving 13.3 to 13.4 liang per catty, is too low, while Chung scale (重秤), giving 18 to 20 liang, is too high. The weighed cotton is removed to the storeroom, and packed into loose bales of 125 catties each, with own trademarks.

The cotton hong sells most of its cotton to the mills, but a small part to the cotton hao and exporters. In both cases the transaction is conducted through another class of brokers known as Mien-K'e (棉客), at a commission of one candareen per picul. The mills or exporters, however, may buy cotton directly from the cotton hong on a contract basis (抄莊), under which whatever amount of cotton collected or purchased by the cotton hong for one day or several days is to be turned over to the mill or exporter exclusively. The commission goes to the cotton hong, varying from ½ to 1 percent, but amounting generally to ten cents per picul. The contract price may be net (洋盤) or gross (毛盤), under the latter of which the buyer, an exporter for instance, may deduct a certain percentage from the contract price as a commission to the person in charge of the transaction, who is usually the compradore in the export firm. At present, although the transaction is carried on directly without any middleman, it has become the practice to claim a rebate of 1.1 candareens per picul for Nan-shi or Pei-shi cotton, but one of 1.4 candareens for Tungchow cotton. The higher rebate for Tungchow cotton is accounted for by the buyer's responsibility to remove the cotton from the Pootung godown.

The ginning of cotton constitutes the chief business of the ginnery, although the ginnery may purchase cotton on its own account, and gins it for sale like the cotton hong. It receives its cotton for ginning from the cotton hong, but sometimes when the cotton is already ginned by the country gin on behalf of the farmer, such cotton can be disposed of by the cotton hong at once. Ginning may also be performed by the hong itself. The scale of operation for a ginnery varies with the type of gins installed. A hand operated gin can be purchased for twenty or thirty dollars, while a power operated gin is not only more costly, but also requires the installation of power facilities. A large ginnery may have a capital investment of twenty to thirty thousand taels. The price for ginning is usually one dollar per picul.

The cotton hao is the key institution in spot trade, as the cotton exchange is in futures trade. It differs from the cotton hong in the greater variety of cotton handled, the larger scale of operation, and the greater risks involved. A cotton hao in Shanghai, which is usually located in the concessions, deals in cotton from all parts of China, and is distinguished by the origin of the cotton handled. Such a hao, for instance, may be

Shanghai (申帮), Hankow (漢帮), Anch'ing (安慶帮), Tungchow (通州帮), Yuyao (姚餘帮), etc. A Hankow hao concentrates its transactions in Hankow cotton, but it may deal in Tientsin or Shantung cotton as a subsidiary line. It is owned and managed by the native merchants from Hankow, and purchases cotton either from the cotton hong in Hankow, or from the branch of the Hankow cotton hao (坐莊) in Shanghai. In still other cases the cotton hao in Shanghai may despatch own agents to Hankow for the collection and purchase of Hankow cotton. A cotton hao, unlike a cotton hong, charges no commission, but makes its profit from the price differences. Its capital investment is also larger, and may run from 30,000 to 50,000 dollars to several hundred thousand dollars. It is mostly organized on a partnership basis, and differs very little from a cotton hong in staff composition except in respect of size. As mentioned below, the cotton hao takes an active part in the futures market, and accepts contracts from the mills for a term of one, two or three months.

The branch office of a cotton hao from other terminal markets, such as Tientsin or Hankow, performs the twin function of marketing and information. It disposes of the cotton received from its respective headquarters, and reports the market conditions in Shanghai for decision. The latter function is the more important, as a cotton hao makes its profit largely from price differences of cotton in different markets.

Cotton mills are the largest buyers in spot cotton, and the position that they occupy in spot trade is the more important because they do not resort to hedging as much as the manufacturers elsewhere. This, undoubtedly, is the case with foreign owned mills also. According to the observation of a foreign expert, "as in Japan, so in China, very large quantities of cotton are bought ahead and not a single bale of such purchases is hedged. Several mill managers in Shanghai did not make any secret of the fact that they were 30,000 bales long in cotton and they spoke of one company that was at least 50,000 bales long. Some of the mills have accumulated a special reserve known as 'Cotton Fluctuation Fund'. It will be readily understood that the business of cotton spinning is only of secondary consideration under such conditions, it will depend upon the luck or otherwise in the purchase of the raw materials whether the mill makes a profit or a loss."[44]

Cotton mills may buy cotton directly from the farmer, or indirectly through one of the three sources, (1) cotton hong, cotton hao or ginnery, (2) cotton exchange, and (3) cotton importer. Cotton is purchased from the farmers through the mill's own agents. At the beginning of the harvesting season in September, the mill despatches some of the staff mem-

44. Pearse, *Cotton Industry of Japan and China*, 1929, p. 196. In Tientsin one Chinese owned mill in 1919 purchased so much cotton for stock that it had to re-sell a part of it and to suffer a loss of $238,613.53. See *Infra, Appendix IVb.*

bers to the local market where a branch office is organized for the purpose of receiving cotton from the farmers. The scale used is of the Szemao type, and a gin may be installed for the ginning of seed cotton. The mill may get a better price for cotton purchased under this method, but several difficulties have tended to discourage it in recent years. The recurrence of civil war interrupts the means of communication. Meantime, it gives rise to the possibility of loss from robbery on the way. The loss from embezzlement by the boatman may be very large at times, while a knowledge of the local market conditions which is the keynote to successful operation is always difficult to acquire. For these reasons, the mills have recently entrusted the purchasing end to the cotton hong as described above. Under such arrangement the mill gives a limit price to the cotton hong, but is responsible for extreme fluctuations in prices. In purchasing from the cotton hao or ginnery, the business is transacted through the medium of brokers or runners. The latter bring the sample from the former to the different mills, with a view to securing business. If the terms are satisfactory to both parties, a contract is immediately drawn up, which is jointly sealed by the mill and the cotton hao. The price is fixed, so also the date and place of delivery. The date of delivery may be spot or futures, the latter varying from one to three months, while the place of delivery may be *ex godown*, at the mill or at the wharf. The price for mill delivery is from ½ to 1½ taels higher in order to allow for the transhipment charges. The place for *ex godown* delivery usually varies according to the kind of cotton purchased. Before the cotton is accepted by the mill, it is first checked with the original sample, and then tested for moisture percentage. From the gross weight are deducted the baggings and the excess moisture, in order to get at the net weight. Payment is made in ten days' sight native bank order, but cash may be demanded with proper allowance for interest. The commission for the broker or runner is one candareen per picul, to be paid by the seller.[45] Cotton purchase from the importer has been described in the preceding chapter, while that from the cotton exchange will be given below.

Future trading in Shanghai:—Trading in cotton futures is often carried on secretly in the terminal markets, but organized dealing may be dated from the establishment of the Japanese Exchange in Shanghai in 1918. Two years later the native merchants there organized the Chinese Stock and Produce Exchange, in which cotton futures were dealt in along with futures in stocks, cotton yarn, and gold bars. In 1921 another exchange, the Chinese Cotton Goods Exchange, was organized under the leadership of Mr. H. Y. Moh, in which futures were transacted in raw cotton and cotton yarn. In Tientsin a Produce Exchange was also organized in that year, with a special department for cotton and cotton yarn.

45 Cotton, *op. cit.*, 48-68.

But as most of the cotton dealers withheld themselves from joining the organization, dealings in the Exchange were never active and the Exchange was soon closed down. In 1927 the Japanese Exchange closed down because of huge loss, while a short time ago futures in cotton and cotton yarn on the Chinese Stock and Produce Exchange were given up due to lack of business. At present, therefore, cotton futures are carried on in the Chinese Cotton Goods Exchange alone.

The Chinese Cotton Goods Exchange, like other exchanges in China, possesses three unique features, of which the first is its organization for the purpose of profit-making. In America or England, the cotton exchange, like other produce exchange, is an association managed and owned by the members—whether brokers or jobbers; in China, the brokers are the clients of the Exchange to which they pay a commission per contract for the use of exchange facilities. On the Chinese Cotton Goods Exchange, the commission is Tls. 12.00 per contract, of which one fourth goes to the Exchange, and the other three fourths belong to the broker. As a profit-making enterprise, the Chinese Cotton Goods Exchange is subject to the Chinese Commercial Associations Law, and is organized as a limited liability corporation, with a capital investment of $3,000,000. It is represented by a Board of Managers elected every three years by the stockholders who must be Chinese citizens. The Board of Managers of the Chinese Exchange is given the same power as that of any American cotton exchange, but its activity is more extensive. In the Chinese Exchange, the work of the various standing committees is performed by the Board of Managers, assisted only by the paid employees. Each member of the Board also receives a salary from the Exchange. A second unique feature is the broker's relationship to the Exchange. In American exchanges, the brokers, being members of the Exchange, represent the exchange and are not apart from it. In the Chinese Exchange, the brokers are subject to the control of the Exchange; and the by-laws and rules of the Brokers' Association—an organization composed exclusively of the brokers licensed by the Exchange and meantime not members of any other cotton exchange—must be approved by the Exchange before they can be put into effect. This rather comprehensive control of the brokers by the Exchange is justified on the ground that the Exchange is legally responsible for any loss arising from the violation of the contract bought by or sold to the broker on the Exchange. On the other hand, the broker must, as a pledge of good faith, deposit a personal bond of Tls. 20,000 with the Exchange, and in addition, must pay various kinds of margins on each contract bought or sold on the Exchange. The third unique feature is the relation of the government to the Exchange. For centuries the Chinese government exercised no control over Chinese industry and trade other than the collection of taxes for revenue purpose. This attitude of indifference would have been possible even today but for the growing complexity of Chinese national economic life in the modern industrial age. In 1921, seven years after the passage of the first Stock Exchange Law, a Produce Exchange Law was adopted and put into effect. The law contains the following provisions that relate to the government regulation of the exchange:—

1. Every produce exchange must be approved and licensed by the Ministry of Agriculture and Commerce. It must submit its constitution and by-laws to the Ministry for approval, as well as any subsequent amendment. If necessary in the opinion of the Ministry, the Ministry may request the exchange to revise its constitution and by-laws.
2. If the exchange commits any act that is unlawful, contrary to public welfare, or opposed to peace or order, the Ministry may take any of the following actions:—
   a) to dissolve the exchange;
   b) to stop the transaction of business on the exchange;
   c) to stop or prohibit the transaction of a part of business on the exchange;
   d) to demand the resignation of the officers of the exchange;
   e) to stop the broker's right to transact business on the exchange or cause him to be expelled from the exchange.
3. If necessary in the opinion of the Ministry of Agriculture and Commerce, the Ministry may appoint at any time an inspector or inspectors to examine the business transactions, books and property of the exchange, as well as the books of the broker or brokers.
4. The exchange must, before the formal opening of its business, deposit with a depositary approved by the Ministry of Agriculture and Commerce a business bond amounting to one third of its capital investment. It shall pay a license fee of $500, and shall, after each annual closing of accounts, pay five percent of its profit as a produce exchange tax, to the Ministry.

The above law, however, was replaced by the new Exchange Law promulgated by the National Government in October, 1929, in which the provision on tax was dropped with the understanding that a new law would soon be promulgated on the exchange tax. No fixed amount was set for the business bond, which under the old law was to be one third of the exchange's capital investment. Again, permission was given to organize the exchange on the basis of membership as well as of profit-making, whereas formerly only profit-making type was allowed.[46]

The Chinese Produce Exchange Law gives the government, through the Ministry of Industries, (formerly Ministry of Agriculture and Commerce), comprehensive control over the affairs of the exchange—control that neither American nor English exchange has been required to acknowledge. The United States Cotton Futures Act, for example, does not possess any of the powers cited above; instead, it touches upon such questions as official standards and spot quotations in fixing differences.

The above description is sufficient for an understanding of the leading features of the Chinese Cotton Goods Exchange. A few words remain

46. For the various laws and regulations, see Yang, Yiu P'u: *Stock and Produce Exchange in China,* Commercial Press, 1930, Appendices 4,5,9,15.

to be said on its actual operation, with particular reference to the nature of the Chinese cotton futures contract. Because of practical difficulties, the Exchange deals in futures in raw cotton and cotton yarn only, not in spots. In raw cotton, the unit of trading per contract is 100 piculs (one picul being equivalent to 133 1/3 lbs.), as contrasted with 100 bales of 500 lbs. each in America. The cotton bought or sold is confined to the Chinese growth, of which Tungchow or Hankow long staple used to be the basis grade. The value difference between the basis grade and other grades tenderable on the contract is fixed twice a year by the Experts' Committee, which is composed of ten persons experienced and well known to the cotton trade, and appointed by the Board of Managers. Trading for the current month and the subsequent five months only, instead of 12 months in England or the United States, is permitted; and margins, in addition to the personal bond required of every broker before his admission to the Exchange, must be paid by either or both parties to the contract. Margins are of several kinds, of which the original (which is now 10% of the contract value) and variation margins are the same as under an American contract. Besides the original and variation margins, a special margin is also required under the Chinese futures contract. A special margin which must not exceed thrice the original margin, is required of either or both brokers whenever there are unusual price fluctuations and other market circumstances, or when the Exchange shall deem it necessary. All these margins, original, variation, or special, can be paid in substitutes other than cash or certified check, which is not the practice on the American exchange. These substitutes, in general, include securities or other negotiable documents. The contract settlement, as well as the margin payment, take place daily, and are handled through the Accounting Department of the Exchange, which is a prototype of the American clearing house. The day preceding the last business day of the month is the only day when the delivery of cotton on contract is permitted, a practice differing considerably from the American custom of issuing five days' delivery notice previous to actual delivery. In case of a default, the contract is settled at the delivery price, with the payment of a penalty of about ten percent to the broker not violating the contract. Any controversy or dispute between the brokers or between the broker and his customer is settled by the Arbitration Committee at the request of the parties involved. The Committee is composed of three persons, to be selected and appointed by the Exchange from the Exchange officers, the committee members of the Brokers' Association and the Experts' Committee.[47]

47. *Constitution and By-laws of the Chinese Cotton Goods Exchange;* Fong, H. D.: The New Cotton Futures Market in China, in *China Weekly Review*, Sep. 29, 1928, pp. 148-9.

According to the Revised Rules of the Exchange dated July 12, 1925, the Exchange limits the number of brokers to 80 in raw cotton, but actually there are only 71 brokers on the Exchange in 1931. These brokers transact business for three classes of clients, namely, cotton mills, cotton hao and cotton hong and a third group including professional and outside speculators. Any client who wishes to buy or sell cotton at the Exchange may do so through his broker. Two copies of the contract are first drawn up specifying the price and quantity of the cotton dealt in, and the terms of delivery, and are sent to the Exchange to be sealed. They are then signed by the broker and the client, after which each party holds a copy for reference. In order to protect the interest of the broker, every client is required to pay the three kinds of margins described above. These margins, which must be paid by the broker to the Exchange, are not always paid by the client. In the case of an unusually reputable client with high credit standing, the original margin may not be paid at all. A broker, being required to deposit a bond of Tls. 20,000 with the Exchange, as well as to pay various kinds of margins on his contracts, must have a large capital at command for sucessful operation. This is more so when the broker is the owner of a cotton hao and deals on own account. Generally, the capital investment of a broker may run from thirty to one hundred thousand dollars.

Trade associations:—The Chinese Cotton Merchants' Association (中華棉業聯合會) is the leading organization in cotton trade, which was organized in 1928 in Shanghai. Its members are composed of the cotton hong, cotton hao, and ginneries, and may be further classified into nine groups: (1) Nan-shi cotton hong, which were formerly organized into the Nan-shi Cotton Merchants' Association, have now united with the Pei-shi cotton hong under the joint organization, the Shanghai Cotton Hong Association. The latter includes about 20 hong from Nan-shi and 15 hong from Pei-shi. (2) Pei-shi cotton hong. (3) Tungchow cotton hao, about 25 in number, are organized into the Tungchow Cotton Merchants' Association. (4) Hankow Cotton Merchants' Association. (5) Shanghai cotton hao, about 20 in number, have joined with the Yuyao cotton hao to form the Cotton Hao Association. (6) Yuyao cotton hao, of which there are nine in Shanghai. (7) Steam ginneries, about 20 in number, are organized into the Steam Ginners' Association. (8) Cotton brokers or runners, about 30 in number. (9) Taich'ang cotton hao. Of these nine groups, the Cotton Hao Association is the most influential, due chiefly to the important financial position occupied by its members.

The Shanghai Cotton Merchants' Association has as its chief objects the protection of trade interests and the promotion of trade activities. It also provides different departments in the headquarter for spot trading in various kinds of native cotton, but not in futures. It issues a daily price report of native and foreign cotton to its members, and a weekly summary report of the amount of cotton in stock and the amount of cotton imported or exported. Besides, the Association prescribes various kinds of blank forms for spot trading.

Among the foreign exporters the only association is the Japanese Cotton Exporters' Association, which has about twenty members.[48]

Packing and warehousing:—In packing Chinese cotton a great deal of confusion exists with respect to form, size, weight and the materials used. In China every cotton district has its own method of packing, which differs not only for the different kinds of cotton, but also for the same kind of cotton produced in different localities. Some cotton is pressed before packing, while others may be packed in a loose state. The result is the considerable variation in size and weight. According to the field investigation by one cotton expert, a bale of Shensi cotton weighs 477 pounds, with a size of $19.5 \times 28 \times 32$ inches or 10 cubic feet and a density of 47.7 pounds per cubic foot; a bale of Yüho cotton weighs 279 pounds, with a size of $22 \times 28 \times 49$ inches or 17.5 cubic feet and a density of 16 pounds per cubic foot; a bale of Tungchow cotton weighs 156 pounds, with a size of $18 \times 30 \times 68$ inches or 21 cubic feet and a density of 7.4 pounds per cubic foot; a bale of Yuyao cotton weighs 78 pounds, with a size of $18 \times 33 \times 34$ inches or 11.7 cubic feet and a density of 6.7 pounds per cubic foot. This investigation reveals a considerable divergence in volume, weight and density for the different kinds of bales. The density, it may be noted, varies from 6.7 pounds per cubic foot for Yuyao cotton to 47.7 pounds per cubic foot for Shensi cotton, the latter being 7.1 times higher than the former. The reasons for this divergence are twofold. When the cotton is transported a long distance before reaching the destination, such as is the case with Shensi cotton, tight packing helps to facilitate transport as well as to reduce freight. This is particularly true when there is a congestion in traffic. Again, even when the distance for transport is the same for two kinds of cotton, the method of packing differs because of difference in trade organization and practice. In Chiahsiang the cotton merchants operate mostly on a large scale, and can afford to install steam or hydraulic press for packing. Tungchow cotton, which is sometimes exported to Japan and has to travel a long distance, is loosely packed because of traditional practice. Each type of packing, however, has its merits, a consideration of which is a necessary pre-requisite to its adoption. Pressing saves space and reduces cost of transport. It reduces loss from leakage and petty theft, as well as the chance for deterioration due to contact with moisture.

48. Cotton, *op. cit.*, pp. 119-22.

From the viewpoint of spinning, loose packing is preferable, for compressed cotton requires a great deal of breaking and opening. Such process is also necessary before the compressed cotton is in a position to absorb the atmospheric moisture essental for successful spinning.

In respect of form and the materials used for packing there is also a lack of uniformity. Shensi cotton, for instance, is packed in rectangular shape, covered with linen bagging and held together by steel bands or ties; while Tungchow cotton is packed in small round shape, covered with cotton bagging and held together by straw ropes. Taich'ang cotton is packed in long round shape, covered by rush bagging and also held together by straw ropes.[49] In Hopei the old method was to cover the bale with cotton bagging and hold it together by means of hempen ropes crosswise, in rectangular shape. These bales may be large, medium or small. The medium bale weighed 160 pounds, and measured about twenty cubic feet, with a density of eight pounds per cubic foot. This method of packing, being loose, was welcomed by the Japanese manufacturers because of facility in spinning, but strongly objected to by the exporters on account of loss from frequent leakage and the larger space that it occupied. A new method is now adopted, under which cotton is packed in 200 pound bales by means of a machine press.[50] It is covered and bound in much the same way as the cotton bag bale, but much more compactly packed.[51]

Warehoursing in Shanghai is mostly a subsidiary undertaking for the steamship companies, both foreign and Chinese, but independent warehouses with pressing facilities have sprung up recently. Besides, because of financial connections, the business of warehousing is also carried on by some of the banks. The steamship companies provide free warehousing facilities to the importers for the first ten days or two weeks after the arrival of the cargo, but not any longer. If a charge is made by the warehouses, whether operated by the steamship companies or by other agencies, it is uniform for all months except the first one. For large steam-pressed bales of 400 catties each, the warehousing fee is Tl. 0.28 for the first month but Tl. 0.20 for every subsequent month; for medium bales of 300 catties each it is Tl. 0.22 for the first month but Tl. 0.15 for every subsequent month; for small bales of 200 catties or below, it is Tl. 0.18 for the first month but Tl. 0.12 for every subsequent month.

At the arrival of the vessel the cotton may be landed for warehousing as soon as the Customs Permit to Land has been secured. It is

49. Tze Yih: Packing the Chinese Cotton, in *China Cotton Journal*, Vol. IV, No. 3, pp. 30-32.
50. Ojima, *op. cit.*, pp. 183-5.
51. Chu, *op. cit.*, p. 28.

received at the warehouse according to the importer's application giving a description of the cotton, number of bales, weight, kind of bale, etc. A receipt is then issued for the cotton received, which the importer exchanges at the business office of the warehouse for the warehouse certificate. In some cases the warehouse requires the importer to produce the fire insurance policy before the cotton is admitted, but in others it undertakes to secure such policy on behalf of the importer. The warehouse certificate, if issued by reputable warehouses, is a valuable security for the obtaining of bank loans.

In withdrawing cotton from the warehouse, the importer must first present the warehouse certificate to the business office for the payment of the warehousing fee. A withdrawal permit is then issued to the importer, with which he may apply for the delivery or release of his cotton at the warehouse. But in case of a bill of lading issued by the steamship company, the importer must first present the bill of lading, together with the pass, to the Customs examiner, who cancels the pass and stamps the bill of lading. The importer then sends the latter to the steamship company for a withdrawal permit, and the same procedure is repeated.[52]

Transport and taxation:—The chief means of cotton transport include the railway, the boat and the cart. Sometimes one of the three means is used, but at other times all of them may have to be employed. The cart, driven by mules or other animals, is employed for short distance transport, but where both railway and boat are not available, as is generally true in the interior, the cart is the sole means of transport. The railway has the advantage of speed, but in war-ridden China, its certainty is questionable. The boat transport is reasonable but slow, so it reduces the rate of capital turnover and thereby increases the interest charges. In North China, furthermore, it is not available during winter season when the river is frozen. Because of the difference in the means of transport employed in each cotton district, the cost differs considerably for the same unit of distance travelled. In Tientsin the cost of transport per kilometre-picul varies from the lowest of 0.25 cent from Shichiachuang to the highest of 0.70 cent per kilometre-picul from Hantan. In Hopei the highest charge for cart transport is from Hantan to Tsangchiao, which amounts to 1.25 cents per kilometre-picul, while the lowest charge for boat transport is that from Yench'ang to Tientsin, which amounts to 0.14 cent per kilometre-picul. From Hantan to the railway station the charge for cart transport runs even higher, namely, 4.5 cents per kilometre-picul.[53]

52. Cotton, *op. cit.*, pp. 146-48.
53. Chu, *op. cit.*, p. 27.

Table 14. Amount of cotton imported into Tientsin by the three means of transport, 1921-1931 (in piculs, as recorded by the Native Customs)

Year	By Rail	By Boat	By cart	Total
1921	496,544	125,761	13,076	635,381
1922	724,514	215,185	4,467	944,166
1923	715,959	230,166	13,671	959,796
1924	381,617	159,255	13,814	554,686
1925	464,338	574,845	18,137	1,057,320
1926	73,055	841,809	30,283	945,147
1927	227,065	956,670	48,693	1,232,428
1928	304,238	846,465	61,732	1,212,435
1929	64,779	421,868	29,909	516,556
1930	167,039	682,812	37,566	887,417
1931 (to May)	170,103	178,181	58,835	407,119
		Percent		
1921	78.1	19.8	2.1	100.0
1922	76.7	22.8	0.5	100.0
1923	74.6	24.0	1.4	100.0
1924	68.8	28.7	2.5	100.0
1925	43.9	54.4	1.7	100.0
1926	7.7	89.1	3.2	100.0
1927	18.4	77.6	4.0	100.0
1928	25.1	69.8	5.1	100.0
1929	12.5	81.7	5.8	100.0
1930	18.8	76.9	4.3	100.0
1931 (to May)	41.8	43.8	14.4	100.0

The tax on Chinese cotton is of three kinds, namely, likin, sales tax and export duty, of which likin is the most irregular and oppressive. In Shansi there is a *tungshui* of one dollar per picul, plus a police surtax of twenty cents, a famine relief surtax of twenty cents, and a special military surtax of eighty cents—a total of $2.20 including *tungshui* and surtax. Shansi cotton meantime has to pay the likin levied by other provinces through which it passes. In Hopei, the likin was fixed in 1919 at Hk. Tl. 0.15 per picul. It was doubled in 1920-21 under the new name *tungshui*, at the rate of Hk. Tl. 0.30 per picul, which was further raised by a surtax of an equivalent amount in 1926. In 1927 it was raised from Hk. Tl. 0.60 per picul to $2.00 per picul, to which a surtax of 60 cents per picul was added during the spring of 1929. In other words, the likin was raised from Hk. Tl. 0.15 or about 20 cents per picul in 1919 to $2.60 per picul in 1929—an increase of thirteen times in the course of but eleven years. An agitation was therefore started by the cotton merchants for a reduction in the tax rate, and it was not until Feb. 15, 1930 that the reduced rate of $1.60 per picul was put into effect. The *tungshui* is collected by the first likin station. The receipt which this station issues on the payment of *tungshui* must be examined each time the cotton passes through a second station, for which process a fee of forty cents is charged. With the abolition of likin on the first of January, 1931, *tungshui* is *ipso facto* abolished, but in Hopei it is still levied at the time of writing (June, 1931).[54]

54. *Textile News*, Nos. 773,778.

In Shansi and Hopei another tax in the nature of sales tax is levied upon raw cotton by provincial authorities. At first the tax was collected directly from the merchants, but later on a lump sum was fixed for each hsien or district, which was collected by the Provincial Tax Bureau or farmed out to some local merchants. Abuses, however, often arose under this system of farming, as a result of which a new method of collection was devised, by delegating the function to a cohong—an association of cotton merchants. The latter was to collect the tax from its own members quarterly, and to turn it over to the Provincial Tax Bureau. In Tientsin most of the cotton imported from the interior have already paid the sales tax, but such tax is levied again at the rate of 1½ percent of the sales price, payable quarterly to the Municipal Tax Bureau through the medium of the Cotton Merchants' Association. The cotton houses are requested to report their sales to the Association, with heavy penalty for failure, so that the tax burden may be equally distributed among the members.

Besides the sales tax and likin, there is a third tax on raw cotton, namely, the export tax, which is fixed at Hk. Tl. 0.35 per picul for any cotton destined for foreign export. But previous to the abolition of likin, it is subject to the payment of likin including the Native Customs duty before its arrival at the port for foreign export. The Native Customs duty is fixed at Hk. Tl. 0.30 per picul, which for foreign merchants is the only kind of likin ever paid under the Outward Transit Pass system. Furthermore, as the Treaty of Tientsin in 1858 provided that the transit duty should not exceed one half of the export duty, the foreign merchant under the Outward Transit Pass system was given the privilege to refund the excess amount of duty paid for raw cotton to the Native Customs, namely, Hk. Tl. 0.125, at the port of export. Before the grant of the same privilege to the Chinese merchant in November, 1925, he had not only no right to the refund, but was also obliged to pay likin other than the Native Customs duty. The new grant, however, was nominal, as the qualifications rendered it ineffective in many ways. Under the Outward Transit Pass system the Chinese merchant has to deposit a bond of thrice the value of the export duty with the Customs. Again, if within the period allowed the merchant fails to have the cotton exported abroad, he is subject to a fine which is one and half times the value of the export duty. If the cotton, having been re-exported to another port, fails to be exported abroad within the period allowed, the fine is raised to two and half times the value of the export duty. The period allowed for the Outward Transit Pass which lasts from the date of issue to the date of foreign export, is generally one year, but for cotton exported from Kansu it is extended to two years.[55]

55. Ojima, *op. cit.*, Chapter VI.

Because of the insufficient production of cotton in China and of the import of foreign cotton to meet the home need, the cotton millowners, through the Chinese Cotton Millowners' Association in Shanghai, presented in June, 1923, a petition to the Governor of Kiangsu, requesting him to levy a cotton export surtax of Hk. Tl. 0.15 per picul. The Association claimed that the surtax would help to curtail the export, and would hasten the improvement of cotton culture in China if it be spent for that purpose. The petition promised some success at first, but was dropped because of the opposition of foreign exporters. Recently, the old Export Tariff, passed in 1858, is revised by the national government, with a general raise in tariff schedule in order to meet the government's deficiency in revenue caused by the likin abolition in January, 1931. The export duty on raw cotton is raised from Hk. Tl. 0.35 per picul to Hk. Tls. 1.20 per picul,—a raise of 3.5 times. Indirectly, the raise more than achieves the purpose of the formerly proposed surtax. Along with the export duty wharfage due amounting to 2% of the duty, and conservancy due, amounting to 3%, have to be paid at Shanghai.

Financing:—In financing the cotton purchase several methods have been developed. The simplest method is to bring cash to the local market for cotton purchase, but in view of the uncertainty of protection from robbery it is rather risky. This method is resorted to when the local market or producing district is not far away from the terminal market, such as in the environs of Shanghai. It is also the only method in regions where no banking facilities are available or where domestic exchange rate, on account of civil war, is unusually high. A second method is to purchase one or two months' sight native bank order from the local bank and discount it at the producing district. For instance, if a Shanghai merchant goes to Hankow for cotton purchase, he may first buy a one month's sight native bank order from some Shanghai bank, and have it discounted at some Hankow bank whenever he is in need of money for cotton purchase after arrival at Hankow. The Hankow bank usually sells the native bank order to some local merchant going to Shanghai for business. The latter, after reaching Shanghai, can have the order cashed at the issuing bank at maturity or discounted before maturity. The issuing bank, however, must be of high credit standing, in order to make its order acceptable elsewhere. A third method is to issue promissory note by the cotton hao itself, which may have to be guaranteed by another person if necessary. These notes, when issued by the cotton hao in Shanghai, may be discounted at the banks in Hankow, and correspond roughly to the single-name and two-name papers in the States. At other times the Hankow cotton hao selling cotton to the agent of a Shanghai cotton hao in Hankow may have its time draft—the trade acceptance—accepted by the agent and discounted at some local bank. With the development of modern banking facilities, a fourth method, telegraphic remittance, is also resorted to. A fifth method is the commercial draft secured by the bill of lading and other documents, which can be more readily discounted at the bank than either promissory note or trade acceptance. The amount of such draft is generally from seventy to eighty percent of the value of the cotton used as security. The difference is called Tien-k'uan (墊款), which varies according to the extent of price fluctuation in the cotton market. The draft may mature within half a month or one month, depending upon the needs of the applicant. If the applicant, say the agent of some cotton hao in Shanghai buying cotton from Hankow, has already sold the cotton on a forward basis, the cotton can be quickly disposed of and paid for as soon as it arrives at Shanghai from Hankow. In that case, the draft matures within half a month. Otherwise, the term of maturity is longer, and it may be necessary for the cotton hao in Shanghai to substitute the cotton with some other goods for security before the bill of lading and other documents can be released by the Shanghai correspondent of the bank. Another way in which commercial draft comes into use is in the grant of book accounts. The representative of the Shanghai cotton hao, after arrival at Hankow for cotton purchase, may need ready cash before the cotton is acutally purchased. He can arrange with some bank and open a book account, which may be converted into commercial draft from time to time as cotton is purchased.[55]

Price movements:—The price movements of raw cotton may be shown after an analysis of the records kept for Shanghai and Tientsin markets by the three institutions, namely, the Chinese Cotton Goods Exchange, the National Tariff Commission and the Nankai Institute of Economics. The Chinese Cotton Goods Exchange has kept a continuous record of the monthly high and low prices for the basis cotton on the Exchange, which is Tungchow cotton from December, 1922 to October 1926, but Hankow long staple since the latter date. The National Tariff Commission, formerly the Bureau of Markets of the Ministry of Finance, has since October, 1922 kept a continuous record of the monthly prices for two kinds of cotton, namely, Tungchow cotton and Shanghai cotton (best steam-ginned) in Shanghai. Previous to 1931 these prices were collected twice a month, on the first and the fifteenth respectively, but since 1931 the collection has been reduced to a monthly basis. The prices for Hsi-ho cotton in Tientsin are collected by this Institute, annually from 1913 to 1927; monthly from January to March, 1928; and weekly since April, 1928.[57] The prices for the four kinds of cotton, namely, basis, Tungchow, Shanghai (best steam-ginned) and Hsi-ho, are given in detail in *Appendices VIII and IX*, but a summary of them is given in Table 15

56. Cotton, *op. cit.*, pp. 79-84.
57. National Tariff Commission, *Shanghai Market Prices Report* (quarterly), April, 1923 to date; Nankai Institute of Economics, *Wholesale Prices and Price Index Numbers in North China*, 1913-1929.

(Fig. 11). This table shows that the prices of raw cotton during the period 1913 to 1931 have on the whole shown a rise until 1924, when the peak is reached. Taking 1926 as the base of 100, the price for Hsi-ho cotton in Tientsin, during the period 1913 to 1930, is the lowest during the first War year (1914), namely, 45.93. Since 1914 it has risen consistently until 1918, when the price movement becomes more or less smooth for a period of five years (1918-1922). The index for Hsi-ho cotton is 81.13 in 1918, 77.74 in 1919, 80.83 in 1920, 81.98 in 1921, and 83.51 in 1922. In 1923 it jumps rapidly to 113.86, and is followed by an equally rapid rise for the following year, the peak year, to 132.09. During the latter year the index for raw cotton in Shanghai shows a similar course of rise, namely, 132.32 for Shanghai cotton, 134.63 for Tungchow cotton, and 137.07 for basis cotton. If we remember the great reduction in China's cotton crop during these two years, the rise in the price of raw cotton is but an expected phenomenon. China's cotton crop, as shown in the preceding chapter, amounted to 8,310,000 piculs in 1922, but was reduced to 7,145,000 piculs in 1923 and 7,809,000 piculs in 1924. Since 1924 the price for raw cotton has tended towards a decline, the index for the various kinds of cotton in Shanghai and Tientsin reaching the lowest point in 1926. After 1926 a rise in the price of raw cotton in Shanghai or Tientsin is again visible, although not uniformly.

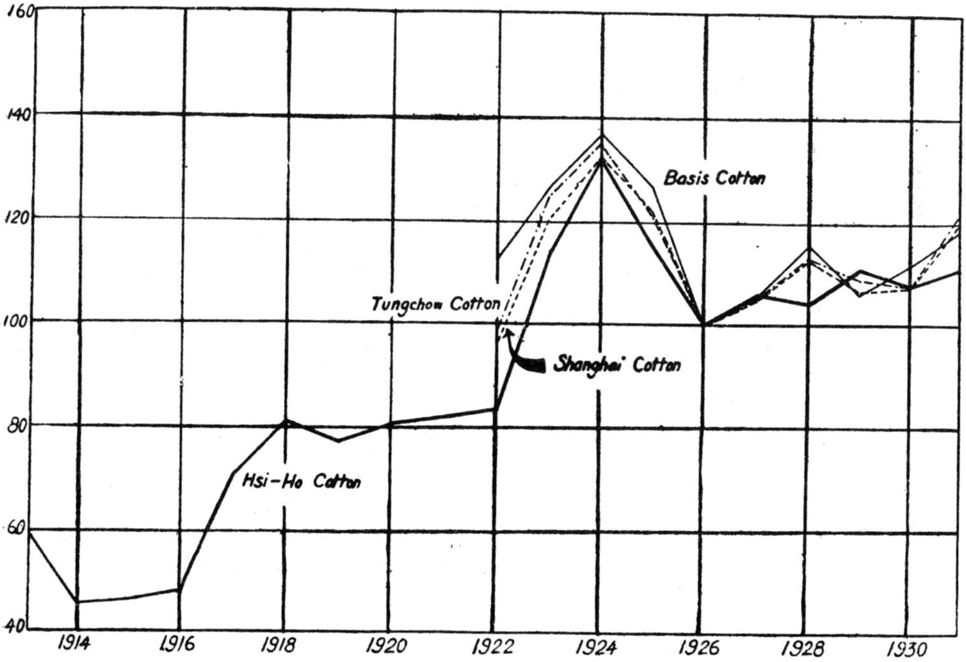

Fig. 11. Prices of raw cotton in Shanghai and Tientsin, 1913-1931 (1926=100) (*See* Table 15)

Table 15. Prices of raw cotton in Shanghai and Tientsin, 1913-1931

Year	Hsi-ho cotton		Shanghai cotton†		Tungchow cotton		Basis cotton*	
	Average price (Tientsin $ per picul)	Relative price (1926=100)	Average price (Shanghai T per picul)	Relative price (1926=100)	Average price (Shanghai T per picul)	Relative price (1926=100)	Average price (Shanghai T per picul)	Relative price (1926=100)
1913	25.76	59.42						
1914	19.91	45.93						
1915	20.34	46.92						
1916	21.04	48.54						
1917	30.54	70.45						
1918	35.17	81.13						
1919	33.70	77.74						
1920	35.04	80.83						
1921	35.54	81.98						
1922	36.20	83.51	30.83	96.83	32.83	98.95	34.73	112.83
1923	49.36	113.86	38.38	120.54	41.38	124.71	39.08	126.97
1924	57.26	132.09	42.13	132.32	44.67	134.63	42.19	137.07
1925	50.18	115.76	38.91	122.20	40.48	121.70	39.14	127.16
1926	43.35	100.00	31.84	100.00	33.18	100.00	30.78	100.00
1927	45.99	106.09	33.47	105.12	34.93	105.27	32.44	105.39
1928	45.05	103.92	35.86	112.63	37.52	113.08	35.73	116.08
1929	48.09	110.93	34.00	106.78	36.31	109.43	32.71	106.08
1930	46.70	107.73	34.23	107.51	35.79	107.87	34.42	111.82
1931	48.03	110.80	38.00	119.34	40.31	121.49	36.45	118.42
Jan.	43.05	99.31	33.63	105.62	36.00	108.50	34.95	113.55
Feb.	50.90	117.42	41.00	128.77	43.00	129.60	41.43	134.60
Mar.	51.35	118.45	40.75	127.98	43.75	131.86	42.25	137.26
Apr.	51.13	117.95	40.00	125.63	43.25	130.35	40.75	132.39
May	50.12	115.62	38.50	120.92	40.50	122.06	38.50	125.08
June	51.82	119.48	39.00	122.49	41.00	123.57	38.88	126.31
July	55.94	129.06	38.25	120.13	41.00	123.57	37.98	123.39
Aug.	51.21	118.13	35.75	112.28	37.75	113.77	34.62	112.47
Sep.	48.48	111.83	35.00	109.92	36.50	109.94	32.90	106.89
Oct.	40.62	93.93					31.80	103.31
Nov.	40.45	93.54					32.18	104.55
Dec.	41.31	95.29					31.18	101.30

* Tungchow cotton from Dec., 1922 to Oct., 1926, but Hankow long staple since the latter date (*Chinese Cotton Goods Exchange*, Shanghai).

† Best steam-ginned.

CHAPTER IV. MANUFACTURING AND MARKETING

Manufacturing

Processes:—The fundamental processes of cotton manufacture are cleaning, carding, drawing, roving, spinning, and lastly weaving, which is usually termed manufacturing. Bleaching, dyeing, printing and finishing are known as the finishing processes. In carding, the fibres are raked parallel; in drawing and roving, the long, loose, thick ropes of cotton fibres laid parallel are drawn out finer and given a slight twist with the object of increasing the cohesion of the threads. Spinning refers to the final stage in the production of yarns, which are weft yarns and loosely twisted, or hard-twisted yarns used chiefly for warps.[1] The process of weaving, finally, consists in interalcing, at right angles, two or more series of flexible materials such as the cotton fibres, of which the longitudinal are called warp and the transverse weft. Bleaching, dyeing, printing and finishing are so well explained by the terms themselves as not to require description. In China the preparatory processes including spinning are carried on in one mill, in which it is not uncommon to take over weaving at the same time. In 1930 China had 127 mills, of which 77 were engaged in spinning, 48 in spinning and weaving, and 2 in weaving. Bleaching and dyeing are mostly carried on in small works, where the products of both power and hand looms are received for treatment. In 1928 Shanghai had 89 bleaching and dyeing works, of which 81 had a total capital of but $601,450, giving an average capital of $7,425 per works.[2] In Tientsin these works are even smaller. In 1929 Tientsin had 39 dyeworks with a total capital of $56,350, giving an average capital of $1,445 per works.[3] But recently there is a tendency to erect large works, especially in Shanghai. A large and modern plant is at present being erected for the Naigai Wata Co., a Japanese firm which has over a dozen mills in China. The Manchester Calico Printers' Association Ltd. has had small works in Shanghai for several years, but they are being extended on a large scale and will have a weekly capacity of 12,000 lumps.[4]

In Table 16 the distribution of spinning and weaving machines in eight of the Shanghai cotton mills is shown, as an illustration of the different processes required in spinning and weaving. The bale breakers, openers, scutchers and mixers are used in cleaning; the cards

1. Chapman, S. J.: *The Cotton Industry and Trade*, London, 1905, p. 22.
2. *Shanghai Industries*, compiled by the Shanghai Social Affairs Bureau and published by the Chung Hua Book Company, 1930.
3. Fong, H. D.: *Rayon and cotton weaving in Tientsin*, Tientsin, 1930, p. 37.
4. Pearse, Arno S.: *The Cotton Industry of Japan and China*, Manchester, 1929, p. 181.

Table 16. Distribution of spinning and weaving machines in Shanghai cotton mills, 1929

No. of mill*	1	2	5	6	7	8	10	11
Counts spun	42	14,16,20	13,16,20	31,32	10,14,16,20, 40, 2/42	10,16,20	10,12,14, 16,20,22, 24,26	10,20, 32,42
Spindles: Spinning	32,000	35,320	44,400	22,920	} 34,888	24,000	38,000	50,000
Doubling	17,600			5,040				10,000
Looms			604	400			1,100	1,000
Hopper bale breaker	2	4	5					
Hopper opener			4					7
Creighton opener		8	10					7
Exhaust opener		4	4					
Scutcher	8	18	16		15	13	7	7
Intermediate		9	8					
Finish		9	8					
Mixer				2	3	4	3	
Card	70	150	182	73	108	96	154	184
Drawing	7	27	20	10	20	14	20	18
Slubber	7	18	23	10	15	14	20	24
Intermediate	14	27	36	14	23	16	29	30
Jack frame								20
Roving	41	54	62	29	42	33	54	54
Ring frame	80	92	121	54	85	60	119	176
Winder	14			4	2			7
Doubler	44			12	8			46
Reeler	80	328	154	53	243	180	160	
Bundler	4		10	4	10	6	} 8	10
Baler	1			1				
Warp and weft winding			44	20			11	14
Beam warping			8	6			8	9
Sizing			3	2			4	3
Drawing-in				8			14	10
Plaiting, shearing, piece stamping				1 each				
Cloth looker			?	?			12	?
Cloth baler			?	?			2	1

* Reference number as given by Pearse, in *Cotton Industry of Japan and China*, Manchester, 1929.

in carding; the drawing, slubbing, intermediate and roving frames in drawing and roving; and the ring frames in spinning. The reeling machines are used in the reeling of yarn, and the winding and doubling machines in the twisting of thread. For packing the bundling and baling presses are employed. In cloth weaving winding machines are resorted to for the winding of warps and wefts, warpers for beam warping, sizers for sizing, drawers-in for drawing-in, and other machines for plaiting, shearing, piece stamping, and cloth baling. Among the eight mills studied, 4 mills were engaged in weaving besides spinning, and 3 mills in doubling.[5]

Machinery:—The machinery used in the cotton mills in China may be British, American, or Japanese, but recently the Chinese have started to make the heavy machinery. Of these, British machinery predominated even in the early years. According to an investigation in 1918, which is shown in Table 17, of the 997,238 spindles in Kiangsu province, 935,804 or 93.84 percent were supplied by the British manufacturers. Platt machinery, being the most popular, supplied 23.45 percent of the total spindleage, after which followed Dobson and Barlow (22.11%), Howard and Bullough (18.61%), Asa Lees (14.68%), John Hetherington (8.94%), Tweedale and Smalley (6.05%). Saco-Lowell, the American manufacturer, supplied only 17,142 spindles or 1.72 percent.[6] The latter were imported into China in 1918, for the Hou Sheng Cotton Mill in Shanghai. Mr. H. Y. Moh, a returned student from the States and meantime manager of the Mill, was a strong advocate of American machinery. Partly through his persuasive influence, and partly on account of the War, American machinery found its way to China quite rapidly. But Since 1921, the tendency to add British machinery in preference to American has been at work again. The latter is said to change quite frequently and thus to become obsolete in a short time. Consequently, the mills have great difficulty in securing new parts for replacement. Indeed, some mills have gone so far as to break up the whole machine in order to furnish new parts for other machine that awaits repair.[7]

The looms, too, were mostly of British make. As shown in Table 17, 3,042 out of 5,438 looms in Kiangsu Province in 1918 were supplied by the British manufacturers. Of the remaining 2,396 looms or 43.82 percent, 1,646 looms or 30.27 percent were supplied by the American

5. The data are given in Pearse, *op, cit.*, pp. 175-180.
6. *The Cotton Spinning and Weaving Industry of Kiangsu*, published by the Kiangsu Industrial Bureau, 1919, pp. 1-7.
7. A technical discussion of the relative merits of American and British machinery may be found in *China Cotton Journal*, Vol III, No. 3, pp. 22-29; No. 4, pp. 14-25.

Table 17. The spindles and looms of cotton mills in Kiangsu in 1918 classified by the name of manufacturer and the year of the mill's establishment

Spindles

Year	Platt Bros.	Dobson & Barlow	Howard & Bullough	Asa Lees	John Hetherington	Tweedale & Smalley	Saco-Lowell	Unknown	Total	%
1890		74,592			9,072				83,664	8.39
1895	100,480	40,768	10,196	36,724		40,096			228,264	21.89
1897		22,568							22,568	2.26
1898		18,200							18,200	1.83
1899			30,590		30,590				61,180	6.13
1905			13,548						13,548	1.36
1906		21,370		21,370					42,740	4.29
1907	4,712	4,712	15,100		15,100			12,700	52,324	5.25
1908		25,480		7,500		7,500		11,592	52,072	5.22
1910		12,788				12,788			25,576	2.56
1911	23,040								23,040	2.31
1913			33,600						33,600	3.37
1914	55,632								55,632	5.58
1915			58,400		19,000				77,400	7.76
1916	50,000			80,808	15,360				146,168	14.66
1917			24,120						24,120	2.42
1918							17,142	20,000	37,142	3.72
Total	233,864	220,478	185,554	146,402	89,122	60,384	17,142	44,292	997,238	100
%	23.45	22.11	18.61	14.68	8.94	6.05	1.72	4.44	100.00	

Looms

Year	Platt Bros.	Saco-Lowell	Henry Livesey	Toyoda	Grayson	Knowles & Marble	Dickinson	Total	%
1890		500		500			356	1,356	24.93
1895	376	250	700		500			1,826	33.58
1897									
1898		300						300	5.51
1899		200	200					400	7.36
1905									
1906									
1907									
1908	510							510	9.38
1910	400							400	7.36
1911									
1913									
1914									
1915									
1916				250				250	4.60
1917									
1918						396		396	7.28
Total	1,286	1,250	900	750	500	396	356	5,438	100
%	23.65	22.99	16.55	13.79	9.19	7.28	6.55	100.00	

manufacturers such as Saco-Lowell, Knowles and Marble; while 750 looms or 13.79 percent were supplied by Toyoda, a Japanese manufacturer. The British manufacturers included, in order of importance, Platt Brothers, Henry Livesey, Grayson, and Dickinson. During the War Crompton and Knowles delivered a good many looms, but the Japanese Toyoda plain loom has recently become a serious competitor. However, when one pays a weaver 69 cents (silver) per day of 12 hours, it is probably not a commercial proposition to invest three or four times the value for an automatic loom as for an ordinary loom. Only one Japanese mill in Shanghai has installed 400 automatic Toyoda looms.[8]

It is hard to tell to what extent China has succeeded in making textile machinery for home demand. In Shanghai it is estimated that there are about 600 machine works of varying size, with a capital ranging respectively from five hundred to several hundred thousand dollars and a working force of twelve thousand. Most of these works are small, and are engaged in the manufacture of minor parts and accessories. It it also estimated that ten of these works are required to meet the demand for accessory parts from a cotton mill with 20,000 spindles. Of the larger works, the China Machine Works (中國鐵工廠) and the Ta Lung Machine Works (大隆機器鐵廠) are the most noted. The former was started by Mr. C. C. Nieh, in 1922. In his trip to Germany Mr. Nieh agreed to buy from the Krupp Works a part of its machinery at a value of ₮300,000, but due to business failure, the proposal was not carried out. The works was thus unable to take orders for textile machinery, but has since its establishment been engaged in the making of accessory parts and weaving looms. It has now a capital of $200,000, a head plant with a premise of 40 *mow* and a working force of 400 at Woosung, and a branch plant in Shanghai. During the Sino-Japanese war in the early spring of 1932, the plant in Woosung was unfortunately destroyed. The Ta Lung Works has a capital of $100,000, with two plants. The plant at Gordon Road has an area of 70 *mow* and a staff of 700 workers. It has a history of about 30 years, and is noted for the production of accessory parts for textile machinery. It has succeeded in putting up the imitations of Toyoda loom. After his visit to the works, Mr. Pearse remarked that the workers "copy faithfully the Toyoda plain loom and the circular winding frame of Toyoda. The firm imports from England only the crank-shaft of the looms. They make at present (1929) four looms per day, but hope to increase their output when they receive a government subsidy".[9] Besides, the works has also imitated

8. Pearse, *op. cit.*, p. 162.
9. *Ibid.*

successfully the mixers and scutchers of Dobson make, and has recently undertaken to produce 20,000 spindles all by itself. In this new adventure which has never been attempted elsewhere in China, the firm takes its model for mixers and scutchers from the Platt Brothers, and that for cards, drawing and roving frames, and ring frames, from Dobson. At present only the scutchers and the ring frames are completed.[10]

In Table 18 China's import of textile machinery is classified according to the origin of import (Fig. 12). Although no subdivision is given for textile machinery in the Customs Returns from which the table is compiled,

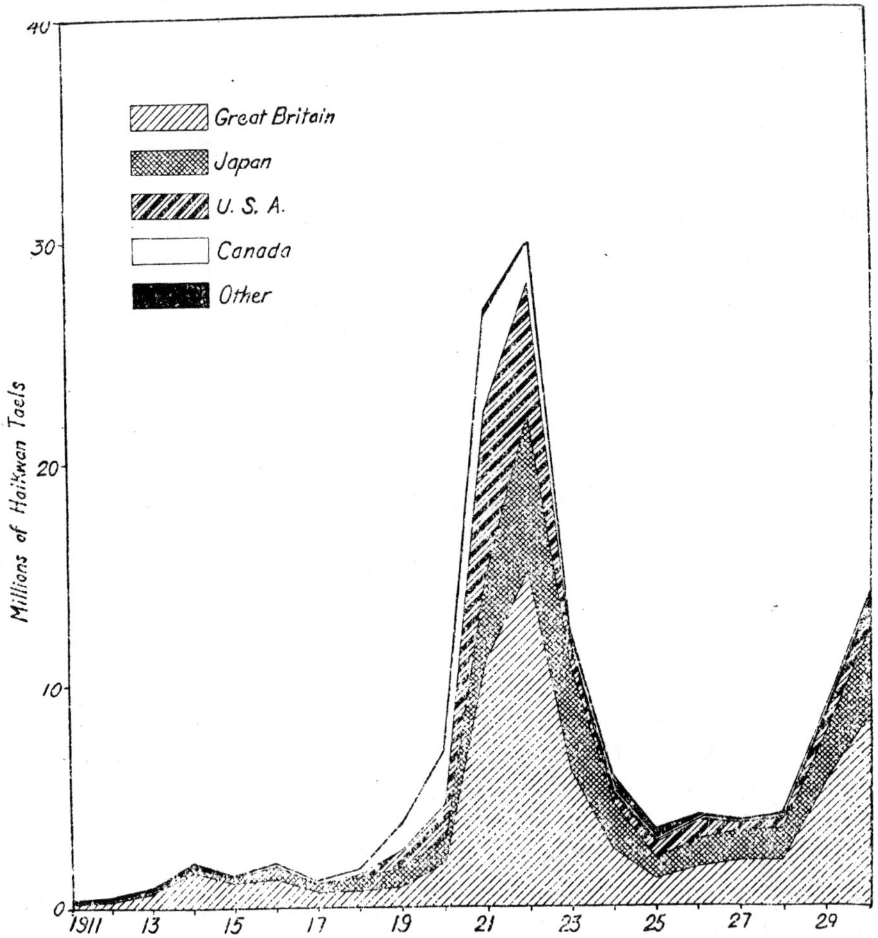

Fig. 12. Distribution of China's import of textile machinery by origin, 1911-1930 (*See* Table 18)

10. Shanghai Industries, *op. cit.*, Part 1, pp. 127, 129; *Textile Industry*, No. 1, pp. 38-40, published by the Nantung Textile Institute, Nantung, April, 1931.

yet in view of the insignificant development of China's textile industry except the cotton branch most if not all of the textile machinery imported may be accepted to represent the cotton machinery. This table shows that during the 20 year period from 1911 to 1930, Great Britain supplied as much as 48.53 percent of the total gross import of textile machinery into China. In terms of value, it amounted to Hk. Tls. 65,295,211. For some years, especially before the year, British share is much higher. In 1913, the highest year, British share amounted to 80.04 percent. Since that year, however, it has shown a progressive decline from 75.55 in 1914 to 65.04 in 1916, 54.03 in 1917, 39.03 in 1918, and 27.80 in 1920. Beginning with 1921, when the conditions had again returned to normalcy, British share rose to 41.66 percent. In terms of absolute value, the increase is almost sixfold, rising from Hk. Tls. 1,925,696 in 1920 to Hk. Tls. 11,160,313 in 1921. In 1922, the peak year during the period under survey, the import from Great Britain was further increased to Hk. Tls. 15,171,830, or 49.7 percent. Since then, although the value of import has on the whole tended towards a decline, yet the share for Great Britain has increased rather than decreased. In 1930, the latest year for which statistics are yet available, British share amounted to Hk. Tls. 8,615,854, or 61.37 percent.

Next to Great Britain Japan occupied the second position in China's gross import of textile machinery from 1911 to 1930. During this period Japan supplied Hk. Tls. 32,137,327 or 23.89 percent of China's gross import of textile machinery. That Japan, being inferior to both Great Britain and the United States in the manufacture of textile machinery except the automatic Toyoda looms, should have supplied almost one fourth of China's textile machinery is easily accounted for by the desire of a large number of Japanese owned mills in China to use machinery of their own make. Japanese owned spindles in China, it may be reiterated, counted for 39.65 percent of China's spindleage.

The United States and Canada supplied 23.51 percent of China's gross import of textile machinery from 1911 to 1930, being 15.95 percent for the former but 7.56 percent for the latter. Both countries, however, occupied a rather insignificant position before the war. As late as 1916, these two countries supplied but Hk. Tls. 115,431 worth of the total import, or 5.97 percent. Since 1916 the share for these two countries has increased rather disproportionately, and at times British machinery seems to be disappearing in face of American competition. Thus, the percentage of total import for the United States and Canada increased from 5.97 in 1916 to 17.72 in 1917, 22.15 in 1918, 51.61 in 1919, and 56.26 in 1920. In 1921 when the British share for the first time in many years showed an increase rather a decrease (from 27.8 percent in 1920 to 41.66 percent in 1921), that for the United States and Canada began to decline, from 56.26 in 1920 to 43.93 in 1921, 25.91 in 1922, and 7.57 in 1923. After 1923 the

Table 18. China's gross import of textile machinery classified by origin, 1911-1930 (in Hk. Tls.)

Year	Great Britain	Japan	U. S. A. (incl. Hawaii)	Canada	Other	Direct Gross Import	%
1911	241,234	60,159	7,161	——	23,028	331,582	0.25
1912	307,283	50,229	9,885	——	91,219	458,616	0.34
1913	672,150	112,500	1,615	1,000	52,459	839,724	0.62
1914	1,540,100	187,661	658	1,872	308,169	2,038,460	1.52
1915	1,076,229	253,490	15,446	——	74,346	1,419,511	1.06
1916	1,257,961	531,437	27,182	88,249	29,312	1,934,141	1.44
1917	667,649	322,607	15,796	203,132	26,616	1,235,800	0.92
1918	669,402	642,948	159,346	220,521	22,777	1,714,994	1.27
1919	813,254	897,760	800,128	1,144,222	112,042	3,767,406	2.80
1920	1,925,696	1,071,201	1,584,315	2,312,889	33,627	6,927,728	5.15
1921	11,160,313	3,622,553	7,471,520	4,296,692	240,994	26,792,072	19.91
1922	15,171,830	6,725,264	6,087,336	1,822,706	722,150	30,529,286	22.69
1923	6,152,364	4,557,784	890,816	42,717	690,736	12,334,417	9.17
1924	2,570,209	2,027,584	595,683	1,761	476,745	5,671,982	4.22
1925	1,189,214	975,571	516,585	9,245	726,271	3,416,886	2.54
1926	1,733,068	1,232,740	806,846	2,737	318,946	4,094,337	3.04
1927	1,990,858	1,325,255	266,166	3,178	251,577	3,837,034	2.85
1928	1,937,165	1,520,210	422,666	450	290,342	4,170,833	3.10
1929	5,603,378	2,090,832	833,317	23,482	434,978	8,985,987	6.68
1930	8,615,854	3,929,542	948,644	——	544,184	14,033,224	10.43
Total	65,295,211	32,137,327	21,461,111	10,174,853	5,470,518	134,539,020	100
Annual Average	3,264,761	1,606,866	1,073,056	508,743	273,526	6,726,951	

Percentage

Year	Great Britain	Japan	U. S. A.	Canada	Other	Direct Gross Import
1911	72.75	18.14	2.16	—	6.95	100
1912	67.00	10.95	2.16	—	19.89	100
1913	80.04	13.40	0.19	0.12	6.25	100
1914	75.55	9.21	0.03	0.09	15.12	100
1915	75.82	17.86	1.09	—	5.23	100
1916	65.04	27.48	1.41	4.56	1.51	100
1917	54.03	26.11	1.28	16.44	2.14	100
1918	39.03	37.49	9.29	12.86	1.33	100
1919	21.59	23.83	21.24	30.37	2.97	100
1920	27.80	15.46	22.87	33.39	0.48	100
1921	41.66	13.52	27.89	16.04	0.89	100
1922	49.70	22.03	19.94	5.97	2.36	100
1923	49.88	36.95	7.22	0.35	5.60	100
1924	45.31	35.75	10.50	0.03	8.41	100
1925	34.80	28.55	15.12	0.27	21.26	100
1926	42.33	30.10	19.71	0.07	7.79	100
1927	51.89	34.54	6.94	0.08	6.55	100
1928	46.45	36.45	10.13	0.01	6.96	100
1929	62.36	23.27	9.27	0.26	4.84	100
1930	61.37	27.99	6.76	—	3.88	100
Annual Average	48.53	23.89	15.95	7.56	4.07	100

share again increased, being 10.53 in 1924, 15.39 in 1925, and 19.78 in 1926, but such increase was incomparable with that for the earlier years. British machinery, in other words, has obtained such a stronghold in China that, but for the vicissitudes of the war, it would have predominated over the Chinese market throughout the whole period from 1911 to 1930.

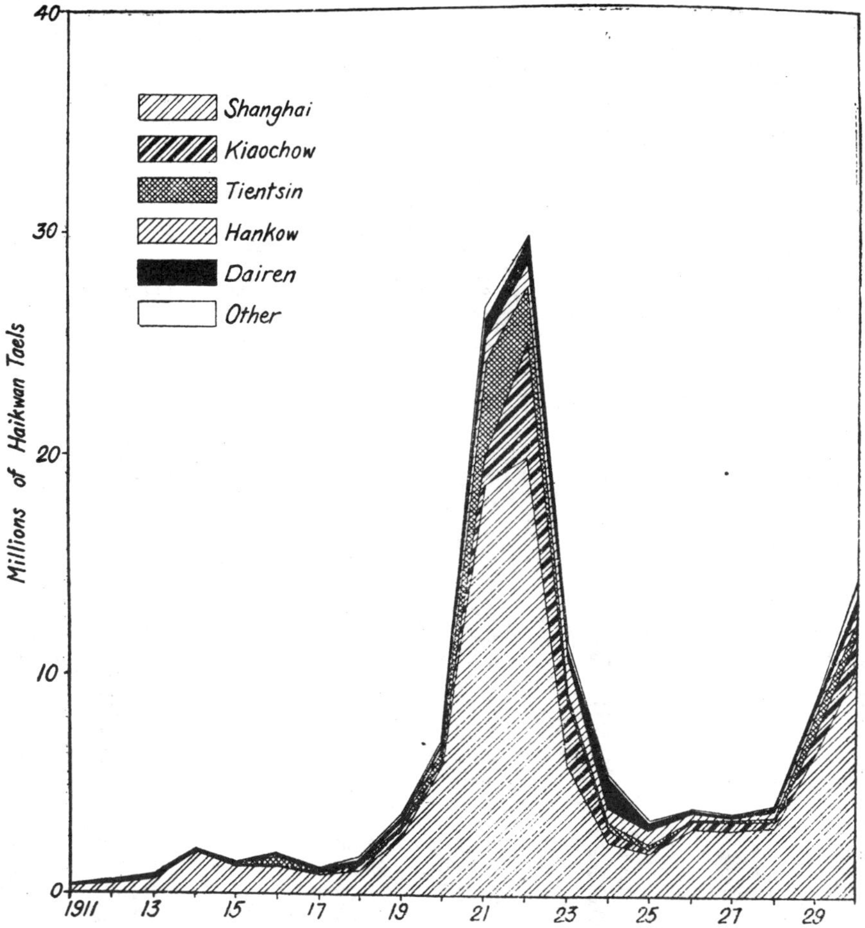

Fig. 13. Distribution of China's import of textile machinery by destination, 1911-1930 (*See* Table 19)

In Table 19 China's net import of textile machinery is classified according to destination (Fig. 13). As is generally expected, Shanghai, China's cotton centre, imported Hk. Tls. 91,853,016 during the 20 year period from 1911 to 1930, or 68.61 percent. Besides Shanghai, Kiaochow imported 11.16 percent, Tientsin 7.54 percent, Hankow 5.69 percent, Dairen 3.84 percent, and other ports, 3.16 percent. These percentages agree closely

Table 19. China's net import of textile machinery classified by destination, 1911-1930 (in Hk. Tls.)

Year	Shanghai	Kiaochow	Tientsin	Hankow	Dairen	Other	Total
1911	271,516	—	14,389	14,065	—	12,915	312,885
1912	424,305	—	4,593	1,054	115	24,988	455,055
1913	675,022	1,140	33,681	1,267	21,955	81,888	814,953
1914	1,873,483	—	41,268	14,252	5,351	99,823	2,034,177
1915	1,238,753	13,328	12,119	14,728	2,766	47,015	1,328,709
1916	1,269,017	26,954	410,881	146,019	4,633	71,329	1,928,833
1917	917,772	109,085	20,750	114,676	698	60,762	1,223,743
1918	1,130,045	201,352	87,101	49,086	5,962	216,891	1,690,437
1919	2,516,528	358,581	290,556	124,482	175,168	259,488	3,724,803
1920	5,951,822	175,740	446,906	202,327	82,030	80,224	6,939,049
1921	18,751,225	1,944,776	3,668,594	1,080,739	671,213	707,846	26,824,393
1922	20,067,240	5,101,992	2,574,730	1,153,774	1,022,143	564,372	30,484,251
1923	6,012,405	2,804,884	251,329	1,752,119	429,390	424,157	11,674,284
1924	2,448,327	541,932	291,881	756,195	1,334,285	156,312	5,528,932
1925	1,946,464	221,441	134,167	844,886	169,844	205,710	3,522,512
1926	3,129,021	279,827	41,242	335,663	187,420	111,111	4,084,284
1927	3,012,801	351,661	96,803	56,967	184,178	19,415	3,721,825
1928	3,163,512	246,299	215,419	197,193	317,505	52,651	4,192,579
1929	6,546,582	975,767	834,987	250,395	219,697	107,686	8.935,114
1930	10,507,176	1,581,946	620,668	509,230	309,930	920,805	14,449,755
Total	91,853,016	14,936,705	10,092,064	7,619,117	5,144,283	4,225,388	133,870,573
Annual Average	4,592,650	746,835	504,603	380,956	257,214	211,268	6,693,529
			Percentage				
1911	86.78	—	4.60	4.49	—	4.13	100
1912	93.24	—	1.01	0.23	0.03	5.49	100
1913	82.83	0.14	4.13	0.16	2.69	10.05	100
1914	92.10	—	2.03	0.70	0.26	4.91	100
1915	93,23	1.00	0.91	1.11	0.21	3.54	100
1915	65.79	1.40	21.30	7.57	0.24	3.70	100
1917	75.81	8.91	1.70	9.37	0.06	4.96	100
1918	66.85	11.91	5.15	2.90	0.35	12.83	100
1919	67.56	9.93	7.80	3.34	4.70	6.97	100
1920	85.77	2.53	6.44	2.92	1.18	1.16	100
1921	69.90	7.25	13.68	4.03	2.50	2.64	100
1922	65.83	16.74	8.45	3.78	3.35	1.85	100
1923	51.50	24.03	2.15	15.01	3.68	3.63	100
1924	44.28	9.80	5.28	13.68	24.13	2.83	100
1925	55.26	6.29	3.81	23.99	4.82	5.84	100
1926	76.61	6.85	1.01	8.22	4.59	2.72	100
1927	80.95	9.45	2.60	1.53	4.95	0.52	100
1928	75.46	5.87	5.14	4.70	7.57	1.26	100
1929	73.27	10.92	9.35	2.80	2.46	1.21	100
1930	72.72	10.95	4.30	3.52	2.14	6.37	100
Annual Average	68.61	11.16	7.54	5.69	3.84	3.16	100

with those for the geographical distribution of China's spindles in 1930. The spindles for Kiangsu, which were imported through Shanghai, amounted to 66.42 percent of China's total,—a percentage which is a little lower than the import value of textile machinery for Shanghai, 68.61 percent. The explanation, if any, lies in the fact that a number of mills in Kiangsu were established before 1911, the year for which the Customs statistics on textile machinery were first kept. The spindles for Shantung, which amounted to 8.80 percent, were imported through Kiaochow, which claimed 11.16 percent in the total import value of the textile machinery. Similarly, the percentage of spindles for Tientsin, 6.91, is close to the percentage of import value, 7.54. Liaoning, with 3.22 percent of the spindles, claimed 3.16 percent of the import value for the chief port of import, Dairen.

Costings:—The cost in cotton manufacture may be divided into two groups, namely, raw materials and other. In the spinning of yarn, the cost for raw materials occupies about four fifths of the total cost. The higher the counts spun, however, the lower the cost of raw materials. In Mill B in Tientsin, for instance, the cost of raw materials occupies 87.92 percent of the total cost for ten counts, 84.87 percent for fourteen counts, 82.61 percent for sixteen counts, and 77.64 percent for twenty counts three ply.

The other costs include those for labor, power, materials, depreciation, interest, tax, and overhead (including insurance, office and sundries). The depreciation of machinery and buildings is thought of only after a dividend (官利) has been fixed and a surplus (公積金) declared. If there is no profit to be divided, there is no depreciation. In his investigation of Shanghai mills in 1929, Mr. Pearse stated that "only in one case a mill manager assured me that he always allowed five percent on both buildings and machinery."[11] This practice of providing for depreciation only after a profit is made is of course very dangerous, as it impairs the assets of the mill.

Contrary to the provisions of the new Company Law, interest on capital stock (or dividend) is usually provided for in fixing the cost prices, in the same way as interest on loans. Interest as an item of cost includes the price for invested as well as borrowed capital. Money is very dear in China; 10 percent per annum is reasonable and as most people overtrade, the question of interest is a vital one to Chinese millowners. According to Mr. Pearse, "a sound concern may provide only Taels 2 per bale of 400 lbs. yarn, whilst a weaker concern must calculate Taels 10 and more for interest on such a bale of yarn".[12] In Table 20, the interest per bale in one of the Tientsin mills is given at $6.03 for ten counts, $10.71 for fourteen counts, $12.34 for sixteen counts, and $16.11 for twenty counts three ply.

11. Pearse, *op. cit.*, p. 189.
12. *Ibid.*

Table 20. Analysis of the cost for yarn and cloth at Mill B, Tientsin, 1929*

Item of cost	Cost of yarn per bale												Cost of cloth per piece		
	10's			14's			16's			20's 3-ply			Sheeting		
	$	%	%	$	%	%	$	%	%	$	%	%	$	%	%
Raw materials	183.32	87.92		179.27	84.87		201.43	82.61		208.71	77.64		6.41	78.84	
Other	25.18	12.08	100.00	31.96	15.13	100.00	42.39	17.39	100.00	60.12	22.36	100.00	1.72	21.16	100.00
Labor	9.53	4.57	37.84	8.01	3.79	25.05	12.71	5.21	29.96	17.85	6.64	29.70	0.63	7.75	
Power	2.35	1.13	9.35	4.18	1.98	13.09	4.80	1.97	11.33	6.27	2.33	10.42	0.15	1.85	
Materials	4.19	2.01	16.64	3.61	1.71	11.30	6.30	2.59	14.90	11.73	4.36	19.50	0.43	5.29	
General	2.03	0.97		3.61	1.71		4.14	1.70		5.41	2.01		0.43	5.29	
Packing	2.16	1.04					2.16	0.89		2.16	0.80				
Doubling										4.16	1.55				
Overhead	3.07	1.48	12.25	5.46	2.58	17.05	6.24	2.56	14.72	8.16	3.04	13.59	0.18	2.22	
Interest	6.03	2.89	23.92	10.71	5.07	33.51	12.34	5.06	29.09	16.11	5.99	26.79	0.32	3.94	
Total cost	208.50	100.00		211.23	100.00		243.82	100.00		268.83	100.00		8.13	100.00	
Selling price	206.96			213.25			236.98			274.91			7.60		
Profit or loss	—1.54			2.02			—6.85			6.08			—0.53		

*The figures given are monthly averages from March to October, 1929.

Table 21. Analysis of the cost per bale of yarn in Shanghai mills, 1929
(Estimate by Mr. Pearse)

Item of cost**	14's		16's		20's	
	Tls.	%	Tls.	%	Tls.	%
Labor	6.20	31.80	9.20	40.21	9.00	31.36
Power	3.00	15.39	3.01	13.16	3.20	11.15
Materials	2.70	13.84	2.52	11.01	3.50	12.20
Overhead	1.53	7.85	1.44	6.29	5.00	17.42
Interest	6.07*	31.12	6.71	29.33	8.00	27.87
Total cost	Tls. 19.50	100.00	Tls. 22.88	100.00	Tls. 28.70	100.00
	$ 27.08		$ 31.78		$ 40.00	

*Estimated by the present writer.

**Tax is omitted here so as to give uniform basis for comparison with Table 20.

There is on every bale a tungshui or excise varying from \$8.25 to \$11.25, depending upon the number of counts. Besides, there is an export duty of Hk. Tls. 2.10. In the case of cloth, there is no tungshui but an export duty of Hk. Tls. 1.50 per picul.

In Table 20 where the cost items for cotton yarn and cloth in one of the Tientsin mills are analyzed, no provision is made for either depreciation or tax. The same is true with Table 21 in which Mr. Pearse's estimate of cost for different items in Shanghai mills is quoted. A comparison of these two tables shows that for the spinning of different counts of yarn, especially of fourteen and sixteen counts, the cost is much higher in Tientsin than in Shanghai. In Tientsin the cost of spinning 14 counts excluding raw materials amounts to \$31.96, while in Shanghai it is only Tls. 19.50 or \$27.08. Similarly, in spinning 16 counts the cost excluding raw materials is \$42.39 in Tientsin but Tls. 22.88 or \$31.78 in Shanghai. It must be remembered, however, that the cost for Tientsin is too high, as it is given by a mill which has been working under loss.

A further analysis of both Tables 20 and 21 shows the percentage distribution of the other costs excluding raw materials. Despite the variation in percentages due to the variation in the kinds of yarn spun, the cost for labor occupies from 30 to 35 percent, that for interest from 25 to 35 percent, and that for materials (i.e. supplies), power and overhead from 10 to 15 percent respectively.

Efficiency:—On the basis of the statistics given in the *List of Cotton Mill in China for 1930* the efficiency of cotton mills in China may be calculated in different ways—by spindle, by loom or by worker. As the 127 mills are not all at work, and even if they do, some of them fail to give statistics on all items, the only solution in correlating any two sets of statistics is to compute the mean average for those mills for which both sets of statistics are given. Such, for instance, has been the case with the motive power per worker, the yarn output per spindle, or the cotton consumption per spindle. But, in correlating motive power with spindle or loom, or worker with spindle, loom, cotton consumption, yarn output or cloth output, the difficulty arises for mills where spinning and weaving are carried on at the same time, and where no apportionment for each of the two branches is made either of the motive power or of the working force. In such case, the first step is to compute the spindle efficiency in terms of the worker or of the motive power, by calculating the mean average for those mills where spinning alone is carried on. The spindle efficiency is then applied to the mills where both spinning and weaving are performed, i.e. to spinning-and-weaving mills, as a basis for calculating the number of workers or the amount of motive power designed solely for weaving. In the following paragraphs, the above methods have been applied in calculating the mill efficiency in various respects. Such calculation, however, must be accepted with great reserve, as the units employed for the calculation are not always uniform. The conditions of one mill vary from those of another. In one mill where the spindles are working on sixteen counts, in another they may be working on twenty counts. Again, even in the same mill the spindles may be working on fourteen counts at one time, but on ten counts at another. Nay, even at the same time some portion of the spindles in the mill may be spinning one count of yarn, while still other portion may be spinning another count. It has to be assumed, besides, that mills are working the same length of time during the year. In our calculation, it is hoped that in a sufficiently large number of mills, the diverse conditions in different mills may tend to offset each other, partly if not wholly.

Statistics on raw cotton consumption are given for 114 mills, and those on yarn production for 116 mills. For the two mills without cotton statistics (nos. 27 and 102) the raw cotton consumption is estimated on the basis of the yarn production, assuming the common proportion of 3.5 piculs of raw cotton for one bale of yarn. Of the other nine mills with neither cotton nor yarn statistics, four mills with a total spindleage of 100,000 (nos. 7, 35, 63, 80) are being planned or suspended, and five mills with a total spindleage of 46,024 (nos. 14, 25, 34, 46, 81) have failed to report. Besides, of the 116 mills that reported, 7 mills (nos. 13, 16, 62, 79, 115-7) possess 107,920 spindles not in operation. In other words, from a total of 4,223,956 spindles for 125 mills, only 3,970,012 spindles in 116 reporting mills are operating, to which the statistics on raw cotton consumption and yarn production refer.

Total spindles in 125 mills		4,223,956
Deduct		253,944
Spindles in 4 planned or suspended mills	100,000	
Spindles in 5 operating mills not reporting	46,024	
Spindles in 7 reporting mills not operating	107,920	
Spindles in 116 reporting mills operating		3,970,012

In these 116 mills where 3,970,012 spindles are operating, the cotton consumption amounts to 8,750,019 piculs and the yarn production amounts to 2,455,177 bales, giving an average cotton consumption of 2.204 piculs per spindle per year and an average yarn production of 0.618 bale or 247 pounds per spindle per year. In both respects the Chinese owned mill is more favorably situated than the Japanese owned mill. For the Chinese mill the cotton consupmtion per spindle amounts to 2.453 piculs, as compared with 1.806 piculs for the Japanese mill. The yarn production per spindle, too, is 0.692 bale or 277 pounds for the Chinese mill but 0.501 bale or 200 pounds for the Japanese mill. A comparison of spindle efficiency between the Chinese and the Japanese mill, therefore, gives a more favorable impression for the former. But as is shown in a later paragraph on per worker efficiency, such impression is reversed. In Chinese mills a worker can take care of only 16.05 spindles, whereas in Japanese mills the average spindles per worker amount to 24.14. In other words, in Japanese mills where each worker takes care of a larger number of spindles than in Chinese mills, the spindle efficiency is necessarily lower because the worker cannot work the spindles as intensively as his comrade in Chinese mills. A further reason is to be found in the different counts of yarn spun in Chinese and Japanese mills. Generally speaking, the Japanese mills spin finer counts such as 32's and 42's, which require greater number of spindles per worker, but return a smaller output in weight. For details see "116a" in Table 22.

Statistics on power capacity and working force are also incomplete. Among the 127 mills the four planned or suspended mills (nos. 7,35,63,80) give no statistics on labor, while two of them give no statistics on power capacity. For one mill where labor statistics are given, those on power capacity are omitted (no. 34); while for 3 mills the reverse is true (nos. 82-84). Besides, 3 mills give neither labor nor power statistics (nos. 25, 46, 81). In other words, only 116 mills give statistics on labor and power capacity, as is shown below.

	Operating	Planned or susended
Power capacity for 119 mills	121,174 K.W. 38,511 H.P.	5,400 K.W.
Deduct power capacity for 3 mills without labor statistics	500 H.P.	5,400 K.W.
Power capacity for 116 mills with labor statistics	121,174 K.W. 38,011 H.P.	
Workers for 119 mills	252,031	
Deduct workers for 3 mills without power statistics	13,000	
Workers for 116 mills with power statistics	239,031	

From the above it may be seen that in the 116 mills where both power and labor statistics are given there are 239,031 workers and 149,682 kilowatts of power (one horse power being converted into 3/4 kilowatt), giving an average power capacity of 0.6262 kilowatt per worker. In Japanese owned mills, however, the power capacity per worker, 0.8281 kilowatt, is higher than that in Chinese owned mills, 0.5301. The explanation for the discrepancy has been partly suggested in the preceding paragraph, in which it is shown that the worker in Japanese mills operate a much larger number of spindles than in Chinese mills. For details see "116b in Table 22.

Among the 125 mills where spinning is carried on independently or jointly with weaving, only 70 spinning mills give statistics on spindles, motive power, workers, cotton consumption and yarn production. These 70 mills employ 2,042,708 spindles, 73,213 kilowatts of motive power and 105,840 workers, giving an average of 19.3 spindles per worker and 0.0358 kilowatt per spindle (for Chinese owned, Japanese owned and British owned mills as a whole). The number of spindles per worker in Japanese owned mill, 24.14, is higher than that in Chinese owned mill, 16.05. Similarly, the amount of motive power per spindle in Japanese mill, 0.0361 kilowatt, is higher than that in Chinese mill, 0.0355 kilowatt. In these 70 mills the cotton consumption amounts to 4,016,545 piculs and the yarn production amounts to 1,132,038 bales, giving an average cotton consumption of 37.95 piculs per worker and an average yarn production of 10.70 bales per worker. Because of the larger number of spindles as well as the higher amount of motive power that a worker operates in Japanese mills, the yarn production per worker in a Japanese mill, 11.95 bales, is higher than that in a Chinese mill, 9.85 bales. For details see "70" in Table 22.

Statistics on cloth production are also incomplete, but not on looms. Among the fifty mills engaged in weaving (two mills, nos. 58 and 100, being exclusively weaving mills, with no spinning) no statistics on cloth production are given for seven mills, of which 750 looms in two mills are not operating (nos. 9, 75), while 2,350 looms in five mills (nos. 40, 49, 82-4) are operating. In other words, in 43 weaving mills there are 26,172 operating looms.

	Operating	Planned of suspended
Power looms in 50 mills	28,522	750
Deduct power looms in 7 mills without cloth statistics	2,350	750
Power looms in 43 mills with cloth statistics	26,172	
Cloth production in 43 mills	14,779,538 pieces	

These 43 mills, with 26,172 operating looms, have a cloth production of 14,779,538 pieces, giving an average cloth production of 564.71 pieces. The cloth production per loom in Japanese owned mills, 717.34 pieces, is much higher than that in Chinese owned mills, 447.52 pieces, due chiefly to the fact that in the former new looms, especially of the automatic type, have been employed, whereas in the latter the looms are partly antiquated. For details see "43" in Table 22.

Table 22a. A comparison of efficiency between Chinese and Japanese owned mills in China, 1930

No. mills included	Nationality of ownership	Spindles	Looms	K. W.	Motive power H. P.§	Total K.W.§	Workers	Raw cotton consumed (piculs)	Yarn spun (bales)	Cloth woven (pieces)
28	Chinese	1,118,300	14,805	34,675	17,061	47,471†	94,990††	3,020,654	844,282	6,625,544
15	Japanese	583,456	11,367	21,969	6,340	26,724†	34,538††	1,146,615	317,133	8,153,994
—	British									
43§§	Total	1,701,756	26,172	56,644	23,401	74,195†	129,528††	4,167,269	1,161,415	14,779,538
42	Chinese	1,015,880		26,538	12,760	36,108	63,296	2,187,160	623,764	
28	Japanese	1,026,828		36,242	1,150	37,105	42,544	1,829,385	508,274	
—	British									
70§§	Total	2,042,708		62,780	13,910	73,213	105,840	4,016,545	1,132,038	
71	Chinese	2,169,048	14,600	62.263	29,838	84,642	159,292	5,320,692	1,500,248	6,225,544
42	Japanese	1,647,644	10,567	57.711	7,490	63,328	76,152	2,976,000	825,407	7,578,994
3	British	153,320	1,900	**	**	**	13,000	453,327	129,522	**
116a§§	Total	3,970,012	27,067	119,974**	37,328**	147,970**	248,444	8,750,019	2,455,177	13,804,538**
73	Chinese	2,184,600	15,255	62,963	30,521	85,854	161,949	5,320,692*	1,500,248*	6,625,544
43	Japanese	1,647,644	11,367	58,211	7,490	63,828	77,082	2,976,000	825,407	8,153,994
—	British									
116b§§	Total	3,832,244	26,622	121,174	38,011	149,682	239,031	8,296,692*	2,325,655*	14,779,538
81	Chinese	2,395,792	16,005	68,363	31,021	91,629	161,949	5,320,692	1,500,248	6,625,544
43	Japanese	1,674,844	11,367	58,211	7,490	63,828	77,082	2,976,000	825,407	8,153,994
3	British	153,320	1,900				13,000	453,327	129,522	
127	Total	4,223,956	29,272	126,574	38,511	155,457	252,031	8,750,019	2,455,177	14,779,538

* Not given for mill 14.

** Not given for mills 82-4.

† Calculating on the basis of 0.0355 K.W. per spindle for Chinese mills, there are 39,700 K.W. for 1,118,300 spindles. The other 7,771 K.W. are assumed to be for 14,805 looms. Calculating on the basis of 0.0361 K.W. per spindle for Japanese mills, there are 21,063 K.W. for 583,456 spindles. The rest 5,661 K.W. are assumed to be for 11,367 looms. The total amount of motive power for spindles is 60,763 K.W., and for looms, 13,432.

†† Calculating on the basis of 16.05 spindles per worker for Chinese mills, there are 69,676 workers to 1,118,300 spindles. The other 25,314 workers are assumed to be weavers. Calculating on the basis of 24.14 spindles per worker for Japanese mills, there are 24,169 workers for 583,456 spindles. The rest 10,369 workers are assumed to be weavers. The total number of spinners is 93,845, and that of weavers, 35,683.

§ One horse power is converted into 3/4 kilowatt.

§§ The numbers for mills not included are as follows:
43: 2, 4-5, 7-9, 11, 13-4, 16, 19, 21-8, 30, 33-5, 38, 40-3, 45-6, 48-9, 52-5, 57, 63-4, 66-7, 69-75, 77-84, 88, 91-9, 101, 103-8, 112, 114-8, 120-1, 125-7.
70: 1, 3, 6-7, 10, 12, 14-5, 17-8, 20, 25, 31-2, 34-7, 39-40, 44, 46-7, 49-51,56, 58-63, 65, 68, 76, 80-7, 89-90, 100, 102, 109-11, 113, 119, 122-4.
116a: 7, 14, 25, 34, 35, 46, 58, 63, 80-1, 100.
116b: 7, 25, 34, 35, 46, 63, 80, 81-4.

Table 22b. A comparison of efficiency between Chinese and Japanese owned mills in China, 1930

No. mills included	Items	All	Chinese	Japanese
70	Spindles per worker	19.30	16.05	24.14
43	Loom per worker	0.73	0.58	1.10
116b	Motive power per worker (K.W.)	0.6262	0.5301	0.8281
70	Motive power per spindle (K.W.)	0.0358	0.0355	0.0361
43	Motive power per loom (K.W.)	0.5132	0.5249	0.4980
70	Yarn output per worker per year (bales)	10.70	9.85	11.95
116a	Yarn output per spindle per year (bales)	0.618	0.692	0.501
70	Yarn output per spindle per year (bales)	0.554	0.614	0.495
43	Cloth output per worker per year (pieces)	414.19	261.73	786.38
43	Cloth output per loom per year (pieces)	564.71	447.52	717.34
70	Cotton consumption per worker per year (piculs)	37.95	34.55	43.00
116a	Cotton consumption per spindle per year (piculs)	2.204	2.453	1.806
70	Cotton consumption per spindle per year (piculs)	1.97	2.15	1.78

The above analysis of the mill efficiency may be supplemented by the statistics on spindle and loom output actually collected from the mills. In Table 23 the spindle output for Shanghai mills is collected by Mr. Pearse, and in Table 24 the spindle output in Tientsin mills is collected by this Institute. Mr. Pearse's figures for Japanese mills under the two shift system of 22 or 23 hours are recomputed on the 24 hour basis, in order to afford a basis of comparison with those for Tientsin mills of Chinese ownership working under the two shift system of 24 hours. In view of the small number of Japanese mills represented, it is hard to reach at any conclusion as to the output per spindle. The spindle output for 14's, 16's, 20's and 32's seem more favorable to the Japanese owned mills, while that for 10's and 42's seem more favorable to the Chinese owned mills. Among the Chinese mills the spindle output in Shanghai is higher than that in Tientsin, which difterence can be explained as much by the lower efficiency of northern workers as by the poorer climatic conditions. The average spindle output for 10's is 2.20 lb. in Shanghai but 1.77 lb. in Tientsin; that for 14's is 1.50 lb. in Shanghai but 1.13 lb. in Tientsin; that for 16's is 1.10 lb. in Shanghai but 0.90 lb. in Tientsin; that for 20's is 0.96 lb. in Shanghai but 0.70 lb. in Tientsin; and that for 42's is 0.38 lb. in Shanghai but 0.26 lb. in Tientsin. In Shanghai, again, the spindle output seems to have increased in recent years. The investigation in 1918 gave an average spindle output of from 1.4 lb. to 1.7 lb. for 10's, but in 1929 it was raised to 2.2 lb. Similarly, the spindle output for 14's was from 1.06 to 1.30 lb. in 1918 but 1.50 lb. in 1929; that for 16's was from 0.90 to 1.09

Table 23. Spindle output in Shanghai and Tientsin cotton mills, 1928-1929

	Shanghai mills,* 1929 (Chinese & Japanese owned)						Tientsin mills, 1928-29 (Chinese owned)		
Count of yarn spun	Ref. no. & nationality of mill		Output per spindle in 24 hours	Average output per spindle in 24 hours: Japanese	Chinese	All	Mill	Output per spindle in 24 hours	Average output per spindle in 24 hours
10's	8	Japanese	2.087				C	1.872	1.768
	9	Chinese	2.200	2.087	2.200	2.162	B	1.841	
	11	”	2.200				A	1.591	
13's	5	”	1.420		1.420	1.420			
14's	2	Japanese	1.745	1.745	1.500	1.622	A	1.259	1.134
	9	Chinese	1.500				B	1.009	
15's							A	1.149	1.149
16's	2	Japanese	1.418	1.283	1.100	1.192	C	.970	.899
	5	Chinese	1.050				B	.879	
	8	Japanese	1.148				A	.847	
	9	Chinese	1.150						
17's							A	.975	.975
20's	2	Japanese	1.113	1.026	.960	.987	B	.697	.697
	5	Chinese	.820						
	8	Japanese	.940						
	9	Chinese	.960						
	11	”	1.100						
23's warp	3	Japanese	1.156	1.156		1.156			
24's warp	3	”	1.309	1.309		1.309			
32's	3	”	.698	.698	.678	.685			
	6	Chinese	.656						
	11	”	.700						
40's	9	”	.400		.400	.400			
42's	1	Japanese	.341	.341	.395	.377	A	.260	.260
	9	Chinese	.390						
	11	”	.400						

* Pearse, *Cotton Industry of Japan and China*, 1929, pp, 175-180.

Table 24. Semi-monthly averages of spindle or loom output per shift of 12 hours, Tientsin cotton mills, 1928-1929

Half Month ending		Yarn output per spindle (in lbs.) 10's A		10's B		10's C		14's A		14's B		15's A		16's A		16's B		16's C		17's A		20's B		42's A		Cloth output per loom (in yards) 11 lbs. A		12 lbs. A		Special A	
		D	N	D	N	D	N	D	N	D	N	D	N	D	N	D	N	D	N	D	N	D	N	D	N	D	N	D	N	D	N
Jan.	15	.826	.798	.954	.954	.9542	.9817	.642	.643	.515	.507	.588	.600	.432	.431			.5323	.5387	.520	.511	.337	.324	.129	.131	39.91	43.81			29.23	26.72
	31	.771	.788	.955	.940	1.0018	1.0171	.619	.617	.503	.499	.550	.542	.439	.435			.5344	.5423	.497	.490	.330	.325	.123	.123	46.82	42.03			29.76	25.83
Feb.	15	.787	.761	.927	.916	.9860	1.0340	.544	.527	.503	.476	.495	.451	.428	.421			.4997	.5030	.438	.455	.321	.313	.122	.121	.30.85	29.11			18.98	21.42
	28	.693	.685	.951	.930	.9892	.9773	.575	.593	.499	.497	.560	.555	.420	.416			.5117	.5088	.460	.467	.335	.338	.111	.113	35.67	37.58			21.61	21.00
Mar.	15	.802	.805	.940	.908	.9493	.9627	.576	.576	.505	.500	.557	.553	.433	.434			.5447	.5160	.465	.472	.374	.380	.177	.170	43.00	37.67			26.12	28.97
	31	.662	.668	.930	.911	.9591	.9810	.545	.558	.506	.502	.516	.514	.398	.391			.4970	.4962	.470	.482	.382	.388	.108	.109	43.97	48.93			22.78	23.88
Apr.	15	.803	.787	.920	.922	.9817	.9753	.637	.625	.511	.501	.596	.586	.427	.423			.4930	.4846	.485	.490	373	.368	.103	.102	58.00	57.64			16.11	15.29
	30	.797	.779	.919	.921	.9672	.9832	.646	.633	.514	.510	.581	.578	.416	.419			.4303	.4545	.452	.448	.366	.367	.118	.113	58.99	59.50			38.48	48.18
May	15	.789	.791	.923	.913	.9282	.9427	.652	.640	.510	.535	.574	.562	.410	.412			.4532	.4542	.448	.463	.380	.378	.114	.109	65.54	64.54				
	31	.814	.823	.925	.913	.9356	.9476	.613	.612	.487	.490	.560	.545	.402	.399			.4890	.4840	.422	.414	.373	.366	.103	.101	56.07	55.63		33.33		
June	15	.761	.700	.914	.916	.9437	.9885	.537	.527	.501	.504	.469	.468	.395	.393			.4601	.4595	.352	.351	.344	.341	.098	.104	41.74	40.35	36.30	41.52		
	30	.748	.741	.917	.901	.9473	.9765	.527	.519	.497	.493	.484	.478	.377	.379			.4723	.4739	.359	.359	.352	.342			44.63	49.57	40.08	39.64		
July	15	.727	.722	.895	.890	.8659	.9033			.522	.522			.446	.437			.4833	.4820	.526	.522					53.10	55.46	51.30	48.54		
	31	.697	.712	.849	.853	.8988	.9028			.499	.502			.384	.417			.4450	.4440	.519	.516		.400	141	.111	47.29	47.70	48.33	46.18		
Aug.	15	.678	.669	.876	.860	.8787	.9266			.493	.480			.421	.416			.4370	.4446	.520	.522	.331	.327	.193	.148			49.75	51.33		
	31	.733	.678	.871	.910	.8369	.8699			.500	.519			.549	.444			.4334	.4320	.526	.526	.344	.345	.124	.116			51.49	51.95		
Sep.	15	.691	.662	.903	.907	.8353	.8359	.669	.673	.506	.503	.655	.624	.367	.367			.4516	.4782	.529	.518	.335	.337	.114	.110	55.57	56.00	52.26	53.47	32.02	33.34
	30	.854	.846	.930	.944	.8613	.8792	.668	.652	.520	.523	.649	.629	.440	.437			.4401	.4441	.470	.464	.335	.343	.185	.144	56.59	54.46	45.14	50.53	31.28	29.98
Oct.	15	.939	.923	.960	.966	.8888	.9142	.715	.701	.510	.509	.641	.609	.452	.443			.4855	.4934	.489	.480	.334	.342	.157	.154	53.12	53.09	50.43	48.69	35.33	32.28
	31	.918	.907	.948	.932	.9418	.9563	.709	.699	.510	.507	.610	.632	.450	.440			.5003	.5044	.552	.573	.349	.344	.148	.154	54.02	52.69	48.28	52.85	31.71	36.71
Nov.	15	.914	.921	.911	.928	.9096	.9259	.720	.707			.618	.607	.435	.427	.437	.445	.5205	.4957	.570	.533	.350	.348	.156	.157	51.39	52.23	45.45	48.53	28.37	34.99
	30	.919	.976	.930	.917	9189	.9543	.683	.688			.614	.608	.437	.429	.444	.440	.5079	.5181	.539	.561	.347	.345	.146	.138	51.12	49.87	50.28	47.17	23.66	28.30
Dec.	15	.974	.968	.938	.940	.9504	.9391	.681	.661			.635	.624	.432	.430	.436	.429	.5017	.5065	.567	.507	.336	.337	.137	.137	45.87	48.54	33.56	44.39	26.29	26.41
	31	.887	.894	.936	.948	.9289	.9026	.676	.686			.630	.632	.450	.446	.448	.437	.4976	.4965	.550	.545	.339	.337	.129	.132	45.53	47.44			24.41	27.50
Grand average		.799	.792	.922	.919	.9274	.9449	.632	.627	.505	.504	.579	.570	.427	.420	.441	.438	.4842	.4856	.489	.486	.348	.349	.133	.127	49.04	49.27	46.36	47.01	27.26	28.80

Note: The data above refer to July, 1928 to June, 1929 for Mill A and Mill B, but Jan to Dec., 1929 for Mill C. D=day shift, N=night shift.

lb. in 1918 but 1.10 lb. in 1929; and that for 20's was from 0.60 to 0.70 lb. in 1918 but 0.96 lb. in 1929.[13]

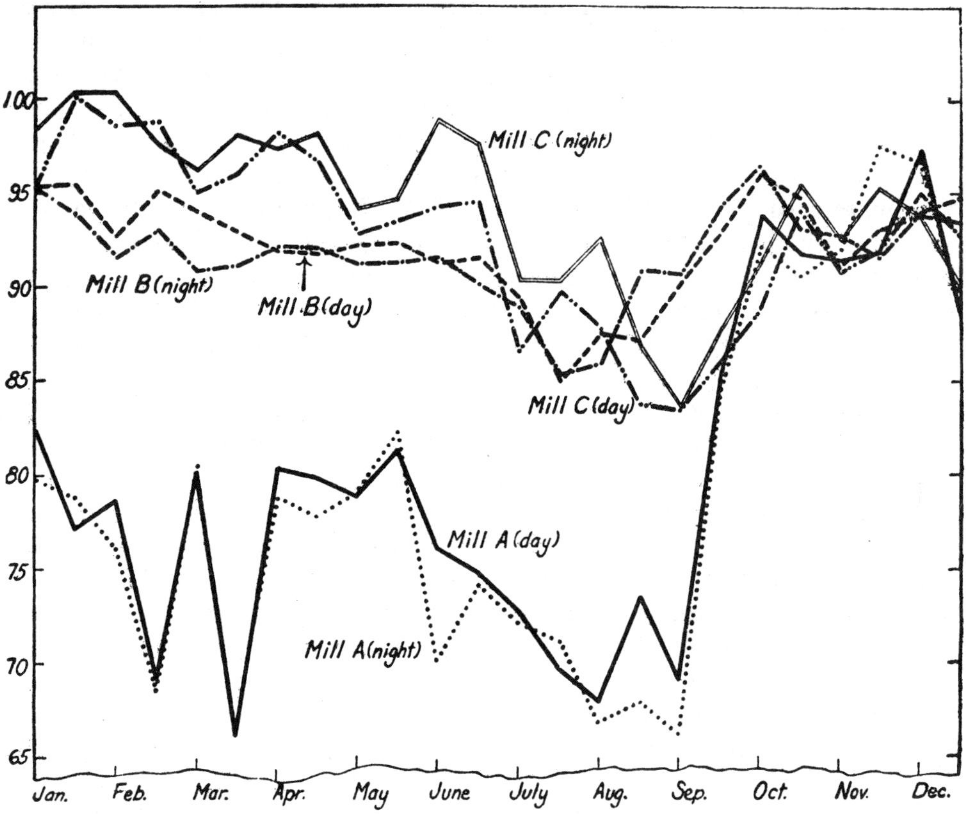

Fig. 14. Semi-monthly fluctuations of the spindle output per day or night shift among Tientsin cotton mills. 1929 (In 1/100 lb. per spindle per shift of 12 hours for ten counts) (*See* Table 24)

A further analysis of Table 24 reveals several other points of interest (Fig. 14). In the first place, taking the ten count yarn as the basis for comparison, the spindle output per shift of 12 hours is the highest for Mill C and lowest for Mill A, with Mill B occupying a middle position between the two extremes. The semi-monthly average output for the day shift during the year 1928 to 1929, as shown in that table, is 0.799 lb. for Mill A, 0.922 lb. for Mill B, and 0.927 lb. for Mill C; while that for night shift is 0.792 lb. for Mill A, 0.919 lb. for Mill B, and 0.945 lb. for Mill C. This discrepancy in output is reflected in or rather confirmed by the financial conditions of these three mills. Mill A is the most un-

13. The Cotton Spinning and Weaving Industry of Kiangsu, *op. cit.*, Part 1, p. 20. For other references to spindle output see Lieu, *China's Cotton Industry*, 1929, p. 28; *Textile News*, Oct. 30, 1930; *China Cotton Journal*, Vol. VII, No. 3, June, 1928; Odell, *Cotton goods in China*, 1916, pp. 162, 164, 167.

favorably situated financially, while the reverse is true with Mill C. Whereas Mill A has during the ten year period from 1919 to 1928 five losing years, Mill C has only one losing year during the same period. Again, while Mill C has four fifths of its paid-up capital invested in fixed assets, the investment in fixed assets for Mill A exceeds the paid-up capital in nine of the ten years covered. In 1921, the worst year, the excess amounts to as high as 59.15% of the paid-up capital. For Mill B although there are four losing years out of nine, the paid-up capital covers approximately the investment in fixed assets. In 1928, the worst year, the excess of the latter over the former is but 15.55%. A more detailed discussion, however, is left to Chapter VII. Secondly, except for Mill C the spindle output is higher for the day than for the night shift. That this is the case needs be briefly stated. Almost in every industry, night labor is always less efficient than day labor, especially under a continuous system as prevails in Chinese cotton mills. It reduces output because the worker is deprived of the health-giving effects of exposure to sunlight, and because, in the case of woman labor, she has to take care of household duties during the day time, partly if not wholly. Night labor is fundamentally unphysiological, not to say unsocial. Man, according to Vernon, "is a diurnal animal, and not a nocturnal one. It is found that during each 24 hours his body temperature shows a regular rhythm. It rises to a maximum at about 6 p.m., and falls gradually to a minimum at about 5 a.m., which is one to two degrees Fahrenheit below the maximum" (*Fatigue and Efficiency,* 1921, p. 90). Thirdly, there is a tendency towards seasonal fluctuation of output, which is especially notable during the summer months. From July to September the output reaches the lowest point during the year for all of the three mills studied, while from October it begins to increase again and with the exception of Mill A, becomes more or less normal throughout almost the rest of the year, with minor fluctuations.

In regard to loom output per shift of 12 hours the same conclusions hold true. The loom output is higher in Japanese than in Chinese owned mills. As shown in Table 25, it is 71 yards for 13 lbs. sheetings in Japanese owned mills, but only 60 yards in Chinese owned mills. To quote Mr. Pearse, "as regards cloth production the Chinese mills state:—

13 lbs. cloth, 36 ins. *60 yds. in 12 hours* per loom, whilst the Japanese-owned mills in China produce:—

13 lbs. cloth, 36 ins. *65-68 yds. in 11 hours* per loom."[14] Again, the loom output in Shanghai is much higher than that in Tientsin. As shown in Tables 24 and 25, the loom output per shift of 12 hours in

14. Pearse, *op. cit.,* pp. 176-180.

Tientsin is only 49.16 yards for 11 lb. cloth and 46.68 yards for 12 lb. cloth, while that in Shanghai is 60 yards for 13 lb. and 49 yards for 12 lb. cloth.[15]

Table 25. Loom output in Shanghai cotton mills, 1929*

Kind of cloth	No. & Nationality of mill	Width (inch)	Length per piece (yards)	Weight (lbs.)	Picks per inch	Picks per minute	Output (yards)	Output in 12 hours (yards)
Shirting	3 Japanese	36	?	12,13,6¾	65	?	48–50 in 11 hrs.	52.36–54.54
,,	4 ,,	36–38	38–40	12,10,6¾	52	190	45 11	49.10
,,	11 Chinese	?	?	?	?	190	50 12	50.00
Sheeting	4 Japanese	36	40	13,11,10	45	194–5	65 11	70.91
,,	5 Chinese	36	?	13	?	180	60 12	60.00
,,	5 ,,	36	?	16	?	180	56 12	56.00
,,	10 ,,	36	?	?	?	210	60 12	60.00

* Pearse, *Cotton Industry of Japan and China*, 1929, pp. 175-180.

Marketing

Cotton Goods:—The native cotton goods may be divided into three classes, namely, yarn, piece goods, and other. Of these, the first is the most important, and the last the least important. The yarns are classified according to the number of counts. Any kind of cotton yarn, one pound of which has a length of 840 yards or one hank, is called one count. If the same weight of yarn has twice or thrice the length of 840 yards, it is called two counts or three counts. It is thus obvious that the higher the number of counts the finer the yarn. Chinese cotton, being of a coarser quality and of a shorter staple, is not fit for the spinning of higher counts of yarn. Generally speaking, for the spinning of 4 to 12 counts raw cotton from Yuyao and Shanghai (called Ho Chi or steam-ginned) and cotton waste are used. For 12 to 20 counts raw cotton from Taich'ang, Ch'angshu, Shensi and British India is used, while for 20 to 45 counts raw cotton from Tungchow and Lingpao (Honan) is used, with American cotton for mixing. For the spinning of counts higher than 45 it is necessary to use raw cotton from Lingpao, the United States, and Egypt. An investigation of the products of 69 mills in China, undertaken by the Chinese Cotton Millowners' Association in June, 1928, shows that 16's is spun by 61 mills, 10's by 57 mills, 20's by 49 mills, 12's by 44 mills, 14's by 44 mills, 32's by 28 mills and 42's by 9 mills. All the other counts are spun by no more than four mills: 24's and 8's by 4 mills, 6's by 3 mills, 60's by 2 mills, 4's, 15's, 26's, 30's, 40's and 80's by 1 mill.[16] These different kinds of yarn may be further classified according to use. 4's yarns are used for the weaving of carpets, 6's to 8's for the weaving of curtains or blinds, 10's for the weaving of shirtings and sheetings, 14's to 16's for the weaving of drills and towels, 20's or above for the weaving of jeans,

15. For other references see Odell, *op. cit.*, pp. 162,167.
16. *Handbook of the Trade-marks of Chinese Cotton Yarn and Cloth*, published by the Chinese Cotton Millowners' Association, 1928.

etc., and 32's or above for the knitting of hoses and underwears. At present, 10's, 16's and 20's are the most extensively used.

The piece goods may be divided into two classes, namely, grey and dyed. The grey piece goods include sheetings, shirtings, drills, jeans and T-cloth, while the dyed piece goods include a far greater number of varieties. The grey shirting requires for both weft and warp from 12's to 15's yarn, and has a width from 30 to 45 inches and a length per piece of from 36 to 50 yards. The sheeting has 14's as warp and 15's as weft, with a width of 36 inches, a length per piece of 40 yards and a weight of 12 to 17 pounds. It is chiefly consumed by the laboring class. The drill requires as warp from 13's to 18's two-ply yarn, and as weft 10's to 14's or 20's, with a width of 30 inches, a length per piece of 40 yards and a weight of 12 to 14 pounds. The jean requires 20's for both warp and weft, with a width of 28 to 31 inches, a length per piece of 30 to 40 yards, and a weight of 11 to 12 pounds. It is either grey or white, but at times the warp may be dyed, the weft being white. The T-cloth is an imitation of the imported variety; it may be grey, dyed or printed. 20's is used for both warp and weft, but occasionally the weft may be of 16's, with 20's as the warp. The width is from 29 to 32 inches, with a length per piece of 24 yards, and a weight of 6 to 8 pounds. Of the five varieties of grey cloth, the sheetings, the drills and the jeans are the most extensively used.[17]

Yarn is packed in the usual manner with 40 bundles, each containing 10 pounds 4 ounces, net, in a bale. The number of skeins in the bundle varies with that of counts. For yarns of 14's or less it is twice the number of counts, for yarns of higher counts, it is the same as the number of counts. For instance, there are 24 skeins in the bundle for 12's, but 16 skeins in the bundle for 16's. Again, for yarns of 14 counts or less every skein is composed of five small skeins, while for yarns of higher counts it is composed of ten small skeins. In other words, the number of small skeins is invariably ten times the number of the count. In order to please the consumer, some mills have added one small skein of 4 ounces in each bundle. Such practice, which is condemned by all the mills, was adopted, it is claimed, after it had been initiated by the Japanese. The Chinese count the extra 10 pounds in the bale as "squeeze", or "cumshaw," and so firmly is the practice established that any mill failing to add the extra 10 pounds would find it difficult to dispose of its yarn on the market.

Cloth is put up in bales of 20 pieces each. A good quality of 10-ounce burlap is used and the bales are firmly bound with hempen ropes. Some of the mills use iron ties around the bales instead of ropes. In order to prevent the ropes or ties from cutting into the contents, a narrow strip of wood or bamboo is usually inserted under them at the four corners

17. *Social Monthly*, published by the Social Affairs Bureau, Shanghai, April, May, 1931.

of the bale. Two bales are sometimes bound together in one truss. This saves handing and freight where the freight charges go by the package. Two bales bound in one truss are counted as one package.[18]

In transporting cotton goods the freight is calculated in terms of foot space on steamships. For Canton and the Strait Settlements every bale counts as 12 square feet; for the Yangtze and northern ports it counts as 11 square feet. As the freight per square foot is fixed at Tl. 0.24, the freight per bale varies from Tls. 2.64 to Tls. 2.88. Besides, every bale has to pay a loading fee of Tl. 0.30 and another Tl. 0.25 as the Customs broker fee, and insurance. The transport of yarn by means of railway is uncommon, but railway freight is fixed at Tl. 0.50 per bale for a distance of 150 kilometres. In transporting cotton cloth on steamships, the freight is also fixed in terms of foot space, at about the same rate as the yarn. The space for one bale of shirtings is 7½ square feet, and that for one bale of drills 10 square feet. The loading charge amounts to Tl. 0.30 per truss of two bales or 40 pieces. The railway freight, too, is the same for cotton cloth as that for cotton yarn, at Tl. 0.50 per truss of two bales, for a distance of 150 kilometres.[19]

The taxes for cotton goods are of two kinds, namely, tungshui or consolidated excise tax and export duty. Tungshui was introduced on the first of February, 1931, as a substitute for likin which was abolished a month earlier. This tax, applicable to cigarettes, flour, cotton yarn, match and cement, divides the cotton yarn into two major classes, namely, (1) cotton yarn, grey, 23 counts or below, and (2) cotton yarn, grey, above 23 counts.[20] For the first class, the tax is fixed at $2.75 per picul; for the second, at $3.75 per picul. Any cloth woven of the taxed yarn is exempted from further taxation, as tungshui literally means one tax for one commodity throughout the whole country. But if the cloth is woven from any yarn that has not paid the tungshui, a new scale is fixed under the Tungshui Act, varying according to the count of yarn used and the weight of the cloth woven.[21]

The Chinese owned mills are opposed to the new tax on several grounds. In the first place, the classification of cotton yarns into two groups does not protect them from the superior competition of the Japanese owned mills in China. The latter, specializing chiefly in yarns of 20 and 42 counts, have relatively lighter burden of taxation than the former specializing in yarns of 10 and 16 counts. The Chinese owned mills claim that a new classification, like that already incorporated into the Customs Import Tariff promulgated on Dec. 29, 1930, should be adopted. This classification divides the grey cotton yarn into five groups, with graduating scale of tax rates, namely, 5.30 gold units per picul for counts up to and including 17, 5.80 units for counts 18 to 23, 7.90 units for counts 24 to 35,

18. The Cotton Spinning and Weaving Industry of Kiangsu, *op. cit.*, Part I, Chapter I, pp. 17-18; Odell *op. cit.*, p. 166.
19. Social Monthly, *op. cit.*,
20. The law and detailed regulation may be found in *Textile News*, Nos. 769-70, 773-76,778.
21. *Ibid.*, No. 773, Feb. 16, 1931.

8.90 units for counts 36 to 45, and 7½% *ad valorem* for counts above 45. Secondly, the new tax rate, being uniform all over the nation, places a heavier burden on the interior mills than on those along the coastal ports. Under the old arrangement some of the interior mills, such as Liaoning, Changsha No. 1, Chiuhsin (in Kiukiang), Yuchung (in Wuhu) and Lufeng (in Tsinan), are wholly exempted from taxation, while others, such as Yufeng (in Chenchow), are taxed lightly. The exemption or reduction is justified on the ground that for the interior mills the cost for machinery, supplies and fuel is higher than for the mills along the coastal port.[22] On the other hand, the new tax is not wholly lacking in protective feature for the mills in China, irrespective of nationality of ownership, as it applies also to the imported yarn which has to pay customs duty in addition. Furthermore, the tax can be refunded when the yarn spun in China is designed for export. The failure of the new Tungshui Act to give superior advantages to the Chinese owned mills is circumstantial, as under the Sino-Japanese Tariff Treaty of 1930, Chinese government is obliged to give equal treatment to the mills in China irrespective of the nationality of ownership.

The export duty on cotton goods, first promulgated in 1843, was revised in 1858 and 1931 respectively. In 1843 an export duty of Hk. Tl. 1.00 per picul was levied on "nankeen and cotton cloth of all kinds", but in 1858 the enumeration was greatly extended as to include not only the nankeens and all other cotton cloth made in China, but also foreign cottons dyed or printed in China, imitation of foreign imports such as drills and jeans, T-cloths, cambrics, muslins, etc., and yarn and thread. The export duty for nankeens, by far the largest item of export, was fixed at Hk. Tl. 1.00 per picul if the warp contained "not more than 70 threads to the inch and the weft not more than 60 threads to the inch", and if the cloth was "not to be a twill weave or woven on a Jacquard or Dobbie loom and the yarn not mercerized". But "if either warp or weft is woven of double threads", the duty was raised to Hk. Tls. 1.25 per picul; it was further raised to Hk. Tls. 1.50 per picul "if both warp and weft are woven of double threads". For "all other cotton cloth made in China, with the exception of the privileged factory products and cotton goods elsewhere enumerated in the Tariff" (i.e. foreign cottons dyed or printed in China and imitations of foreign cotton goods etc.) the export duty was fixed at five percent *ad valorem.* The export duty on cotton thread was fixed at Hk. Tl. 0.72 per picul, while that on cotton yarn at Hk. Tl. 0.70 per picul. The Revised Export Tariff of 1931 simplifies considerably the duty on cotton piece goods, which is fixed at Hk. Tl. 1.50 per picul *in toto.* The duty on "cotton thread, sewing, on spools or cops (or 50 yds or less)" is fixed at Hk. Tl. 0.037 per gross, while that for "cotton thread, not otherwise provided for", is, like that for cotton yarn, fixed at Hk. Tls. 1.10 per picul. The export duty on cotton piece goods is fixed at Hk. Tls. 1.50 per picul, while that on "piece goods, not otherwise

22. *Ibid,* Nos. 761, 775.

provided for", is fixed at 7½% *ad valorem*. Cotton socks and stockings, however, are exempted from the export duty.

The dealers:—The dealers in cotton goods distribute not only native, but also imported products. Indeed, the first dealers rose at a time when the import of foreign cotton goods had been put on a more or less permanent basis, after the seventies. At that time only piece goods were traded in, as yarns were not imported on a large scale until around the nineties. The rapid development of China's cotton industry since the World War, however, resulted in the replacement of a large portion of foreign imports by native products, especially yarns, and consequently the dealers were able to trade directly with own manufacturers instead of with foreign importers. Meantime, there has also grown up a specialization in business which did not exist in former years. The yarn dealers are organized into what is known as Sha-hao or yarn shop, and those in piece goods into what is known as Pu-chwang or cloth shop. The organization for both types of shops is similar, and does not differ much except in the kinds of goods traded in. Indeed, a yarn shop may also trade in cloth and a cloth shop in yarn. But a major portion of the trade for each type of shops is devoted to its own specialities.

In Shanghai a recent investigation by the Social Affairs Bureau estimates the number of yarn shops at 63, and that of cloth shops at 87. In Tientsin the number of yarn shops is estimated at 32, and that of cloth shops at 44, also by the Social Affairs Bureau. The number of cloth shops is, therefore, larger than that of yarn shops, indicating the preponderance of piece goods over yarns in both markets.[23]

Some insight may be gained into the capital, equipment, staff and trading methods of these shops by a brief summary of the previous surveys of the two Bureaus in Shanghai and Tientsin. In Tientsin the paid-up capital of a shao-hao varies from fifty to two hundred thousand dollars, but the working capital, including a large portion of the paid-up capital, as well as loans and deposits, reaches at least one hundred thousand dollars, especially in recent years when cash transaction is preferred to credit. The loans are secured from the native banks called ning-hao, and their rate of interest depends upon the credit standing of the shop. Commonly speaking, it is 1% per month, payable monthly or at one of the three festivals. The deposits are derived largely from the owners, relatives or friends. The rate of interest is lower, being 0.6% per month. Sometimes, a surplus may be appropriated from the business profits either in cash or in stock. For some shops the practice is to fix a cost value for the ending inventory during the calendar year, and write it off as a surplus.

23. Social Monthly, *op. cit.*; *Annual Report*, Tientsin Social Affairs Bureau, Aug., 1928 to July, 1929, pp. 570, 576, 577.

Such surplus is often used to strengthen the working capital, and is thus called the 'protecting capital'.

The equipment of a shao-hao is simple enough. A few rooms for office use are indispensable, but it is not uncommon to have the warehouse at the back of the office, and the staff dormitory at the second floor. A safe is also to be found, along with other necessary furnitures and fixtures. The books are still kept in the old Chinese manner, and are preserved for reference for a decade or so. These books are useful documents for historical analysis, but many owners still entertain the fear that once they are in the possession of others, business secrets may be divulged to their disadvantage.

The staff of a shao-hao is composed of a manager who is oftentimes the owner himself, a vice-manager, an accountant-treasurer, and several runners, clerks and apprentices. The staff members must be introduced or recommended by the owners and approved by the manager. They have to secure some one as guarantor before admission. Besides, a few janitors are employed to look after the handling end of the business, and to carry cash money, bills or other despatches for the shop.

Trading methods:—The dealers may buy directly from the mills or indirectly through the Exchange, and may sell directly to the clients or indirectly through the 'runners'. They may also act as brokers, receiving a commission of from Tl. 0.25 to Tl. 0.50 for every bale of cotton yarn transacted. In all these transactions, trading may be carried on either in spots or in futures. Both types of contracts, especially the futures, used to be transacted in the two exchanges in Shanghai, namely, the Chinese Cotton Goods Exchange and the Chinese Stock and Produce Exchange. The latter has suspended future contracts in cotton yarn since June, 1929, and consequently, the former is the only future market for cotton yarn in China. Future contracts in cotton cloth are provided for in the regulations of the Chinese Cotton Goods Exchange, but have seldom been traded in. The history and organization of this exchange, as well as the nature of its future contract, have been described in Chapter III on raw cotton, and need not be reiterated here. But a few words may be said that apply only to the futures trading in cotton yarn and cotton cloth. In cotton yarn, the unit of trading per contract is 50 bales (of 40 bundles per bale), while in cotton cloth it is 10 bales (of 20 pieces each). The quantity unit for quotation is one bale for cotton yarn and one piece for cotton cloth. For cotton yarn the unit for price fluctuation is one mace or one tenth of a tael, while for cotton cloth it is one candareen or one hundredth of a tael. The cotton yarn bought or sold on the Exchange is confined to the Chinese make, of which 16's, Man and Bell Brand (of the Shen Hsin Cotton Mill), was taken as the basis grade for the period from July to December, 1928. Similarly, the 14 pound cloth, of the Man and Horse Brand (of Heng Feng mill), was taken as the basis grade on the first of May, 1926. The products of Japanese owned mills in China, whether yarn or cloth, are excluded from trading on the Exchange, as a consequence of the recurrent embarrassment arising from the Anti-Japanese boycotts.

The Exchange brokers are composed of the dealers referred to above. According to the revised rules of the Exchange dated July 12, 1925, the Exchange limits the number of brokers to 80 in raw cotton, 80 in cotton yarn. The same broker, however, may trade in raw cotton and cotton yarn simultaneously. It is for this reason that there were only 72 brokers in the Exchange in 1931.[24] Each broker represents one of the yarn or cloth shops, and may have one or two agents to assist him on the Exchange floor. These brokers are organized into the Brokers' Association, and have frequent dealings with the Exchange to which they have to pay commissions not exceeding one percent of the contract value.

In the following table the extent of the Exchange's transactions in cotton yarn futures is given for the first half year period of 1926.[25]

Table 26. Amount of cotton yarn transacted and delivered at Chinese Cotton Goods Exchange, January to June, 1926

(16's Man and Bell Brand as basis grade)

Month	No. bales transacted	No. business days during month	No. bales transacted per day	No. bales delivered	Range of price per bale (Tls.) High	Low
Jan.	253,950	23	11,041	2,400	152.10	146.40
Feb.	248,350	15	16,557	1,350	151.50	142.00
Mar.	640,900	26	24,650	3,350	148.90	138.00
Apr.	438,350	25	17,534	2,100	147.30	136.60
May	551,800	25	22,072	1,500	145.70	135.20
June	393,300	24	16,388	2,350	143.40	134.00
Total	2,526,650	138	18,309	13,050	152.10	134.00

Price movement:—The price movement of native cotton goods may be analyzed from the records kept for the two leading markets in China, namely, Shanghai and Tientsin. In respect of cotton yarn, the National Tariff Commission, formerly the Bureau of Markets of the Ministry of Finance, has since 1922 collected prices for two brands of cotton yarn spun in Shanghai mills, namely, 16 counts "Water and Moon" brand spun by the Naigai Wata Mill (Japanese owned) and 16 counts "Pao Ding" (Incense Burner) brand spun by the Hung Yu Mill (now a branch mill of Wing On, Chinese owned). The price was collected monthly from October, 1922 to March, 1925; but semi-monthly after the latter date.[26] In Tientsin this Institute has collected the prices of cotton yarn spun in Tientsin since 1913 for two brands, namely, 16 counts Sung Hao (Pine

24. Social Monthly, *op. cit.*
25. Yang, Y. P.: *Stock and Produce Exchanges in China*, Commercial Press, Shanghai, 1930, Part IV, pp. 191-2.
26. *Shanghai Market Prices Report* (Quarterly), April, 1923 to date.

and Crane) and 10 counts Sung Hao, both brands being spun by the Yu Yuan Mill of Chinese ownership. The prices were collected annually from 1913 to 1927; monthly from January to March, 1928; and weekly from April, 1928 to date.[27] In Tables 27 and 28, the prices and price relatives of native cotton yarn in Shanghai and Tientsin are given respectively (Fig. 15). From these tables it may be noted that the price movement of native cotton yarn in general is the same for Shanghai as that for Tientsin. In Tientsin where data are available for the period 1913 to 1931, there has been a rapid upward movement of cotton yarn price since 1914, when the price relative for 16 counts Sung Hao relative to 1926 as 100 amounts to 52.11. It reaches the peak of 134.77 in 1919. Similarly, the price relative for 10 counts Sung Hao also increases from 51.63 to 122.83 during the same period. After 1919 the price relative for 16 counts drops continuously to the lowest point of 102.53 in 1922, so also that for 10 counts to 99.22. After 1922 an improvement in the price of native cotton yarn is visible in Shanghai as well as in Tientsin, until another peak is reached in 1924. At the latter date the price relative in Tientsin is 124.43 for 10 counts and 123.05 for 16 counts, and that in Shanghai is 123.8 for 16 counts spun by the Chinese owned mill and 124.2 for 16 counts spun by the Japanese owned mill. From 1924 on the price relative for native cotton yarn keeps

Table 27. Prices of native cotton yarn in Shanghai, 1922-1931 (in Shanghai taels per bale)

Date	Cotton yarn, 16's (Chinese owned mill)			Cotton yarn, 16's (Japanese owned mill)		
	Average price per bale	Relative price (1926=100)	Percent of increase (+) or decrease (—) as compared with preceding period	Average price per bale	Relative price (1926=100)	Percent of increase (+) or decrease (—) as compared with preceding period
1922	137.000	97.9		138.833	97.8	
1923	158.000	112.9	+15.3	157.292	110.8	+13.3
1924	173.333	123.8	+ 9.7	176.333	124.2	+12.1
1925	169.167	120.9	— 2.4	171.369	120.7	— 2.8
1926	139.958	100.0	—17.3	141.927	100.0	—17.2
1927	139.740	99.8	— 0.2	141.594	99.8	— 0.2
1928	160.604	114.8	+14.9	160.667	113.2	+13.5
1929	171.271	122.4	+ 6.6	167.042	117.7	— 4.0
1930	161.146	114.3	— 7.1	162.292	114.3	— 3.0
1931	172.222	123.1	+ 7.7	172.917	121.8	+ 6.5
Jan.	159.000	113.6	— 0.6	158.750	111.9	— 2.1
Feb.	173.500	124.0	+ 9.2	176.250	124.2	+11.0
Mar.	177.500	126.8	+ 2.3	179.000	126.1	+ 1.5
Apr.	174.500	124.7	— 1.7	177.000	124.7	— 1.1
May	171.500	122.5	— 1.8	171.500	120.8	— 3.2
June	173.500	124.0	+ 1.2	176.000	124.0	+ 2.6
July	174.00	124.3	+ 0.2	176.000	124.0	
Aug.	175.000	125.0	+ 0.6	174.250	122.8	— 1.0
Sep.	171.500	122.5	— 2.0	167.500	118.0	— 3.9
Oct.						
Nov.						
Dec.						

27. *Wholesale Prices and Price Index Numbers in North China*, 1913-1929.

Table 28. Prices of native cotton yarn in Tientsin, 1913-1931
(in Tientsin dollars per bale)

Date	Cotton yarn, 16's Average price per bale	Cotton yarn, 16's Relative price (1926=100)	Cotton yarn, 16's Percent of increase (+) or decrease as (—) compared with preceding period	Cotton yarn, 10's Average price per bale	Cotton yarn, 10's Relative price (1926=100)	Cotton yarn, 10's Percent of increase (+) or decrease as (—) compared. with preceding period
1913	122.83	61.68		112.62	61.12	
1914	103.77	52.11	—15.52	95.14	51.63	—15.53
1915	122.83	61.68	+18.36	112.61	61.11	+18.36
1916	169.84	85.28	+38.26	155.70	84.50	+38.28
1917	191.27	96.04	+12.62	175.33	95.15	+12.60
1918	216.96	108.94	+13.43	198.88	107.93	+13.43
1919	268.40	134.77	+23.71	226.33	122.83	+13.81
1920	240.92	120.97	—10.24	204.78	111.14	— 9.52
1921	210.28	105.59	—12.71	184.84	100.31	— 9.74
1922	204.19	102.53	— 2.90	182.82	99.22	— 1.09
1923	228.12	114.55	+11.72	202.64	109.98	+10.84
1924	245.06	123.05	+ 7.42	229.27	124.43	+13.14
1925	235.75	118.38	— 3.80	218.74	118.71	— 4.60
1926	199.15	100.00	—15.53	184.26	100.00	—15.76
1927	195.78	98.31	— 1.69	180.52	97.97	— 2.03
1928	218.99	109.96	+11.85	193.65	105.10	+ 7.28
1929	242.60	121.82	+10.79	209.59	113.75	+ 8.23
1930	225.92	113.44	— 6.88	191.68	104.03	— 8.55
1931	235.62	118.31	+ 4.29	202.35	109.82	+ 5.57
Jan.	220.62	110.78	+ 6.36	189.11	102.64	— 6.54
Feb.	238.39	119.70	+ 8.05	205.49	111.52	+ 8.65
Mar.	245.79	123.42	+ 3.11	218.62	118.65	+ 6.39
Apr.	240.42	120.72	— 2.19	209.32	113.60	— 4.26
May	236.60	118.80	— 1.59	203.70	110.55	— 2.68
June	238.31	119.66	+ 0.72	202.22	109.75	— 0.72
July	239.12	120.07	+ 0.34	202.91	110.12	+ 0.34
Aug.	236.39	118.70	— 1.14	199.51	108.28	— 1.67
Sep.	229.33	115.15	— 2.99	197.24	107.04	— 1.15
Oct.	229.47	115.22	+ 0.06	197.19	107.02	— 0.02
Nov.	242.69	121.86	+ 5.76	204.37	110.91	+ 3.63
Dec.	230.39	115.69	— 5.06	198.51	107.73	— 2.87

on dropping until another lowest point is again reached in 1927, namely, 97.97 for 10 counts and 98.31 for 16 counts in Tientsin, and 99.8 for 16 counts Chinese and 99.8 for 16 counts Japanese in Shanghai. After 1927 the price again rises and reaches the peak in 1929, when the price relative is 113.75 for 10 counts and 121.82 for 16 counts in Tientsin, but 122.4 for 16 counts Chinese and 117.7 for 16 counts Japanese in Shanghai. In short, the price of native cotton yarn in Tientsin and Shanghai since 1913 has undergone three waves of changes, reaching the peak in 1919, 1924 and 1929 respectively.

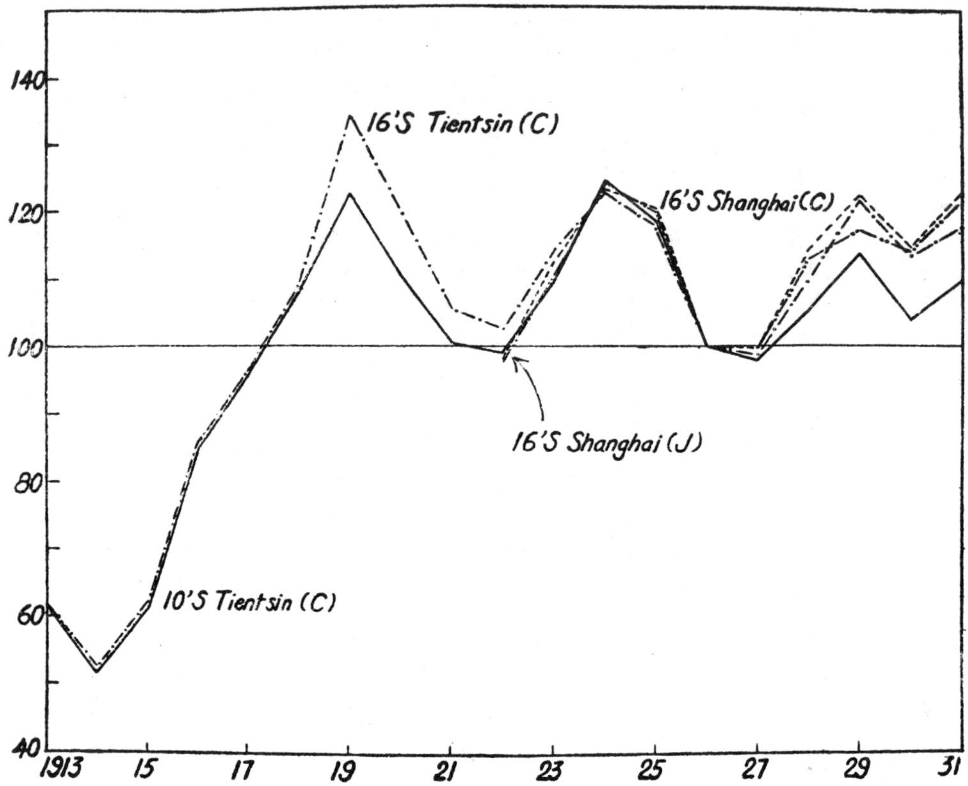

Fig. 15. Prices of native cotton yarn in Shanghai and Tientsin, 1913-1931 (1926=100) (*See* Tables 27-28). J represents yarn spun by Japanese owned mill, and C that by Chinese owned mill.

In Table 29 the comparison is made between the price relatives of native cotton yarn and the index numbers of wholesale prices in Shanghai and Tientsin, from 1913 to 1931. It is obvious that the general price level has maintained an unbroken upward trend in Shanghai as well as in Tientsin since 1914, as compared with the erratic changes in the price level of native cotton yarn. The change in the price level of cloth and clothing in Tientsin and of textile goods in Shanghai coincides generally with that in the price level of native cotton yarn, but the former is much less violent than the latter.

The prices for native cotton cloth are collected for the two markets in Shanghai and Tientsin by the National Tariff Commission and this Institute respectively, referring in both cases to the 14 pound cloth woven by the Heng Feng Cotton Mill in Shanghai and covering the same period as that for the cotton yarn. The brand sold in Shanghai is Man and Horse, while that sold in Tientsin is Human Head. These prices, as given in Table 30, show a similar trend of development as those for cotton yarn, although the three peak years, namely, 1919, 1924, 1929, do not apply invariably to those for cotton cloth. (Fig. 16). For the latter both 1919 and 1929 are peak years, but not 1924. In 1919 the price ratio in Tientsin reaches as high as 129.61, while in 1929 it is 109.73 in Tientsin and 111.99 in Shanghai. In Shanghai there is another peak year in 1925, when the price ratio reaches 115.12, but in Tientsin the price movement from 1921 to 1925 is rather smooth, the price ratio being 111.39, 106,31, 111.18, 109.73 and 111.59 for the respective years. In 1926 there is a rapid fall of the price ratio in both markets, which is from 111.59 to 100 in Tientsin, and from 115.12 to 100 in Shanghai.

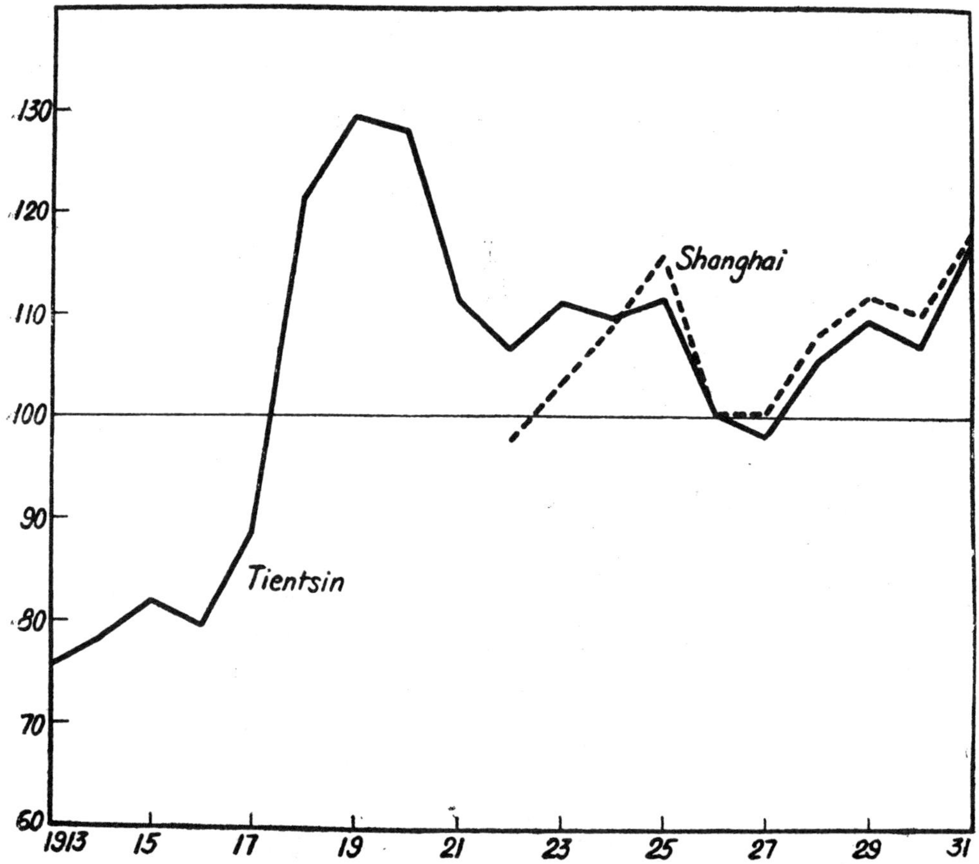

Fig. 16. Prices of native cotton cloth in Shanghai and Tientsin, 1913-1931 (1926=100) (*See* Table 30)

Table 29. Price relatives of native cotton yarn and index numbers of wholesale prices compared, 1913-1931 (1926=100)

Year	Price relative of cotton yarn				Index numbers of wholesale prices			
	10's (Chinese) Tientsin	16's (Chinese) Tientsin	16's (Chinese) Shanghai	16's (Japanese) Shanghai	Cloths & Clothing Tientsin	Textile goods Shanghai	General Tientsin	General Shanghai
1913	61.62	61.68			65.47		67.18	
1914	51.63	52.11			61.20		66.89	
1915	61.11	61.68			65.53		68.78	
1916	84.50	85.28			72.98		74.19	
1917	95.15	96.04			83.29		79.95	
1918	107.93	108.94			96.64		82.21	
1919	122.83	134.77			107.06		81.07	
1920	111.14	120.97			104.33		88.92	
1921	100.31	105.59			99.78	103.5	88.91	104.6
1922	99.22	102.53	97.9	97.8	99.33	104.1	86.40	98.6
1923	109.98	114.55	112.9	110.8	107.41	110.6	90.35	102.0
1924	124.43	123.05	123.8	124.2	109.70	107.5	93.61	97.9
1925	118.71	118.38	120.9	120.7	108.21	106.8	97.28	99.3
1926	100.00	100.00	100.0	100.0	100.00	100.0	100.00	100.0
1927	97.97	98.31	99.8	99.8	99.96	100.9	103.20	104.4
1928	105.10	109.96	114.8	113.2	103.26	102.1	107.98	101.7
1929	113.75	121.82	122.4	117.7	107.35	101.9	111.08	104.5
1930	104.03	113.44	115.1	114.3	103.76	105.6	115.85	114.8
1931	109.82	118.31	123.1	121.8	117.03	118.8	122.55	126.7

Table 30. Prices of native cotton cloth in Shanghai and Tientsin, 1913-1931 (Sheeting, 40 yds. x 36 in., 14 lbs. Heng Feng Cotton Mill, Shanghai)

Date	Tientsin			Shanghani		
	Average price per piece	Relative price 1926=100	% of increase (+) or decrease (—) as compared with preceding period	Average price per piece	Relative price 1926=100	% of increase (+) or decrease (—) as compared with perceding period
1913	$ 7.32	75.78				
1914	7.56	78.26	+ 3.27			
1915	7.93	82.09	+ 4.89			
1916	7.68	79.50	— 3.16			
1917	8.56	88.61	+11.46			
1918	11.72	121.33	+36.93			
1919	12.52	129.61	+ 6.82			
1920	12.37	128.05	— 1.20			
1921	10.76	111.39	—13.01			
1922	10.27	106.31	— 4.56	$ 5.775	97.47	
1923	10.74	111.18	+ 4.58	6.109	103.19	+ 5.78
1924	10.60	109.73	— 1.30	6.427	108.56	+ 5.20
1925	10.78	111.59	+ 1.70	6.815	115.12	+ 6.04
1926	9.66	100.00	—10.39	5.920	100.00	—13.13
1927	9.47	98.03	— 1.97	5.925	100.08	+ 0.08
1928	10.16	105.18	+ 7.29	6.386	107.87	+ 7.78
1929	10.60	109.73	+ 4.33	6.621	111.99	— 3.68
1930	10.34	107.04	— 2.45	6.513	110.02	— 1.63
1931	11.26	116.56	+ 8.89	6.983	117.96	+ 7.22
Jan.	10.31	106.73	— 8.43	6.525	110.22	— 6.56
Feb.	10.58	109.52	+ 2.61	6.675	112.75	+ 2.30
Mar.	10.75	111.28	+ 1.61	7.050	119.09	+ 5.62
Apr.	10.86	112.42	+ 1.02	7.200	121.62	+ 2.12
May	10.92	113.04	+ 0.55	7.050	119.09	— 2.08
June	11.11	115.01	+ 1.74	7.050	119.09	—
July	11.15	115.42	+ 0.36	7.050	119.09	—
Aug.	11.34	117.39	+ 1.71	7.150	120.78	+ 1.42
Sep.	11.79	122.05	+ 3.97	7.150	120.78	—
Oct.	12.08	125.05	+ 2.46			
Nov.	12.35	127.85	+ 2.24			
Dec.	11.93	123.50	— 3.40			

CHAPTER V. LABOR: I

Extent and Character

Number of cotton workers, 1912-1930:—Cotton industry, the largest factory industry of China today, employs the greatest number of workers. According to the *Statistical Annuals* of the former Ministry of Agriculture and Commerce for the period 1912-1920, cotton workers, including ginners, spinners, doublers, weavers, dyers and bleachers, count as one fourth of the total factory workers in China. As shown in Table 31, which is an abstract from the *Annuals*, the percentage for cotton workers is 21.2 for 1915, 20.3 for 1916, 21.8 for 1917, 24.3 for 1918, and 23.7 for 1919. The high percentage for 1920, 33.6, is due to the increase of cotton spinners from 9.7 percent to 15.9 percent,—an increase which can be partly explained by the rapid gowth of the industry during the post-war period.

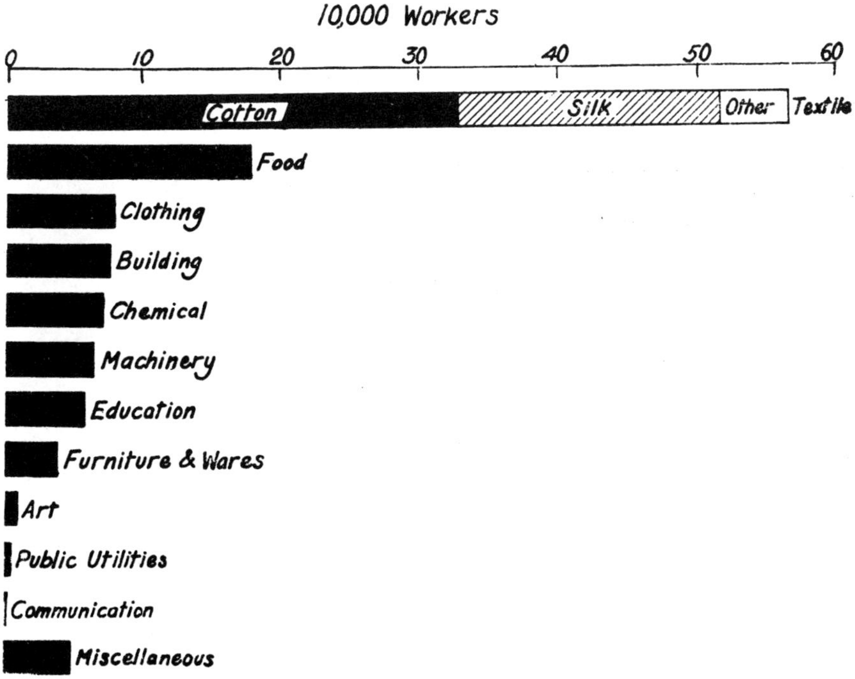

Fig. 17. Distribution of factory workers in nine provinces of China by industries, 1930 (*See* Table 32)

In a recent investigation of the factory workers in nine provinces including Kiangsu, Chekiang, Anhwei, Kiangsi, Hupeh, Shantung, Kwangtung, Kwangsi and Fukien, the percentage for cotton workers is found to be 27.22, which is quite close to that given by the earlier investigation

Table 31. Cotton factory workers in China, 1912-1920 (in thousands)

Type of worker	1912		1913		1914		1915		1916		1917		1918		1919		1920§	
	No.	%	No.	%	No.	%	No.	%	No.	%	No.	%	No.	%	No.	%	No.	%
Factory workers	661.8	100.0	630.9	100.0	624.5	100.0	619.7	100.0	565.3	100.0	555.6	100.0	523.0	100.0	410.3	100.0	323.0	100.0
Textile workers	228.5	34.5	249.2	39.5	288.3	46.2	295.0	46.7	276.4	48.9	293.4	52.8	270.0	51.6	241.1	58.8	211.8	65.6
Cotton spinning	18.0	2.7	19.0	3.0	34.4	5.5	43.0	6.9	36.5	6.5	43.0	7.7	43.8	8.4	39.8	9.7	51.3	15.9
Cotton weaving	*		*		*		78.3	12.6	66.7	11.8	60.8	10.9	73.7	14.1	51.1	12.5	51.0	15.8
Other cotton workers							10.3	1.7	11.7	2.0	17.3	3.2	9.6	1.8	6.5	1.5	6.1	1.9
Cotton gining	1.8		26.0		6.7		1.3		2.5		2.1		2.0		2.4		2.7	
Cotton doubling	3.3		0.6		0.8		0.7		1.1		8.1		0.2		0.8		0.3	
Cotton & silk weaving	*		*		*		0.1		0.1		0.1		0.3		0.3		—	
Dyeing & bleaching	3.6		3.4		15.8		8.2		8.0		7.0		7.1		3.0		3.1	
Total cotton workers							131.6	21.2	114.9	20.3	121.1	21.8	127.1	24.3	97.4	23.7	108.4	33.6

* Included under "Textile Weaving".

§ For 1920 the total factory workers is given at 413,000. The present figure has been revised in view of the fact that whereas in Hopei there were only 3,517 male spinners and 941 female spinners in 1919, in 1920 the male spinners had increased to 93,000, with a decrease of female spinners to 727. The 93,000 male spinners are probably a mistake for 3,000, and accordingly, 90,000 workers are deducted from the total "factory workers", the "textile workers" and the "cotton spinners" respectively.

referred to above. However, the later investigation, which was undertaken by the Ministry of Industries in 1930, covered factories employing thirty or more workers, whereas the earlier one included all factories employing seven or more workers.[1] As shown in Table 32, there were in the nine provinces 1,204,318 factory workers, including 566,301 textile workers or 47.02 percent and 327,842 cotton workers or 27.22 percent (Fig. 17).[2]

Table 32. Distribution of factory workers in nine provinces of China by industries, 1930

Industry	No.	%	Industry	No.	%
Textile	566,301	47.02	Food	176,504	14.66
Cotton	327,842	27.22	Clothing	80,078	6.65
Spinning	206,532	17.15	Building	77,737	6.45
Weaving	109,809	9.12	Chemical	72,020	5.98
Other		0.95	Machinery	65,501	5.44
Ginning	6,510	0.54	Education	59,006	4.90
Doubling	1,432	0.12	Furniture & wares	40,195	3.34
Mixture weaving	3,265	0.27	Art	10,216	0.85
Finishing	294	0.02	Public utilities	5,432	0.45
Silk	188,750	15.69	Communication	1,284	0.10
Other	49,709	4.11	Miscellaneous	50,044	4.16

In the above tables two classes of cotton workers seem to overlap each other, namely, cotton spinners and cotton weavers. The former are employed in the so-called cotton mills—spinning or spinning-and-weaving plants, while the latter can be found in smaller weaving plants employing either power looms or handlooms. The Ministry's survey on the number of cotton spinners (i.e. cotton mill workers) are, however, incomplete, as it fails to cover five provinces where cotton mills also exist, including Hopei, Honan, Hunan, Liaoning and Shansi. Besides, for the six provinces covered in the Ministry's survey, including Kiangsu, Chekiang, Hupeh, Shantung, Kiangsi and Anhwei, the number of workers does not agree with that given by the Chinese Cotton Millowners' Association. Whereas the Association reported altogether 212,683 cotton mill workers in the six covered provinces, the Ministry's returns gave only 206,532 cotton mill workers for the same region—a difference of 6,151 workers. Meantime, the five provinces not covered in the Ministry's survey employed 39,348 workers.[3]

1. This distinction, however, does not seriously affect the cotton factories, as they are generally quite large in size.
2. As a matter of fact, these workers are located in 6 of the 9 provinces, the other 3 provinces having no cotton workers.
3. Ministry of Industries, *a National Survey of the Worker's Livelihood and Industrial Production*, Bulletin No. 1, Nanking, 1930; *Nankai Weekly Statistical Service*, Feb. 16, 1931.

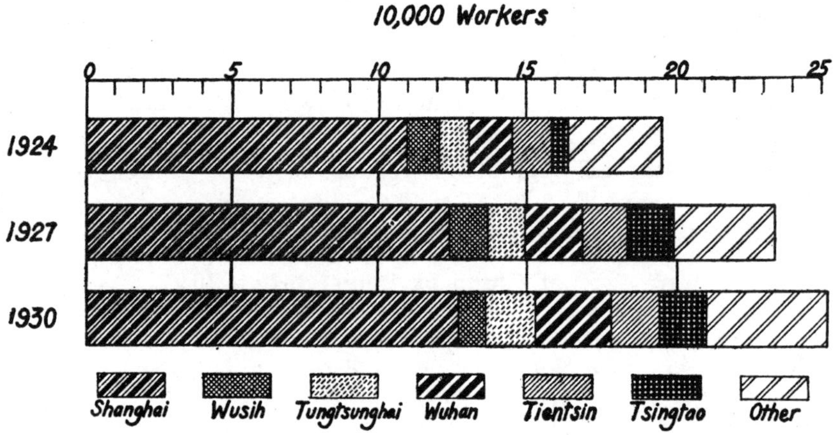

Fig. 18. Distribution of cotton mill workers in China by cities, 1924, 1927 and 1930 (*See* Table 33)

In Table 33 the cotton mill workers in China are classified by cities, for the period 1924 to 1930 (Fig. 18). Six cities, including Shanghai, Wusih, Tungtsunghai, Wuhan, Tientsin and Tsingtao, claim about 85 percent of the total cotton mill workers in China during the period. In 1930 the percentage is the highest for Shanghai, namely, 50.6%, after which follow 10.4% for Wuhan, 6.9% for Tungtsunghai, 6.1% for Tientsin, 6% for Tsingtao, and 3.7% for Wusih. For the other cities, the percentage is 16.3. Because of the great prominence that Shanghai occupies in China's cotton industry, as well as the comparative wealth of data for that city, our analysis of the labor conditions in China's cotton industry will be confined chiefly to that city. Tientsin, however, will also be given special consideration, since the present investigation is undertaken under the auspices of the *Nankai Institute of Economics* located in that city.

Table 33. Cotton mill workers in China classified by cities, 1924-1930

	1924		1925		1927		1928		1930	
City	No.	%	No.	%	No.	%	No.	%	No.	%
Shanghai	109,865	56.1	117,922	56.2	124,521	53.1	116,678	48.3	127,604	50.6
Wusih	11,358	5.8	14,440	6.9	12,803	5.4	12,156	5.0	9,346	3.7
Tungtsunghai	10,800	5.5	11,690	5.6	12,840	5.5	15,221	6.3	17,331	6.9
Wuhan	14,900	7.6	19,570	9.3	19,476	8.3	26,384	10.9	26,084	10.4
Tientsin	14,100	7.2	12,496	5.9	15,432	6.6	16,018	6.6	15,338	6.1
Tsingtao	5,200	2.7	5,200	2.5	16,147	6.9	16,523	6.9	15,184	6.0
Other	29,468	15.1	28,641	13.6	33,321	14.2	38,630	16.0	41,144	16.3
Total	195,691	100	209,959	100	234,540	100	241,610	100	252,031	100

Nativity, age, sex, height and weight of cotton workers:—The workers in cotton mills are mostly recruited from the neighboring districts or provinces, as shown in Table 34. According to that table, of a total of 1,919 workers in a Japanese owned mill in Shanghai, only 231 workers or 12.04% are natives of Shanghai, the rest being born elsewhere in Kiangsu or other provinces. In another investigation of 100 cotton mill workers' families in Yangtzepoo District, it is again shown that only 12% of the family heads are natives of Shanghai. However, Kiangsu, the province in which Shanghai is located, claims a rather high percentage in the nativity of workers, namely, 82.96% for the workers in the Japanese owned mill, 67.83% for those in Jessfield Village and 57% for those in Yangtzepoo District.[4] In Tientsin, a sample survey of 3,898 workers in three mills shows that 927 workers or 23.78% are natives of Tientsin, the rest being born elsewhere in Hopei or other provinces, especially Shantung and Honan. Hopei, the province in which Tientsin is located, claims 79.06% of the workers in Tientsin cotton mills.

Table 34. Shanghai and Tientsin cotton mill workers classified by nativity

	Shanghai						Tientsin	
Nativity	Japanese mill		Jessfield		Yangtzepoo			
	No.	%	No.	%	No.	%	No.	%
Kiangsu	1,592	82.96	156	67.83	57	57.00	32	0.82
Shanghai	231	12.04	?	?	12	12.00		
Chekiang	22	1.15	15	6.53	33	33.00	6	0.16
Anhwei	217	11.32	38	16.52	2	2.00	2	0.05
Hupeh	6	0.31	7	3.04				
Hunan	34	1.77	7	3.04				
Kwangtung	3	0.16						
Shansi							4	0.10
Shantung	29	1.51	5	2.17	8	8.00	409	10.50
Hopei							3,082	79.06
Tientsin							927	23.78
Honan	3	0.15					293	7.52
Liaoning							2	0.05
Other	13	0.67	2	0.87			68	1.74
Total	1,919	100	230	100	100	100	3,898	100

In Table 35 the age distribution of the workers in Shanghai, Tsingtao and Tientsin mills is given (Fig. 19).[5] In looking over the table it is striking to note that about three quarters of the workers fall within the age group of 11-25. The percentage of workers in that group is 89.86 in a Japanese owned mill in Tsingtao, 79.12 in another Japanese owned mill in

4. *China Labor Yearbook*, I: 362; Yang, *The Standard of Living in Shanghai*, p. 26; *Chinese Economic Journal*, Aug., 1930, p. 870.
5. *China Labor Year book*, I: 379, 380.

Shanghai, 78.97 in a Chinese owned mill in Tsingtao, and 70.06 in three Chinese owned mills in Tientsin. In other words, in Japanese owned mills the workers on the whole are younger than in Chinese owned mills. Again, the percentage for child workers below 16 years of age, 23.07, is the highest for the Japanese owned mill in Shanghai, after which follow 21.23 for a Chinese owned mill in Tsingtao, 11.62 for 3 Chinese owned mills in Tientsin, and 6.57 for a Japanese owned mill in Tsingtao. Table 35 also shows that the percentage of female workers is the highest in Shanghai, with 69.83%, after which follow 16.94% in Tsingtao and 2.54% in Tientsin.

Table 35. Age distribution of workers in cotton mills in Shanghai, Tsingtao and Tientsin

	Shanghai		Tsingtao				Tientsin	
Age	Japanese mill		Japanese mill		Chinese mill*		Chinese mills	
	No.	%	No.	%	No.	%	No.	%
10	1	0.05					10	0.26
11-15	441	23.02	83	6.57	107	21.23	442	11.36
16-20	693	36.17	754	59.70	206	40.87	1,254	32.23
21-25	382	19.93	298	23.59	85	16.87	1,030	26.47
26-30	232	12.11	71	5.62	35	6.94	564	14.49
31-35	138	7.20	34	2.69	30	5.95	224	5.76
36-40			23	1.82	11	2.18	145	3.73
41-45	22	1.15			15	2.98	97	2.49
46-50					9	1.79	71	1.82
51-55	7	0.37			3	0.60	37	0.95
56-60					3	0.60	12	0.31
61-65							5	0.13
Total	1,916	100	1,263	100	504	100	3,891	100
Unknown	3						7	
Grand total	1,919	100	1,263	100	504	100	3,898	100
Males	579	30.17			469	83.06	3,799	97.46
Females	1,340	69.83			35	16.94	99	2.54

* Resident workers only.

The height and weight of the workers have seldom been measured in Chinese industries. In the cotton industry, however, some attempt has been made towards that direction since the publication of the *Report of the Child Labor Commission* of the Shanghai Municipal Council in 1924, with a view to obtaining some definite standard for the restriction of child labor. Dr. Chen, in a recent study of 49 cotton mills in Shanghai, stated that "every one of 34 foreign and some Chinese cotton mills have adopted a height standard of not less than 4 feet 2 inches as minimum for entry, aiming toward a standard of 14 years...... In the determination of this standard the heights of 1,000 children were taken by an important cotton mill company, correlating these with the stated age of the young workers. Upon the basis of the result the determination of entry standard was

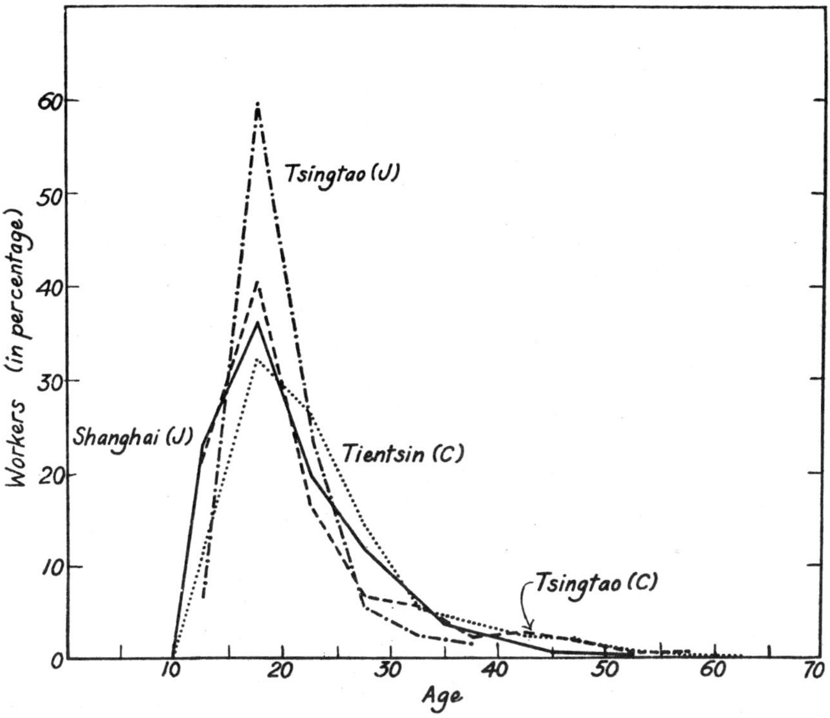

Fig. 19. Age distribution of cotton mill workers in Shanghai and Tientsin (*See* Table 35)

made."[6] In Tientsin a similar but more elaborate study has been made by the Hua Hsin mill, under the nominal requirement that any applicant for work must have a height of not less than 4½ feet. The regulation, however, is not strictly enforced, as a consequence of which statistics are available for 604 of the 2,041 workers whose height falls below 4½ feet.

In *Appendix XIIa* the height of the 2,041 workers in Hua Hsin mill, including 1,637 males and 404 females, is classified according to age. The average height for male workers, which as shown in the Appendix, is 4' at 11, rises to 4' 2" at 12, 4' 5" at 15, 5' at 18, and 5' 4" at 21. After 21, however, the height shows little change, as it fluctuates within the small range of only three inches, from 5'4" to 5'7". The same holds true for the female workers, although their height is on the whole lower than that for the male workers of the same age. But, the statistics for female worker must be used with greater reserve than those for male workers, because they cover a limited number of workers (404). The average height for all ages, which is 5' for male workers, is 4'6" for female workers.

6. Chen Ta, *Study of the Applicability of the Factory Act of the Chinese Government*, China Institute of Scientific Management, 1931, p. 15.

In *Appendix XIIb* the age distribution of the height of 2,041 workers in Hua Hsin Cotton Mill is given. The average weight for the male workers, which is 66 pounds at 10, rises to 68 at 11, 75.8 at 14, 81.3 at 16, 114.9 at 19, 122.8 at 22, 125.8 at 26, 134.6 at 30, and 146 at 33. After 33, the weight tends to decrease with an increase in age, reaching the lowest point of 127.6 pounds at 40. For the female workers the weight increases with an increase in age, up to 22 years of age. After 22 the statistics, being related to only 58 workers, are less reliable and more erratic, and fail to show any correlation between age and weight. It is nevertheless true that for the same age the weight is much heavier for male than female worker. At 20, for instance, the weight is 114.4 pounds for male worker but 93.5 pounds for female worker. For all ages the average weight is 106.5 pounds for male worker but 78.6 pounds for female worker.

In *Appendix XIIc* the sex distribution of the height and weight of 2,041 workers in Hua Hsin Cotton Mill is given. Making allowance for some exceptions due to the limited number of workers studied, the average weight for the male worker increases from 67.1 pounds at 4 feet to 83 pounds at 4½ feet, 107.2 pounds at 5 feet, and 127.5 pounds at 5½ feet. For the female worker the increase is from 65.5 pounds at 4 feet to 74.1 pounds at 4½ feet, 87.1 pounds at 5 feet and 126 pounds at 5½ feet. The average weight for all height is 107.7 pounds for male worker but 78.6 pounds for female worker.[7]

Labor Conditions

Employment and labor mobility:—A decade ago when cotton mills were just established, the first group of workers were recruited from outside districts or provinces, especially those parts where cotton mills were already in existence. When Yu Yuan Mill was first organized in 1918 the skilled workers, including the mechanics, were recruited from Shanghai, while the semi-skilled workers came from Chuangteh in Honan. These workers were offered better conditions of work as an inducement, oftentimes with free travelling expenses. In 1919, for instance, Yu Yuan mill spent $3,057 for the purpose of labor recruiting. In Hua Hsin another practice was resorted to, namely, that of training up apprentices for the skilled jobs. These apprentices were recruited from the neighborhood of Tientsin by the mill's agents, mostly janitors, police cops and workers. The latter were sent back by the mill to their native districts, where they could better persuade fellow countrymen to join the mill in Tientsin. An advertisement was posted, in which the conditions of work, including free travelling expense, free provision for room, board and

7. Cf. an earlier study on the same subject by S. M. Shirokogoroff, *Process of Physical Growth among the Chinese*, Vol. I, Commercial Press, Shanghai, 1925.

clothing, one hour physical training, two hour continuation education, and a term of apprenticeship for three years, were described in detail. Besides, a small monthly subsidy was promised to the apprentice for pocket money, varying all the way from twenty cents to $2.60, and depending upon the length of stay with the mill. In case of separation before the end of the three year term the apprentice or his guarantor was held responsible for the refunding of living expenses, at six dollars per month. These apprentices, unfortunately, were poorly treated after admission into the mill. Not a few of them died, and were buried in the workers' cemetry a few miles away from the mill.

At present when Tientsin mills have already a history of more than a decade, the situation is reversed. There are more workers than the mills can employ, and consequently, the latter are in a position to lay down rather strict rules in admitting new workers. In Hua Hsin, for instance, any applicant for work, whether male or female, must be from 16 to 40 years of age, with a height of not less than 4½ feet, must be in good health and not deformed. He must possess good temperament and common sense, and must secure a reliable person with a regular occupation, but not a worker of the mill, as his guarantor. He must not be a former employee who was fired by the mill or quit for more than three times, nor must he have been imprisoned or known as a trouble-maker in other mills. If the applicant is a skilled hand, he (or she) must have passed the job test of the mill. If the applicant is a new hand, he must have passed the test after a minimum training of one month. Moreover, a new hand is not allowed to continue his training if he fails to satisfy the minimum requirement after two months' training. If an applicant has met all these requirements, he must have the employment contract signed by himself and counter-signed by his guarantor. He is then given a pay slip with which he is admitted into the mill and identifies himself for the receipt of his wages. The employment contract, however, becomes ineffective if the worker fails to secure a substitute for the guarantor when the latter has withdrawn his responsibility towards the mill. The same also applies if (1) the worker is unable to perform his work because of sickness or of sickness leave for over two months, (2) the worker is unfit for the job because of incompetency, (3) the worker is on leave for over one month on account of reasons other than sickness (excluding the time spent on journey), (4) the worker, if a new hand, fails to attain the standard of workmanship after half a year of stay with the mill, (5) the mill, in contracting the scale of operation or in reducing the output, has to reduce the working force, (6) the mill under *force majeure* suspends work for over one month. Under all these circumstances the worker is asked to leave the mill. He is fired outright if (1) he forges his name, nativity, and age, (2) violates the important prohibitive rules of the mill, (3) does serious damage to the mill's property, (4) is absent without leave for over five days within half a month, or for eight days within one month, or for over two months within a year, (5) is a trouble-maker interfering with the work of his fellow worker or violating the criminal code, (6) secretly manipulates the machinery such as gears, resulting in a reduction of output, (7) disregards orders and sabotages purposely, (8) abuses publicly the staff members of the mill. These regulations, of course, are not strictly enforced, but represent rather the mill's attempt to introduce a set of guiding principles upon which to determine the selection of new applicants.

The applicant is customarily introduced to the mill through the medium of foremen. Whenever new hands are needed, the news spreads out immediately among the foremen, who in turn are responsible for introducing them to the management. Indeed, under the notorious contract system which prevailed formerly in foreign owned mills and still prevails in some of them in Shanghai, the foreman who is usually the native contractor supplies the requisite labor and is paid on production. This system is obviously open to grave abuse, particularly in regard to child labor. The *Shanghai Child Labor Commission* appointed in 1924 heard evidence to the effect that "in some instances contractors obtain young children from the country districts, paying the parents $2 a month for the services of each child. By employing such children in the mills and factories the contractor is able to make a profit of about $4 a month in respect of each child. These children are frequently most miserably housed and fed. They receive no money and their conditions of life are practically those of slavery".[8] Although the system of contract labor is gradually giving way, yet because of the key position which these foremen still hold in regard to employment, their earnings are frequently enhanced by illegal tribute from fellow workers.

The method of employment, as above described, is commonly adopted in Tientsin mills, but in Yu Yuan another method is employed in securing the casual coolies. Every morning at about six o'clock, a group of coolies are seen waiting in front of the mill's gateway. In a few minutes a staff member comes forth with a bundle of numbered sticks and throws them towards the coolies. A struggle immediately ensues and those coolies are employed for the day who are in possession of the sticks. The method employed is repeated day after day, and is evidently against the interests of the coolies. But in view of the keen competition for jobs, the mill is able to retain the method and to dispense with the obligation of having to maintain the casual staff on regular payroll.

Labor turnover is a term which has been commonly identified with three aspects of labor mobility, namely, the number of employees hired (accessions), (2) the number leaving (separations), and (3) the number

8. Report reprinted in *China Yearbook*, 1925, pp. 548-9.

of replacements required to keep up the working force.[9] The rate at which employees leave may be called the separation rate, and the rate at which they are hired, the accession rate. Whichever of these two rates is the lower, may, for all practical purposes, be used as the replacement rate. In Tientsin mills statistics on all these aspects of labor mobility are seldom kept with uniformity or completeness, Hua Hsin mill being excepted. In the fiscal year of March, 1929 to February, 1930, the Mill, with an average work force of 2,348 on the payroll, hired 1,175 workers, while 988 workers separated from the Mill. The separation rate, expressed in terms of percentages, is therefore 42.1, which is also the replacement rate, while the accession rate is 50.1. For other mills only separations are recorded, and in a rather haphazard manner. In Yu Yuan 1,012 workers separated from July to December, 1927; 1,266 workers from January to December, 1928; and 392 workers from January to June, 1929. In Heng Yuan 405 workers separated from July to December, 1927; 502 workers from January to December, 1928; 214 workers from January to December, 1929; and 79 workers from January to May, 1930. In Peiyang 768 workers separated from April to September, 1930. Dividing the average payroll employees[10] into the number of separations, the separation rate can be computed for the different mills. In this way, the separation rate for Yu Yuan, expressed in percentages, is 35.5 in 1927, 20.8 in 1928 and 12.3 in 1929; that for Heng Yuan is 28.4 in 1927, 15.7 in 192.8, 6.6 in 1929 and 5.8 in 1930; that for Hua Hsin is 42.1 in 1929; and that for Peiyang is 76.8 in 1930. For some mills the data for earlier years were kept, but at the time of our investigation they have already been mislaid or destroyed. The data now at our disposal show, however, that the separation rate in Tientsin mills, except Peiyang, is not high, and the tendency towards a decrease is visible in recent years.

In Table 36 the separations of the workers in one Shanghai mill and four Tientsin mills, including quits, discharges and layoffs, are classified by reasons. According to this table, among the 3,968 workers in Tientsin

9. Brissenden and Frankel, *Labor Turnover in Industry*, New York, 1922, p. 8.

10. The average payroll employees are given in the following table. The figures for 1928 are given in *Annual Report*, Aug., 1928-July, 1929, by the Bureau of Social Affairs, Special Municipality of Tientsin. Those for 1929-1930 are estimated by myself. All these figures for Tientsin mills, it may be noted, are higher than those reported by the Chinese Cotton Millowners' Association.

Mill	1927	1928	1929-30
Hua Hsin	2,156	2,235	2,348
Yu Yuan	5,700	6,083	6,395
Heng Yuan	2,850	3,200	3,262
Peiyang	1,800	1,950	2,000
Yu Ta	1,526	1,700	1,700
Pao Cheng	1,400	1,630	1,630
Total	15,432	16,798	17,335

mills, 1,583 or 39.9 percent separated on account of long absence. Such a phenomenon, separation on account of long absence, is a common one in Chinese mills, and is largely due to the long hours of work under the two shift system. During the summer time in particular, the workers are so tired after work that they are induced to take a few days off for rest, if not for personal affairs. The frequent recurrence of absence, however, interferes with the efficient operation of the mill, and gives rise to several practices designed to minimize the evil. In the first place, it is common

Table 36. A comparison of reasons for workers' separations in Shanghai and Tientsin cotton mills, 1929

	Shanghai		Tientsin	
Reason	No.	%	No.	%
Absence without leave			86	2.2
Long absence	608	28.3	1,583	39.9
Frequent absence			43	1.1
Violation of rules			159	3.9
Stealing	61	2.8	247	6.2
Disobedience	30	1.4	53	1.3
Loafing, laziness	105	4.9	173	4.4
Fighting	32	1.5	66	1.7
Strike and picketing	44	2.0		
Flirting			5	0.1
Runaway			40	1.0
Bad work	280	13.0	149	3.8
Discontent with work	33	1.5		
Other job	58	2.7	78	2.0
Return to native place	257	12.0	511	12.9
Marriage and birth	129	6.0	56	1.4
Sickness or injury	244	11.4	428	10.8
Sickness of family member			19	0.5
Death	25	1.2	123	3.1
Death of family member			13	0.3
Insufficient height of body	46	2.1		
Domestic affairs	168	7.8		
Elimination	30	1.4		
Other			136	3.4
Total	2,150	100.0	3,968	100.0

for a Chinese mill to keep more workers on the payroll than are actually needed, so that there will always be a marginal work force on reserve. In Heng Yuan Mill, for instance, the average percentage of the workers on the wage list that attend amounts only to 90.05 in 1928 and 91.35 in 1929. As shown in Table 37, such average is lower in some months than in others, particularly in February, June, July and August (Fig. 20). In February the celebration of the Chinese New Year keeps many workers away from work, while in June, July and August the discomfort of summer heat is

Table 37. Workers' attendance in a Tientsin cotton mill, 1928-1929

	1928			1929		
Month	Wage list	Attendance	%	Wage list	Attendance	%
January	2,601	2,421	93.08	3,015	2,832	93.93
February	2,818	2,523	89.53	3,003	2,702	89.90
March	2,905	2,651	91.26	3,209	2,907	90.59
April	3,021	2,726	90.24	3,284	2,946	89.71
May	3,042	2,758	90.66	3,304	3,038	91.95
June	3,021	2,686	88.91	3,325	2,992	90.08
July	2,996	2,641	88.15	3,383	3,039	89.83
August	3,027	2,746	90.72	3,361	3,024	89.97
September	3,034	2,766	91.17	3,336	3,052	91.49
October	3,010	2,768	91.96	3,315	3,066	92.49
November	3,024	2,823	93.35	3,306	3,099	93.74
December	3,027	2,838	93.76	3,292	3,050	92.65
Average	2,961	2,696	90.05	3,261	2,979	91.35

responsible for the same phenomenon. In Yu Yuan the average percentage of attendance in 1929 is 89.77 in May but 89.04 in June. A second practice

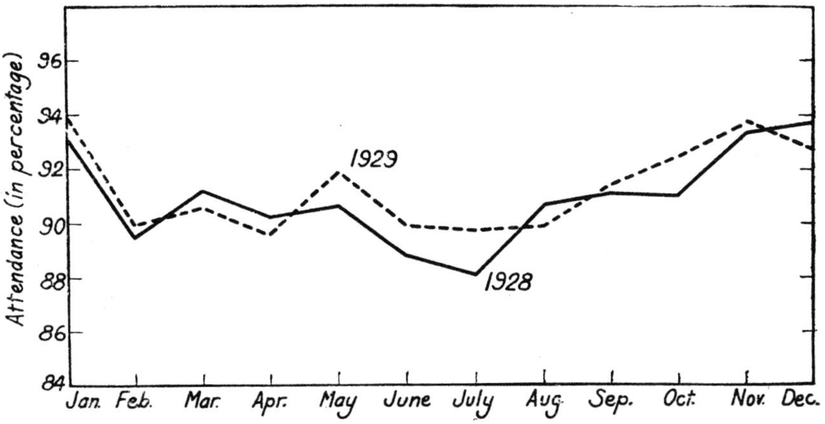

Fig. 20. Monthly fluctuations of workers' attendance in a Tientsin cotton mill, 1928-1929 (average payroll number=100) (*See* Table 37)

to minimize the evil of frequent absence is to prevent it through the grant of a full attendance bonus for a certain period, which may run from one half to one month. In Yu Yuan mill the practice is to give a bonus of fifty cents to any worker for uninterrupted attendance of one month. This practice started from October, 1927, but in June, 1929 the period was shortened from one month to half a month. Even so, the percentage of workers receiving the bonus is rather low, being 66% for October to December 1927, 58.7% for 1928, and 63.6% for January to September, 1929. In Hua Hsin, a more refined practice has been adopted since April 16, 1929, under which a full attendance bonus, being equivalent to one day's wage, is given to any worker who has not been absent for half a month. But no bonus is given if he has been absent for one day. Further than this, a fine is levied on any worker who has been absent without leave for two or more days, according to the following scale: one day's wage for two days' absence, two days' wage for three days' absence, three days' wage for four days' absence, and dismissal for five days' absence. No fine, however, is levied on the worker if he has secured permission for absence from the management. At the end of the Chinese (lunar) year a bonus of ten dollars is given for full attendance during the year, one of five dollars for absence of less than ten days, and one of two dollars for absence of less than fifteen days.

Referring again to Table 36, return to native place is the second important reason for separation, which accounts for 12.9 percent of all separations in Tientsin mills. This is due to the fact that most of the workers in Tientsin are recruited from the neighboring districts and provinces. Whenever these workers have accumulated enough savings, they prefer to return home rather than stay away from their family members. A third important reason, which accounts for 10.8 percent of the separations, is sickness. This indirectly serves as an index of the poor physical condition of Chinese workers, and their inability to stand the strain of continuous machine work. A fourth reason is stealing, which accounts for 6.2 percent of the separations, and is responsible for the familiar scene of the mill police searching every worker on his exit from the mill's gateway. The percentage for marriage and birth, 1.4, is rather small, and is explained by the small number of women workers in Tientsin mills.

Table 36 also compares the reasons for workers' separation in Tientsin mills with those in a Japanese mill in Shanghai.[11] It is striking to note that the percentage for many of the reasons in Tientsin coincides with that in Shanghai. Long absence, which claims 39.9 percent in Tientsin, claims 28.3 percent in Shanghai. The percentage for return to native place is very close, being 12.9 in Tientsin and 12.0 in Shanghai. Similarly, the percentage for sickness is 10.8 in Tientsin and 11.4 in Shanghai. The percentage for marriage and birth in Shanghai, 6.0, is much higher than that in Tientsin, 1.4. The predominance of woman labor in Shanghai mills is largely responsible for this.

11. *China Labor Year book*, I: 369-370.

In the absence of other data, the length of stay may also serve as an index of labor mobility. In a study of 3,898 workers in three cotton mills in Tientsin in 1930 it is found that 1,095 workers, or 27.8 percent,

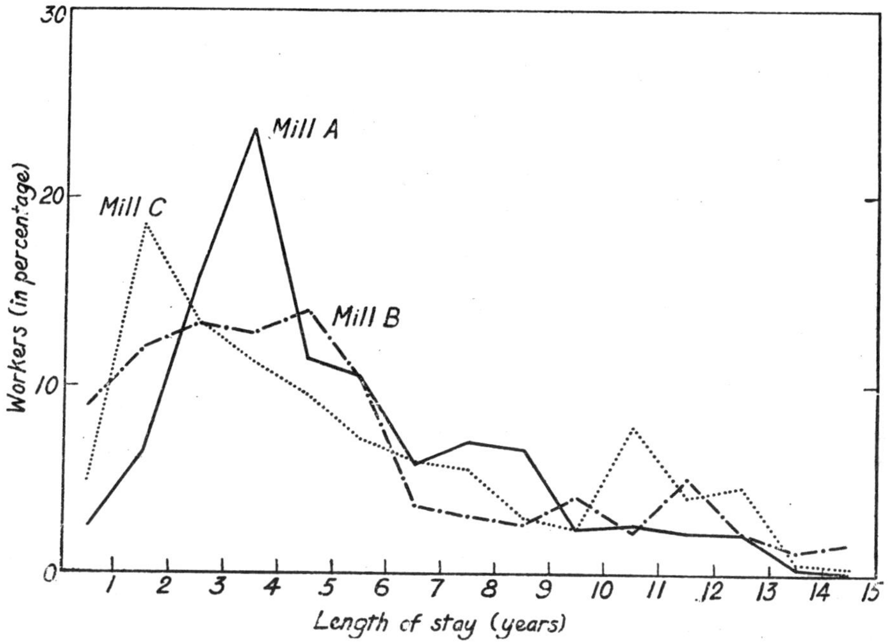

Fig. 21. Distribution of cotton mill workers in Tientsin by length of stay, 1930 (*See* Table 38)

have been with the mills for three years or less, while 2,326 workers or 59.4 percent have been with the mills for five years or less. In other words, 2,803 workers or 72.2 percent have been with the mills for three years or more, while 1,572 workers or 40.6 percent have been with the mills for five years or more (Fig. 21). The length of stay, on the whole, is rather long, and coincides with the tendency towards a lower labor turnover in Tientsin mills in recent years. This long length of stay may be attributed to several factors. The recurrence of civil war, which prevents the development of industry, deprives the workers of the opportunity for other employment. The rise of labor organizations, again, makes it more difficult for the management to discharge the workers. In Table 38 the workers in Tientsin cotton mills are classified by length of stay.

Comparing Table 38 with Table 39, in which the length of stay for the workers in a Japanese mill in Shanghai is shown, it may be seen that the length of stay in Tientsin is longer than that in Shanghai. Whereas in Tientsin 72.2 percent of the workers have a length of stay of over three years, in Shanghai the length of stay of over three years

Table 38. Workers in Tientsin cotton mills classified by length of stay, 1930

Length of stay	Mill A No.	Mill A %	Mill B No.	Mill B %	Mill C No.	Mill C %	Total No.	Total %
Under 1 year	72	2.6	31	8.9	38	4.9	141	3.6
1 & under 2	179	6.4	42	12.1	141	18.4	362	9.0
2 " " 3	441	15.9	47	13.5	104	13.6	592	15.2
3 " " 4	660	23.7	45	12.9	87	11.3	792	20.3
4 " " 5	316	11.4	49	14.1	74	9.6	439	11.3
5 " " 6	293	10.5	36	10.4	55	7.2	384	9.9
6 " " 7	164	5.9	13	3.7	46	6.0	223	5.8
7 " " 8	197	7.1	11	3.2	42	5.5	250	6.4
8 " " 9	190	6.8	10	2.9	24	3.1	224	5.7
9 " " 10	70	2.5	15	4.3	19	2.5	104	2.7
10 " " 11	73	2.6	8	2.3	61	7.9	142	3.6
11 " " 12	62	2.2	18	5.2	32	4.2	112	2.9
12 " " 13	55	2.0	7	2.0	37	4.8	99	2.6
13 " " 14	5	0.2	4	1.2	5	0.6	14	0.4
14 " " 15	3	0.1	6	1.7	3	0.4	12	0.3
15 " above	1		5	1.6			6	0.2
Unknown	2	0.1					2	0.1
Total	2,783	100	347	100	768	100	3,898	100

applies only to 47.3 percent of the male spinners, 42.8 percent of the female spinners, 18.3 percent of the male weavers and 22 percent of the female weavers. In Shanghai, the length of stay of one year or less is the commonest, which applies to 28.2 percent of the male spinners, 44.7 percent of the female spinners, 57.1 percent of the male weavers and 44.2 percent of the female weavers.[12] Evidently, Shanghai, as the industrial and commercial metropolis of China, offers greater opportunity for work, which is one way or the other responsible for the higher mobility of labor.

Table 39. Length of stay of workers in a Japanese cotton mill in Shanghai, 1928 (in percentages)

Length of stay	Spinner Male	Spinner Female	Weaver Male	Weaver Female
1 month	2.3	6.9	9.7	6.0
3 months	9.9	12.6	13.7	12.5
6 "	13.7	16.9	21.1	19.7
1 year	2.3	8.3	12.6	6.0
1½ years	4.6	3.7	11.4	10.2
2 "	5.3	3.7	7.4	17.3
3 "	14.5	5.1	5.7	6.3
Above 3 years	47.3	42.8	18.3	22.0

12. Pearse, *Cotton Industry of China and Japan*, Manchester, 1929, p. 172.

Wages and standard of Living:— Generally speaking, three systems of wage payment prevail in cotton mills, namely, time, piece and time-plus-piece. Under the time system of payment, the workers are paid by day or by month, while under the piece system the amount of wage is determined by multiplying the quantity of output by the wage rate per unit of output. Under the time-plus-piece system a time rate is fixed, but a standard is also set for the day's work, above which a piece rate is given in addition to the time rate. In Yu Yuan Mill in Tientsin, the last two systems are in operation. Mixers, scutchers, card tenders, balers, mechanics, smiths, carpenters, power tenders, sizers, finishers, and coolies are paid under the time system, while rovers, spinners, reelers, bundlers, warp and filling winders, warpers, drawers and weavers are paid under the time-plus-piece system. The time-plus-piece system assures the worker of a minimum daily rate, while securing for the management the increase in output generally expected under the piece system. The guarantee of a minimum daily wage is important, for in some departments in the weaving plant the work is not always regular. Nevertheless, the time-plus-piece system is not wholly satisfactory, either to the worker or to the management. Under this system, the slack worker who fails to produce the standard output is not penalized, while on the other hand, the quick worker is penalized for not having been paid a fair extra work rate. In Yu Yuan Mill the slubbers in the roving department in plant No. 1 are given a time rate of fifty cents per day for ten, fourteen or sixteen counts, with an output of seven hanks as the standard, but they are paid an extra work rate of four cents for the first hank above the standard, and one of two cents for every additional hank. On the basis of fifty cents for seven hanks under the time system, the wage rate per hank is about seven cents. To pay an extra work rate of four cents for the first hank and one of two cents for every additional hank is obviously unjust. The injustice is greater if we consider the possibility that under the time system the worker need not produce seven hanks in order to receive the full-time rate of fifty cents. Similarly, the bobbers in the spinning department in plant No. 1 are paid a time rate of forty-eight cents per day, with an output of 2,395 pounds for the fourteen counts, that is to say, 23.3 cents per thousand pounds provided the worker produces the standard output. The extra work rate, however, is only 22.2 cents per thousand pounds. Besides, the time-plus-piece system shares the defects common to the time and the piece systems respectively. Under the time system, which applies to such work as cannot be accurately measured, the worker is inclined to steal leisure, especially in hot and dry summer. The means adopted is either to slow down the machinery by lubricating the motor belt, or to stop it entirely by setting it out of order. The latter action sometimes results in serious damage to the machinery. Under the piece system the abuse is of a different nature. The rovers, whose output is measured by means of a hank meter, are noted for hank stealing through meter manipulation. The mill, at last, has to guard the meter with iron fence which is locked. The weavers, again, may manipulate the gear in such a way as to give greater distance between the wefts. In that way, the texture of the cloth woven is loosened, but the length is increased without additional effort on the part of the weaver. The mill, consequently, suffers from the inferior quality of its output, and not infrequently it is unable to sell 110 pieces of its cloth at an equivalent price for 100 pieces.

In our investigation of wage statistics for Yu Yuan Mill, the wage rates are tabulated for the different classes of workers during the two dates, namely, January 1st and June 30th, 1929. These rates apply to 4,828 workers out of a total of 6,395, that is, to those workers who have worked with the mill more or less continuously for a period of six months. The tabulation, as given in Table 40, shows the wage rates for the workers in different departments during the two dates. The average wage rate

Table 40. Average daily wage rates for workers in a Tientsin cotton mill, 1929 (in silver cents)

Department and occupation	No. workers investigated			Daily wage rates					
	Male	Female	All	Male		Female		All	
				Jan. 1	June 30	Jan. 1	June 30	Jan 1	June 30
Blowing	76		76	45.5	47.2			45.5	47.2
Mixing	13		13	52.5	55.2			52.5	55.2
Scutching	63		63	44.0	45.6			44.0	45.6
Carding	135	15	150	44.1	45.8	40.5	41.8	43.7	45.4
Roving	447	185	632	49.5	51.0	48.3	49.2	49.1	50.5
Slubbing	126	17	143	45.6	47.2	41.3	42.8	45.1	46.5
Roving	321	168	489	51.1	52.5	49.0	49.9	50.4	51.6
Spinning	1,264	140	1,404	43.1	46.9	35.9	40.2	42.4	46.2
Reeling	410	205	615	35.3	41.0	28.6	32.8	33.1	38.3
Baling	99		99	38.3	40.8			38.3	40.8
Mechanics and smiths	154		154	65.6	68.4			65.6	68.4
Carpenters	41		41	52.7	54.2			52.7	54.2
Coolies	118		118	38.6	40.2			38.6	40.2
Power	230		230	66.0	67.5			66.0	67.5
Warping	165	228	393	42.1	45.2	22.4	24.0	30.7	32.9
Warp winding	62		62	37.6	41.0			37.6	41.0
Warping	25	125	150	38.9	41.3	21.9	24.7	24.7	27.5
Drawing-in	9	30	39	41.4	42.5	23.2	23.8	27.4	28.1
Sizing	42		42	52.4	56.1			52.4	56.1
Filling winding	27	73	100	39.5	42.1	22.8	23.0	27.3	28.2
Weaving	850		850	44.6	49.6			44.6	49.6
Finishing	66		66	41.9	45.2			41.9	45.2
All	4,055	773	4,828	45.3	48.9	33.0	35.6	43.4	46.8

per day for all workers is 43.4 cents on January first, but 46.8 cents on June 30th, giving an increase of 3.4 cents or 7.8 percent in the course of half a year. Again, the average wage rate for male workers on January first, 45.3 cents, is higher than that for female workers on the same date, 33 cents—the latter being only 72.8 perecent of the former. In respect of the distribution by departments, the daily wage rate on January first is the highest for power department, 66 cents, and lowest for warping department, 30.7 cents. For other departments the daily wage rates are as follows: mechanics and smiths, 65.6 cents; carpenters, 62.7 cents; roving, 49.1 cents; blowing, 45.5 cents; weaving, 44.6 cents; carding, 43.7 cents; spinning, 42.4 cents; finishing, 41.9 cents; coolies, 38.6 cents; baling, 38.3 cents; and reeling, 33.1 cents. However, the wage rates for some of the departments, especially spinning and weaving, are nominal but not actual, as under time-plus-piece system, they refer to time rate which is inclined to be low rather than high.

Although the nominal wage rates are lower than the actual wage rates for such departments as spinning and weaving in Yu Yuan, yet they are higher than the actual wages for the workers in Hua Hsin. We have, in our investigation, computed the average daily wages for the workers in Hua Hsin during the year 1929. The process here is to divide the number of workers in each department into the total wage payment for that department for the fifth and twentieth of each month in 1929. A general average, as given in Table 41, is then found for the 24 daily averages during the year. Except for the baling and inspection departments this *average daily wage* is lower than the *average daily wage rate* for Yu Yuan workers. The grand average for Hua Hsin, which is 39.4 cents, is much lower than that for Yu Yuan, 43.4 cents. The difference would have been greater if we consider the fact that the average for Yu Yuan workers refers only to wage rates, while that for Hua Hsin workers includes other items—bonus of one kind or another.

Table 41. Average daily wages for the day shift workers in a Tientsin cotton mill, 1929 (in silver dollars)

Department	Av. no. of workers	Total average wages	Av. wages per worker	Av. wage rates per Yu Yuan worker
Blowing	28.1	10.831	.385	.455
Roving	198.1	82.402	.416	.481
Spinning	363.0	116.460	.321	.424
Reeling	255.5	83.296	.326	.331
Baling	55.7	31.373	.563	.383
Waste cotton picking	61.9	17.973	.290	
Inspection	71.7	43.270	.603	
Mechanical	28.3	20.230	.715	.656
Power	75.7	42.095	.556	.660
Total or average	1,138.0	447.930	.394	.446

Table 42. Average daily wage rates in Shanghai cotton spinning mills, 1929 (in silver dollars)

Department and job		No. workers investigated				Average wage rates per day			
		Male	Female	Child	All	Male	Female	Child	All
Blowing		824	26		850	.470	.480		.470
Mixing		249			249	.468			.468
Scutching		469	26		495	.480	.480		.480
Ginning &c.		106			106	.432			.432
Carding		796	56		852	.488	.408		.483
Stripping		216			216	.552			.552
Carding		417	56		473	.468	.408		.461
Others		163			163	.456			.456
Roving		515	7,410	181	8,106	.463	.486	.318	.468
Foremen		65			65	.636			.636
Forewomen no. 1			220		220		.792		.792
Drawing		11	684		695	.480	.384		.386
	P.W.*		1,362		1,362		.444		.444
Roving		66	1,339	89	1,494	.396	.444	.336	.415
	P.W.*		3,799		3,799		.516		.516
Others		373	6	92	471	.444	.396	.300	.415
Spinning		726	9,638	594	10,958	.451	.450	.313	.442
Foremen		48			48	.600			.600
Forewomen no. 1			273		273		.804		.804
Ring spinning		7	1,062		1,069	.288	.492		.491
	P.W.*		7,809	101	7,910		.456	.408	.455
New hands			335		335		.204		.204
	P.W.*		124		124		.240		.240
Yarn testing			35		35		.480		.480
Bobbing		180		388	568	.372		.288	.315
Others		491		105	596	.468		.312	.441
Reeling		334	9,624		9,958	.468	.435		.436
Forewomen no. 1			289		289		.732		.732
Reeling		334			334	.468			.468
	P.W.*		9,199		9,199		.425		.425
Others			33		33		.384		.384
	P.W.*		103		103		.468		.468
Baling		543	41		584	.700	.370		.677
Weighing		62			62	.492			.492
Bundling		105	4		109	.552	.360		.545
	P.W.*	311			311	.845			.845
Others		65	33		98	.444	.372		.420
	P.W.*		4		4		.360		.360
Waste cotton		77	610	76	763	.705	.355	.252	.380
Picking		35	123		158	.408	.336		.352
	P.W.*	42	478	76	596	.952	.360	.252	.388
Others			9		9		.372		.372
Mechanical		3,743	169	310	4,222	.578	.324	.263	.545
Repairers		1,780		25	1,805	.576		.252	.572
Mechanics		263			263	.756			.756
Smiths		789			789	.679			.679
Coolies		911	169	285	1,365	.444	.324	.264	.392
Total		7,558	27,574	1,161	36,293	.552	.452	.300	.468

*P.W. refers to piece wages. All other workers are paid time wages.

Table 43. Average daily wage rates in Shanghai cotton weaving mills, 1929 (in silver dollars)

Department and job	No. workers investigated				Average wage rate per day			
	Male	Female	Child	All	Male	Female	Child	All
Warping	378	2,102	345	2,825	.510	.537	.363	.512
Foremen	7			7	.924			.924
Forewomen no. 1		8		8		.936		.936
Warping	70	14		84	.475	.571		.491
P.W.*		314		314		.557		.557
Warp winding	48	80		128	.480	.743		.644
P.W.*		188	314	502		.511	.363	.418
Filling winding		226		226		.469		.469
P.W.*		974		974		.539		.539
Drawing P.W.*		190		190		.583		.583
Sizing	54			54	.581			.581
P.W.*	11			11	.682			.682
Others	188	12	31	231	.484	.360	.368	.462
P.W.*		96		96		.381		.381
Weaving	1,014	4,958		5,972	.944	.550		.617
Foremen	47	131		178	.816	.804		.807
Forewomen no. 1								
Weaving	134			134	.525			.525
P.W.*	776	4,827		5,603	1.057	.543		.614
Others	57			57	.496			.496
Finishing & Mechanical	1,166	68	49	1,283	.581	.502	.350	.568
Finishing	347	46	29	422	.484	.475	.310	.471
P.W.*	65	8	20	93	.794	.888	.408	.719
Mechanics & smiths	497			497	.673			.673
Coolies	257	14		271	.482	.372		.476
Total	2,558	7,128	394	10,080	.722	.545	.357	.581

* P.W. refers to piece wages. All other workers are paid time wages.

Table 44. Average daily wage rates for workers in Shanghai and Tientsin cotton mills, 1929 (in silver cents)

Department	Male		Female		Child		All	
	S.	T.	S.	T.	S.	T.	S.	T.
Blowing	47.0	47.2	48.0				47.0	47.2
Carding	48.8	45.8	40.8	41.8			48.3	45.4
Roving	46.3	51.0	48.6	49.2	31.8		46.8	50.5
Spinning	45.1	46.9	45.0	40.2	13.3		44.2	46.2
Reeling	46.8	41.0	43.5	32.8			43.6	38.3
Baling	70.0	40.8	37.0				67.7	40.8
Waste cotton	70.5		35.5		25.2		38.0	
Mechanical &c.	57.8	55.9	32.4		26.3		54.5	55.9
Power		67.5						67.5
All	55.2	49.0	45.2	38.4	30.0		46.8	47.7
Warping	51.0	45.2	53.7	24.0	36.3		51.2	32.9
Weaving	94.4	49.6	55.0				61.7	49.6
Finishing	58.1	45.2	50.2		35.0		56.8	45.2
All	72.2	48.6	54.5	24.0	35.7		58.1	44.4
All	59.5	48.9	51.9	35.6	25.0		49.3	46.8

Note: S. refers to Shanghai, and T. to Tientsin. The wage rates in Tientsin are represented by those in Yu Yuan Mill, on June 30, 1929.

The daily wage rates in Tientsin, as represented by Yu Yuan Mill, are lower than those in Shanghai. In a study of the wage situation in Shanghai undertaken by the Social Affairs Bureau of the City Government of Greater Shanghai on September 25, 1929, the daily wage rates were computed for 36,293 workers in the cotton spinning industry and 10,080 workers in the cotton weaving industry.[13] As shown in Table 44 whereas the average daily wage rates amount to 46.8 cents in Tientsin, those in Shanghai are higher, namely, 49.3 cents. This difference, however, is nominal. As a matter of fact, the average daily wage rates for the spinners (in a broad sense) in Tientsin, 47.7 cents, are higher than those in Shanghai, 46.8 cents. But for the weavers (in a broad sense) the average daily wage rates, 44.4 cents, are much lower than those in Shanghai, 58.1 cents.[14] As has been explained in a previous paragraph, the weavers in Tientsin are paid under time-plus- piece system, and their rates refer to time rates only. Actually speaking, such time rates are minimum rates, for it is not uncommon for the weaver to receive a much higher rate than the time rate through extra work. The weaver receives a time rate only if his output fails to exceed the standard requirement, but once it exceeds the standard, a piece rate is paid for the extra work.

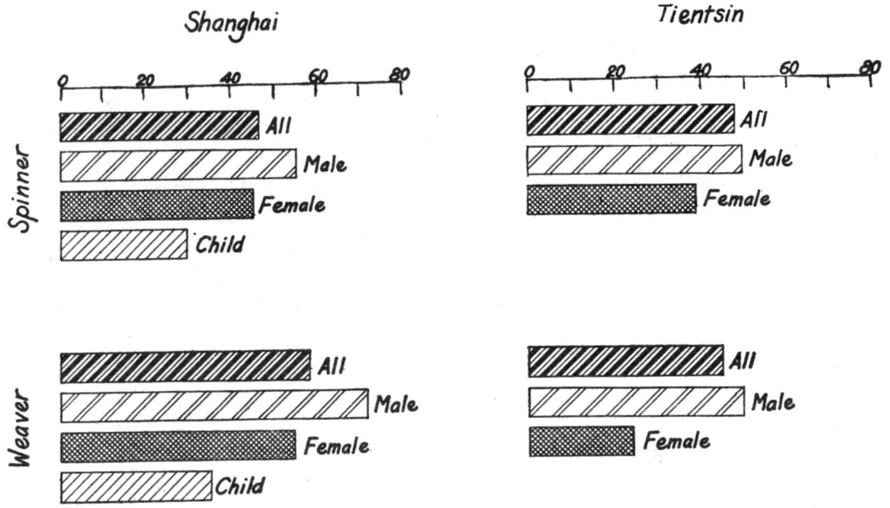

Fig. 22. Wages of cotton workers in Shanghai and Tientsin compared, 1929 (in silver cents) (*See* Table 44)

13. *Wages and Hours of Labor in Greater Shanghai*, 1929, published by the Social Affairs Bureau, City Government of Greater Shanghai, 1931.

14. In a study of 49 cotton mills and 13 cloth weaving factories in Shanghai the daily wage rates appear to be much higher for both spinners and weavers. *See Infra, Appendix XIII.*

In Tientsin as elsewhere it is customary to pay a higher rate for overwork. In Hua Hsin, Peiyang and Paocheng the hourly overwork rate is equivalent to 1½ hours of ordinary wage rate. In Yu Yuan, the system is more complicated. No premium is given for overwork within less than half an hour. From half an hour to six hours the overwork rate is raised to 20% above the ordinary rate. It is raised to 30% from six to nine hours, and to 40% from nine to twelve hours. Overwork in all these mills is uncommon except for power tenders and repairers. If any tender fails to report for the night shift, in the power plant, the day shift man must not leave the job because of the serious consequence that may entail upon his departure. He will have to continue his work on an overwork basis. The same also happens in the repair department, as delay in repair increases the mill's overhead cost. Moreover, the repairers are generally kept working at the mill while other workers go on their rest during the weekly or ten day change of shift. It is only on such occasions that the mill can undertake considerable repair.

Besides the ordinary rate and the overwork rate, several kinds of bonus are given in Tientsin. First, there is the full attendance bonus, which has been touched upon in connection with labor turnover. A second bonus is given on the basis of good work and discipline, and takes the form of rewards. Such a bonus is irregular in amount, and is fixed at the personal whim of the superintendent. It may be mentioned here that fines are levied upon the worker for poor work and lack of discipline. Fines, however, are less frequent and smaller in amount than bonus. During the year July, 1928 to June, 1929, the total amount of bonus given in Yu Yuan mill, $596,320, is almost thrice the fines, $203,443. The difference between bonus and fines is borne by the mill, amounting to $392,877. In summer time a third bonus of fifty cents is given by Yu Yuan as a melon bonus—a petty subsidy with which the worker may buy melons or anything else that meets his needs more urgently. At the end of the year, a fourth bonus, the year-end bonus, is also given, but the scale for it varies according to the nature of the job and the length of service. It begins with the minimum of one dollar for workers who have stayed with the mill for less than three months to the maximum of twenty dollars for the foremen in different departments. Between these two extremes, there are eight classes with following scales: $18, $15, $12, $10, $8, $6, $4, $2.

In Shanghai similar kinds of bonus are given, with local variations in practice. Because of the frequent fluctuations in the price of rice, the staple food for the Southerners in China, a rice allowance is frequently given in order to dodge the issue of constant revision in wage scales.

Wage rates differ from earnings, as the latter include besides the former the different kinds of bonus mentioned above, which vary in nature and in amount with different mills. Wherever fines are levied, the difference between the sum total of wage rates and bonus on the one hand, and the fines on the other, constitute the earnings. In our investigation of the Yu Yuan Mill in Tientsin, such earnings have been computed directly from the Mill's payroll during the period from January to June, 1929. There were altogether 6,395 workers on the payroll in Yu Yuan, but earnings were computed for 4,828 workers only. As shown in Table 45a the average monthly earnings for these 4,828 workers amount to $14.69, being $14.51 for the spinning plant and $15.18 for the weaving plant. This average, as shown in Table 45b, is higher than that for cotton workers in Shanghai, which is compiled by the Social Affairs Bureau for the year 1929. Whereas the average monthly earnings for cotton workers amount to $14.69 in Tientsin, those for Shanghai, $14.51, are lower by 1.2 percent. But if further analysis be made, the average monthly earnings for spinners in Tientsin, $14.51, are higher than those in Shanghai, $12.93; while the reverse is true with the weavers. The average monthly earnings for weavers in Shanghai, $19.22, are much higher than those in Tientsin, $15.18.

Table 45a. Average monthly earnings of cotton workers in Tientsin,* 1929 (in silver dollars)

Department	Male	Female	All	Department	Male	Female	All
Blowing	14.22		14.22	Coolies	13.03		13.03
Mixing	17.60		17.60	Power	23.53		23.53
Scutching	13.53		13.53	All (Spinning)	14.98	11.98	14.51
Carding	13.20	11.30	13.02	Warping	13.34	9.85	11.38
Roving	15.32	14.60	15.10	Warp winding	12.72		12.72
Slubbing	13.93	12.18	13.72	Warping	12.08	9.48	9.92
Roving	15.87	14.83	15.52	Drawing-in	13.20	9.95	10.27
Spinning	13.72	11.58	13.50	Sizing	15.72		15.72
Reeling	12.80	9.93	11.85	Filling winding	12.23	10.43	10.93
Baling	12.93		12.93	Weaving	17.10		17.10
Mechanical	17.87		17.87	Finishing	13.17		13.17
Mechanics and smiths	21.55		21.55	All (Weaving)	16.29	9.85	15.18
Carpenters	18.00		18.00	All (S & W)	15.33	11.35	14.69

* As represented by the workers in Yu Yuan Cotton Mill.

The recording and computation of wages is carried out in more or less the same manner in different mills. In entering the mill the worker exchanges his pay card, which serves also as the employment contract, for a numbered stick. The card is then turned over to the pay department, which puts a seal on it. Whether the wage be paid on time or on piece basis, the seal serves as a register of the worker's attendance. After the seal has been put on, the card is returned to the worker in each de-

Table 45b. Average monthly earnings of cotton workers in Shanghai, 1929 (in silver dollars)

Month	Spinning Male	Spinning Female	Spinning Child	Spinning All*	Weaving Male	Weaving Female	Weaving Child	Weaving All*	Spinning & Weaving all*
January	17.49	14.22	9.37	14.75	24.51	13.89	11.40	16.49	15.13
February	14.75	12.50	8.94	12.85	15.29	12.21	8.77	12.86	12.85
March	15.93	13.70	7.70	13.97	24.99	18.48	12.85	19.91	15.26
April	15.71	13.32	7.09	13.62	25.14	18.25	12.16	19.74	14.95
May	14.89	12.32	8.72	12.74	23.75	17.82	12.33	19.11	14.12
June	14.95	11.32	8.50	11.98	23.01	17.63	11.50	18.76	13.45
July	14.44	11.45	8.17	11.97	20.15	16.34	9.89	17.05	13.07
August	14.50	11.52	7.65	12.02	22.37	17.54	11.56	18.53	13.44
September	14.79	12.40	8.18	12.76	25.30	15.67	12.19	17.98	13.89
October	14.85	13.42	7.28	13.52	24.78	17.07	12.05	18.83	14.67
November	15.29	12.64	7.63	13.03	25.54	17.95	13.84	19.71	14.48
December	15.59	11.64	7.82	12.34	25.30	17.94	11.50	19.56	13.91
Average	15.28	12.50	8.07	12.93	23.54	18.09	11.69	19.22	14.51
No. workers Investigated	7,558	27,574	1,161	36,293	2,559	7,128	394	10,080	46,373

* Weighted arithmetic average.

partment, in exchange for the numbered stick. For the time worker the seal serves as the basis for computing his wages, but for the piece worker, the department in which he works has to send in a separate report on which is recorded the amount of work performed by him during the day. In one mill, the wage for each worker is computed daily, but in majority of the mills in Tientsin it is computed semi-monthly. The worker, in other words, has to wait for two weeks before he receives his pay. In this way, the worker is depositing two weeks' wages with the mill as a guarantee, from which may be deducted any fine or compensation for damage done to the machinery etc. For special reasons, such as a wedding or funeral, the worker is permitted to apply for earlier payment of his due wages.

In computing the wages the following rules are observed in some mills. Whether for time or for piece worker, an absence of two hours is counted as one fourth of a day's work or 'kung', an absence of five hours is counted as one half of one 'kung'. For the piece worker the wage for the average amount of output per day is considered as one 'kung'. Again, no wage is paid for any period of rest arising from the change of shift, or from cessation of work caused by *force majeure*. But for legal holidays the wage is paid accordingly. Besides, if no rest is ordered on such holidays, double wage is paid, while if the worker fails to report on the day following a holiday, not only does he lose the wage for the day's absence, but is fined to an equivalent amount.

The standard of living for cotton workers has been investigated for Shanghai and Tientsin respectively, the former by the *Social Research Institute of Peiping* and the latter by the *Nankai Institute*. The Shanghai inquiry covers 230 families selected from among the cotton mill workers in Jessfield Village for the period November, 1927 to October, 1928,[15] while the Tientsin investigation covers 87 families selected from among the

15. Yang, *op. cit.*

cotton mill workers in Hsiao Liu Chuang for the period November, 1929 to October, 1930. Although the period of investigation differs by two years, yet a comparison of the two investigations is not greatly affected by such difference because of the fixity of living standard. In this connection, it may be noted that whereas the Shanghai survey was conducted from day to day by means of the account keeping method, the Tientsin survey was conducted from month to month, with the same method. The former is necessarily more laborious and expensive than the latter.

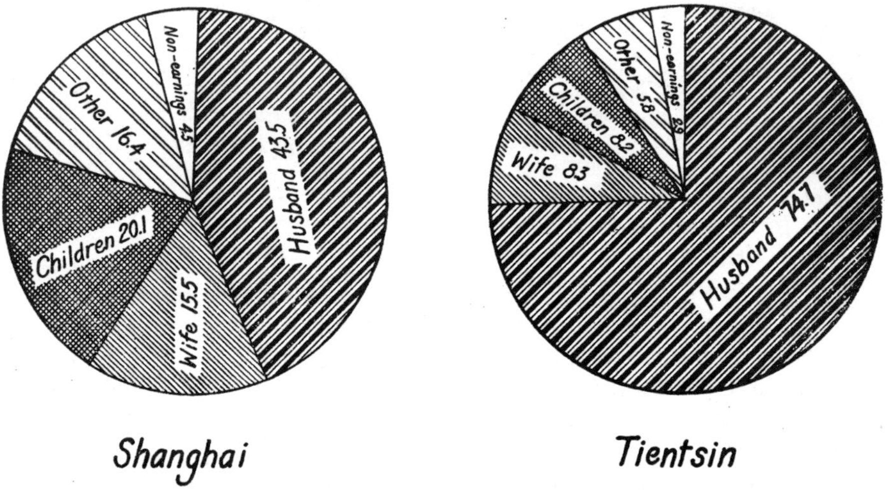

Fig. 23. Distribution of the income of cotton worker's family in Shanghai and Tientsin compared (in percentages) (*See* Table 46)

In Table 46 the average amount and percentage distribution of income per family for the cotton mill workers in Shanghai and Tientsin are given (Fig. 23). In Shanghai the average income per family per month amounts to $32.56, which is equivalent to an annual average of $390.72. It is 34.1 percent higher than the annual average for Tientsin, $291.37. This difference in family income is partly due to the difference in family size. In terms of male adults, the family size in Shanghai, 3.75 persons, is 35 percent larger than that in Tientsin, 2.80 persons. Table 46 also shows that the percentage of income derived from earnings is 95.5 for Shanghai, but 97.07 for Tientsin. In Tientsin the husband contributes 74.71 percent of the total family income; while the percentage is 8.34 for wife, 8.23 for children, 3.49 for brother and sister, and 2.30 for parents. In Shanghai, while the percentage for husband is only 43.5, which is much lower as compared with 74.71 in Tientsin, the percentage for wife or children is 15.5 or 20.1, which is higher as compared with 8.34 or 8.23 in Tientsin. This again confirms the fact that in Shanghai child and woman labor is a much commoner phenomenon than in Tientsin.

Table 46a. Average amount and percentage distribution of income per family per month by income groups for the cotton workers in Shanghai

Income group	No. of families	Earnings: Husband	Wife	Son	Daughter	Other males	Other females	Total	Non-earnings: House rent	Boarders	Other	Total	Grand total
Under $20	42	$13.43	$1.64	$0.25	$0.64	$0.33	$0.30	$16.59	$0.03	$0.01	$0.04	$0.08	$16.67
$20-29.99	90	12.11	5.41	2.49	1.84	1.15	1.10	24.10	0.13	0.49	0.42	1.04	25.14
$30-39.99	46	15.20	5.21	3.55	4.32	2.81	2.30	33.39	0.45	0.87	0.05	1.37	34.76
$40-49.99	34	15.09	7.30	4.55	5.95	4.30	5.49	42.68	0.68	0.49	0.75	1.92	44.60
$50-59.99	18	20.25	4.63	7.99	7.10	6.91	11.69	58.57	0.04	3.25	1.69	4.98	63.55
All income	230	14.17	5.05	3.21	3.33	2.42	2.92	31.10	0.26	0.75	0.46	1.47	32.56
						Percent							
Under $20	42	80.6	9.8	1.5	3.8	2.0	1.8	99.5	0.2	0.1	0.2	0.5	100
$20-29.99	90	48.2	21.5	9.9	7.3	4.6	4.4	95.9	0.5	1.9	1.7	4.1	100
$30-39.99	46	43.7	15.0	10.2	12.4	8.1	6.6	96.1	1.3	2.5	0.1	3.9	100
$40-49.99	34	33.8	16.4	10.2	13.3	9.6	12.3	95.7	1.5	1.1	1.7	4.3	100
$50-59.99	18	31.9	7.3	12.6	11.2	10.9	18.4	92.2	0.1	5.1	2.7	7.8	100
All income	230	43.5	15.5	9.9	10.2	7.4	9.0	95.5	0.8	2.3	1.4	4.5	100

Table 46b. Average amount and percentage distribution of income per family per year by income groups for the cotton workers in Tientsin

Income group	No. of familes	Earnings: Parent	Husband	Wife	Brother	Sister	Children	Total	Non-earnings: Relief	Rent &c.	Interest	Total	Grand total
$200 or under	5		149.22	39.08				188.30	4.00			4.00	192.30
$201-300	46	1.56	206.59	21.36	0.42	0.24	5.55	235.72	7.50	0.98		8.48	244.20
$301-400	27	18.55	237.29	20.33		6.82	47.02	330.01	3.63	7.07	1.67	12.37	342.38
$401-500	9	1.11	253.54	42.90	74.54		62.36	434.45					434.45
All income	87	6.70	217.68	24.29	7.92	2.24	23.99	282.82	5.32	2.71	0.52	8.55	291.37
							Percent						
$200 or under	5		77.60	20.32				97.92	2.08			2.08	100
$201-300	46	0.64	84.60	8.75	0.17	0.10	2.27	96.53	3.07	0.40		3.47	100
$301-400	27	5.42	69.31	5.94		1.99	13.73	96.39	1.06	2.06	0.49	3.61	100
$401-500	9	0.26	58.36	9.87	17.16		14.35	100.00					100
All income	87	2.30	74.71	8.34	2.72	0.77	8.23	97.07	1.83	0.93	0.18	2.93	100

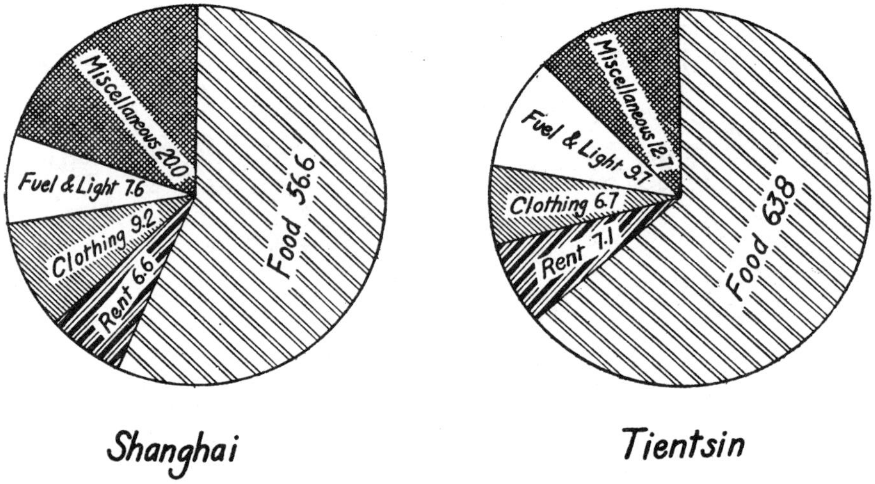

Fig. 24. Distribution of the expenditure of cotton worker's family in Shanghai and Tientsin compared (in percentages) (*See* Table 47)

In Table 47 the average amount and percent distribution of the items of expenditure for the cotton workers' families in Tientsin and Shanghai are given by income groups (Fig. 24). In both places, the following observations may be drawn:

(1) As the income increases, the expenditure for food, rent, fuel and light tends to decrease;

(2) As the income increases, the expenditure for clothing and miscellaneous items tends to increase.

The percentage distribution of the items of expenditure in Shanghai, however, differs from that in Tientsin. Taking the all income group as a basis for comparison, the percentage for food occupies as much as 63.79 in Tientsin, but 56.62 in Shanghai. One reason for this discrepancy is, of course, the difference in the size of family. The average family size, which is 3.75 adult males for Shanghai, is only 2.80 adult males for Tientsin. The percentage for food decreases proportionately when the size of family increases. A second reason is the difference in the cost for food during the respective period of investigation. According to the Shanghai cost of living index which is compiled on the basis of the family budget inquiry for the 230 families of cotton workers referred to above, whereas there is a decrease in the general index of cost of living from 106.7 in 1927 to 102.5 in 1928, there is a more rapid decrease in the group index for food from 106.7 to 92.1 during the same period. Considering the fact that the Shanghai inquiry was undertaken from November, 1927 to October, 1928, this great decrease in the cost for food, amounting to 15.9%, which took place at a time when the general cost of living index showed a decrease of but 4.1%, is responsible for

Table 47a. Average amount and percent distribution of the monthly expenditure of the families of cotton workers in Shanghai

Income group / Item of expenditure	Under $ 20	$20—29.99	$30—39.99	$40—49.99	$50 & over	All incomes
	Amount ($)					
Food	12.53	15.06	18.67	22.61	30.32	18.04
Rent	1.63	1.84	2.25	2.46	2.90	2.09
Clothing	1.09	2.13	3.06	4.34	6.48	2.92
Fuel and light	1.90	2.08	2.46	2.80	4.03	2.43
Miscellaneous	3.26	4.85	6.38	9.21	13.07	6.38
Communication	0.11	0.20	0.29	0.51	0.37	0.27
Sanitary expenses	0.32	0.43	0.53	0.62	0.94	0.51
Cigarettes, wines, etc.	0.76	0.94	1.11	1.13	1.70	1.05
Doctor's fee & medecine	0.14	0.31	0.23	0.33	0.25	0.26
Toilet Articles	0.03	0.08	0.10	0.13	0.30	0.11
Amusements	0.02	0.06	0.11	0.10	0.25	0.09
Education	0.01	0.05	0.08	0.09	0.14	0.06
Social expenses	0.34	0.66	0.75	1.15	1.44	0.78
Rates & contributions	0.10	0.16	0.35	0.47	0.36	0.26
Water	0.42	0.47	0.47	0.57	0.62	0.49
Religious worship	0.08	0.16	0.37	0.30	0.33	0.23
Occasional expenses	0.52	0.42	0.49	2.30	3.05	1.00
Other	0.41	0.91	1.50	1.51	3.32	1.27
Furniture & utensils	0.14	0.35	0.44	0.57	0.97	0.43
Interest on debt	0.13	0.22	0.59	0.43	1.72	0.45
Remittances to relatives	—	0.16	0.29	0.24	0.27	0.19
Sundries	0.14	0.18	0.18	0.27	0.36	0.20
Average expenditure	20.41	25.96	32.82	41.42	56.70	31.86
Average income	16.68	25.15	34.77	44.61	63.55	32.56
Surplus (+) or deficit (—)	— 3.73	— 0.81	+ 1.95	+ 3.19	+ 6.85	+ 0.70
Average size family (adult males)	2.62	3.04	3.95	4.82	6.27	3.75
Number of families	42	90	46	34	18	230.
	Percent					
Food	61.39	58.01	56.89	54.59	53.30	56.62
Rent	7.99	7.09	6.86	5.94	5.11	6.55
Clothing	5.34	8.21	9.32	10.48	11.43	9.17
Fuel and light	9.31	8.01	7.49	6.76	7.11	7.63
Miscellaneous	15.97	18.68	19.44	22.23	23.05	20.03
Communication	0.54	0.77	0.88	1.23	0.65	0.85
Sanitary expenses	1.57	1.66	1.61	1.50	1.66	1.60
Cigarettes, wines, etc.	3.72	3.62	3.38	2.73	3.00	3.29
Doctor's fee & medecine	0.69	1.19	0.70	0.80	0.44	0.82
Toilet articles	0.14	0.31	0.31	0.31	0.53	0.34
Amusements	0.10	0.23	0.34	0.24	0.44	0.28
Education	0.05	0.19	0.24	0.22	0.25	0.19
Social expenses	1.66	2.54	2.29	2.77	2.54	2.45
Rates & contributions	0.49	0.62	1.07	1.13	0.63	0.82
Water	2.06	1.81	1.43	1.38	1.09	1.54
Religious worship	0.39	0.62	1.13	0.72	0.58	0.72
Occasional expenses	2.55	1.62	1.49	5.55	5.38	3.14
Other	2.01	3.50	4.57	3.65	5.86	3.99
Furniture & utensils	0.68	1.35	1.34	1.38	1.71	1.35
Interest on debt	0.64	0.84	1.80	1.04	3.03	1.41
Remittances to relatives	—	0.62	0.88	0.58	0.48	0.60
Sundries	0.69	0.69	0.55	0.65	0.64	0.63

Table 47b. Average amount and percent distribution of the annual expenditure of the families of cotton workers in Tientsin

Item of expenditure	$ 200 or below	$ 201—300	$ 301—400	$ 401—500	All incomes
			Amount ($)		
Food	134.39	163.50	207.16	260.01	185.36
Rent	14.98	20.85	19.46	27.12	20.50
Clothing	11.34	18.28	25.60	34.88	19.58
Fuel and light	21.63	25.34	31.72	35.30	28.14
Miscellaneous	19.29	30.13	46.07	54.67	36.99
Communication	0.32	0.77	2.33	0.83	1.23
Sanitary expenses	3.25	4.77	6.56	10.06	5.79
Cigarettes, wine, &c.	4.10	4.88	10.81	9.58	7.16
Doctor's fee & medecine	0.82	2.86	4.18	6.30	3.51
Amusements	0.54	1.08	2.57	5.70	1.99
Education	0.07	0.52	0.75	0.13	0.52
Social expenses	0.50	2.09	2.37	1.98	2.07
Rates & contribution		0.05	0.22	0.11	0.10
Toilet articles	1.80	2.42	3.65	4.74	3.01
Water	3.84	4.41	5.66	6.46	4.98
Religious worship		0.34	0.46	0.51	0.38
Occasional expenses	4.05	5.94	6.51	8.27	6.25
Average expenditure	201.63	258.10	330.01	411.98	290.57
Average income	192.30	244.20	342.38	434.45	291.37
Surplus (+) or deficit (—)	— 9.33	— 13.90	+ 12.37	+ 22.47	+ 0.80
Average family size (adult males)	2.38	2.55	3.07	3.48	2.80
Number of families	5	46	27	9	87
			Percent		
Food	66.65	63.35	62.77	63.11	63.79
Rent	7.43	8.08	5.90	6.58	7.06
Clothing	5.63	7.08	7.76	8.47	6.74
Fuel and light	10.73	9.82	9.61	8.57	9.68
Miscellaneous	9.56	11.67	13.96	13.27	12.73
Communication	0.16	0.30	0.70	0.20	0.42
Sanitary expense	1.61	1.85	1.99	2.44	1.99
Cigarettes, wine, &c.	2.03	1.89	3.27	2.33	2.46
Doctor's fee & medecine	0.41	1.11	1.27	1.53	1.21
Toilet articles	0.89	0.94	1.11	1.15	1.04
Amusements	0.27	0.42	0.78	1.38	0.68
Education	0.03	0.20	0.23	0.03	0.18
Social expenses	0.25	0.81	0.72	0.48	0.71
Rates & contribution		0.02	0.07	0.03	0.03
Water	1.90	1.70	1.71	1.57	1.71
Religious worship		0.13	0.14	0.12	0.13
Occasional expenses	2.01	2.30	1.97	2.01	2.15

the small percentage that food occupies in the total family expenditure. On the other hand, the workers' cost of living index in Tientsin, which is compiled on the basis of a family budget inquiry of the handicraft workers from September, 1927 to June, 1928 by the *Nankai Institute*, shows an increase in the cost of living index from 118.39 in November, 1929 to 122.47

in October, 1930, as well as an increase in the food index from 118.35 to 121.27 during the same period,—the period during which the Tientsin inquiry was undertaken.

The percentage that clothing occupies in the total expenditure is 6.74 in Tientsin, but 9.17 in Shanghai. This may be attributed to the higher standard of living among the Shanghai workers. The percentage for fuel and light, however, is higher in Tientsin than in Shanghai, being 9.68 and 7.63 respectively. In Tientsin because of the cold weather it is a common practice to burn coal balls in winter time, whereas in Shanghai even well-to-do families seldom resort to fire. The miscellaneous expense, which occupies 20.03 percent in Shanghai, occupies only 12.73 percent in Tientsin. This, again, is due to the higher standard of living among the Shanghai workers. Among the miscellaneous items social expense, for instance, occupies 2.45 percent in Shanghai, but 0.71 percent in Tientsin. Similarly, the expense for cigarettes, wine etc. occupies 3.29 percent in Shanghai, but 2.46 percent in Tientsin.

Hours of work:—The hours of work are generally twelve in Chinese owned mills, but eleven in Japanese owned mills. Actually, however, the hours of work are about equal, as in Chinese owned mills more loafing and sitting about is allowed.[16] During the noon time or midnight, from one half to one hour is allowed for meals. In Tientsin the working period lasts from 7 A.M. to 7 P.M. in Peiyang and Hua Hsin; 6:30 A.M. to 6:30 P.M. in Heng Yuan; and 6 A. M. to 6. P. M. in Yu Yuan, Pao Cheng and Yu Ta. In all these mills two shift system prevails.

Rest days are arranged to suit individual cases. Some stop every Sunday afternoon, others every ten days, still others allow two days per month. In Tientsin the first arrangement prevails. It is during rest days that the change of shift takes place. The holidays for the year include five days for the New Year, but one day for each of the three festivals (Spring Festival on the 15th day of the 1st month, Dragon Festival on the 5th day of the 5th month, and Moon Festival on the 15th day of the 8th month, all in lunar calendar), Sun Yat-Sen's birthday on Nov. 12 and death day on March 12, the 72 patriots' day on Mar. 29, the beginning of the Nationalist Revolution on July 9, the National Independence Day on Oct. 10 and other legal holidays sanctioned by the National government. On such holidays wages are paid at the mill's expense. Some mills take advantage of the holidays to change shift, still others offer double wages to their workers for continuous operation. In recent years the increase in the number of legal holidays is putting a serious drain on the mills. In 1929, for instance, Yu Yuan Mill, employing an average working force of 6,395, had to suffer a total wage loss of $49,616 for 17 holidays, or

16. In Dr. Chen's study, *op. cit.*, the average working hours per shift in 49 cotton spinning mills amount to 11.3 hours.

an average loss of $2,919 per holiday. These holidays include five days for the Lunar New Year, one day each for the Solar New Year, Spring Festival, Labor Day (May 1st), May 30th incident, Dragon Festival, Moon Festival, Double Tenth (i.e. National Independence day) and five days for the birth, death and burial of President Sun Yat-sen.

On February 16, 1930, Pao Cheng Mill in Tientsin put into effect the three shift system for the first time in China's cotton industry. Under this system the working hours were reduced from twelve to eight: they were changed from the old arrangement of 6 A.M. to 6 P.M. to the new arrangement of 2 P.M. to 10 P.M., 10 P. M. to 6 A. M. and 6 A. M. to 2 P. M. No change, however, was made in the number of workers, as the 1,500 workers employed in the mill, who were formerly divided into two shifts of 750 each, were now re-arranged into three shifts of 500 workers each. As most departments of the mill worked under piece system, an increase in efficiency, rather than an increase in wages, was expected to make up for the workers' loss arising from the shorter hours of work.

Immediately after the introduction of the three shift system at Pao Cheng Mill, opposition to the change was unanimous among the Chinese mills, for fear that their own workers might demand a similar change which would involve a considerable recruiting of workers. Such a change, which was quite feasible for Pao Cheng, was claimed to be difficult for other mills. In the first place, it is claimed that the efficiency of the workers in Pao Cheng is lower than that in other mills. According to the investigation of the Social Affairs Bureau of the Special Municipality of Tientsin in 1928, the yarn output per worker (6.63 bales), is the lowest for Pao Cheng, as it is only 59 percent of that for Heng Yuan (11.25 bales).[17] Secondly, Pao Cheng has suffered successive losses during the last three years, amounting to $197,083 in 1926, $58,819 in 1927 and $61,566 in 1928. 1926 was a bad year for other mills, but in 1927 and 1928 both Hua Hsin and Yu Yuan made a fair profit. Peiyang, which lost more than Pao Cheng during 1927 and 1928, has now been reorganized.

17. *Annual Report,* op. cit.

Statistics on Tientsin cotton mills, 1928

Name of mill	No. spindles Total	Per worker	No. looms Total	Per worker	No. workers Spinners	Weavers	Yarn output (bales) Total	Per worker	Cloth output (pieces) Total	Per worker
Hua Hsin	27,000	12.80			2,235		20,000	8.95		
Yu Yuan	75,000	17.20	1,000	.58	4,359	1,724	37,000	8.49	770,000	446.64
Heng Yuan	31,000	11.63	310	.58	2,666	534	30,000	11.25	100,000	187.27
Peiyang	28,000	14.36			1,950		20,000	10.26		
Yu Ta	35,000	20.59			1,700		15,000	8.82		
Pao Cheng	27,000	16.56			1,630		10,800	6.63		

But Pao Cheng is heavily in debt to the Anderson Meyer & Co., and has been under the latter's supervision since 1923. The mill, in other words, is on the verge of bankruptcy. But for the increase in efficiency, its closing-down may have resulted in the loss of employment for many workers.[18]

The increase in efficiency from the change of two shift to three shift system is, as a matter of fact, a possibility, and has been admitted by the Mill in its reply to Professor Chen Ta on March 20, 1931.[19] In that reply the mill appended a table of statistics showing the increase in output, with an increase in wages, which is here reproduced in Table 48. This table shows that the average daily output for the one and half month period from January 1 to February 15, 39.18 bales, is approximately the same as that for the one and half month period from Feb. 16 to March 31, 39.09 bales. In other words, there is apparently no reduction in output after the decrease of the work force per shift from 750 under the 12 hour shift to 500 under the 8 hour shift system. The absence of the reduction in output under the 8 hour system, with a work force which is only two thirds of that under the 12 hour system, means one third increase in efficiency,—an increase which can be explained by several factors. In the first place, whereas under the two shift system the mill is handicapped by the presence of too many workers whom it is unable to dismiss for fear of union opposition, under the three shift system these workers are spread out in three instead of two shifts. Each worker, as a result, is given an opportunity to do his best under the new arrangement. The card tender is now in charge of 20 instead of 10 cards under the two shift system; similarly, whereas three tenders used to be in charge of two roving machines, now each tender is allowed to take care of one machine. Secondly, the weekly change of shift under the two shift system requires a cessation of work for 12 hours, but under the three shift system only 8 hours are needed for such change. This means an economy of sixteen hours per month. Finally, shorter hours of work necessarily result in greater output, as the workers get greater opportunity for rest and recuperation, and are less likely to loaf during the working hours.

---

18. *Ibid.*

Nominal profit and loss for Tientsin cotton mills, 1926-28

Year	Hua Hsin		Yu Yuan		Heng Yuan		Peiyang		Pao Cheng	
	Amount	%	Amount	%	Amount	%	Amount	%	Amount	%
1926	– 88,312	–3.65	–245,017	–4.41	256,256	6.41	–526,281	–19.57	–197,083	–6.57
1927	33,809	1.40	365,531	6.57	–140,932	–3.52	–134,433	– 5.00	– 58,819	–1.96
1928	181,376	7.49	345,885	6.22	–152,174	–3.80	–329,035	–12.23	– 61,566	–2.05

19. *Current Events*, May, 1931, p. 320. Dr. Chen, in his recent pamphlet on the *Applicability of the Factory Act of the Chinese Government*, stated that in Shanghai "a group of cotton mills estimate the loss from all causes as 9%, the reduction in output alone would amount to 17% if the working hours were changed from 12 to 10 per day" (p. 9).

Table 48. A comparison of output and wages under the 12-hour (or two shift) and 8-hours (or three shift) system in Pao Cheng Mill, Tientsin, January 1 to April 15, 1930

Item	12 hour shift (2 shifts per day)			8 hour shift (3 shifts per day)			
	Jan. 1-15	Jan. 16-31	Feb. 1-15	Feb. 16-28	Mar. 1-15	Mar.16-31	Apr. 1-15
Working days	13.00	12.50	13.00	12.33	13.66	15.33	14.33
Yarn output (bales)	532.59	490.70	484.93	482.58	534.70	597.75	581.44
Average count of yarn spun	18.15	19.18	18.99	18.47	17.82	17.97	18.14
Average yarn output per day (bales)	40.97	39.26	37.30	39.14	39.14	38.99	40.57
Wages paid (not including wages for monthly workers) ($)	11,526.84	11,542.13	11,706.30	11,164.07	12,996.31	13,517.61	12,839.68
Average wages paid per day ($)	886.68	923.37	900.48	905.44	951.41	881.77	896.00
Average wages per bale of yarn ($)	21.64	23.52	24.14	23.13	24.31	22.62	22.09

Besides the increase in efficiency, other advantages are claimed for the three shift system. The latter anticipates the eight hour work under the new Factory Act, the enforcement of which was to take place on the first of August, 1931. This, however, is not true, as under the new Factory Act, half hour rest is to be given for every 5 hours of continuous work. Again, it anticipates the prohibition of night work for child and woman labor under the same Act, as child and woman labor can now be put on the first shift from 6 A.M. to 2 P.M. The worker, too, has sixteen instead of twelve hours to himself under the three shift system, and is not inclined to take frequent leave for personal affairs. The mill, in this way, is able to cut down losses arising from a higher frequency of absence. Finally, from the viewpoint of the society at large and of the workers in particular, shorter hours of worker are conducive to better health and greater welfare. Although the provision for education and recreation is still highly inadequate, yet it is hoped that its improvement in the future will enable the workers under the three shift system to make good use of their spare time.

The change from the two shift to the three shift system, however, is difficult for other mills. For some mills especially of Japanese ownership, where the labor force is not superfluously abundant, such a change creates at the beginning the problem of having to recruit a large labor force for the extra shift. Again, if the mill has already achieved a high degree of efficiency, a reduction of hours may give rise to one of the two results, a reduction or an increase in wages. If either party has to bear the loss, it is more likely the mill rather than the worker, as the former is in a better position to shift the increased cost to the consumer.

Child and woman labor:—The employment of child and woman labor is a common feature in the cotton industry. Indeed, of the 327,842 cotton workers in the 28 cities of China, there are 202,738 woman workers or 61.84 percent and 20,633 child workers or 6.29 percent—a total of 223,371 woman and child workers or 68.13 percent.[20] As shown in Table 49, of the 432,940 woman workers in the factory industries for the 28 cities in the nine provinces as investigated by the Ministry of Industries, the cotton industry, with 202,738 woman workers, claims 46.83 percent, which is the highest for any factory industry. The silk industry, employing 143,469 woman workers or the next largest number, claims only 33.14 percent. In respect of child labor, cotton industry ranks only next to silk industry in importance. The cotton industry, employing 20,633 child workers, claims 32.60 percent of the total child workers in 28 cities; while the silk industry, employing 22,572 child workers, claims 35.67 percent.

Table 49. Child and woman labor in Chinese factory industries in 28 cities, 1930

Industry	Woman labor		Child labor		All labor	
	No.	%	No.	%	No.	%
Cotton	202,738	46.83	20,633	32.60	327,842	33.97
Spinning	143,767	33.21	12,330	19.48	206,532	21.40
Weaving	55,476	12.81	7,037	11.12	109,809	11.39
Other	3,495	0.81	1,266	2.00	11,501	1.18
Silk	143,469	33.14	22,572	35.67	197,229	20.44
Reeling	126,200	29.15	19,632	31.02	148,814	15.42
Weaving	7,611	1.76	1,994	3.15	26,448	2.74
Other	9,658	2.23	946	1.50	21,967	2.28
Other	86,733	20.03	20,082	31.73	439,882	45.59
Total	432,940	100.00	63,287	100.00	964,953	100.00

20. Ministry of Industries, *op. cit.*, Bulletin No. 1; *Nankai Weekly Statistical Service*, March 2,1931.

Table 50a. Child and woman labor in China's cotton industry, 1930, classified by branches and localities

Province or city	Woman labor Spinning	Woman labor Weaving	Woman labor Other	Woman labor Total No.	Woman labor Total %	Child labor Spinning	Child labor Weaving	Child labor Other	Child labor Total No.	Child labor Total %	All labor Spinning	All labor Weaving	All labor Other	All labor Total No.	All labor Total %
Kiangsu	137,921	24,745	793	163,459	80.63	11,721	4,005	236	15,962	77.36	182,071	46,523	4,227	232,821	71.02
Shanghai	126,654	14,768	96	141,518	69.80	9,238	1,872	12	11,122	53.90	164,752	29,244	214	194,210	59.24
Soochow	1,691	1,597	562	3,850	1.90	855	35	84	974	4.72	2,902	3,056	3,637	9,595	2.93
Wusih	7,951	1,526		9,477	4.67	1,055	220		1,275	6.18	11,770	2,158		13,928	4.25
Wuchin	1,625	1,325	135	3,085	1.52	573	625	134	1,332	6.46	2,647	2,102	310	5,059	1.54
Chinkiang		1		1				6	6	0.03		162	66	228	0.07
Nantung		5,215		5,215	2.57		1,176		1,176	5.70		9,228		9,228	2.81
Ihing		100		100	0.05		50		50	0.24		152		152	0.05
Nanking		213		213	0.11		27		27	0.13		421		421	0.13
Chekiang	1,068	3,668		4,736	2.34	409	190		599	2.90	2,000	4,425	72	6,497	1.98
Hangchow		2,520		2,520	1.24							2,738	72	2,810	0.86
Chiahsin		900		900	0.44		180		180	0.87		1,200		1,200	0.37
Ningpo	1,068	248		1,316	0.65	409	10		419	2.03	2,000	487		2,487	0.76
Anhwei	850	1,937		2,787	1.37	200	269		469	2.27	1,500	4,189		5,689	1.74
Anch'in		135		135	0.07		45		45	0.22		875		875	0.27
Wuhu	850	902		1,752	0.86	200	224		424	2.05	1,500	1,514		3,014	0.92
Pêngpu		900		900	0.44							1,800		1,800	0.55
Kiangsi	1,200	100		1,300	0.64						1,700	309	282	2,291	0.70
Kiukiang	1,200			1,200	0.59						1,700			1,700	0.52
Nanchang		100		100	0.05							309	282	591	0.18
Hupeh	1,763	20,363	2,290	24,416	12.04		1,600	1,030	2,630	12.75	4,112	47,398	6,030	57,540	17.55
Hankow		9,500	2,290	11,790	5.82		1,600	1,030	2,630	12.75		29,860	6,030	35,890	10.95
Wuchang	1,763	10,863		12,626	6.22						4,112	17,538		21,650	6.60
Shantung	965			965	0.48						15,149			15,149	4.62
Tsingtao	965			965	0.48						15,149			15,149	4.62
Kwangtung		4,663		4,663	2.30		973		973	4.72		6,965		6,965	2.12
Foshan		2,763		2,763	1.36		73		73	0.35		3,965		3,965	1.21
Swatow		1,900		1,900	0.94		900		900	4.36		3,000		3,000	0.92
Fukien			412	412	0.20								890	890	0.27
Foochow			412	412	0.20								890	890	0.27
Total	143,767	55,476	3,495	202,738	100.00	12,330	7,037	1,266	20,633	100.00	206,532	109,809	11,501	327,842	100.00

In Table 50a the geographical distribution of child and woman labor in China's cotton industry is given. Kiangsu province, above all others, employs the highest percentage of child and woman workers in the cotton industry. 163,459 woman workers or 80.63 percent of all woman workers and 15,962 child workers or 77.36 percent of all child workers in the cotton industry are found in this province, which employs altogether 238,821 child and woman workers or 71.02 percent of all workers in the cotton industry. As shown in Table 50b, in Kiangsu woman labor occupies 70.21 percent of the total labor in cotton industry, while child labor occupies 6.85 percent. Man labor, which occupies 22.94 percent, takes a middle position between child and woman labor. In Chekiang, where only 2.34 percent of total woman labor and 2.90 percent of total child labor in the cotton industry are found, the percentage for child or woman labor is

Table 50b. Child and woman labor in China's cotton industry, 1930, classified by branches and localities (in percentages)

Province	Woman labor				Child labor			
of city	S*	W*	O*	T*	S*	W*	O*	T*
Kiangsu	75.75	53.19	18.76	70.21	6.44	8.61	5.58	6.85
Shanghai	76.87	50.53	44.86	72.87	5.61	6.41	5.61	5.73
Soochow	58.27	52.26	15.45	40.13	29.46	1.14	2.31	10.15
Wusih	67.55	70.71		68.04	8.97	10.20		9.16
Wuchin	61.37	63.04	43.55	60.98	21.65	29.73	43.22	26.33
Chinkiang		0.62		0.44			9.09	3.63
Nantung		56.51		56.51		12.75		12.75
Ihing		65.79		65.79		32.89		32.89
Nanking		50.53		50.59		6.41		6.42
Chekiang	53.40	82.89		72.90	20.45	4.30		9.22
Hangchow		92.04		64.20				
Chiahsin		75.00		75.00		15.00		15.00
Ningpo	53.40	50.92		52.91	20.45	2.06		16.85
Anhwei	56.67	46.24		48.99	13.33	6.42		8.24
Anch'in		15.43		15.43		5.14		5.14
Wuhu	56.67	59.58		58.13	13.33	14.79		14.07
Pêngpu		50.00		50.00				
Kiangsi	70.59	32.36		56.74				
Kiukiang	70.59			70.59				
Nanchang		32.36		16.92				
Hupeh	42.87	42.96	37.98	42.43		.3.38	17.08	4.57
Hankow		31.81	37.98	32.85		5.36	17.08	7.33
Wuchang	42.87	61.94		58.32				
Shantung	6.37			6.37				
Tsingtao	6.37			6.37				
Kwangtung		66.95		66.95		13.97		13.97
Foshan		69.69		69.69		1.84		1.84
Swatow		63.33		63.63		30.00		30.00
Fukien			46.29	46.29				
Foochow			46.29	46.20				
Total	69.61	50.52	30.39	61.84	5.97	6.41	11.01	6.29

* S represents spinning, W weaving, O other, and T total.

even higher than that in Kiangsu, namely, 9.22 or 72.90. In other southern and central provinces, the percentage for child or woman labor is also high. The percentage that woman labor occupies in total labor for the cotton industry is 66.95 for Kwangtung, 56.74 for Kiangsi, 48.99 for Anhwei, 46.29 for Fukien, and 42.43 for Hupeh. In respect of child labor, such percentage is 13.97 for Kwangtung, 8.24 for Anhwei and 4.57 for Hupeh. In northern provinces, the employment of woman labor is rather uncommon because of social prejudice. In Shantung, woman labor occupies but 6.37 percent of the total cotton labor. In Hopei, statistics in 1928 show that of the 16,798 workers employed in Tientsin mills, only 1,842 workers or 10.97 percent are women. However, the percentage for child workers, 8.68 (1,459 child workers), compares well with that for the southern or central provinces.[21]

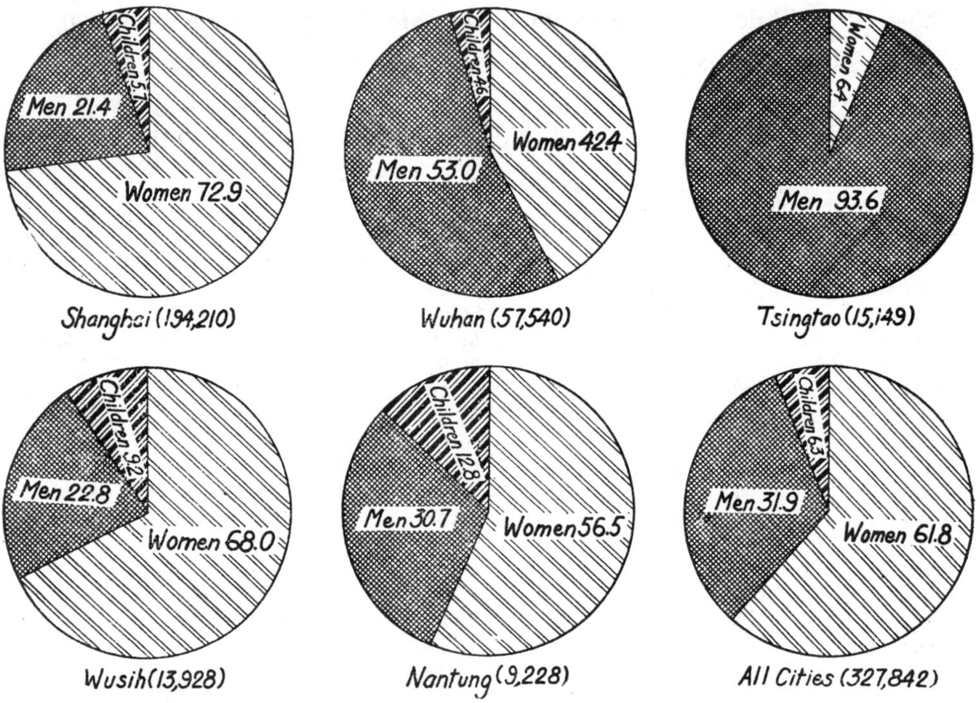

Fig. 25. Distribution of man, woman and child labor in China's cotton manufacturing centres, 1930 (*See* Table 51)

In Table 51 the distribution of man, woman and child labor in the important cotton centres is shown. According to this table, of the total cotton workers (327,842) in the 28 cities, Shanghai, Wuhan, Tsingtao, Wusih and Nantung claim 290,053 workers or 88.47%. The proportion of woman labor in these centres is the highest for Shang-

21. Social Affairs Bureau, Annual Report, *op. cit.*

hai (72.9%), after which follow Wusih (68%), Nantung (56.5%), and Wuhan (42.4%). The lowest is that for Tsingtao in North China, namely, 6.4%. As to child labor, the proportion is the highest for Nantung (12.8%), after which follow Wusih (9.2%), Shanghai (5.7%), and Wuhan (4.6%). In Tsingtao no child labor is employed at all (Fig. 25)

Table 51. Distribution of man, woman and child labor in China's cotton industry by cities, 1930

City	Women		Men		Children		Total		% for each city
	No.	%	No.	%	No.	%	No.	%	
Shanghai	141,518	72.9	41,570	21.4	11,122	5.7	194,210	100.0	59.24
Wuhan	24,416	42.4	30,494	53.0	2,630	4.6	57,540	100.0	17.55
Wuchang	12,626	58.3	9,024	41.7			21,650	100.0	6.60
Hankow	11,790	32.9	21,470	59.8	2,630	7.3	35,890	100.0	10.95
Tsingtao	965	6.4	14,184	93.6			15,149	100.0	4.62
Wusih	9,477	68.0	3,176	22.8	1,275	9.2	13,928	100.0	4.25
Soochow	3,850	40.1	4,771	49.7	974	10.2	9,595	100.0	2.93
Nantung	5,215	56.5	2,837	30.7	1.176	12.8	9,228	100.0	2.81
Wuchin	3,085	61.0	642	12.7	1,332	26.3	5,059	100.0	1.54
Other	14,212	61.4	6,797	29.4	2,124	9.2	23,133	100.0	7.06
Total	202,738	61.8	104,471	31.9	20,633	6.3	327,842	100.0	100.0

In Table 52 the child and woman workers in Shanghai and Tientsin cotton mills are classified by occupations. In Shanghai mills the blowing, carding, baling, mechanical and finishing departments are predominated by man workers, and the roving, spinning, reeling, waste cotton picking, warping and weaving departments by woman workers. Over seventy percent of workers are men or women in each of these departments.[22] In Tientsin mills woman workers occupy a far less important position in all these departments except warping, where woman workers account for 57.22 percent of the workers employed in that department. In reeling and roving departments their percentage is only 41.05 and 32.19 respectively, which compares poorly with that of 96.65 and 91.41 respectively in Shanghai mills. Child labor is of little importance as compared with man or woman labor in Shanghai or Tientsin mills. In Shanghai mills, in no department does child labor claim a percentage higher than 13, the figures being 12.21% in warping, 9.96% in waste cotton picking, 7.34% in mechanical, 5.42% in spinning, 3.82% in finishing and 2.23% in roving. In Tientsin an investigation in 1929 of 195 child workers of 16 years of age or below in Yu Yuan Mill shows that there were 87 child workers in spinning department, 57 in reeling department and 51 in warping department. Since the Mill was reported to have employed only 184 child workers in 1928, the 195 child workers in 1929 covered approximately all the child workers in the Mill. As there were in 1929 1,758 workers in the spinning

22. Wages and hours of labor in Greater Shanghai, *op. cit.*

department, 899 workers in the reeling department, and 526 workers in the warping department, the percentage of child labor in each of the three departments was therefore 4.95, 6.34 and 9.70 respectively.

Table 52. Occupational distribution of man, woman and child labor in Shanghai and Tientsin cotton mills

Occupation	Shanghai						Tientsin			
	Male		Female		Child		Male		Female	
	No.	%	No.	%	No.	%	No.	%	No.	%
Blowing	824	96.94	26	3.05			100	100.00		
Carding	796	93.43	56	6.57			189	91.30	18	8.70
Roving	515	6.35	7,410	91.41	181	2.23	615	67.81	292	32.19
Spinning	726	6.63	9,638	87.95	594	5.42	1,584	90.10	174	9.90
Reeling	334	3.35	9,624	96.65			530	58.95	369	41.05
Baling	543	92.98	41	7.02			131	100.00		
Waste cotton	77	10.09	610	79.95	76	9.93				
Mechanical	3,743	88.65	169	4.00	310	7.34	724	100.00		
Warping	378	13.38	2,102	74.41	345	12.21	225	42.78	301	57.22
Weaving	1,014	16.98	4,958	83.02			1,064	100.00		
Finishing	1,166	90.88	68	5.30	49	3.82	79	100.00		
Total	10,116	21.82	34,702	74.83	1,555	3.35	5,241	81.95	1,154	18.05

The above investigation of 195 child workers shows that 146 of them are boys and 49 girls. 77 of the child workers are 15 years of age, 54 14 years of age, and 42 13 years of age. Of the remaining 22 workers the age distribution is as follows: 10 years, 3; 11 years, 4; 12 years, 15. Of these 195 child workers 40 joined the mill at 11 years of age, 47 at 12 and 44 at 13. Of the other 64 workers 6 joined the mill at 9, 22 at 10, 24 at 14 and 12 at 15. Before they joined the mill, 77 of them were idle; 48 were pupils; and 70 were engaged in the following occupations: gleaning, 30; farming, 20; cotton spinning, 5; weaving etc., 7; handicraft, 5; and peddling, 3. The length of stay of the 195 workers may be distributed as follows: 24 under one year, 52 under two years, 56 under three years, 39 under four years and 24 for four years or more. Among the 195 child workers 86 workers had 115 other members of the family working in the mill, including 30 fathers, 1 mother, 54 brothers, 13 sisters, 3 sisters-in-laws and 14 others. 181 of the 195 workers were earning the following wages per day: 21-25 cents, 18; 26-30 cents, 31; 31-35 cents, 40; 36-40 cents, 37; 41-45 cents, 31; 46-50 cents, 22; 51-55 cents, 2. The average daily wage rates, therefore, amount only to 35.4 cents.

In Shanghai an investigation in 1924 by the *Shanghai Child Labor Commission* reported that "the children are mostly employed in the Spinning Department, and in the great majority of cases have to stand the whole time they are at work. It is difficult to state definitely the lowest age at which the children commence work. The Commission, however, saw many children at work who could not have been more than six or seven years of age. Some of these children are not on the payroll but are allowed to be brought by their mothers in order that they may be under their care. In many mills the conditions during the night shift are, according to Western ideas, most unusual. Rows of baskets containing babies and children, sleeping or awake as the case may be, lie placed between the rapidly moving and noisy machinery. Young children, who are supposed to be working, but who have been overcome by fatigue or who have taken advantage of the absence of adequate supervision, lie asleep in every corner, some in the open, others hidden in baskets under a covering of raw cotton. The discipline appears to be lax, and those in charge seem to wink at much that goes on in this respect".[23]

Industrial accident and sickness:—Statistics on industrial accidents and sickness in cotton mills are seldom compiled, as millowners in China have not yet appreciated the value of such statistics. Fortunately, one charitable organization, the Industrial Hospital of Shanghai, has kept systematic records of the industrial accidents and sickness of the cotton mill workers in Yangtzepoo District. This Hospital was financed by the mills in the District, to which the workers, chiefly of foreign owned mills, were sent in case of accident or sickness. Because of the frequent inquiry on the subject, the Hospital in March, 1924 published a statistical summary of 880 cases of cotton mill workers treated by the Hospital since its establishment in September, 1919. Yangtzepoo District had at the time of investigation approximately 15,000 cotton mill workers, of whom about 55% were females, 25% males, and 20% children. The 880 cases analyzed, including 566 males or 65%, 164 females or 18% and 150 children (under 15 years of age) or 17%, represent an unusually small sample. This is especially true in regard to female workers, as female workers have greater prejudice against western medical practice than male workers.

Table 53. Distribution of 880 cotton mill workers by accident and sickness, Shanghai

Type of patient	Industrial accident cases		Other cases		Total cases	
	No.	%	No.	%	No.	%
Male	231	41	335	59	566	65
Female	43	26	122	74	164	18
Child	100	67	50	33	150	17
Total	374	43	507	57	880	100

23. Report reprinted in *China Yearbook*, 1925, pp. 548-9.

According to the Hospital's analysis, which is reproduced above in Table 53, among the male, female and child patients the percentage of the injured is the highest among child patients (67), next to which are 41 among male patients and 26 among female patients. Since male workers can be found practically in every department of a cotton mill, from a fitter to a carrying coolie, it is not surprizing that the percentage of the injured among the males should be as high as 41. But female and child workers perform more or less the same type of work, which is light and easy, and does not involve much danger. It is, therefore, to be wondered at that the percentage of the injured among child workers, 67, is almost two and half times higher than that among female workers, 26. However, the industrial experience elsewhere in the world has proved to us that accidents usually take place among workers who possess neither training nor experience, and it is practically impossible to eliminate accidents among these workers even if safety devices, such as the fencing of machinery, be put into effect. Here lies the explanation why child workers, being inexperienced and untrained, are more subject to accidents than female workers. Again, as has been pointed out above, female workers are more prejudiced against western medical practices, and seldom come to the Hospital for treatment.

Table 54. Percentage distribution of the location of injury arising from accidents among cotton mill workers, Shanghai

Location of injury	Male	Female	Child	All
Upper extremity	35	53	51	42
Lower extremity	34	18	30	31
Head	16	20	15	16
Trunk	10	6	3	7
Other	5	3	1	4
Total	100	100	100	100

In Table 54 is given the percentage distribution of the site of bodily injury among the male, female and child workers in cotton mills. It may be noted that the location of injury for male workers is different from that for female or child workers. Here the explanation again lies in the fact that the work for male workers is quite varied, while female and child workers are mostly machine tenders, and more frequently use the upper extremities for their work. For the latter, 95% of the wounds are of the hand or just above. Consequently, many of the disabilities in women and children come from disabled hands. It is most deplorable that the hand which is so useful, especially to the textile worker, is the part of body most often mangled.

Table 55. Percentage distribution of the nature of accidents and sickness among cotton mill workers, Shanghai

Nature of injury or sickness	Male	Female	Child	All
Sickness	100	100	100	100
Tuberculosis	5	14	22	9
Non-tuberculosis respiratory	7.5	15	8	9
Beri-beri	6	3	—	5
Parasitic	22	4	32	19
Chronic ulcer of leg	5	10	—	5
Other	54.5	54	38	53
Injury	100	100	100	100
Laceration	67	37	57	59
Compound fracture	13	35	21	18
Simple fracture	3	2	9	5
Burns	8	6	12	8
Other	9	20	1	10
Accident cases resulting in:—	100	100	100	100
Permanent disability	20	44	29	25
Death	1.7	—	3.0	1.8

In Table 55 the nature of injury and sickness is given in detail (Fig. 26). It is significant to note the common occurence of lacerations among all classes of workers, which is more or less inherent in the occupation. Approximately 75% of the lacerations were infected. Compound fracture, which comes next in order of importance, occurs generally in the bones of the hand or of the lower forearm. Because of the inflammability of cotton and the large number of steam-pipes in the mills, a considerable number of patients were affected by burns, some of which were quite severe. In respect of permanent disability the percentage for child workers, 29, is higher than that for male workers, 20, which can again be explained by the lack of training and experience of the child workers. The percentage for female workers, 44, is the highest, due chiefly to the frequent occurrence of partial or total blindness caused by the injury from the sharp pointed instrument that pierces many a worker's eye in the weaving department. In respect of death from injury, the percentage for child workers, 3, is the highest, due again to the lack of experience and training. The percentage for male workers is 1.7, and that for female workers, zero. In respect of sickness, an examination of Table 55 reveals that no sickness can be considered as inherent in the occupation, as occupational sickness is generally caused by chemical matters, which the cotton mills seldom use except for the purpose of bleaching. The use of bleaching powder, however, accounts for the frequent occurrence of tuberculosis and other respiratory diseases, especially for female and child workers. The hot, humild atmosphere also plays a part in these diseases.[24]

24. Decker: Industrial Hospital, Shanghai: A Review of 880 Cases from the Cotton Mills, in *China Medical Journal*, March, 1924.

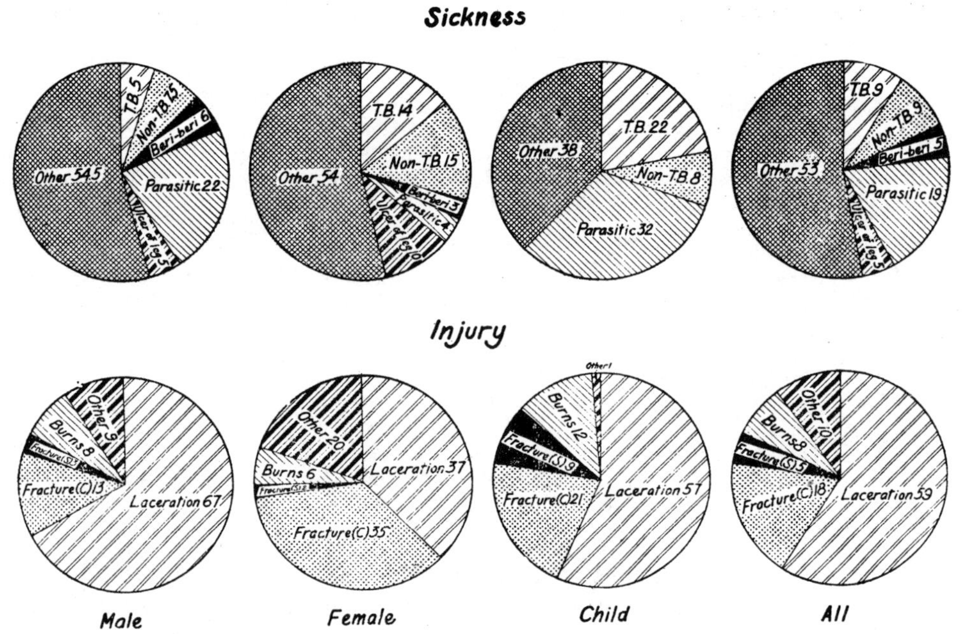

Fig. 26. Distribution of the nature of accidents and sickness among cotton mill workers in Shanghai (in percentages) (*See* Table 55)

In Tientsin every mill has a so-called hospital, which in its simplest form is composed of one or two rooms for visiting patients, with a small stock of medicine. In some mills, such as Hua Hsin, Yu Yuan and Peiyang, several beds are provided for indoor patients, while in others any patient with serious sickness or injury is sent to outside hospital for treatment, at the cost of the mill. In Yu Yuan and Heng Yuan, the two largest mills in Tientsin, records of a very elementary character are kept for the patients. The records for Yu Yuan, which are relatively more complete, classify the patients according to the method of treatment which may be Chinese or western. But unfortunately, no reference is made to the occupation of the patient or the duration of the sickness. The patients in both Chinese and western hospitals are further classified into five departments, namely, surgical; medical; dermatology; ophthalmology; ears, nose and throat. As shown in Table 56 there were during the year July, 1928 to June, 1929 a total of 10,482 patients for the five departments in the two hospitals. As the average working force was 6,083 for 1928 and 6,395 for 1929, (or 6,239 for July, 1928 to June 1929), the fact that the number of patients is greater than that of workness is because one worker may have become patient at more than one department during the year. This table also shows that surgical cases alone occupy as much as 26.8 percent in the number of patients and 35.8 percent in the number of visits. In absolute figures, there are 2,804 patients with 5,562 visits for the surgical cases, giving an average of 1.98 visits per patient. Among these surgical cases are included almost all the cases arising from accidental injury, for which reason the high percentage of patients and visits in surgical department may be taken as an index of the extent of accidents in the mill. The medical cases, which rank first in importance, claim 55.2 percent of the patients and 45.3 percent of the visits, with an average of 1.22 visits per patient. The ophthalmology cases, which rank third in importance, claim 8.3 percent of the patients and 8.9 percent of the visits, with an average of 1.58 visits per patient. This phenomenon is significant, as it confirms the conclusion of Shanghai study on the high percentage of eye cases.

Table 56. The patients and visits to the worker's hospital of a Tientsin cotton mill classified by departments, July 1928 to June 1929*

Department	No. patients					No. visits				
	Chinese		Western		Total	Chinese		Western		Total
	No.	%	No.	%		No.	%	No.	%	
Medical	5,440	92.4	342	7.6	5,782	6,307	89.7	725	10.3	7,032
Surgical	682	24.3	2,122	75.7	2,804	841	15.1	4,721	84.9	5,562
Dermatology	24	6.0	376	94.0	400	34	5.3	607	94.7	641
Ophthalmology	488	55.8	387	44.2	875	763	55.2	619	44.8	1,382
Ears, Nose & Throat	320	51.5	301	48.5	621	382	41.4	541	58.6	923
Total	6,954	66.3	3,528	33.7	10,482	8,327	53.6	7,213	46.4	15,540

* During the year July, 1928 to June, 1929 the Chinese hospital treated 1,358 family members and the western hospital treated 1,030 family members—a total of 2,388 patients who are not included in our present study.

Table 56 also shows that the workers prefer Chinese treatment for medical cases, but western treatment for surgical cases. Thus, 92.4 percent of the cases treated in the Chinese hospital are medical, and 75.7 percent of the cases treated in the western hospital are surgical. Again, the female workers prefer the Chinese hospital to the western, even for surgical cases. While there are 416 female visits to the Chinese hospital, only 36 female visits are registered to the western hospital.

In Table 57 the monthly distribution of the patients and visits is given. Taking the twelve month average as the base of 100, the indices for the first three months, 65.8 for July, 70.7 for August, and 78.6 for September, are unusually low. The low indices must not be taken to represent the actual condition, but rather explain the fact that the hospital, being newly established, had to win over the patients slowly. Beginning with October, the data become more representative, for by that time almost all the workers had learnt to take advantage of the facilities offered

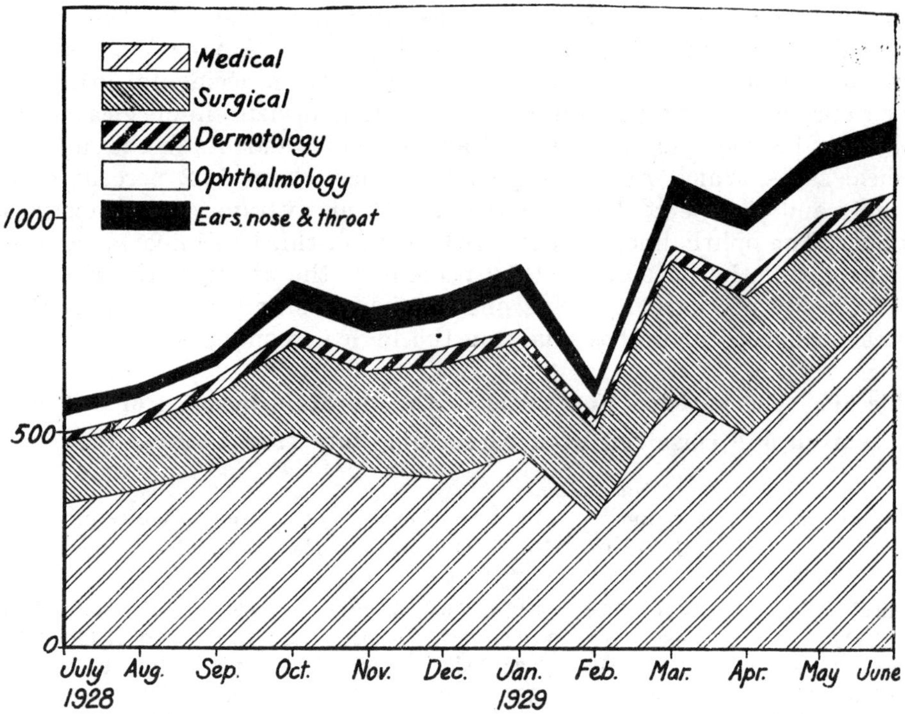

Fig. 27. Monthly fluctuations of the number of patients to the various departments of a Tientsin cotton mill hospital, July 1928 to June 1929 (*See* Table 57)

by the hospital. The great fall from 102.9 in January to 71.9 in February may have been a seasonal phenomenon, as in February when the Chinese new year takes place, the workers have generally five days' vacation, and are given a chance for recreation and rest. In May and June the index again rises to 136.2 and 143.2 respectively, as these months mark the beginning of the hot dry summer when epidemics commence to spread and accident is more frequent under the pressure of heat. However, the above interpretation is purely tentative, and further data are needed in order to reach at final conclusions.

In Shanghai 49 cotton mills with an average size of 2,069 workers per mill reported in 1930 an average of 2,667 times of sickness arising from employment and 132 times of injuries attributed to the self-same cause. Wages were paid by 36 mills for sickness, and by 44 mills for injury, while medical care was given by 47 mills for both sickness and injury. The average wage cost per mill is estimated at $134.84 for sickness, and $43.61 for injury, while the average medical cost per mill amounts to $5,454.6 for sickness and $274.67 for injury. In case of permanent

Table 57. Monthly fluctuation of the patients and visits to the workers' hospital of a Tientsin cotton mill, July 1928 to June 1929

	Medical			Surgical			Dermatology			Ophthalmology			Ears, nose & throat			All			Index (12 mos. av.=100)	
Month	P	V	V/P	P	V	V/P	P	V	V/P	P	V	V/P	P	V	V/P	P	V	V/P	P	V
1928 July	328	398	1.21	149	255	1.71	21	51	2.43	45	56	1.24	32	41	1.28	575	801	1.39	65.8	61.9
Aug.	364	439	1.21	154	377	2.45	22	30	1.36	41	54	1.32	37	76	2.05	618	976	1.58	70.7	75.4
Sep.	418	508	1.22	172	385	2.24	34	34	1.00	34	42	1.20	28	30	1.07	687	999	1.45	78.6	77.1
Oct.	500	578	1.16	209	346	1.65	39	59	1.51	55	84	1.53	53	76	1.43	856	1,143	1.34	97.9	88.3
Nov.	412	490	1.19	235	525	2.23	29	48	1.65	62	107	1.73	60	82	1.37	798	1,252	1.57	91.3	96.7
Dec.	401	485	1.21	260	450	1.73	39	65	1.67	65	110	1.69	61	77	1.26	826	1,187	1.44	94.5	91.7
1929 Jan.	460	530	1.15	256	457	1.78	34	63	1.85	88	146	1.66	62	100	1.61	900	1,296	1.44	102.9	100.1
Feb.	301	343	1.14	210	367	1.75	25	37	1.48	53	69	1.30	40	51	1.27	629	867	1.38	71.9	66.9
Mar.	588	761	1.30	324	569	1.76	36	65	1.80	100	178	1.78	66	117	1.77	1,114	1,690	1.52	127.4	130.5
Apr.	501	654	1.31	326	706	2.16	42	62	1.48	119	172	1.44	49	77	1.57	1,037	1,671	1.61	118.6	129.0
May	669	833	1.25	306	712	2.33	43	63	1.47	111	181	1.63	61	86	1.41	1,190	1,875	1.58	136.2	144.8
June	840	1,013	1.21	203	413	2.03	36	64	1.78	101	183	1.81	72	110	1.53	1,252	1,783	1.42	143.2	137.7
Total	5,782	7,032	1.21	2,804	5,562	1.98	400	641	1.60	875	1,382	1.58	621	923	1.49	10,482	15,540	1.48		
Average	482	586	1.21	234	464	1.98	33	53	1.60	73	115	1.58	52	77	1.49	874	1,295	1.48	100.0	100.0

P = patients, V = visits V/P = visits per patient.

injury wages were paid by 2 mills, and in case of death no wages were paid by any mill. In both cases medical care was given by only 13 mills.[25]

The above general survey may be further supplemented by a few concrete cases. In the Japanese owned mills in Shanghai, the injured are given free medical treatment at the mill hospital, in addition to which 50 to 70 percent of the wage is paid during their absence. In Shanghai Mill a compensation of nine months' wage is given in case of permanent disability. In case of death, some mills merely pay for the funeral expense, while others give a subsidy, amounting to eight or nine months' wage of the deceased, to the family members. In Kung Ta Mill, such a subsidy is derived from a fund, which is built up by deducting 1/50th of the workers' monthly wages. In case of death from accident, the family members of the deceased may receive a subsidy of ten to fifteen dollars from the fund.[26] In Tientsin most of the mills give full-time wage to the injured during their absence from work. In case of permanent disability the injured are given a light and easy job in the mill. In case of death, the arrangement is similar to that of the Japanese owned mills in Shanghai, including the payment of the funeral expense with a subsidy to the family members. The funeral expense covers, however, only the cost for the coffin, which is about ten to fifteen dollars. It is also paid to any worker who dies of sickness instead of injury. In one mill, Hua Hsin, even the worker's parent is entitled to four dollars' coffin subsidy in case of death.

25. Chen, *op. cit.* p. 38.
26. *China Labor Yearbook,* III: pp. 29-30.

CHAPTER VI. LABOR: II

Labor Organization

Labor unions:—The union movement, which received its impetus chiefly from South China, especially from Canton and Hongkong, spread to the Yangtze Valley towards the end of 1922. Along this Valley are located the two cotton centers, Shanghai and Wuhan (i.e. Hankow and Wuchang), where cotton workers, the largest body of industrial labor, are among the first group to come under the influence of unionization. Indeed, a strike in May, 1925 in Naigai Wata Kaisha, the largest Japanese cotton mill in China, led to the famous May 30th incident—the incident that was mainly responsible for the rapid growth of unions in China during the following few years.[27] On the 20th of August when the Shanghai Cotton Mill Workers' Union was organized as one of the 16 industrial unions under the Shanghai General Labor Union, it had a total of 118,223 members—nearly all the workers in the cotton mills in Shanghai at that time. As the General Labor Union had only 217,804 members, the members from cotton mills constituted about 54 percent.[28] In 1926 the cotton mill workers in Wuhan were also organized, with a membership of 20,800 which constituted about one third of the total organized labor in Wuhan (63,900).[29] In May 1927 when the Pan-Pacific Trade Union Conference met, the Chinese delegates reported a total of 3,065,000 organized workers in China, of whom 180,000 were cotton mill workers.[30] In 1928 the unionization movement among cotton workers spread to Tientsin, as a consequence of which unions were organized for five of the six cotton mills there. The Pao Cheng workers were first organized on May 25, after which followed the workers in Yu Yuan and Heng Yuan on July 21, those in Hua Hsin on July 22, and those in Peiyang on Jan. 1, 1929. In Yu Ta, the only cotton mill under Japanese ownership in Tientsin, no union was organized until after a long strike in October, 1930. As a result of that strike 800 of the 1,400 workers in the mill were organized. For the other five mills, an investigation by the Social Affairs Bureau in December, 1929 showed a total organized membership of 13,318, with 10,794 (81.05%) males, 1,884 (14.15%) females, and 640 (4.80%) children under 16 years of age. As there were altogether 29,542 organized workers in Tientsin at that time, the cotton mill workers occupied 45.08 percent.

In April, 1927, when the Kuomingtang Party decided to wipe out the communists, the organized labor movement in China met with a serious setback. Many unions were abolished and dissolved, while a small number

27. A brief description of the incident is given in Chen Ta, Analysis of strikes in China from 1918 to 1926, in *Chinese Economic Journal*, November, 1927, p. 947.
28. *China Labor Yearbook*, II: 46, 63-5.
29. Tso, *Labor movement in China*, Shanghai, 1928, p. 100.
30. *Chinese Economic Bulletin*, Nov. 27, 1926.

of others were re-organized. Since February, 1928 when the Fourth Plenary Session of the Central Executive Committee of the Kuomingtang resolved to abolish the Peasants', the Workers', the Youth, and the Merchants' departments of the Central Party headquarters, and instead to establish a department for the organization and training of mass movements, the promotion and training of peasant and labor organizations was placed under the sole direction of the Party organs. All peasant and labor unions of a questionable character were to be either abolished or re-organized in accordance with the proper procedure promulgated by the Kuomingtang. The cotton workers' unions, like other unions, were considerably reduced in number, and as a consequence, an investigation by the Shanghai Social Affairs Bureau in 1929 reported only 73,903 organized workers in the clothing group, in which the cotton workers were included.[31] In 1930, another investigation by the Ministry of Industries reported only 6,874 organized workers in the cotton industry in Shanghai, of whom 5,211 were cotton mill workers.[32] That investigation, covering 29 cities in the nine provinces of Kiangsu, Chekiang, Anhwei, Kiangsi, Hupeh, Shantung, Kwangtung, Kwangsi and Fukien, gives 76,132 organized workers in the cotton industry, which is equivalent to 54.79 percent of all organized workers in the textile industry (138,946), and 13.21 percent of

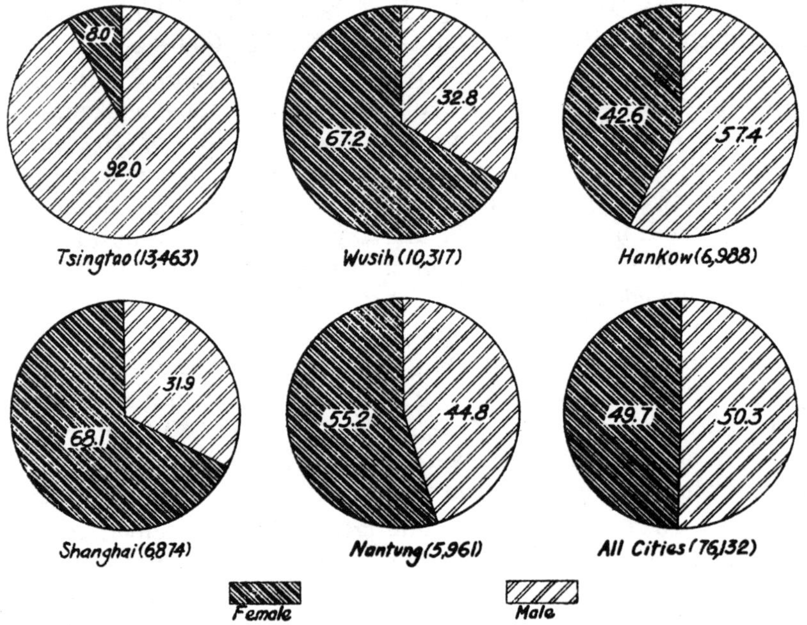

Fig. 28. Sex distribution of the organized cotton workers in leading centres, 1930 (in percentages) (*See* Table 58)

31. Fang, *Chinese Labor*, 1931, p. 75.
32. Ministry of Industries, *op.cit.*, Bulletin No. 3.

Table 58. Organized labor in China's cotton industry classified by branches and localities, 1930

Province or city	Spinning Male	Spinning Female	Spinning Total	Weaving Male	Weaving Female	Weaving Total	Other Male	Other Female	Other Total	Total (Cotton industry) Male	Total (Cotton industry) Female	Total (Cotton industry) Total No.	Total (Cotton industry) Total %	Textile Industries	% of cotton industry	All industries	% of cotton industry
Kiangsu	8,343	16,146	24,489	898	741	1,639	237	14	251	9,478	16,901	26,379	34.67	58,715	44.93	155,405	16.97
Shanghai	1,287	3,924	5,211	737	741	1,478	171	14	185	2,195	4,679	6,874	9.03	17,062	40.29	68,133	10.09
Wusih	3,394	6,923	10,317							3,394	6,923	10,317	13.55	13,187	78.24	20,886	49.40
Wuchin	992	2,008	3,000							992	2,008	3,000	3.94	3,000	100.00	4,210	71.26
Chinkiang				161		161	66		66	227		227	0.30	813	27.92	4,834	4.70
Nantung	2,670	3,291	5,961							2,670	3,291	5,961	7.83	5,961	100.00	6,925	86.08
Chekiang				227	46	273				227	46	273	0.36	16,531	1.65	52,438	0.52
Hangchow				223		223				223		223	0.29	12,974	1.72	33,906	0.66
Chiahsin				4	46	50				4	46	50	0.07	2,577	1.94	3,864	1.29
Anhwei	1,390	985	2,375							1,390	985	2,375	3.12	3,184	74.59	32,263	7.36
Anch'in	740	135	875							740	135	875	1.15	875	100.00	11,349	7.71
Wuhu	650	850	1,500							650	850	1,500	1.97	2,309	64.96	20,914	7.17
Hupeh	13,452	16,447	29,899							13,452	16,447	29,899	39.27	36,167	82.67	84,220	35.50
Hankow	4,014	2,974	6,988							4,014	2,974	6,988	9.18	13,256	52.72	57,625	12.13
Wuchang	9,438	13,473	22,911							9,438	13,473	22,911	30.09	22,911	100.00	28,084	81.58
Shantung	12,393	1,070	13,463							12,393	1,070	13,463	17.68	13,581	99.13	25,639	52.51
Tsingtao	12,393	1,070	13,463							12,393	1,070	13,463	17.68	13,581	99.13	25,639	52.51
Kwangtung				1,202	2,261	3,463				1,202	2,261	3,463	4.55	10,252	33.78	182,582	1.90
Foshan				1,202	2,261	3,463				1,202	2,261	3,463	4.55	9,949	34.81	17,396	19.91
Fukien							175	105	280	175	105	280	0.37	516	54.26	32,855	0.85
Foochow							175	105	280	175	105	280	0.37	516	54.26	26,370	1.06
Kiangsi																1,300	
Kwangsi																9,548	
Total	35,578	34,648	70,226	2,327	3,048	5,375	412	119	531	38,317	37,815	76,132	100.00	138,946	54.79	576,250	13.21
%	50.66	49.34	100.00	43.29	56.71	100.00	77.59	22.41	100.00	50.33	49.67	100.0					
%			90.24			7.06			0.70			100.0					

all organized workers in all industries (576,250). As shown in Table 58, the 76,132 organized workers in the cotton industry are equally divided between males and females, there being 38,317 (50.33%) for the former and 37,815 (49.67%) for the latter. However, as female workers account for 61.84 percent and male workers 31.87 percent of the workers in the cotton industry we may conclude that male workers are organized to a much larger extent than female workers (Fig. 28).

In terms of georgaphical distribution, Wuhan cities lead with 39.27 percent of the total organized labor in the cotton industry, after which follow Tsingtao with 17.68 percent, Wusih with 13.55 percent, Shanghai with 9.03 percent,[33] and Nantung with 7.83 percent. The other cities occupy altogether but 12.64 percent.

Labor disputes:—Partly due to unionization and partly due to other causes, the labor strikes in Shanghai cotton mills showed an abnormal increase during the three years from 1925 to 1927. During the twelve year period from 1918 to 1929 in Shanghai, the chief cotton mill centre in China, there were altogether 209 strikes, of which 171 or 81.8 percent occurred within these three years, namely, 38 strikes in 1925, 78 in 1926, and 55 in 1927. In 1925 the famous May 30 incident led to a series of political strikes in foreign owned mills, which spread to the Chinese owned mills when they were forced to cease operation by the stoppage of electric supply from the Shanghai Municipal Council on July 6. These strikes, at first political in character, gradually assumed an economic significance. They showed no decrease in the following year, but instead, increased from 38 to 78 in number. These 78 strikes in 1926, however, were more evenly distributed among the twelve months than in 1925, although June still led with 19 strikes, due partly to the influence exerted by the anniversary of the May 30 incident. In 1927 when the tide of labor had somewhat turned against the extremists, the number of strikes in Shanghai cotton mills did not show any considerable decrease, but remained at the high figure of 55. This is because in February a general strike was called in Shanghai, in order to help the Northern Expedition, resulting in 17 strikes in 17 mills. In Table 59 the monthly distribution of labor strikes in Shanghai cotton mills is given for the period from 1918 to 1929.[34]

33. In a recent study of 49 cotton mills in Shanghai by Dr. Chen, only five were reported to have organized the labor unions. See Chen, Applicability of the Factory Act of the Chinese Government, *op. cit.*, p. 37.

34. The strike data are gathered from the following sources: Chen, Ta: An analysis of strikes during the last eight years, in *Tsing Hua Journal*, June, 1926; *China Labor Yearbook*, II: 218-235; *Annual Report on Labor Strikes in Greater Shanghai*, 1928, by Bureau of Social Affairs, City Government of Greater Shanghai; *Strikes and Lockouts in Greater Shanghai*, 1929, by Bureau of Social Affairs, City Government of Greater Shanghai. The author, however, is responsible for the analysis of the data.

Table 59. Monthly distribution of labor strikes in Shanghai cotton mills, 1918-1929

	1918	1919	1920	1921	1922	1923	1924	1925	1926	1927	1928	1929	Total
Jan.			1						7	2		2(2)	12
Feb.		1	1		2			1	6	19	1(1)	1(1)	32
Mar.					1	2		2	11	12		(1)	28
Apr.	1	1			1				5	3		1(1)	12
May		2			1		2	1	5			(2)	11
June			1					15	19				35
July									8		3(3)	(3)	11
Aug.	2			1					3	5			11
Sep.			2					3	4	6			15
Oct.	2	1		1				1	2	1	(1)		8
Nov.					1			7	3	7	(1)	1(2)	19
Dec.					1			8	5		(2)	1(2)	15
Total	5	5	5	2	7	2	2	38	78	55	4(8)	6(14)	209

Note: The bracketed figures refer to the number of labor disputes.

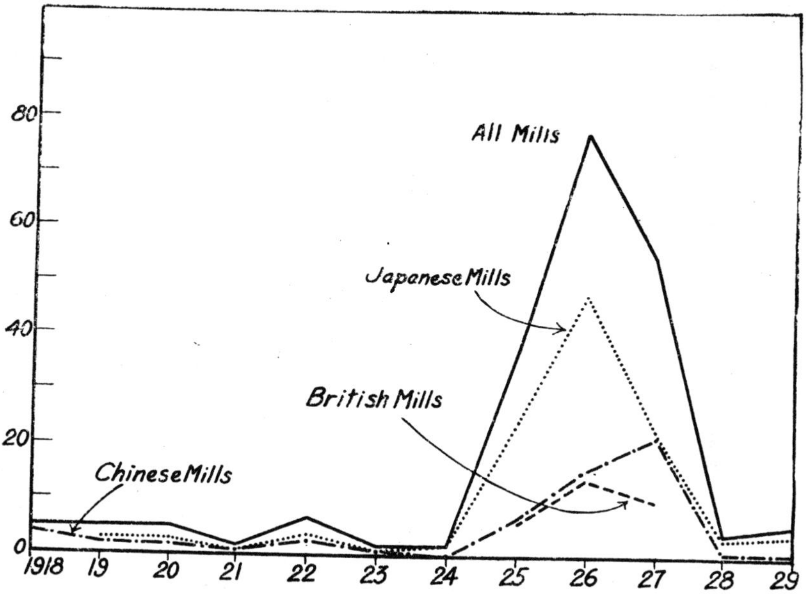

Fig. 29. Labor strikes in Shanghai cotton mills, 1918-1929 (*See* Table 60)

In respect of the nationality of mill ownership, Table 60 shows that the largest number of strikes, 119 or 56.94%, took place in Japanese owned mills from 1918 to 1929. The Chinese owned mills had 58 strikes or 27.74%, while the British owned mills had 30 strikes or 14.35%. The high frequency of strikes in Japanese owned mills is partly accounted for by the predominance of Japanese owned mills. According to the *1930 List of Cotton Mills in China*, of a total of 127,604 workers in Shanghai cotton mills, 58,029 workers or 45.48 percent are to be found in Japanese owned mills, with 56,575 workers or 44.33 percent in Chinese owned mills and 13,000 workers or 10.19 percent in British owned mills. According to the *1925 List of Cotton Mills in China,* the percentage of workers that Japanese owned mills claim is even higher, namely, 47.90%, with 38.10% for Chinese owned mills and 14.00% for British owned mills. A second factor which is responsible for the high frequency of strikes in

	Japanese owned mills	Chinese owned mills	British owned mills
Workers in 1930	58,029(45.48%)	56,575(44.33%)	13,000(10.19%)
Workers in 1925	56,488(47.90%)	44,934(38.10%)	16,500(14.00%)
Strikes, 1918-1929	119(56.94%)	58(27.74%)	30(14.35%)

Japanese owned mills is the racial difference, especially because the workers there are under the supervision of a Japanese instead of a Chinese staff.

Table 60. Labor strikes in Shanghai cotton mills, 1918-1929

	1918	1919	1920	1921	1922	1923	1924	1925	1926	1927	1928	1929	Total
Chinese mills		3	3	1	3	1		7	16	22	1	1	58
San Hsin		2	3	1	1			1	3	1			12
Shen Hsin					1			1	2	4			8
Heng Feng								2	2	3			7
Wing On									2	3			5
Hou Sheng		1								3			4
Wei Tung									2	2			4
Tung I									1	2			3
Hung Chang								2		1			3
P'u I								1		1			2
Heng Ta					1	1							2
Cheng Hua										1			1
Ta Chung Hua									1				1
Cheng Ta											1		1
Hua Feng												1	1
Tai Lai									1				1
Shen Yih									1				1
Chin Chen									1				1
Hsin Ta										1			1
British mills								6	14	10			30
Yangtszepoo									7	2			9
Ewo								3	3	3			9
Oriental								2	2	3			7
Kung I								1	2	2			5
Japanese mills	4	2	2	1	4	1	2	25	48	23	3	4	119
Naigai Wata								5	29	11	1	1	47
Japan-China	3	1	2	1	4		1	5	9	3	2	2	33
Tung Shing						1		5	3	4			13
Shanghai	1	1						3	2				7
Hsi Ho								1	4				5
Dai Nippon							1	2		1			4
Tokwa								1		2			3
Toyo								1		1		1	3
Kung Ta								1	1	1			3
Toyoda								1					1
Unknown	1											1	2
Total	5	5	5	2	7	2	2	38	78	55	4	6	200

In Table 61 the number of workers involved in Shanghai labor strikes from 1918 to 1929 is given. The number of workers involved is reported for 172 of the 209 strikes, and is estimated for the other 37 strikes on the basis of the average workers per strike for the strikes with reported workers during the respective years. In this way, the total number of workers involved in the 209 strikes is calculated at 577,239, giving an average of 2,762 workers per strike. As is expected after the above analysis, the 171 strikes from 1925 to 1927 or 81.8% affected 469,941 workers or 81.42%. 1925, with 38 strikes or 18.18%, leads with 199,296 workers or 34.53%, after which follow 1927 with 55 strikes (26.3%) and 146,891 workers (25.45%), and 1926 with 78 strikes (37.32%) and 123,754 workers (21.44%). In other words, the average workers per strike is the highest for 1925 (5,244), second for 1927 (2,671), and third for 1926 (1,586).

Table 61. The number of workers involved in labor strikes in Shanghai cotton mills, 1918-1929

Year	No. strikes		No. workers involved			%
	All strikes	Strikes with no. workers reported	Reported	Estimated	Total	
1918	5	3	5,300	3,533	8,833	1.53
1919	5	3	18,600	12,400	31,000	5.37
1920	5	5	22,000		22,000	3.80
1921	2	1	4,000	4,000	8,000	1.39
1922	7	4	14,200	10,650	24,850	4.30
1923	2	2	1,500		1,500	0.26
1924	2	1	600	600	1,200	0.22
1925	38	28	146,850	52,446	199,296	34.53
1926	78	65	103,128	20,626	123,754	21.44
1927	55	50	133,537	13,354	146,891	25.45
1928	4	4	2,771		2,771	0.48
1929	6	6	7,144		7,144	1.24
Total	209	172	459,630	117,609	577,239	100.00

In Table 62 the strikes in Shanghai cotton mills from 1918 to 1929 are classified by matters in and results of strike. This table shows that of the 209 strikes 151 or 72.25 percent are related to collective bargaining, the remaining 58 strikes or 27.75 percent being not so related. The strikes related to collective bargaining are classified into two groups, namely, (1) those concerning trade unions or collective agreement; and (2) those concerning the conditions of work including (a) wages, (b) hours of labor, (c) engagement or dismissal of workers, (d) treatment, (e) factory regulations, (f) system of work, and (g) others. The strikes not related to collective bargaining are also divided into three groups, namely, (1) sympathetic, (2) political, and (3) others. Among all these groups the engagement or dismissal of workers leads with 50 strikes, after which

Table 62. An analysis of labor strikes in Shanghai cotton mills by subject matters and results, 1918-1929

Matters in dispute			Entirely accepted	Partially accepted	Rejected	Indeterminate or unknown	Total
A. Disputes related to collective bargaining	I. Concerning trade unions or collective agreement	1. Trade unionism	1		2	1	4
		2. Collective agreement	2				2
	II. Concerning conditions of work	1. Wages	22	11	9	3	45
		2. Hours of labor	3	2	5		10
		3. Engagement or dismissal of workers	10	17	19	4	50
		4. Treatment	3		2	1	6
		5. Factory regulations	3	2	7	2	14
		6. System of work	4	1	3		8
		7. Others	2	1	5	4	12
B. Disputes not related to collective bargaining	I. Sympathetic		1	3	2	7	13
	II. Political		14	19	2		35
	III. Others		2	1	5	2	10
Total			67	57	61	24	209

follow wages with 45 strikes and political causes with 35 strikes. These three groups claim 130 of the 209 strikes. The prominence of political strikes is chiefly due to the May 30 incident in 1925 and the Northern Expedition in February, 1927. Among the other groups the more important include the following: 14 strikes for factory regulations, 13 sympathetic strikes, 10 strikes for hours of work, 8 strikes for systems of work, and 6 strikes for treatment. Of these 209 strikes, the results are given for 185 strikes. The demands for 67 strikes are entirely accepted, those for 57 strikes partially accepted, and those for 61 strikes rejected (Fig. 30).

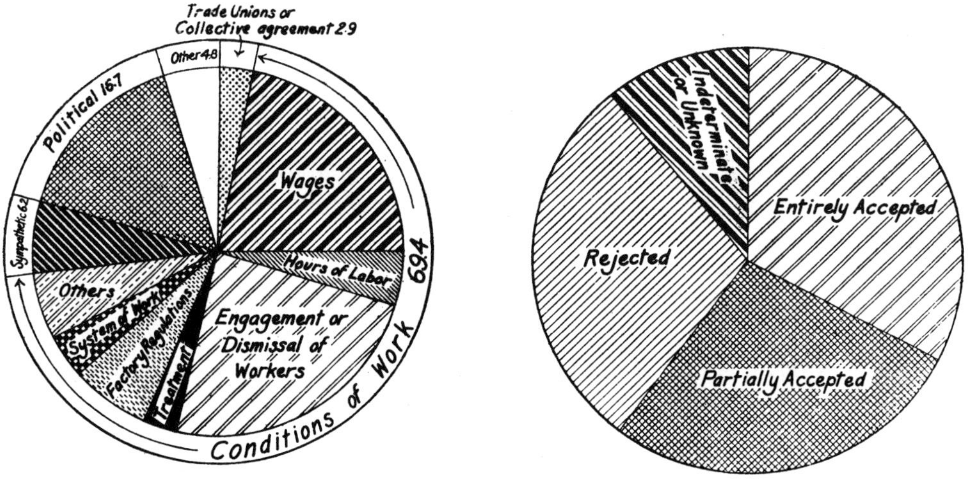

Fig. 30. Distribution of labor strikes in Shanghai cotton mills according to subject matters and results, 1918-1929 (*See* Table 62)

The methods of mediation for the labor strikes are not always given in every case, especially during the first few years of the period covered. The workers' representatives may negotiate directly with the management, but if that fails, the local police whose presence is quite common in early strikes may serve as the mediator. Sometimes when the strike assumes a more serious character, the local gentry and other public bodies such as the Chamber of Commerce, the Students' Association and the Women's Association may be called in for settlement. In 1925 when the General Labor Union was organized, it began to play a leading part as the negotiator for workers. It served as a mediator when the cotton workers' union failed to reach at an agreement with the management. In 1927 the labor unions were placed under the supervision of the Kuomingtang party, and a move towards their reorganization, with a view to eliminating the radical elements, was initiated. As a result, the Labor Purification Committee was formed, which also served as the mediator in industrial disputes including strikes, independently or jointly with the local Kuomingtang party. Beginning with 1928 the newly promulgated Labor Disputes Act placed a large share of responsibility upon the Conciliation Committee of the Bureau of Social Affairs of the City Government of Greater Shanghai. Usually a case of dispute is first referred to the Committee. Indeed, according to the Regulations for Labor Disputes promulgated by the National Government, and the rules governing their application in Greater Shanghai, the Committee is the only legal authority for the conciliation of labor conflicts. The decision of the Conciliation Committee is not enforceable, however, unless accepted by both parties. In case of acceptance this decision has the force of an agreement between the parties. If the conciliation proceedings lead to no result, arbitration by the Arbitration Committee of the City Government may be requested by common agreement between the parties, or ordered by the administrative authorities. The latter has the force of an agreement between the parties.[35]

The importance of the strikes may be judged by the number of mills affected, the number of workers involved, the duration of strikes, and the number of man-days lost. Since the basic unit of a strike is for our purpose defined as the mill, or several mills of one company when they strike at the same time for the same subject matter, the number of mills affected seldom exceeds one, except for a few mills each of which possesses several plants. Naigai Wata, a Japanese mill, possesses 11 plants, while Japan-China, also a Japanese mill, possesses 4 plants. Consequently, of the 209 strikes, the number of mills affected is one for 194 strikes, two for 7 strikes, three for 2 strikes, five for 1 strike, ten for 2 strikes, and eleven for 3 strikes.

Statistics are not always given on the number of workers involved and the duration of strikes. Again, when the number of workers involved is given, its duration is omitted. But both sets of statistics are essential to the calculation of the number of man-days lost during the strike . In our study of the 209 strikes in Shanghai mills, statistics on the number of workers involved are given for 172 strikes, those on the duration of strikes for 184 strikes, and those on both aspects for 155 strikes. In Tables 63, 64 and 65 the labor strikes in Shanghai mills are distributed by the number of workers involved, the duration of strikes, and the number of man-days lost. Table 63 shows that among the 155 strikes, 1,001-10,000 workers are involved in each of the 100 strikes, 101-1,000 workers in each of the 40 strikes, less than 10 workers in each of the 10 strikes, and over 10,000 workers in each of the 5 strikes. Table 64 shows that among the 155 strikes 2-10 days are lost in each of the 87 strikes, 11-50 days in each of the 33 strikes, less than 2 days in each of the 30 strikes, over 100 days in each of the 3 strikes, and 51-100 days in each of the 2 strikes.

35. *Strikes and lockouts in Greater Shanghai*, 1929, pp. 8-9.

Table 63. Distribution of labor strikes in Shanghai cotton mills according to the number of workers involved, 1918-1929

No. workers	1918	1919	1920	1921	1922	1923	1924	1925	1926	1927	1928	1929	Total
Less than 10													
10 - 100									6	1	1	2	10
101 - 1,000	1	1	(1)			2	1	4 (2)	23(1)	6	1(1)	1	40 (5)
1,001 - 10,000	2	2	4	1	4			8(10)	33(1)	42	1	3	100(11)
Over 10,000								3 (1)	1	1			5 (1)
Total	3	3	4(1)	1	4	2	1	15(13)	63(2)	50	3(1)	6	155(17)

Note: The bracketed figures indicate the number of strikes for which only the number of workers involved is given.

Table 64. Distribution of labor strikes in Shanghai cotton mills according to duration, 1918-1929.

No. days	1918	1919	1920	1921	1922	1923	1924	1925	1926	1927	1928	1929	Total
Less than 2					(2)			3(5)	20(6)	6		1	30(13)
2 - 10	3	3(1)	3	1(1)	4	2	1	4(3)	33(4)	28(3)	2	3	87(12)
11 - 50			1		(1)			4	10(2)	15	1	2	33 (3)
51 - 100								1	(1)	1			2 (1)
Over 100								3					3
Total	3	3(1)	4	1(1)	4(3)	2	1	15(8)	63(13)	50(3)	3	6	155(29)

Note: The bracketed figures indicate the number of strikes for which only the duration of strikes is given.

Table 65. Distribution of labor strikes in Shanghai cotton mills according to man-days lost, 1918-1929

No. man-days lost	1918	1919	1920	1921	1922	1923	1924	1925	1926	1927	1928	1929	Total
Less than 20											1		1
20 - 1,000	1							2	21	5		3	32
1,001 - 50,000	2	3	2	1	3	2	1	4	38	35	2	2	95
50,001 - 1,000,000			2		1			8	4	10		1	26
Over 1,000,000								1					1
Total	3	3	4	1	4	2	1	15	63	50	3	6	155

Table 65 shows that from 1,001 to 50,000 man-days are lost in each of the 95 strikes, 20-1,000 man-days in each of the 32 strikes, 50,001-1,000,000 man-days in each of the 26 strikes, and less than 20 days or over 1,000,000 days in one strike respectively. This table may be read together with Table 66, in which the actual number of man-days lost is given for the strikes during the 12 years from 1918 to 1929. According to that table 6,721,956.5 man-days were lost during the 155 strikes, giving an average loss of 43,367 man-days per strike. The highest number of man-days lost, however, is that for 1925, 231,657; while the lowest is that for 1923, 3,000.

Table 66. The number of man-days lost in Shanghai cotton mill strikes, 1918-1929

Year	No. strikes	No. workers involved	No. strikes	No. days lost	No. strikes	No. man-days lost	Average man-days lost per strike
1918	3	5,300	3	15	3	42,900	14,300
1919	3	18,600	3(1)	17	3	86,800	28,933
1920	4(1)	21,000(1,000)	4	33	4	177,000	44,250
1921	1	4,000	1(1)	4	1	16,000	16,000
1922	4	14,200	4(3)	30	4	121,600	30,400
1923	2	1,500	2	8	2	6,000	3,000
1924	1	600	1	10	1	6,000	6,000
1925	15(3)	98,750(48,100)	15(8)	547	15	3,474,850	231,657
1926	63(12)	98,928(4,200)	63(13)	355.5	63	964,101	15,303
1927	50	133,537	50(3)	623.3	50	1,659,623.5	33,192
1928	3(1)	2,441(330)	3	26	3	38,268	12,756
1929	6	7,144	6	64.2	6	128,814	21,469
Total	155(17)	406,000(53,630)	155(29)	1,733	155	6,721,956.5	43,367

Note: The bracketed figures refer to the strikes for which only the number of workers involved or the duration of strikes is given.

In Tientsin the strikes in cotton mills are much fewer in number than in Shanghai. Whereas the number of strikes from 1925 to 1929 is 181 in Shanghai, in Tientsin it is only 6. In 1925 there were four strikes in Tientsin, but after that year only one strike had taken place in 1926 and 1928 respectively. Since 1929, however, strikes have become more frequent in Tientsin. In 1930 there were three strikes, while in 1931 four strikes have taken place up to June.[36]

Besides the 13 strikes during the period 1925-1931, there were 7 disputes not resulting in strikes. There were, in other words, 20 labor disputes in Tientsin mills, if the term labor dispute be broadly interpreted

36. The strike data are compiled from the local newspapers.

as to include the strike. In Table 67 these disputes are distributed among different years as follows: 4 in 1925, 1 in 1926 and 1928 respectively, 2 in 1929, 6 in 1930 and 6 in 1931 up to the end of June. Yu Yuan mill, employing 6,395 workers or 36.9% of the total (17,335) workers in Tientsin mills, leads with 7 disputes during the period, after which follows Yu Ta with six disputes. Both mills, incidentally, are directly or indirectly affiliated with Japanese interests. The former is heavily indebted to the Japanese banks, while the latter is already under Japanese ownership. Pao Cheng, which is heavily indebted to the American firm, Andersen Meyer & Co., has two disputes during the period.

Table 67. Monthly distribution of labor disputes in Tientsin cotton mills, 1925-1931

	1925	1926	1927	1928	1929	1930	1931	Total
Jan.							1	1
Feb.							2(1)	2(1)
Mar.		1(1)						1(1)
Apr.							1(1)	1(1)
May					1			1
June				1(1)			2(2)	3(3)
July	1(1)					1		2(1)
Aug.	3(3)					1(1)		4(4)
Sep.						1(1)		1(1)
Oct.						1		1
Nov.					1	2(1)		3(1)
Dec.								
Total	4(4)	1(1)		1(1)	2	6(3)	6(4)	20(13)

Note: In this and the following tables the bracketed figures refer to strikes.

Table 68. Labor disputes in Tientsin cotton mills, 1925-1931

	1925	1926	1927	1928	1929	1930	1931	Total
Yu Yuan		1(1)			2	2(1)	2(2)	7(4)
Heng Yuan				1(1)			1	2(1)
Peiyang						1		1
Hua Hsin						1(1)		1(1)
Pao Cheng	2(2)							2(2)
Yu Ta	1(1)					2(1)	3(2)	6(4)
All	1(1)							1(1)
Total	4(4)	1(1)		1(1)	2	6(3)	6(4)	20(13)

The workers involved in the 13 strikes amount to 44,900, giving an average of 3,454 workers per strike, while the workers involved in the 20 disputes amount to 67,200, giving an average of 3,360 workers per dispute. 1925, however, leads with the largest number of workers in dispute, 19,500, after which follow 1930 with 17,400 workers, and 1931 with 12,600 workers.

Table 69. The number of workers involved in labor disputes in Tientsin cotton mills, 1925-1931

	Strikes		Disputes	
	No.	Workers	No.	Workers
1925	4	19,500	4	19,500
1926	1	5,700	1	5,700
1927				
1928	1	2,000	1	2,000
1929			2	10,000
1930	3	9,800	6	17,400
1931	4	7,900	6	12,600
Total	13	44,900	20	67,200

In Table 70 the matters in and results of the disputes are shown. Among the 20 disputes 11 disputes are caused by wages, 3 by engagement or dismissal of workers, 2 by systems of work and the other 4 by trade unionism, hours of labor, factory regulations and others. The results of these disputes, on the whole, are more favorable to the workers than the management, as the demands for 10 disputes are entirely accepted and those for 4 disputes partially accepted. The demands for five disputes are rejected, thus leaving one dispute with indeterminate result.

Table 70. An analysis of labor disputes in Tientsin cotton mills by subject matters and results, 1925-1931

Matters in dispute			Entirely accepted	Partially accepted	Rejected	Indeterminate or unknown	Total
A. Disputes related to collective bargaining	I. Concerning trade unions or collective agreement	1. Trade unionism	1				1
		2. Collective agreement					
	II. Concerning conditions of work	1. Wages	6(4)		4(4)	1	11(8)
		2. Hours of labor	1				1
		3. Engagement or dismissal of workers	1(1)	2(1)			3(2)
		4. Treatment					
		5. Factory regulation			1		1
		6. System of work	1(1)	1(1)			2(2)
		7. Others					
B. Disputes not related to collective bargaining	I. Sympathetic						
	II. Political						
	III. Others			1(1)			1(1)
Total			10(6)	4(3)	5(4)	1	20(13)

In Tables 71 and 72 the importance of the disputes is measured by the number of workers involved and the duration of dispute. Table 71 shows that 1,001 to 10,000 workers are involved in each of the 16 disputes, 101 to 1,000 workers in each of the 3 disputes, and over 10,000 workers in 1 dispute. Table 72 shows that the duration of dispute is 2 to 10 days for 10 disputes, less than 2 days for 6 disputes, and 11 to 50 days for 4 disputes.

Table 71. Distribution of labor disputes in Tientsin cotton mills according to the number of workers involved, 1925-1931

No. workers	1925	1926	1927	1928	1929	1930	1931	Total
Less than 10								
10 - 100								
101 - 1,000						1	2(2)	3(2)
1,001 - 10,000	3(3)	1(1)		1(1)	2	5(3)	4(2)	16(10)
Over 10,000	1(1)							1(1)
Total	4(4)	1(1)		1(1)	2	6(3)	6(4)	20(13)

Table 72. Distribution of labor disputes in Tientsin cotton mills according to duration, 1925-1931

No. days	1925	1926	1927	1928	1929	1930	1931	Total
Less than 2	2(2)					(2)	4(3)	6(7)
2 - 10	2(2)	1(1)		1(1)		4(1)	2(1)	10(6)
10 - 50					2	2		4
51 - 100								
Over 100								
Total	4(4)	1(1)		1(1)	2	6(3)	6(4)	20(13)

In Table 73 the number of man-days lost during the 13 strikes is shown, according to which the number of man-days lost is 1,001 to 50,000 for 9 strikes and 20 to 1,001 for 4 strikes. This table may be read together with Table 74, in which the actual number of man-days lost is shown. For the 13 strikes from 1925 to 1931 95,442 man-days were lost, giving an average loss of 7,342 man-days per strike. Because of the two prolonged strikes in 1926, the one lasting 13 days and the other 17 days, the average loss is the highest for that year, namely, 28,500 man-days.

Table 73. Distribution of labor strikes in Tientsin cotton mills according to man-days lost, 1925-1931

No. man-days lost	1925	1926	1927	1928	1929	1930	1931	Total
Less than 20								
20 - 1,000						1	3	4
1,001 - 50,000	4	1		1		2	1	9
50,001 - 1,000,000								
Over 1,000,000								
Total	4	1		1		3	4	13

Table 74. The number of man-days lost in Tientsin cotton mill strikes, 1925-1931

Year	No. strikes	No. workers involved	No. days lost	No. man-days lost	Average no. man-days lost per strike
1925	4	19,500	7.	24,000	6,000
1926	1	5,700	5	28,500	28,500
1927					
1928	1	2,000	3	6,000	6,000
1929					
1930	3	9,800	5	6,700	2,233
1931	4	7,900	5.7	30,242	7,561
Total	13	44,900	25.7	95,442	7,342

Labor Legislation

Labor conditions:—Apart from the workers' attempt to organize for collective bargaining, and to enforce such bargaining through strike as the last resort, labor legislation offers another solution to the labor problems in Chinese industries. Recently, several labor laws have been passed by the National Government which have a significant bearing upon all industries, especially the cotton industry. These laws include the Labor Disputes Act promulgated on June 9, 1928 and amended on March 17, 1930; the Labor Union Act promulgated on October, 21, 1929 and enforced on November 1, 1929; and the Factory Act promulgated on December 30, 1929 and enforced on the first of August, 1931.

The Factory Act, the most important of the labor laws so far promulgated, regulates the conditions of work in power driven plants employing 30 or more workers, of which cotton mills offer the best example. As it now stands, the Act may produce significant effects upon the parties concerned,—the worker, the employer and the public. From the worker's viewpoint, the Act, if effectively enforced, constitutes his *Magna Carta* or bill of rights. In the first place, it reduces the risks of labor. The provisions on the termination of contracts insure him against sudden and unreasonable loss of employment, as employers desiring to cancel a contract for which no time stipulation is made can only do so by serving to the worker a notice in advance, according to the length of service. Thus a worker with from 3 to 12 months' service is entitled to 10 days' notice, and the periods of notice range up to 30 days in case of a worker with more than three years' service. Where the employer terminates the contract with advance notice he must pay, in addition to due wages, an extra sum equal to one half of the due wages for the notice period; where the employer terminates the contract forthwith he must pay besides the due wages an extra sum equal to the full amount of the due wages for the notice period. A worker under notice is entitled to leave of absence, not exceeding two days a week, without loss of wage, in order to enable him to find other work. Again, the provisions on health and safety protect the workers against the risks of accident and sickness which have been very much neglected by the cotton mills in China. Safety provisions are to be made against life and bodily risks of the workers, in the structural details of the factory, in the fencing of machines, and in the prevention of fire and flood. Health provisions are to be made in respect of good ventilation, pure drinking water, suitable lavatories and toilet facilities, good lighting, and poison prevention. Before the passage of the social insurance laws the factory is to be responsible for the medical and living expenses of the sick or the injured according to the following scales. For temporary disability through injury or sickness arising from the performance of his work, the worker is to receive, besides free medical treatment, a benefit amounting to two-thirds of his regular daily wages for a period of six months, and upon the expiration of that period, if the worker is still not recovered, he is to receive a benefit amounting to one half of the regular daily wages, for the period of one year. For permanent total or partial disability the benefit is to be fixed in proportion to the worker's loss of earning capacity. The maximum amount of such benefit is not to exceed the average wages for three years and the minimum amount is not to fall below the average wages for one year. In case of death the legal heirs are to receive from the factory fifty dollars for funeral expenses, plus a compensation amounting to 300 dollars and two years' average wages.

A second favorable effect of the Factory Act from the worker's viewpoint is the improvement in wages. The Act introduces a new principle under which women are to be paid the same rate as men if they perform the same kind of work with equal efficiency. Again, employers are not allowed to deduct in advance a part of the worker's wages as a deposit for compensation of damages, or security for fines in case of breach of contract. Other provisions, relating to higher pay for overtime work and bi-weekly payment of wages, are already in force in many of the mills. The requirement that minimum wages be fixed according to local conditions and standard is difficult of application. Although figures on family budget inquiry have been collected for Shanghai and Tientsin, yet those for other districts are still lacking. In southern mills the price of rice has always been taken as the criterion that measures more accurately than any other single factor what it costs the workers to live. Many agreements have involved the payment of a "rice allowance" if the price of rice rises above a certain amount.

A third favorable effect relates to the hours of work. The enforcement of the Factory Act may lead to the replacement of the present two shift system by the three shift system, as in China cotton mills operate continuously from day to night. The law provides that the regular working day for adults is to be eight hours, but for local circumstances and if the nature of the work require the working day may be increased to 10 hours, and in the case of *force majeure* even to 12 hours, although overtime work (above 10, not 8) may not exceed 36 hours a month. Since the law also provides that workers are not to work longer than five hours without a period of rest of half an hour, the working hours per day and night may be reduced from 24 to 22½ under the three shift system, with a reduction of the actual working hours per shift from 8 to 7½ hours. In view of this further loss the mills may possibly ask for an extension of the working hours from 8 to 10 under the two shift system. If under the ten hour system a further grant of overtime limit be granted, which is 36 hours per month, the hours of work in cotton mills will not be much altered after the operation of the law. The mill, in that case, will have 18 days of the month working under the 12 hour shift, leaving about 10 days at the ten hour length. The number of days per month on which overtime may be worked is not specified, and the allowance of 36 hours per month is liberal enough to nullify the ten-hour day, completely setting aside the eight hour day suggested. Thus the number of hours suggested is not widely different from that now existing in the cotton industry. Provision for overtime payment, however, is a safeguard.[37]

As is the practice in some of the cotton mills today, the law provides that one day's rest per week is to be given and all factories are to stop work on holidays designated by law or by order of the government. However ,a new feature is introduced under which workers with one to three years' service are to be given seven days' rest a year, those with three to four years' service, 10 days' rest, five to ten years' service, 14 days' rest, and over 10 years' service an additional day for each year, but no more than 30 days altogether. The clause of importance in all these cases is that workers are to be given their regular wages for the statutory holidays and all rest days; if they do not wish to take the rest days they are to be paid additional wages. Here, as is pointed out by an experienced lady inspector from the West, "lies the crux of the situation. The economy of the country generally is adjusted to the provision of a weekly wage which, for working six days, provides maintenance for seven. If work is upon a piece work basis, it is usually such that it needs both skill and full working time to earn sufficient wages. The application of this clause, just though it is, and essential if the workers are to be prevented from working on Sunday—or a seventh day—will mean much immediate adjustment for managements. From the point of the annual holidays' payment, if it is meant to replace the custom of half or full

37. Hinder, Eleanor M.: China's New Factory Law, in *Chinese Recorder*, March, 1931, p. 152.

months' wages at Chinese New Year, the situation will not change much from that at present obtaining."[38]

A fourth favorable effect relates to child and woman labor. The employment of child workers under the age of 14 is prohibited in all factories, but those who are now 12 and over and at present employed may continue in employment. The presumption is that any child worker now under 12 shall cease forthwith to work. Child workers, i.e. those between the ages of 14 and 16, are not to work later than 7 p.m. or earlier than 6 a.m. Women are not to be employed later than 10 p. m. or earlier than 6 a. m. The restriction on the age of child labor, the reduction in the hours of work and the prohibition of night work for child and woman labor, reduce the unfair competition of child and woman labor to man labor on the one hand; while on the other, they help to safeguard the health and welfare of child and woman labor. It is true that the immediate effects of these provisions will be rather unfavorable, as their enforcement may result in the temporary unemployment for the classes affected—the child and woman workers. In the long run, however, the beneficial features of the Act will more than counteract the losses arising from the new adjustment.

Finally, the workers are given the right to 'joint control' under the new Factory Act. The latter provides for workers' representation, which is still an unknown practice in China. The works council, which is to be composed of equal number of representatives of the employer and the workers, is to promote the efficiency, to improve industrial relations and settle industrial disputes, to assist in the enforcement of contracts and factory regulations, to deliberate and decide upon the overtime work, to propose improvements in the factory and to make plans for the workers' welfare. The employers' representatives are to be selected by the employers from those familiar with the factory or labor conditions, while the workers' representatives are to be elected by the workers over 18 years of age from among themselves in the same factory, who must be Chinese citizens over 24 years of age and having worked at the factory for at least half a year. The representatives from each side are to elect a chairman, to preside in turn at the works council meetings, which are to be held regularly once a month, but special meetings may be convened if necessary.

In short, the new Act reduces the risks of labor such as unemployment, accident and sickness; improves the wage scale; shortens the hours of work; minimizes the evils of child and woman labor; and gives the worker the right to joint control in his workshop. It is a bill of right for the workers. But from the viewpoint of the employer, the Factory Act is a highly costly measure. The reduction in working hours

38. *Ibid*, p. 153.

may lead to a reduction of output, with a simultaneous increase in overhead cost. Whether the wages be paid on time or on piece basis, the workers will not stand for a decrease of wages because of shorter working hours. It is reasonable to argue that with shorter hours of work, an increase in efficiency may offset the losses from higher wages. Such an argument, however, remains to be proven in the cotton industry where machine labor rather than manual work predominates. Further, the economic losses of the employer will be enhanced by the provisions for health, safety, education, motherhood pension, and workmen's compensation, as well as those on wage payments for rest days, rest periods, and legal holidays. The provisions on child and woman labor, under which the age for child labor is raised to 14 and the night work for child and woman is prohibited entirely, not only confront the mill owners with the difficult problem of recruiting new hands, but also impose upon them the heavy expenses arising from the recruiting of new workers. Eventually, the employer will pass on all these losses to the consuming public, in the form of higher price. Indeed, labor legislation, like any other piece of social legislation, is an outlay for the nation at large, although its beneficial effects, in terms of greater social welfare, cannot be accurately measured.

It is plain from the above analysis that some sections in the Factory Act require further consideration, and cannot be uniformly enforced at one time. Dr. Chen Ta, in a recent study on "The Applicability of the Factory Act", suggests that a time limit of varied length be granted for the enforcement of the different sections of the Act. His conclusions are based upon a personal investigation of 228 factories in Shanghai, including 62 factories or 27.2% in the cotton industry; and are rather conservative. According to Dr. Chen some sections of the Act may be enforced at once if somewhat modified, while others, with or without modification, require a period of one, two, or three years for enforcement. Among the sections for immediate enforcement Dr. Chen recommends a day and night shift of ten hours each for women and children in all industries except when women are engaged in seasonal industries with special permits for each occasion worked and when national and other emergency situations arise. Night work for child and woman labor is permitted with the same working hours until after three years. The rest days are to be reduced from four days per month with pay under the Act to two days without pay; but no change is made in the number of legal holidays (8 per year with pay). The sections on health and safety are accepted *in toto*, with the condition however that benefits be given for industrial disease instead of sickness. Motherhood pension, which includes four weeks' leave with pay, is to be enforced only after one year, while after two years the hours of work in the day shift are to be reduced from ten to eight for child labor, so that supplementary education may be provided for during the extra two hours. The age limit for child labor, however, is to be reduced from fourteen to twelve, at the very beginning of the enforcement of the Act. Still other sections, relating to minimum wage, annual leave, employment contract, and sickness benefit, are to be postponed indefinitely.[39]

That the Factory Act cannot be enforced *in toto* at one time is plain enough; it has now become an established fact. Although the date set for the enforcement of the Act, August, 1, 1931, has abready passed, no concrete action has yet been taken towards its enforcement. Indeed, the Act as it now stands requires considerable revision. As has been well remarked by an experienced lady factory inspector of the West who is also familiar with Chinese conditions, the Act is "a goal the reaching of which in five or seven years of steady progress might be regarded as a splendid achievement."[40]

Labor unions and disputes:—Labor unions and labor disputes are provided for respectively in the Labor Union Act and the Labor Disputes Act. According to the former, all workers at least 16 years of age of the same industry or trade with a view to increasing their knowledge, skill, productive capacity, maintaining or improving their working conditions and standard of living may gather together at least 100 in number employed in the same industry or at least 50 in number employed in the same trade and organize a union, provided that such union be duly registered with the proper authority, and be the only one of its kind in the district. Further, such union may be permitted to form a federation with the other unions of the same industry or trade in other districts, although approval must be obtained of the government for affiliation with a foreign labor union. The union is a juristic person, which is to be concurrently held responsible if the directors of a union or their agents do damage to other persons. A worker shall be allowed to become the member of only one labor union, whether it be an industrial or a trade union. A union, meantime, shall not compel any person to become a member nor shall it prevent any person from resigning his membership. It shall not interfere with the work of non-member workers. On the other hand, an employer or his agent is not to reject an applicant for work or dismiss an employee or accord other unfavorable treatment to him because of his affiliation with a union, nor is he to demand his employee as a condition of employment to refrain from participating in the activities of the union or from enrolling as members of the union or to resign their membership. The duties and functions of a union are largely economic, which are however beyond the financial resources of a union if faithfully carried out. These duties, according to the Act, shall be (1) to conclude, revise or

39. The Chinese version is published in *Shun Pao*, a noted Chinese newspaper in Shanghai, July 31, Aug. 1-2, 1931; but an English version has recently been issued by the China Institute of Scientific Management, 1931, Shanghai.
40. Hinder, *op. cit.*, p. 149.

cancel collective agreements, (2) to recommend its members for employment and to establish employment offices, (3) to establish savings institutions, labor insurance organizations, hospitals, clinics and day nurseries, (4) to organize cooperative societies, (5) to provide vocational and workers' education, (6) to establish libraries and reading rooms, (7) to issue printed matters, (8) to organize social gatherings, clubs and other recreational activities, (9) to settle disputes between labor unions or between own members of the union, (10) to settle disputes between the employers and the employees, (11) to submit its views to the administrative, judicial or legislative authorities on the enactment, revision or cancellation of labor laws and ordinances, (12) to investigate the workers' home, living and economic conditions and their state of employment or unemployment and to compile labor statistics, and (13) to undertake other measures to improve working conditions and to further the interests of its members. It is provided that the proper authority may render necessary assistance to the union in performing these duties and functions, but despite such provision, the union will certainly be unable to perform one half of the duties enumerated for the coming decade or so. Not to mention the presence of the high degree of illiteracy as well as the lack of experience of the workers in all these matters, the financial strength of the union alone will disqualify it from the performance of some of them. The Act provides that a union may collect fees from its members, but the amount of admission fee shall not exceed the small sum of one dollar for each member and the regular dues shall not exceed two percent of each member's income. The latter, according to our study of wages, amount only to $2.94 per year in Tientsin and $2.86 per year in Shanghai. Indeed, in Tientsin mills an investigation of the Social Affairs Bureau in 1929 shows that among the five cotton workers' unions in the five mills the union in Heng Yuan was the only one that succeeded in collecting fifty dollars per month from membership dues, which if distributed among the 3,076 members in the union, amounted only to 1.62 cents per month or 31.44 cents per year per member. Each of the five unions, meantime, derived its income partly or solely from the mill's subsidy, amounting to $250 per month for the union in Yu Yuan (5,011 members), $85 for that in Peiyang (1,740 members), $70 for that in Hua Hsin (2,212 members), $30 for that in Pao Cheng (1,279 members), and $30 for that in Heng Yuan (3,076 members). In addition, the unions in Hua Hsin and Pao Cheng derived respectively an income of $30 per month from the sale of night soil. In Pao Cheng the union had an additional income of about $20 per month from fines.[41]

In respect of labor disputes including strikes, the Labor Union Act provides that in case of dispute between the employer and the workers,

41. *Social Affairs Monthly*, published by the Social Affairs Bureau of the Special Municipality of Tientsin, Vol. I, Nos. 5-6, December, 1931.

no strike shall be declared unless attempts have first been made to settle it by means of conciliation and arbitration, and unless the case has subsequently been referred to a general meeting of the union, at which at least two-thirds of its members have voted by secret ballot in favor of the strike. On the other hand, an employer or his agent shall not dismiss any of his employees when the dispute is pending during the period of conciliation and arbitration. In the Labor Disputes Act the machinery for conciliation and arbitration is provided for. The conciliation board, which is to be composed of one or three representatives from the administrative authority and two representatives appointed by the employer and the employees respectively, is to be convened by the administrative authority *ex officio*, or at the request of one or both of the parties concerned. When a dispute is submitted for conciliation, the parties shall appoint their representatives within three days of the receipt of the official notification. The conciliation board, after having been convened, shall begin the investigation of the dispute not more than two days after the convention, the duration of which shall not exceed seven days except on special grounds. On the conclusion of such investigation, the conciliation board shall issue its decision within two days except under special circumstances, which shall have the force of contract between the parties concerned. If the attempt at conciliation is not successful the case, at the request of one or both of the parties, shall be referred to an arbitration board for arbitration, which is to be composed of five representatives from the administrative authority, the Kuomingtang, the court, the employer and the employees respectively. The board shall be convened as soon as written application is filed by the parties concerned, which shall draw up within two days a statement of its decisions in writing. Such decisions, which shall be adopted by a majority vote of the entire board, shall have the force of contract if either party make no objection within five days of receiving the award of the arbitration board. Like the Labor Union Act, the Labor Disputes Act provides that during the time of conciliation and arbitration neither strike nor lockout shall be ordered by the party concerned.

Welfare work

Living accommodations:—Strictly speaking, welfare work refers to all activities undertaken by the management for the workers' benefit, the commonest forms of which in Tientsin mills include the hospital, the school, and the employee store. The workers' hospital has been dealt with in a previous section on industrial accident and diesease, while the school, the employee store and other welfare activities, both in Shanghai and in Tientsin, may be reviewed here in a broader sense, embracing those activities not necessarily promoted under the management's initiative.

These activities include living accomodations, education and recreation, and savings.

In respect of living accomodations, it is a widespread practice among the cotton mills to provide for the workers' dining room. Although in a few mills the workers take their meals in working rooms, yet in a great majority of them separate rooms have been built for such purpose. Next to the dining room a public kitchen is maintained together with a water pot, where the workers may steam their rice or bread and get hot water for drinking or washing. Sometimes, a nursery is built where female workers may leave their babies during work time. The housing of workers in the dormitories at a low rent is also a common practice. Indeed, the Kung Ta Mill in Shanghai, the property of the wealthy Kanegafuchi Company in Japan, "has its own Chinese village in the compound, provides supervision, hospitals, baths, clubhouses, stores, schools, gardens, play-grounds, dining halls, etc."[42] In Tientsin the workers' dormitories are found in Yu Yuan, Heng Yuan, Hua Hsin, Peiyang and Pao Cheng. In Heng Yuan, even meals are prepared for the workers, especially the apprentices. A third form of living accomodations is the employee store. In Yu Yuan the store is an employee store *par excellence,* as it is supervised and financed by the mill. In Heng Yuan it is nominally a consumers' co-operative organized by the workers, but actually receives financial support from the mill. In Yu Yuan the employee store was organized on the first of October, 1927. It deals in necessaries such as flour, rice, cloth, etc., not in luxuries; and confines its business to the employees only. The latter are allowed to purchase at the store on credit, at an amount not exceeding their wage claim against the mill. As the wage is paid at the end of every half month period, such claim cannot exceed the wages for fourteen days. The employee, moreover, is not allowed to purchase on credit until he has accumulated five days' wage claim on his paybook. Since the chief object of the store is to sell below the market price to the employees, the regulation that no employee is allowed to purchase an amount above his wage claim, even in cash, is enforced in order to prevent any purchase on behalf of non-employees. For the monthly worker (i.e. those paid on a monthly basis) the maximum purchase is equivalent to his monthly wage. However, in case of funeral or wedding, this regulation does not apply, and the employee is allowed to purchase according to needs. The business hours for the store are from 9 A.M. to 7 P.M., but during the first few days when credit sale is allowed (i.e. when five days' wage has been accumulated on the pay book), they may be postponed until 11 P.M.

In Yu Yuan store the total sale during 1929 amounted to $313,405.49, giving a monthly average of $26,117.12; it was equivalent to about one third of the total money wages (excluding bonus) for 1928, namely,

42. Pearse, *op. cit.,* p. 169.

$973,233. Judging by the large amount of sales, the profit made, $1,531.06, is rather small, as the chief object of the store is to reduce the cost of distribution for the employees. Among the selling expenses the largest item goes to interest, amounting to as much as $1,710.98 or 33.7 percent of the total selling expense, as the store is financed by loans from the local banks, at a monthly interest rate of one percent. A total interest charge of $1,710.98 for the whole year, or an average monthly charge of $142.58, means an average monthly loan of $14,258.00 from the banks, in order to finance an average monthly sale of $26,117.12. On the whole, the store is meeting a real need of the workers, but it is not without its objections. The local retailers opposed it on the ground that the store took away their business not only from the employees, but also from the non-employees or local residents. Since it is difficult for the store to detect in all cases the employees' purchases on behalf of non-employees, the local retailing trade is indirectly affected. Again, instead of cultivating a sense of economy among the workers, the store has produced the contrary effect with its system of credit sale. It often happens that the worker has very little left on his paybook during the pay day, as a good part of his wages are already deducted against his purchases at the store. In 1929, the credit purchase, which amounted to a monthly average of $22,671.99, accounted for 86.81% of the average monthly sales ($26,117.12). As there were on the average 6,770 purchasers per month, each purchaser had an average credit purchase of $3.35 per month. Considering the fact that the account is settled every half month, most of the clients, if not all, must have purchased at the store for at least twice per month. The actual amount of purchase per client, therefore, must have been twice the amount given above, or $6.70. Since the average monthly earnings of a client or worker amounts to $14.69, the credit sale per month, $6.70, accounts for 45.61 percent of the average monthly earnings.

The store in Heng Yuan, the Heng Yuan Consumers' Cooperative Society, was started by the union in August, 1929, with a loan of five thousand dollars from the mill. This store, unlike that in Yu Yuan, approaches in many respects the Rochdale type. The capital of the store is subscribed by the members, at one dollar per share. No member is allowed to have more than ten shares, and each member is given one vote irrespective of the number of shares owned. The goods are sold at the market price, to both members and non-members, on a cash basis. Credit sale, however, is extended to the members for a period of half a month, which is not to exceed the amount of the member's wage claim against the mill during the period. The store does not have the right to deduct the member's purchase from the wage, as is the case in Yu Yuan store, but has to send own clerks to the member's home for collection. The profit is divided among the various participants according to the following percentages:

50% for the members, 10% for the directors, 5% for the manager and 5% for the employees, the other 30% being apportioned equally between the surplus and the public benefit fund. The profit for the members is calculated on the basis of purchase, not of capital subscription. An annual interest of five per cent is paid on the capital, provided that the member purchase at the store to the extent of at least one tenth of his average purchase. If any member wishes to withdraw, resell or mortgage his subscription, he must communicate his wish to the Board of Auditors one month in advance, and have it accepted by the Board. Unless because of removal or of death, such withdrawal deprives the member of the interest as well as the profit.

The Heng Yuan store is a limited liability organization. It had 945 members with a capital subscription of $1,171 for the first half year (August 4 to December 25, 1929), while for the second half year (December 26, 1929 to June 25, 1930) the membership was reduced to 897, and the capital subscription to $1,078. During the two half-year periods, the store reaped a profit of $1,003.12 during the first period and one of $1,678.23 during the second. The accounts receivable, however, amounted to $3,894.10 during the first period and $5,647.54 during the second. As the total purchase of the members amounted to $21,617.69 during the first period of $4\frac{2}{3}$ months and $25,277.06 during the second of 6 months, thus giving an average monthly purchase of $5,895.73 for the first period and one of $5,055.41 during the second, the ratio of accounts receivable to monthly purchase had increased from 0.66 for the first period to 1.08 for the second. This increase in the ratio is a serious drain upon the financial resources of the store, and may eventaully upset its operation. It ties up the working capital of the store, and disables it from a better and wider selection of goods for sale. The credit standing of the store is impaired, and as a result of all these factors, there is an increase in price, with a simultaneous reduction in sales. The further fact that the store, with as little circulating capital as it possessed, made a loan of $1,104.47 to the No. 1 Branch, crippled further its financial strength. This branch was started in March, 1930, but up to June 22 of the same year it had suffered a loss of $267.42.

Heng Yuan, with a working force of 3,262 in 1929, had only 945 workers or 29 percent enlisted as members of the Co-operative Society. These members, with an average monthly purchase of $5,895.73, received an average monthly wage of $6,735.40 in 1928. In other mords, they spent 86 percent of their wages for purchases at the Society. The percentage is rather high, although we are not unaware of the fact that the board for these 945 workers, amounting to an average monthly cost of $1,723.37, was provided for gratis by the mill.

Education and recreation:—Until recently workers' education is a novelty in China. Large industrial enterprises have sporadically started schools for the education of the workers and their children, but no government undertaking has been attempted until recent years. In Shanghai only 33 of the 49 mills studied by Dr. Chen provided education to the workers, at an average annual cost of $1,648.12.[43] In Tientsin workers' education was at first confined to the workers' children, but has now been extended to the workers themselves. In 5 of the 6 mills in Tientsin the schools for the workers' children can now be found. Hua Hsin School, which was started in 1920, is the oldest, and has since then graudated six classes with several hundreds of pupils. It has a fine building, with a large athletic ground. At the time of the *Institute's* investigation in 1930 the school had 122 pupils distributed among the four grades, including 90 boys and 32 girls. The first grade had 49 pupils; the second grade, 37; the third grade, 27; and the fourth grade, 9. The age of the pupils ranged from 5 to 16, but 96 pupils or 78.7% fell within the age group of 7 to 11. The curriculum was composed of Chinese, calligraphy, science, arithmetic, music, art, gymnastics, and the Three People's (or Kuomingtang) doctrine. All expenses, including tuition, books, stationery, uniform etc, were borne by the mill. The school had a faculty of six, including the principal, two men teachers and three women teachers. Yu Yuan School, which compares more favorably with Hua Hsin School in equipment, was built in the summer of 1929, at a cost of $4,000 for the building alone. The school occupies an area of 2.67 mow, with 1.9 mow for the athletic ground and 0.77 mow for the school building. For the first academic year of 1929-1930, it had an annual budget of $2,412, with three teachers and 98 pupils (82 boys and 16 girls whose age ranged from 6 to 9). During the first year the school had two grades, the first and the second, with about the same curriculum as that for Hua Hsin School. Heng Yuan School, unlike the other two schools mentioned above, was started by the Union in the Spring of 1930; it was financed partly by the public benefit fund from the Workers' Cooperative Society, and partly by voluntary contributions from the mill and the workers. Because of lack of funds, the equipment is inadequate, while the faculty is recruited from the workers without pay. Instruction is confined to the first grade, with only five hours of class work per day. No tuition is charged, but books and stationery are provided for by the pupils. For the first term the school had seven teachers and sixty pupils. Like in other schools there were more boys than girls, a phenomenon largely due to the social premium on boys under the Chinese family system.

The continuation schools for the workers were first started by the Educational Bureau of the Special Municipality of Tientsin, but because of lack of funds they are now taken over by the workers' unions in the

43. Chen, *op. cit.*, p. 39.

different mills. Such schools give daily instructions in the three subjects of Kuomingtang doctrine, arithmetic and Chinese for two hours. Each class has 40 to 80 pupils, with free tuition and free supply of books and stationery. In Yu Yuan there were two schools in the Spring of 1930, with 230 pupils. The age of these pupils ranged from 12 to 27: 12-15, 29; 16-20, 107; 21-25, 80; and 26-27, 14. In Hua Hsin the School graduated a class of 82 pupils in the Spring of 1929, and another one of 87 pupils in the winter of 1929. Since then, the school had been suspended because of the Bureau's lack of funds, but on the first of June, 1930 it was again opened under the union's support, at a monthly expenditure of 70 dollars. There were then two classes, one of 52 pupils and the other of 32 pupils, with only one teacher. In all these schools, the pupils were male workers. In the fall of 1930, a school was started for the female workers in Yu Yuan under the auspices of the local Y. W. C. A. The school held two classes of one hour each on Tuesday, Thursday, and Saturday afternoons, with instructions in Chinese and caligraphy. The books and stationery were supplied freely, and no tuition was charged. There were 36 pupils when the school opened in July, but one month later 17 of them had left on account of domestic duties and distance from home. The pupils were all young girls whose age ranged from 11 to 19, but 11 of them were from 13 to 14 years of age.

Besides the two types of schools, the worker's union in Heng Yuan has also started a library, a weekly and a technical discussion group. The library was organized in 1928, with the small appropriation of one hundred dollars left over from the workers' year-end bonus. It does not even possess a reading room, but a depository from which the workers may draw books for a period of two weeks. The library had about two hundred books in Chinese, with 500 volumes, in March, 1930. From March, 1929 to March, 1930 it had a record of 314 readers, averaging less than one reader per day. The weekly, edited by the union and known as the "Heng Yuan Union Weekly", was started in 1929, printing items interesting chiefly to the cotton workers. It contained only one mimeographed sheet of one foot and two inches by three feet per issue. The technical discussion group, also organized by the union, studied the common problems of machine technique and exchanged experience among the members. Once awhile the results of these discussions are mimeographed and circularized among the members, or turned over to the Weekly for publication.

Workers' recreation varies all the way from Chinese drama and music, story telling, novel reading, to boxing, gymnastics etc. Of these Chinese drama is the commonest choice, as many of the workers can sing a few popular songs learnt from childhood. In two of the mills in Tientsin, Yu Yuan and Heng Yuan, the workers have organized a dramatic society, with expenses partly borne by the mill, and partly defrayed from the membership dues. There are two hours of coaching every day during the week, from 7 P.M. to 9 P.M. in the evening. Occasionally a performance is staged in order to raise sufficient funds for the purchase of equipments. Both societies cater to what is called the Peking drama. But in Yu Yuan another society is formed which caters to modern drama, laying emphasis on acting rather than on singing, and dispensing with the colorful gowns and the incongruous music of the old drama. Chinese music is closely related to Chinese drama, and oftentimes a worker sings while playing on the native violin. To play on violin is not an organized recreation like drama; it is reasonable as the cost of a native violin does not exceed thirty or forty silver cents. Story telling is given in a tea house, and in this way offers double attraction to the clients. Novel reading appeals to a limited group of workers, because of the literacy requirement. Chinese boxing is also an organized undertaking. In Heng Yuan, the workers were organized into a society for the same purpose, in April, 1930, with about 80 members. In Yu Yuan an athletic ground is set aside for the workers by the mill, where boxing also is practiced. Boxing, however, is not so common as other forms of sports which can be practiced at a reasonable cost and in small groups. The raising of stone discs is one example. Such discs, two pieces of which are usually connected by a wooden handle at both ends, have a weight of 40, 80, 120,200 or 240 catties. The raising of stone discs is a common pastime for the workers in North China, as is also the throwing of sandbags. These sandbags, filled with small iron sands, are thrown from one worker to the other, at a distance of about ten feet. A third game is foot pulling, for which purpose a worker is first covered with a canvas shirt and then girded around his loins with a heavy cloth band. When one worker pulls the foot of the other by means of his own foot, the former wins if the latter falls.

Savings:—Savings is still a personal affair, for very few mills have started saving institutions on behalf of the workers. The fact that most of the workers live from hand to month and have very little left for savings is one reason. Besides, the workers prefer the old Chinese method of providing for emergency needs, in the form of borrowings or lendings. An investigation of 230 families of the cotton workers in Jessfield Village in Shanghai shows that of the various forms of borrowing, receipts from loan society, or drawings of subscriptions in advance or at the conclusion of the term of membership, were quite popular, with borrowing as the next choice. "Yin tze chien" or stamp money represents a kind of usury. The loan is contracted in a lump sum but is repaid by the debtor during stipulated periods of time in installments, which include both the principal and the interest or simply the interest. It

Table 75. Forms and amounts of borrowing for the families of cotton mill workers in Shanghai

		Receipts from loan society	Borrowing	Yin-tze-chien	Receipts from pawned articles	Purchase on credit	Loans returned
No. of families having		70	77	11	45	12	12
Highest	Amount	$221.00	$250.00	$ 36.00	$ 52.50	$ 11.00	$ 60.00
	No. of months	12	12	11	12	10	12
Lowest	Amount	$ 0.77	$ 2.00	$ 3.00	$ 0.80	$ 0.07	$ 0.20
	No. of months	11	10	9	9	1	10
Average	Amount	$ 30.03	$ 23.60	$ 13.01	$ 9.34	$ 3.98	$ 15.18
	No. of months	10.1	9.7	10.0	9.8	9.5	11.1

Table 76. Forms and amounts of lending for the families of cotton mill workers in Shanghai

		Loan society subscription	Payment of debt	Yin-tze-chien	Redeeming of pawned articles	Savings	Lending
No. of families having		159	91	23	62	6	1
Highest	Amount	$419.00	$125.00	$ 88.00	$ 28.90	$120.00	
	No. of months	12	10	11	9	10	
Lowest	Amount	$ 1.00	$ 0.02	$ 0.21	$ 0.77	$ 1.40	
	No. of months	12	2	10	11	10	
Average	Amount	$ 44.03	$ 21.14	$ 15.47	$ 7.27	$23.57	$ 19.00
	No. of months	9.3	9.7	9.2	10.1	8.8	10.0

goes without saying that the interest charged on "Yin tze chien" is exorbitant and few people care to borrow under such an arrangement unless very hard pressed. Its name is derived from the fact that a seal is stamped for each payment on a folder kept by the creditor and how the loan stands is calculated according to the number of seals stamped. In respect of lendings, loan society subscriptions, as is to be expected, were found to be quite popular among the families, next to which were savings and payment of debts. Indeed, to join a loan society either for saving or for advancing sums of money in times of need has become an institution among the Shanghai workers.[44]

Several mills, however, have started savings institutions on behalf of the workers. In Shanghai the Naigai Wata Mill gives an annual interest rate of 12 percent to any worker who deposits one half percent of his wages with the mill, at his own choice.[45] In Tientsin the Yu Yuan Mill used to require workers to deposit five percent of their wages with the Mill, but no interest was paid. Such deposit served more as a guarantee fund than a form of savings. In 1928 when the workers' union was organized, it demanded the Mill to pay interest on the deposits. Because of the complicated procedure that such payment of interest might involve, the Mill stopped the practice of requiring five percent deposit from the first of January, 1929, but instead required the workers to deposit, during each pay period, any amount below ten cents on his paybook. The latter, which nominally served as a guarantee fund, actually simplified the Mill's routine in wage computation and payment.

44. Yang, *op. cit.*, pp. 45-7.
45. *China Labor Yearbook*, III: 63-4.

CHAPTER VII. INDUSTRIAL ORGANIZATION

Introduction

As the largest factory industry of China today, cotton manufacturing is carried on in large mills with considerable outlay of capital and a great number of workers. A statistical measurement of the scale on which the industry is organized, on the basis of the data contained in the *List of Cotton Mills in China* published annually[1] since 1920 by the Chinese Cotton Millowners' Association, is perhaps the best approach to the subject. Such a list, which is highly useful but seldom compiled for any other industry in China, unfortunately fails to meet modern requirements in several respects. The statistics given are incomplete and not uniformly up-to-date, as may be shown from an analysis of the 1930 list. For some mills for which 1930 data are not available, those for earlier years are used. For the 127 mills in 1930, of which three have not yet started operation and another one has suspended work, capital investment is given for 120 mills, motive power for 119 mills, workers for 119 mills, cotton consumption for 114 mills and yarn production for 116 mills. While there are 50 weaving or weaving-and-spinning mills, statistics on cloth production are given for only 43 mills. The statistics on spindles and looms, however, are given for all of the 127 mills, including 77 spinning mills, 48 spinning-and-weaving mills and 2 weaving mills.

The statistics on cotton consumption, being the most incomplete, are also inaccurate. Fortunately, cotton statistics and yarn statistics serve as a mutual check wherever gross inconsistencies occur, for it is generally accepted that 3.5 piculs of raw cotton are required in order to produce one bale of yarn. Accepting the statistics on yarn production as being the more likely correct, statistics on cotton consumption are revised whenever for any mill they fail to bear a proportion that is 3 or 4 times to those on yarn production. The preference for 3 or 4 instead of 3.5 gives allowance for possible divergence from the commonly accepted average of 3.5, as the amount of cotton waste per bale of yarn spun varies with different mills. The revision in such a case is made by substituting the original figure on raw cotton consumption by another one which is 3.5 times that for yarn production.[2] However, for some mills where the statistics on raw cotton consumption bear a proportion more than four times to those on yarn production, the revision is made in yarn instead of in cotton statistics. This is due to the fact that in such a

1. No list, however, was issued for 1926 and 1929. A revised list for 1930 is given in the pocket at the back of the book.
2. For instance, mill 88 produced 40,643 bales of yarn, but consumed 256,744 piculs of raw cotton, giving an average cotton consumption of 6.3 piculs per bale of yarn, which is impossible under any circumstance. The revised figure, 142,250, is substituted which is obtained by multiplying 40,643 by 3.5. Again, mills 82-4 reported a total yarn production of 129, 522 bales, but a total cotton consumption of only 300,000 piculs, giving an average cotton consumption of 2.3 piculs per bale of yarn, which is also impossible under any circumstance. The revised figure, 453,327, is likewise substituted which is obtained by multiplying 129,522 by 3.5.

mill cloth is also woven, but the yarn spun by the mill and consumed in weaving the cloth is not included.[3] Again, in two mills (nos. 110-111) with 100,000 spindles and 2,000 looms, there are a cloth production of 1,440,000 pieces, a yarn production of 10,000 bales and a cotton consumption of 48,000 piculs. Here not only do the yarn statistics fail to agree with the cotton statistics, but both cotton and yarn statistics fall far short of the truth, as 1,440,000 pieces of cloth production would have required, assuming 1/40 bale of yarn for each piece of cloth, about 36,000 bales of yarn. Assuming 3.5 piculs of cotton for every bale of yarn, it would have required a cotton consumption of 126,000 piculs. Judging by the large number of spindles and looms that the mill possesses, the error lies more in an under-estimate of cotton consumption and yarn production rather than in an over-estimate of cloth production. Accordingly, we have used the revised figure in place of the original one. Applying the revision as outlined above to the original figures for cotton consumption and yarn production for the 116 mills, there is to be a decrease of 480,337 piculs in raw cotton consumption and an increase of 98,744 bales in yarn production for the mills in China. The result is that the 116 mills produced 2,445,177 bales of yarn and consumed 8,750,019 piculs of raw cotton, giving an average cotton consumption of 3.56 piculs per bale of yarn spun, which is quite close to the commonly accepted average of 3.5 piculs per bale.[4]

---

3. Thus, mill 124 wove altogether 376,000 pieces of cloth, which, if estimated at a consumption of 1/40 of a bale of yarn per piece, would have consumed 9,400 bales of yarn. The mill, in other words, produced 18,500 bales of yarn instead of the original figure of 9,100 bales, for which no revision, according to the criterion given above, need be made in the original figure of 56, 690 piculs of raw cotton.
4. The revision in statistics on cotton consumption and yarn production for 26 mills in 1930 is given below in detail.

No. of mill	Cotton consumption (piculs)		Yarn production (bales)		Cloth woven (pieces)
	Original	Revised	Original	Revised	
10			15,579	25,061	379,264
26	2,100	1,575			
27		31,500			
29	338,460	178,164	44,376	50,904	261,125
30	88,324	66,360			
36	50,000	105,000			
44	20,000	24,500			
47	21,000	17,675	4,600	5,050	18,000
52	600,000	66,500			
55	4,500	2,800			
60	151,800	112,612	24,750	32,175	297,000
73	40,000	49,000			
74	42,000	75,600			
77-8	11,500	31,500			
82-4	300,000	453,327			
88	256,744	142,250			
96	23,733	33,677			
102		52,500			
104	39,556	32,340			
109				18,459	738,360
110-1	48,000	126,000	10,000	36,000	1,440,000
113	203,000	157,500	24,000	45,000	840,000
124			9,100	18,500	376,000
Total	2,240,717	1,760,380	132,405	231,149	4,349,749

Next to cotton statistics, capital statistics are the most unsatisfactory. They are given for 120 mills only, of which one has suspended operation. Their usefulness is vitiated by several shortcomings, the greatest being the lack of uniformity. The unit of currency differs, as it may be taels, dollars, or yen. For one mill in Liaoning the capital is quoted in Fengpiao—the paper currency for the province that has depreciated greatly since the establishment of the mill in 1922. It is converted into dollars at the 1926 rate of exchange which is one dollar for 375.11 Fengpiao. The taels may be converted into dollars by assuming the common rate of exchange of one dollar to 0.72 tael or one tael to 1.39 dollars, but the exchange rate for yen fluctuates considerably. Taking 1913 as 100, in which year one yen is equivalent to 0.7167 tael in Tientsin, or about one Chinese dollar, the ratio rose to 117.90 in 1915, but fell from that year to the lowest figure of 54.97 in 1919. It rose again to the highest figure of 94.91 in 1921, but with the exception of 90.57 for 1923, it fell continuously until another lowest figure was reached in 1925, namely, 72.00. Since 1925 the rise was rapid, reaching as high as 159.77 in 1930.[5] Under such circumstances it is quite difficult to reduce the capital investment for Japanese mills in China into dollars instead of yen. However, as such investment is always quoted in yen, and remains for the most part unchanged, it seems justifiable to convert it at the rate of exchange prevailing during the year of the mill's establishment. Practically, however, a process of conversion of this kind is hardly possible. The Japanese mills in China are mostly combines, several mills being owned by one company. Consequently, as is the case with Naigai Wata Kaisha, the capital investment for the eleven mills in Shanghai owned by the company is reported in one lump sum, although the years of establishment for these eleven mills differ considerably, from the earliest of 1896 to the latest of 1923. In view of these difficulties, we have arbitrarily applied the rate of exchange in 1913 to the capital investment for all Japanese mills, in order to reduce it from the yen to the dollar basis for the purpose of comparison. That is, one Japanese yen is converted into 0.7167 tael or approximately one Chinese dollar. Another shortcoming in the capital statistics is the ambiguous interpretation of the term "capital investment." For some mills capital investment refers to the authorized capital, whereas for others it may mean the paid-up capital. But the actual capital of a mill may exceed its authorized capital, because of successful operation during the interval. On the other hand, the actual capital may have fallen below the paid-up capital, not to say the authorized capital, due to the recurrence of bad years. As there is no basis for making such a distinction in the statistics given, no revision is made, with the hope that among a sufficiently large number of mills, excesses and deficiencies may

5. Ho, Franklin L.: An Index of Foreign Exchange Rates, 1898-1926, in *Chinese Economic Journal*, February, 1928.

Table 77. Revised statistics of cotton mills in China, 1930

	Chinese			Japanese			British			Total		
	Mills	Amount	% of all mills	Mills	Amount	% of all mills	Mills	Amount	% of all mills	Mills	Amount	% of all mills
No. mills	81		63.8	43		33.9	3		2.4	127		100.0
Capital and surplus	74	126,908,222	44.0	43	148,919,916	51.6	3	12,500,000	4.4	120	288,328,138	100.0
Spindle	74	117,518,506	44.5	42	135,764,277	51.0	3	10,827,193	4.5	116	264,109,976	100.0
Loom	31	9,389,716	38.8	15	13,155,639	54.3	3	1,672,807	6.9	49	24,218,162	100.0
Spindles (Spinning)	80	2,326,872	58.6	42	1,489,360	37.5	3	153,320	3.9	125	3,969,552	100.0
Spindles (Doubling)	20	68,920	27.1	16	185,484	72.9				36	254,404	100.0
Looms	32	16,005	54.7	15	11,367	38.8	3	1,900	6.5	50	29,272	100.0
Motive power: K. W.	51*	68,363	54.0	40*	58,211	46.0				91*	126,574	100.0
H. P.	36*	31,021	80.6	6*	7,490	19.4				42*	38,511	100.0
Total K. W.*	76	91,629	58.9	43	63,828	41.1				119	155,457	100.0
No. workers	73	161,949	64.3	43	77,082	30.6	3	13,000	5.2	119	252,031	100.0
Cotton consumed (piculs)	72	5,320,692	60.8	41	2,976,000	34.0	3	453,327	5.2	116	8,750,019	100.0
Yarn spun (bales of 400 lbs)	72	1,500,248	61.1	41	825,407	33.6	3	129,522	5.3	116	2,455,177	100.0
Cloth woven (pieces)	28	6,625,544	44.8	15	8,153,994	55.2				43	14,779,538	100.0

* 11 Chinese and 3 Japanese mills employ both electric and steam power. 1 horse power is converted into ¾ kilowatt.

offset each other. A third shortcoming, which is corrected wherever it occurs, is that for some branch mills, especially of Japanese ownership, the capital investment reported refers to the mill as a whole, not to the branch alone. The two branch mills for Dai Nippon, one in Shanghai and the other in Tsingtao, were reported to have a capital investment of Yen 52,000,000 respectively, while actually both together might not have even one third of the sum, namely, Yen 17,334,000. For Naigai Wata Kaisha, having 504,440 spindles and 1,600 looms, as compared with 144,080 spindles and 759 looms for the two branch mills of Dai Nippon, has a capital investment and surplus of but Yen 42,043,426.

Technical size and size distribution

The technical aspect of a mill refers to machinery, labor, raw materials, and output, and the technical size and size distribution in these repects may be determined after a critical analysis of the statistics contained in the *List of Cotton Mills in China for 1930*. Since many of the mills in the *List* are owned by one company, their statistics are merged together in the name of the company, not in that of the mills individually. In analyzing the statistics from the standpoint of the mills individually, not of the company as a whole, some procedure has to be adopted in order to distribute the statistics among the different mils belonging to the same company. The spindle statistics, which are with the exception of a few cases reported for every mill instead of for every company, may serve as the basis for distributing the other statistics.[6] The proportion that the spindles in one mill bear to those in the other mill of the same company is applied to the cotton and labor statistics.[7] However, when the statistics for a spinning mill and a weaving mill are merged together—such as the labor statistics, the problem of distributing the workers is more complicated. The way out is to discover, as in the case of Chinese owned mills 57-58, the number of workers required to spin the given quantity of yarn (54,300 bales). Since the average yearly production per worker for Chinese owned mill is estimated at 9.85 bales on page 94, the number of workers required to spin 54,300 bales at mill 57 may be estimated at 5,513, thus leaving 1,687 workers for mill 58—the weaving mill. In mills 110-111, the statistics on looms are merged together like those on spindles or workers; so also in mills 89-90. In both cases the workers are apportioned equally between the two mills. In still another case for mills 82-84 where

6. The exceptions here referred to include mills 89-90, 91-92, 93-94, 98-99, 110-111, 115-117, for which the spindles are reported together, and are distributed for each mill equally. For instance, the 100,000 spindles for mills 110-111 are distributed equally by giving 50,000 spindles to mill 110 and another 50,000 spindles to mill 111.

7. In mills 82-84, the spindle statistics are given for each of the three mills as follows: 72,312, 25,376, 55,632; but the labor statistics are merged together, namely, 13,000. The latter is therefore distributed according to the proportion for the spindles in the three mills, as follows: 6,131, 2,151, 4,718.

the spindles, not the looms, are given for each of the three mills, the workers for the three mills are also distributed according to the spindle proportion.

In respect of looms and cloth production, for mills whose statistics are merged together, the principle of equal distribution is also followed as in the case of spindle statistics. But where on the one hand the loom or the cloth statistics are merged, but on the other hand the spindle statistics are not merged, the former are arbitrarily distributed according to the proportion for the latter.[8]

In respect of motive power, for mills where statistics are merged together, the distribution for different mills is based upon the proportion for workers instead of that for spindles or looms, as power, like labor, may be employed for the working of spindles or looms or both.

Table 78. Size distribution of cotton mills in China, 1930

Nationality of ownership		Chinese	Japanese	All
Spindles per mill	Mean	29,947	39,877	33,792
	Median	25,334	34,168	28,588
	Mode	27,692	31,328	27,358
Looms per mill	Mean	500	758	585
	Median	401	751	501
	Mode	254	267	257
Motive power per mill (K.W.)	Mean	1,206	1,484	1,307
	Median	921	1,230	1,030
	Mode	731	801	756
Workers per mill	Mean	2,218	1,793	2,118
	Median	1,769	1,615	1,711
	Mode	1,212	858	1,671
Cotton consumption per mill (piculs)	Mean	74,939	70,857	75,431
	Median	64,168	60,001	63,531
	Mode	23,685	52,345	53,207
Yarn output per mill (bales)	Mean	21,130	19,653	21,165
	Median	17,501	15,626	17,263
	Mode	7,500	12,970	12,826
Cloth output per mill (pieces)	Mean	236,627	543,599	343,710
	Median	177,778	583,334	262,501
	Mode	147,067	722,340	53,269

8. In mills 82-4 where the spindles given are 72,312, 25,376 and 55,632 respectively, the 1,900 looms for the three mills are distributed in the same proportion as follows: 896, 314, and 690.

With these revisions[9] in mind the statistics on spindle, loom, motive power, labor, cotton consumption, yarn and cloth output, may now be examined in greater detail, in respect of the size distribution. In an analysis of the size distribution, three types of averages, namely, the mode, the median and the mean, have been computed for the Chinese owned mills, the Japanese owned mills and all mills in China. The British owned mills, of which there are only three in China, are not separately analyzed. Among the three types of averages, the mode is generally the lowest and the mean the highest, with the median standing between the two extremes. These three types of averages are summed up in Table 78, but detailed statistics may be found in Tables 79-85.

In Table 79 the cotton mills in China are classified by the number of workers (Fig. 31). This table shows that the greatest number of mills fall within the class of 1,501-2,000 workers. 25 mills with 41,779 workers or 16.6 percent belong to this class, giving an average of 1,671 workers per mill. The mode average, however, is lower than the median (1,711) or the

9. The revision, which applies to 23 mills, is given in detail below.

No. of mill	Workers Original	Workers Revised	Spindles Original	Spindles Revised	Looms Original	Looms Revised	Motive power Original K.W.H.P.	Motive power Revised K.W.H.P.	Raw cotton (piculs) Original	Raw cotton (piculs) Revised	Yarn spun (bales) Original	Yarn spun (bales) Revised	Cloth woven (pieces) Original	Cloth woven (pieces) Revised
57-8	7,200	5,513	90,000	90,000				2,417	200,000	200,000	54,300	54,300		
		1,687			655	655	3,100	683					400,000	400,000
77-8	1,000	398	13,600	13,600			1,400	1,400	31,500	12,530	9,000	3,580		
		602	20,000	20,000			500	500		18,970		5,420		
		6,131	72,312	72,312		896				213,808		61,088		
82-4	13,000	2,151	25,376	25,376	1,900	314	?	?	453,327	75,030	129,522	21,437	?	
		4,718	55,632	55,632		690				164,489		46,997		
89-90	3,542	1,771	52,256	26,128	500	250	2,000	1,000		50,956		12,820	181,726	90,863
		1,771		26,128		250		1,000		50,956		12,820		90,863
91-92	3,070	1,535	55,552	27,776			1,800	900		54,169		13,629		
		1,535		27,776				900	549,558	54,169	138,269	13,629		
93-94	5,560	2,780	136,864	68,432			4,500	2,250		133,548		33,578		
		2,780		68,432				2,250		133,548		33,578		
95	3,799	3,799	37,120	37,120			1,150	1,150		72,392		18,215		
98-99	1,800	900	73,600	36,800			2,000	1,000	55,220	27,610	17,290	8,645		
		900		36,800				1,000		27,610		8,645		
110-1	5,600	2,800	100,000	50,000	2,000	1,000	3,500	1,750	126,000	63,000	36,000	18,000	1,440,000	720,000
		2,800		50,000		1,000		1,750		63,000		18,000		720,000
		833		30,134				2,500		62,000		1,900		
115-7	2,500	833	90,400	30,134			7,500	2,500	186,000	62,000	57,000	1,900		
		834		30,132				2,500		62,000		1,900		
125-6	1,960	1,662	53,600	53,600			1,850	1,569	53,822	45,647	15,718	13,331		
		298	9,600	9,600				281		8,175		2,387		

Table 79. Cotton mills in China classified by the number of workers per mill, 1930

Workers per mill	Chinese Mills	Chinese Workers	Chinese % of workers	British Mills	British Workers	British % of workers	Japanese Mills	Japanese Workers	Japanese % of workers	Total Mills	Total Workers	Total % of workers
Below 501	6	1,919	1.2				2	768	1.1	8	2,687	1.1
501 - 1,000	8	6,285	3.9				11	9,440	12.2	19	15,725	6.2
1,001 - 1,500	15	18,182	11.2				6	8,021	10.4	21	26,203	10.4
1,501 - 2,000	14	24,648	15.2				11	18,818	24.4	25	41,779	16.6
2,001 - 2,500	11	24,944	15.4	1	2,151	16.5	2	4,343	5.6	14	33,563	13.3
2,501 - 3,000							6	16,461	21.4	6	16,461	6.5
3,001 - 3,500	4	13,044	8.1				1	3,440	4.5	5	16,484	6.5
3,501 - 4,000	7	26,947	16.6				3	11,662	15.1	10	38,609	15.3
4,001 - 4,500	3	12,573	7.8				1	4,129	5.4	4	16,702	6.6
4,501 - 5,000	1	4,604	2.8	1	4,718	36.3				2	9,322	3.7
Above 5,000	4	28,803	17.8	1	6,131	47.2				5	34,496	13.7
Total	73	161,949	100	3	13,000	100	43	77,082	100	119	252,031	100

Table 80. Cotton mills in China classified by the amount of power capacity per mill, 1930 (in kilowatts)

Motive power per mill	Chinese Mills	Chinese Motive power	Chinese % of Motive power	Japanese Mills	Japanese Motive power	Japanese % of Motive power	Total Mills	Total Motive power	Total % of Motive power
Below 501	17	5,712	6.23	2	781	1.22	19	6,493	4.17
501-1,000	25	18,278	19.95	14	11,213	17.57	39	29,491	18.97
1,001-1,500	14	18,432	20.12	12	15,051	23.58	26	33,483	21.53
1,501-2,000	9	15,913	17.37	6	10,469	16.40	15	26,382	16.97
2,001-2,500	3	6,875	7.50	6	14,500	22.72	9	21,375	13.75
2,501-3,000	4	11,862	12.95				4	11,862	7.63
3,001-3,500	3	9,700	10.58	1	3,215	5.04	4	12,915	8.32
3,501-4,000				1	3,600	5.64	1	3,600	2.32
Above 4,000	1	4,856	5.30	1	5,000	7.83	2	9,856	6.34
Total	76	91,628	100	43	63,829	100	119	155,457	100

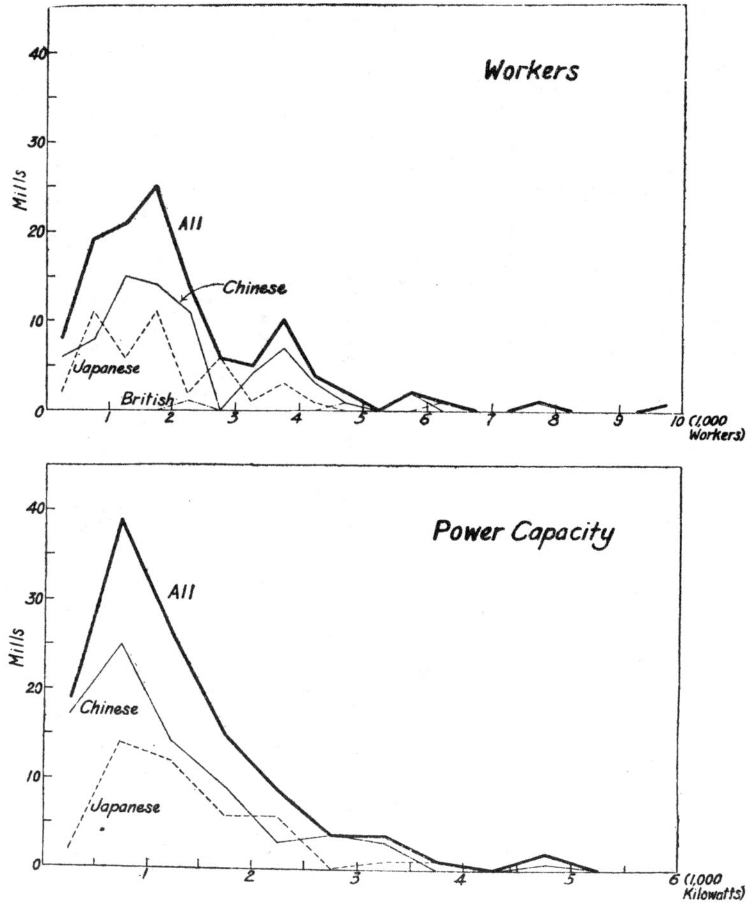

Fig. 31. Distribution of cotton mills in China by workers and power capacity per mill, 1930 (*See* Tables 79-80)

mean (2,118). Hankow No. 1, a Chinese mill in Wuchang, and Ta Sheng No. 1a, a Chinese mill in Nantung, are the largest mills, with 9,556 and 7,779 workers respectively. On the other hand, Lee Sheng, a Chinese mill in Paoti (Hopei), is the smallest, having only 110 workers. In respect of the nationality of ownership, whereas the commonest size for the Chinese mill varies from 1,001 to 1,500 workers, that for the Japanese mill is lower, varying from 501 to 1,000 workers. In exact figures, the mode average is 1,212 for the former but 858 for the latter. The same is true with the median or the mean average, being 1,769 or 2,218 for the Chinese mill but 1,615 or 1,793 for the Japanese mill.

In Table 80 the cotton mills in China are classified by the amount of power capacity (Fig. 31). This table shows that the greatest number of mills fall within the class of 501-1,000 kilowatts. 39 mills with 29,491

Table 81. Cotton mills in China classified by the number of spindles per mill, 1930

Spindles per mill	Chinese			British			Japanese			Total		
	Mills	Spindles	% of spindles	Mills	Spindles	% of spindles	Mills	Spindles	% of spindles	Mills	Spindles	% of spindles
Below 5,000	3	7,280	0.3							3	7,280	0.2
5,001 - 10,000	6	44,760	1.9				1	9,600	0.6	7	54,360	1.3
10,001 - 15,000	13	169,336	7.1							13	169,336	4.0
15,001 - 20,000	8	141,164	5.9				1	19,836	1.2	9	161,000	3.8
20,001 - 25,000	9	202,012	8.4				5	118,024	7.1	14	320,036	7.6
25,001 - 30,000	15	415,386	17.3	1	25,376	16.5	7	188,464	11.3	23	629,226	14.8
30,001 - 35,000	3	103,340	4.3				9	281,952	16.8	12	385,292	9.1
35,001 - 40,000	6	229,640	9.6				5	185,520	11.0	11	415,160	9.9
40,001 - 45,000	5	210,634	8.8							5	210,634	5.0
45,001 - 50,000							4	199,200	11.9	4	199,200	4.7
50,001 - 55,000	2	106,844	4.4				1	53,600	3.2	3	160,444	3.8
55,001 - 60,000	1	57,000	2.4	1	55,632	36.2	1	58,000	3.5	3	170,632	4.1
60,001 - 65,000	2	123,504	5.2				3	186,256	11.1	5	309,760	7.3
65,001 - 70,000	2	135,776	5.7				3	203,200	12.1	5	338,976	8.0
70,001 - 80,000	2	149,716	6.2	1	72,312	47.2				3	222,028	5.3
80,001 - 90,000	1	90,000	3.7				2	171,192	10.2	3	261,192	6.2
90,001 - 100,000	1	90,400	3.8							1	90,400	2.1
Above 100,000	1	119,000	5.0							1	119,000	2.8
Total	80	2,395,792	100.0	3	153,320	100.0	42	1,674,844	100.0	125	4,223,956	100.0

kilowatts of motive power or 18.97 percent belong to this class, giving an average of 756 kilowatts per mill. The mode, however, is lower than the median (1,030) or the mean (1,306). Dai Nippon, a Japanese mill in Tsingtao, and Yu Yuan, a Chinese mill in Tientsin, are the largest mills in respect of power capacity, having 5,000 and 4,856 kilowatts respectively. On the other hand, Tung Ch'ang and Hsieh Feng, both being Chinese mills in Shanghai, are the smallest, having 187 and 60 kilowatts respectively. In respect of the nationality of ownership, the commonest size for the Chinese and Japanese mills fall within the same class of 501-1,000 kilowatts, but in exact figures the Japanese average, 801, is higher than the Chinese average, 731. The same is true with the median or the mean, being 1,230 or 1,484 for the former, but 921 or 1,206 for the latter.

In Table 81 the cotton mills in China are classified by the number of spindles (Fig. 32). This table shows that the greatest number of mills fall within the class of 25,001-30,000 spindles. 23 mills with a total spindleage of 629,226 or 14.8 percent belong to this class, giving an average of 27,358 spindles per mill. The mode average, however, is lower than the median (28,588) or the mean (33,792). Wing On No. 2, a Chinese mill in Shanghai, has the largest number of spindles which is 119,000. Hankow No. 1, a Chinese mill in Wuchang, has the next largest number, namely, 90,400. On the other hand, three Chinese mills including Fu Ta in Changchow, Cheng Shing in Wuchih (Honan), and Fu Min in Dihhua (Sinkiang) have the smallest number of spindles, namely, 3,200, 2,800, and 1,200. In respect of the nationality of ownership, whereas the commonest size for the Chinese mill varies from 25,001 to 30,000 spindles, that for the Japanese mill is higher, varying from 30,001 to 35,000 spindles. In exact figures, the mode average is 27,692 for the former but 31,328 for the latter. The same is true with the median or the mean, being 34,168 or 39,877 for the Japanese mill but 25,334 or 29,947 for the Chinese mill.

In Table 82 the cotton mills in China are classified by the amount of raw cotton consumption (Fig. 32). This table shows that the greatest number of mills fall within the class of 45,001-60,000 piculs. 17 mills with a total cotton consumption of 904,523 piculs or 10.4 percent belong to this class, giving an average of 53,207 piculs per mill. The mode average, however, is lower than the median (63,531) or the mean (75,431). Hankow No. 1, a Chinese mill in Wuchang, and Ewo, a British mill in Shanghai, are the two mills that have the largest amount of cotton consumption, 490,000 and 213,808 piculs respectively, On the other hand, Hsieh Feng in Shanghai, Lee Sheng in Paoti, and Cheng Shing in Wuchih are the three mills that consume the smallest quantity of raw cotton, namely, 1,575, 2,800 and 4,293 piculs respectively. They are all owned by the Chinese. In respect of the nationality of ownership, whereas the commonest size for the Chinese mill varies from 15,001 to 30,000 piculs, that for the Japanese

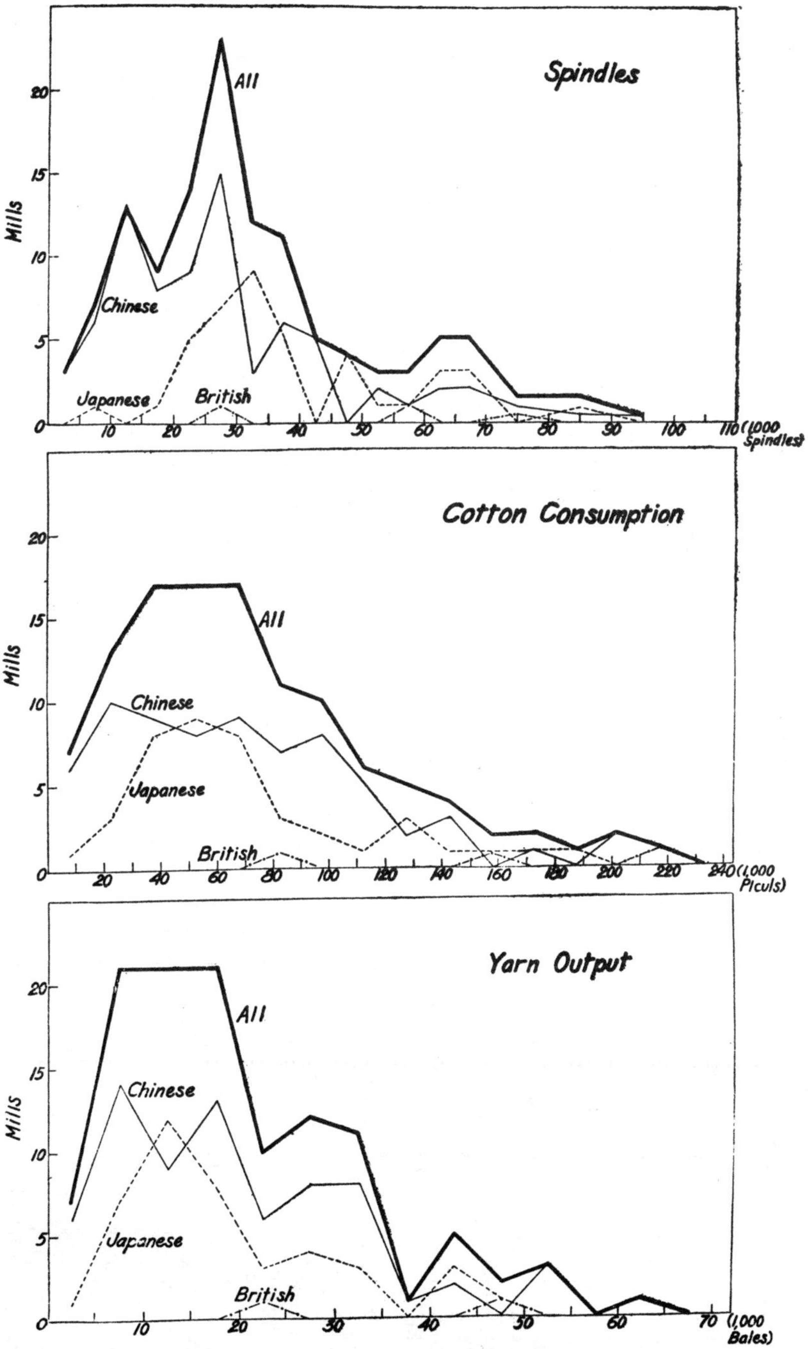

Fig. 32. Distribution of cotton mills in China by spindles, cotton consumption and yarn output per mill, 1930 (*See* Tables 81-83)

Table 82. Cotton mills in China classified by cotton consumption per mill, 1930 (in piculs)

Cotton consumption per mill	Chinese Mills	Chinese Cotton	%	British Mills	British Cotton	%	Japanese Mills	Japanese Cotton	%	Total Mills	Total Cotton	%
Under 15,001	6	41,148	0.8				1	8,175	0.3	7	49,323	0.6
15,001 - 30,000	10	236,845	4.5				3	74,574	2.6	13	311,419	3.5
30,001 - 45,000	9	329,416	6.2				8	283,571	9.5	17	612,987	7.0
45,001 - 60,000	8	433,414	8.1				9	471,109	15.8	17	904,523	10.4
60,001 - 75,000	9	599,201	11.3				8	531,229	17.9	17	1,130,430	12.9
75,001 - 90,000	7	565,199	10.6	1	75,030	16.5	3	248,797	8.3	11	889,026	10.1
90,001 - 105,000	8	780,967	14.7				2	199,179	6.7	10	980,146	11.2
105,001 - 120,000	5	572,612	10.8				1	117,000	3.9	6	689,612	7.9
120,001 - 135,000	2	265,000	4.9				3	389,416	13.1	5	654,416	7.5
135,001 - 150,000	3	431,665	8.1				1	142,250	4.8	4	573,915	6.6
150,001 - 165,000				1	164,489	36.3	1	157,500	5.3	2	321,989	3.7
165,001 - 180,000	1	178,164	3.3				1	168,200	5.6	2	346,364	3.9
Above 180,000	3	887,061	16.7	1	213,808	47.2	1	185,000	6.2	5	1,285,869	14.7
Total	71	5,320,692	100	3	453,327	100	42	2,976,000	100	116	8,750,019	100

Table 83. Cotton mills in China classified by yarn output per mill, 1930 (in bales)

Yarn output per mill	Chinese Mills	Chinese Yarn output	% of yarn output	British Mills	British Yarn output	% of yarn output	Japanese Mills	Japanese Yarn output	% of yarn output	Total Mills	Total yarn output	% of yarn output
Below 5,001	6	11,491	0.77				1	2,387	0.29	7	13,878	0.57
5,001 - 10,000	14	105,001	7.00				7	58,485	7.09	21	163,486	6.66
10,001 - 15,000	9	113,772	7.58				12	155,638	18.86	21	269,410	10.97
15,001 - 20,000	13	235,179	15.68				8	148,174	17.95	21	383,353	15.61
20,001 - 25,000	6	132,301	8.82	1	21,437	16.55	3	65,392	7.92	10	219,130	8.93
25,001 - 30,000	8	215,662	14.37				4	114,732	13.90	12	330,394	13.46
30,001 - 35,000	8	262,245	17.48				3	101,156	12.25	11	363,401	14.80
35,001 - 40,000	1	39,080	2.60							1	39,080	1.59
40,001 - 45,000	2	86,050	5.74				3	129,443	15.68	5	215,493	8.78
45,001 - 50,000				1	46,997	36.28	1	50,000	6.06	2	96,997	3.95
50,001 - 55,000	3	159,707	10.64							3	159,707	6.50
55,001 - 60,000												
60,001 - 65,000				1	61,088	47.16				1	61,088	2.49
Above 65,000	1	139,760	9.32							1	139,760	5.69
Total	71	1,500,248	100	3	129,522	100	42	825,407	100	116	2,455,177	100

mill is higher, varying from 45,001 to 60,000 piculs. In exact figures, the mode average is 23,685 for the former, but 52,345 for the latter. The reverse is true with the median or the mean, being 64,168 or 74,939 for the Chinese mill but 60,001 or 70,857 for the Japanese mill.

In Table 83 the cotton mills in China are classified by the amount of yarn output (Fig. 32). This table shows that the greatest number of mills fall within the class of 10,001-15,000 bales. 21 mills, with a total yarn output of 269,410 bales or 10.97 percent, belong to this class, giving an average of 12,826 bales per mill. The mode average, however, is lower than the median (17,263) or the mean (21,165). Like in cotton consumption, Hankow No. 1 and Ewo are also the largest mills in yarn output, namely, 139,760 and 61,088 bales respectively. Hsieh Feng, Lee Sheng, Cheng Shing and Tung Ch'ang are the four smallest mills, producing respectively 450, 800, 1,171 and 1,920 bales. They are all owned by the Chinese. In respect of the nationality of ownership, whereas the commonest size for the Chinese mill varies from 5,001 to 10,000 bales, that for the Japanese mill is higher, varying from 10,001 to 15,000 bales. In exact figures, the mode average is 7,500 for the former but 12,970 for the latter. The reverse is true with the median or the mean, being 15,626 or 19,653 for the Japanese mill but 17,501 or 21,130 for the Chinese mill.

In Table 84 the cotton mills in China are classified by the number of looms (Fig. 33). This table shows that the greatest number of mills fall within the class of 201-300 looms. 11 mills with 2,830 looms or 9.67 percent belong to this class, giving an average of 257 looms per mill. The mode average, however, is lower than the median (501) or the mean (585). Toyoda, a Japanese mill in Shanghai with 1,296 looms, is the largest, next to which is Fu Yuan, a Chinese mill in Wuchang with 1,200 looms. On the other hand, Kwang Ch'in in Wusih and Tung Cheng in Changchow are the smallest mills, both being of Chinese ownership and having 82 and 40 looms respectively. In respect of the nationality of ownership, the commonest size for the Chinese or the Japanese mills falls within the same class of 201-300 looms, but in exact figures the Japanese average, 267, is higher than the Chinese average, 254. The same is true with the median or the mean, being 751 or 758 for the Japanese mill but 401 or 500 for the Chinese mill.

In Table 85 the cotton mills in China are classified by the quantity of cloth output (Fig. 33). This table shows that the greatest number of mills fall within the class of less than 100,001 pieces. 10 mills, with a total cloth output of 532,686 pieces or 3.6 percent, belong to this class, giving an average of 53,269 pieces per mill. The mode average, however, is much lower than the median (262,501) or the mean (343,710). Shanghai Nos. 1 and 3, and Toyoda are the three largest mills in cloth output, producing respectively 821,134, 883,335 and 840,000 pieces. They are all Japanese mills in

Table 84. Cotton mills in China classified by the number of looms per mill, 1930

Looms per mill	Chinese Mills	Chinese Looms	Chinese % of looms	British Mills	British Looms	British % of looms	Japanese Mills	Japanese Looms	Japanese % of looms	Total Mills	Total Looms	Total % of looms
Below 101	2	122	0.76							2	122	0.42
101 - 200	3	600	3.75							3	600	2.05
201 - 300	8	2,030	12.68				3	800	7.04	11	2,830	9.67
301 - 400	3	1,036	6.47	1	314	16.53				4	1,350	4.61
401 - 500	5	2,278	14.23							5	2,278	7.78
501 - 600							2	1,086	9.55	2	1,086	3.71
601 - 700	2	1,267	7.92	1	690	36.32	1	664	5.84	4	2,621	8.95
701 - 800	2	1,520	9.50				3	2,359	20.75	5	3,879	13.25
801 - 900	1	852	5.32	1	896	47.16				2	1,748	5.97
901 - 1,000	3	2,920	18.24				3	2,984	26.25	6	5,904	20.17
1,001 - 1,100	2	2,180	13.62				1	1,052	9.25	3	3,232	11.04
1,101 - 1,200	1	1,200	7.50				1	1,126	9.91	2	2,326	7.95
1,201 - 1,300							1	1,296	11.40	1	1,296	4.43
Total	32	16,005	100	3	1,900	100	15	11,367	100	50	29,272	100

Table 85. Cotton mills in China classified by cloth output per mill, 1930 (pieces)

Cloth output per mill	Chinese Mills	Chinese Cloth output	Chinese %	Japanese Mills	Japanese Cloth output	Japanese %	All Mills	All Cloth output	All %
Below 100,001	7	264,960	4.00	3	267,726	3.28	10	532,686	3.60
100,001 - 200,000	9	1,323,605	19.97				9	1,323,605	8.96
200,001 - 300,000	4	1,108,925	16.74				4	1,108,925	7.50
300,001 - 400,000	3	1,139,264	17.20	1	376,000	4.61	4	1,515,264	10.25
400,001 - 500,000	1	473,920	7.15	1	408,000	5.00	2	881,,920	5.97
500,001 - 600,000	3	1,672,888	25.25	3	1,668,439	20.46	6	3,341,327	22.60
600,001 - 700,000	1	641,982	9.69				1	641,982	4.34
700,001 - 800,000				4	2,889,360	35.43	4	2,889,360	19.55
800,001 - 900,000				3	2,544,469	31.22	3	2,544,469	17.23
Total	28	6,625,544	100	15	8,153,994	100	43	14,779,538	100

Shanghai. On the other hand, Kwang Ch'in in Wusih and Tung Cheng in Changchow, both being owned by the Chinese, are the smallest mills in cloth output, producing respectively 15,000 and 18,000 pieces. In respect of the nationality of ownership, whereas the commonest size for the Chinese mill varies from 100,001 to 200,000 pieces, that for the Japanese mill is much higher, varying from 700,001 to 800,000 pieces. In exact figures, the mode is 147,067 pieces for the former but 722,340 for the latter. The same is true with the median or the mean, being 583,334 or 543,599 for the Japanese mill but 177,778 or 236,627 for the Chinese mill.

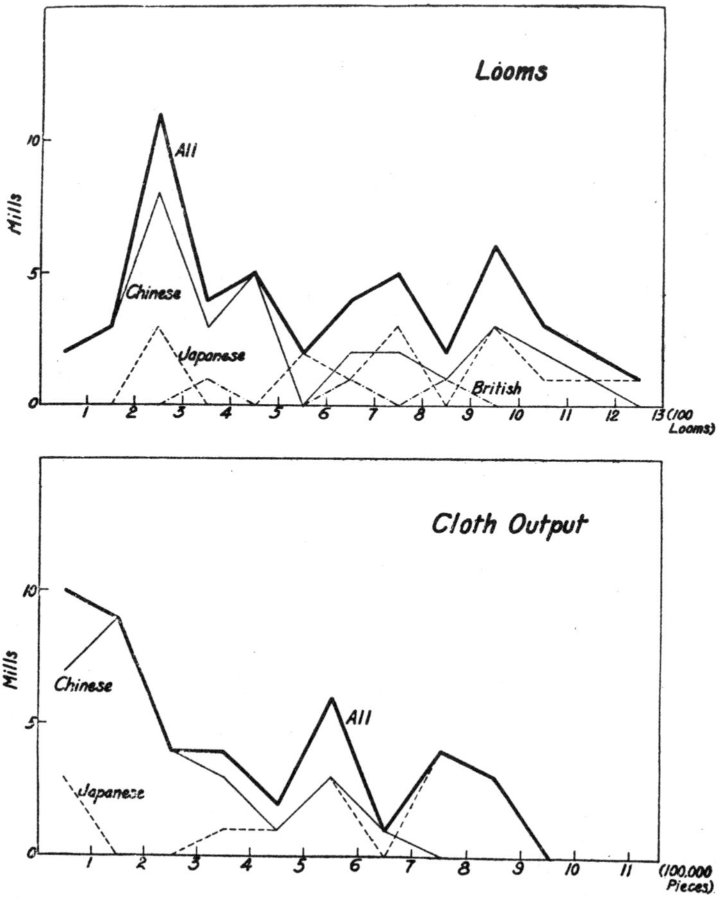

Fig. 33. Distribution of cotton mills in China by looms and cloth output per mill, 1930 (*See* Tables 84-85)

Financial size and size distribution

In an analysis of the financial size and size distribution of cotton mills in China, two types of indices may be computed from the data contained in the *List of Cotton Mills in China for 1930*, namely, the capital

Table 86. 40 Chinese owned mills classified by capital investment per spindle, 1930 (in dollars)

Capital per spindle	Mills Shanghai No.	%	Mills Elsewhere No.	%	Mills Total No.	%	Spindles Shanghai No.	%	Spindles Elsewhere No.	%	Spindles Total No.	%	Capital investment Shanghai Amt.	%	Capital investment Elsewhere Amt.	%	Capital investment Total Amt.	%
Below 11*	1	7.1	1	3.8	2	5.0	40,200	13.1	25,340	4.8	65,540	7.9	416,667	3.4	222,222	0.6	638,889	1.4
11 - 20†	2	14.3	2	7.7	4	10.0	21,120	6.9	27,744	5.3	48,864	5.9	393,056	3.2	320,000	0.9	713,056	1.5
21 - 30	1	7.1	1	3.8	2	5.0	5,200	1.7	2,880	0.6	8,080	1.0	138,889	1.1	60,000	0.2	198,889	0.4
31 - 40	4	28.6	3	11.5	7	17.5	101,468	33.1	50,500	9.6	151,968	18.3	3,313,889	26.9	1,850,000	5.4	5,163,889	11.0
41 - 50	2	14.3	4	15.4	6	15.0	52,072	17.0	63,648	12.2	115,720	13.9	2,311,111	18.8	2,970,000	8.6	5,281,111	11.3
51 - 60			2	7.7	2	5.0			59,000	11.3	59,000	7.1			3,156,807	9.1	3,156,807	6.7
61 - 70	2	14.3	6	23.1	8	20.0	49,552	16.2	119,684	22.9	169,236	20.4	3,097,222	25.1	8,040,000	23.3	11,137,222	23.7
71 - 80	1	7.1	1	3.8	2	5.0	8,500	2.8	14,000	2.7	22,500	2.7	645,833	5.2	1,001,011	2.9	1,646,844	3.5
81 - 90	1	7.1	2	7.7	3	7.5	28,120	9.2	58,112	11.1	86,232	10.4	2,003,333	16.3	5,000,000	14.5	7,003,333	14.9
91 - 100			1	3.8	1	2.5			27,000	5.2	27,000	3.3			2,585,170	7.5	2,585,170	5.5
Above 100**			3	11.5	3	7.5			75,480	14.4	75,480	9.1			9,369,500	27.1	9,369,500	20.0
Total	14	100	26	100	40	100	306,232	100	523,388	100	829,620	100	12,320,000	100	34,574,710	100	46,894,710	100

*8.77, 10.36. † 11.13, 11.92, 18.22, 19.53. **107.14, 122.07, 143.31.

per spindle or loom, and the total capital. The first index serves chiefly to determine the financial standing of a mill, while the second points to the extent of the mill's operation. The second index, however, cannot be computed before the first is completed, as for some mills where capital statistics for both spindles and looms are merged in a lump sum in the name of one company, there is no basis on which to apportion the capital among the different mills other than by the aid of some average for the capital per spindle or per loom. But it is admitted that the capital per spindle or per loom is not the only factor that affects the financial standing of a mill.

In calculating the capital per spindle, the process for the spinning mill is to divide the number of spindles into the amount of capital invested. Among the 81 Chinese owned mills 7 mills are omitted which give no statistics on capital investment, so are 34 others for which capital statistics are given in one lump sum for both spindles and looms. The mills for which the capital per spindle is computed are therefore 40 in number. In Table 86 the capital per spindle for each of the 40 mills is distributed. As shown in that table, the capital per spindle in Chinese owned mills varies from the lowest of 8.77 dollars to the highest of 143.31 dollars. The range of fluctuation is high, and can be attributed to several factors. In the first place, for some mills which are rented the capital investment given refers to the circulating capital, not to the fixed capital. As the fixed capital occupies more than two thirds of the total capital in a Chinese mill, the circulating capital per spindle is naturally small. Indeed, among the six mills having a capital per spindle of below 21 dollars, five mills are rented (nos. 4, 22, 28, 42, 43). However, it sometimes also happens that the capital investment of a rented mill includes something else than the circulating capital—a part if not all of the fixed capital. Mill 14, a rented mill, has a capital per spindle of $64.30, while mill 41, also a rented mill, has a capital per spindle of $31.40. Secondly, under capital investment are included both capital and surplus whenever such surplus is provided for. Among the 40 mills 11 mills have also surplus, which amounts to $1,902,810 or 12.4 percent of the total capital ($15,329,122) for these mills. Thirdly, as the capital investment of a mill refers usually to that for the year of establishment, and as the machinery is bought in terms of gold, not of silver, the fiuctuation in the rate of exchange is an important factor in the size of a mill's capital investment. A fourth factor is the effciency of the mill. If a mill is losing money, its capital investment is often larger than another mill which is not. This is because the mill's capital investment includes, besides the actual capital as represented by the current and fixed assets, the losses that have been accumulated in the years past and that have not yet been written off. In Tientsin where several mills have been suffering from losses for several years, the capital per spindle is unusually high, being 143.31 for Peiyang mill and 107.14 for Paocheng mill. Of course, it may also be said that such a high figure for the capital per spindle may, on the contrary, represent the sound financial position of a mill, as is true with the Japanese mills. Still other factors that affect the size of the capital per spindle include the location of the mill, the availability of coal and raw materials, the comparative cost of labor, the facility of transport and finance, and the proximity of market. A mill in the interior has a higher capital per spindle than another one in the treaty port, especially Shanghai. In Shanghai, the mill can have the motive power supplied by the Municipality, whereas in the interior it has to erect a power house itself for the purpose. In the interior again, the mills have to provide for living accommodations to the workers who may have been recruited from other provinces or cities. It may have to bear the initial cost of building up a new community with all its requirements. In the interior the land is cheaper, but the materials for building are more costly, due to the higher cost of transport. Finally, the interior mills have a greater difficulty in obtaining credit facilities, for which reason a part of the capital investment will have to be laid aside for the financing of current expenses.

Despite the many factors that account for the great variation in the size of a mill's capital per spindle, it is justifiable, for the purpose of getting at an average figure, to eliminate from the above table certain mills for which the capital per spindle is unusually high or low. We may eliminate from the table all those mills for which the capital per spindle either falls below 21 dollars or exceeds 80 dollars. In other words, out of the 40 Chinese owned mills given in Table 86, 13 mills, representing 36.6 percent of the total spindles and 43.3 percent of the capital investment, may be eliminated. The remaining 27 mills possess 526,504 spindles and a capital investment of $26,584,762, giving an average capital per spindle of $50.49. Applying this average to the 34 mills possessing both spindles and looms, the spindle capital for these mills may be eliminated from the total capital, and the loom capital may thus be obtained. In actual figures, these 34 mills possess 1,398,768 spindles, 15,559 looms and a total capital investment of $80,013,512. Deducting from the total capital of $80,013,512 the spindle capital of $70,623,796.32, which is obtained by multiplying the number of spindles (1,398,768) by the average capital per spindle ($50.49), there is a total loom capital of $9,389,715.68 for 15,559 looms, giving an average capital per loom of $603.50.

Having obtained the average capital per spindle or per loom for the 34 Chinese owned mills possessing both spindles and looms, the capital investment for seven of them (nos. 15-17, 29-30, 57-58), which is reported in three lump sums, may now be distributed separately for each mill. Since these seven mills possess 152 times more spindles than looms (there being 408,440 spindles but 2,685 looms), the chance for error in using the average capital per loom is smaller than that in using the average capital per spindle. In this way, the capital investment for each of the seven mills is obtained. In Table 87 these seven mils, together with the other 67 mills for which capital investment is given separately for each mill, are distributed according to the size of capital investment (Fig. 34). According to that table there are 24 Chinese owned mills in Shanghai with a total capital investment of $40,736,666, giving an average capital investment per mill of $1,697,361, while elsewhere there are 50 Chinese owned mills with a total capital investment of $86,171,556, giving an average capital per mill of $1,723,431. The mean size for Shanghai mills is therefore quite close to that elsewhere, the former being a little lower than

Table 87. 74 Chinese owned mills classified by capital investment per mill, 1930 (in dollars)

Capital per mill	Shanghai Mills	Shanghai Capital	Shanghai % of capital	Elsewhere Mills	Elsewhere Capital	Elsewhere % of capital	Total Mills	Total Capital	Total % of capital
Below 500,001	7	2,179,168	5.3	9	2,386,959	2.8	16	4,566,127	3.6
500,001 - 1,000,000	2	1,645,833	4.0	12	9,788,026	11.4	14	11,433,859	9.0
1,000,001 - 1,500,000	2	2,311,111	5.7	6	7,311,011	8.5	8	9,622,122	7.6
1,500,001 - 2,000,000	1	1,930,556	4.7	4	7,211,251	8.4	5	9,141,807	7.2
2,000,001 - 2,500,000	7	14,892,220	36.6	6	14,082,694	16.3	13	28,074,914	22.8
2,500,001 - 3,000,000	3	8,543,261	21.0	7	19,482,948	22.6	10	28,026,209	22.1
3,000,001 - 3,500,000	1	3,285,252	8.1	1	3,420,500	4.0	2	6,705,752	5.3
3,500,001 - 4,000,000				1	3,869,500	4.5	1	3,869,500	3.0
4,000,001 - 4,500,000				3	12,538,667	14.5	3	12,538,667	9.9
4,500,001 - 5,000,000									
5,000,001 - 5,500,000									
5,500,001 - 6,000,000	1	5,949,265	14.6				1	5,949,265	4.7
Above 6,00,000				1	6,080,000	7.0	1	6,080,000	4.8
Total	24	40,736,666	100.00	50	86,171,556	100.00	74	126,908,222	100.00

the latter. For China as a whole, the 74 mills of Chinese ownership have a total capital investment of $126,908,222, giving an average capital per mill of $1,714,976. The median size for Shanghai mill, $2,000,001, is higher than that for the mill elsewhere, $1,333,334. The same is true with the mode, being $2,127,460 for the former but $815,669 for the latter. For China as a whole, the median size is $1,437,501, which is higher than the mode, $285,387.

The statistics on capital investment for Japanese owned mills are more unsatisfactory than those for Chinese owned mills. Out of the 43 Japanese mills in China, 6 mills have to be eliminated, as the capital statistics for each of them refer to the company of which the mill is but a branch (Nos. 112-3, 119-22). Of the remaining 37 mills 12 are further eliminated, for which capital statistics for both spindles and looms are given together. Among the 25 spinning mills the capital for 16 is given in the name of the company which has more than one mill in the first place, and secondly possesses both spindles and looms. Consequently, the basis upon which the average capital per spindle is computed rests upon 9 mills only (nos. 107,114,115-7,118,125-6,127). These nine mills possess 290,508 spindles with a total capital investment of $23,550,000, giving an average capital per spindle of $81.06. Applying this average to the 28 mills whose capital is reported together either for several mills or for both spindles and looms, the spindle capital for these mills may be eliminated from the total capital, and the loom capital may thus be obtained. In actual figures, these 28 mills possess 1,050,696 spindles and 8,328 looms, with a total capital investment of $94,807,871. Deducting from the total capital of $94,807,871 the spindle capital of $85,169,418, there is a loom capital of $9,638,453 for 8,328 looms, giving an average capital per loom of $1,157.35.

Having obtained the average capital per spindle or per loom, the capital statistics for the 6 branch mills may be revised in the light of these averages.[10] The two branch mills of Dai Nippon, for instance, are reported to have a capital investment of $52,000,000 respectively. The

10. The revision in capital statistics for 6 Japanese owned mills is given below in detail.

No. of mill	Spindles	Looms	Original capital	Revised capital Spindle	Revised capital Loom	Revised capital Total
112	86,080		$52,000,000	$6,977,645		$6,977,645
113	66,336	1,296	14,981,944	5,377,196	$1,499,926	6,877,122
119	64,096	984	14,458,333	5,195,622	1,138,831	6,334,453
120	26,360		31,650,000	2,136,742		2,136,742
121	32,768		7,830,000	2,656,174		2,656,174
122	58,000	759	52,000,000	4,701,480	878,429	5,579,909
Total	333,640	3,039	172,820,277	27,044,859	3,517,186	30,562,045
			30,562,045			
Excess of original over revised capital			142,358,232			

first branch in Shanghai (No. 112), which possesses only 86,080 spindles, has a capital investment of but $6,977,645 if revised according to our average of $81.06 per spindle. Similarly, the second branch in Tsingtao (no. 122), which possesses 58,000 spindles and 759 looms, has a capital investment of $5,579,909, including a spindle capital of $4,701,480 and a loom capital of $878,429.

Of the 43 Japanese mills in China, capital investment is given individually for 9 spinning mills, and similarly computed for 6 branch mills referred to above. For the other 28 mills for which capital statistics are given either in the name of the company having more than one mill or for both spindles and looms in the mill, the capital investment for each mill may be estimated on the basis of the average capital per spindle or per loom.[11] After such estimates have been made, the 43 Japanese owned mills in China are classified by the capital investment per mill in Table 88. (Fig. 34). According to that table, there are 30 mills in Shanghai with a total capital investment of $106,112,638, giving an average capital investment per mill of $3,537,088, while elsewhere there are 13 mills with a total capital investment of $42,807,278, giving an average capital investment of $3,292,868

---

11. The revision in capital statistics for 28 Japanese owned mills, 1930, is given below in detail.

No. of mill	Original capital ($)	Revised capital ($) Spindle	Loom	Total	Spindles	Looms
85		815,335	768,480	1,583,815	22,432	664
86	8,930,555	955,781	673,578	1,629,359	26,296	582
87		3,093,656	1,217,532	4,311,183	85,112	1,052
88		1,406,193		1,406,193	38,688	—
89		1,117,871	289,338	1,407,209	26,128	250
90		1,117,871	289,338	1,407,209	26,128	250
91		1,188,379		1,188,379	27,776	
92	12,635,000	1,188,379		1,188,379	27,776	
93		2,927,832		2,927,832	68,432	
94		2,927,832		2,927,832	68,432	
95		1,588,160		1,588,160	37,120	
96		2,015,551		2,015,551	23,040	
97		5,318,814		5,318,814	60,800	
98		3,219,282		3,219,282	36,800	
99		3,219,282		3,219,282	36,800	
100			925,880	925,880		800
101	32,543,426	2,804,975		2,804,975	32,064	
102		2,165,317	925,880	3,091,197	24,752	800
103		2,010,652		2,010,652	22,984	
104		2,799,380		2,799,380	32,000	
105		2,799,380		2,799,380	32,000	
106		4,339,033		4,339,033	49,600	
108	16,810,000	10,647,924		10,647,924	61,360	
109		4,858,900	1,303,176	6,162,076	28,000	1,126
110	13,888,889	5,787,095	1,157,350	6,944,445	50,000	1,000
111		5,787,094	1,157,350	6,944,444	50,000	1,000
123	5,000,000	4,652,795	347,205	5,000,000	24,816	300
124	5,000,000	4,416,696	583,304	5,000,000	31,360	504

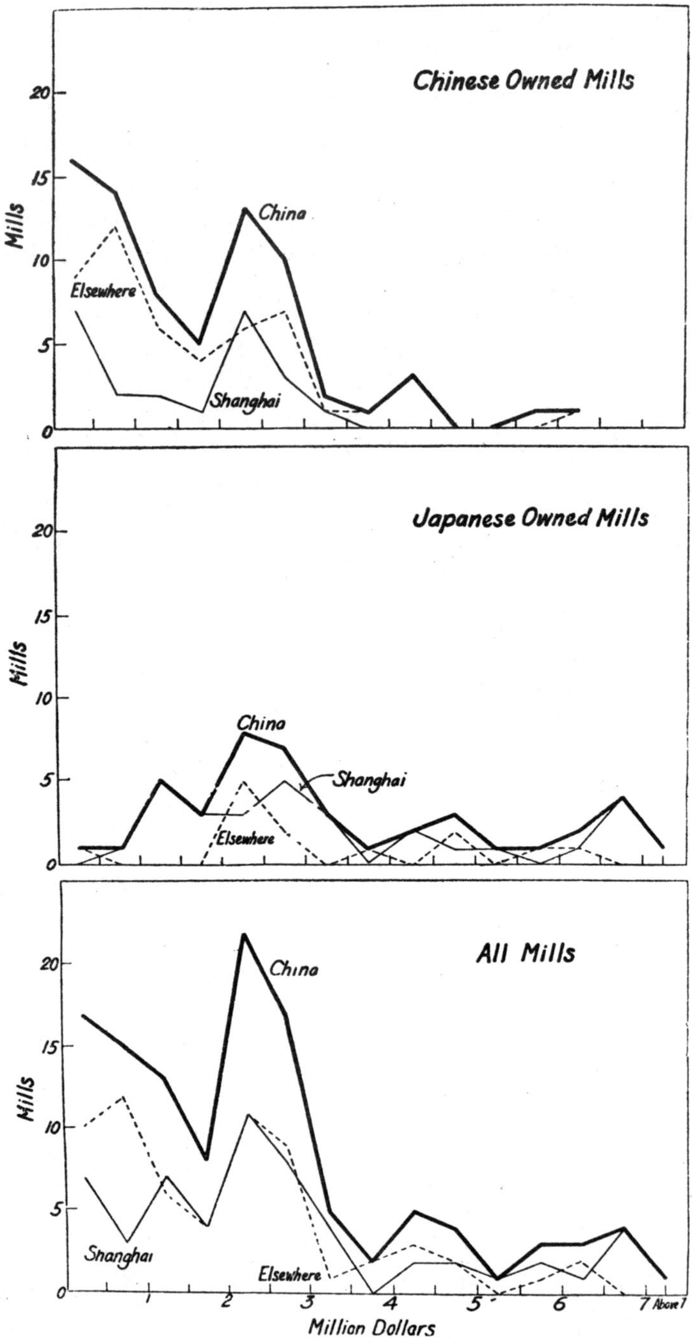

Fig. 34. Distribution of cotton mills in China by capital investment per mill, 1930 (*See* Tables 87-89)

per mill. The mean size for Shanghai mills is therefore quite close to that for the mills elsewhere, the former being a little higher than the latter. For China as a whole 43 Japanese owned mills have a total capital investment of $148,919,916, giving an average capital investment per mill of $3,463,254. The median size for Shanghai mill, $2,800,001, is higher than that for the mill elsewhere, $2,625,001. Similarly, the mode size for Shanghai mill, $2,851,880, is also higher than that for the mill elsewhere, $2,251,399. For China as a whole, the median size is $2,750,001, which is higher than the mode, $2,216,650.

Table 88. Japanese owned mills classified by capital investment per mill, 1930 (in dollars)

Capital per mill	Shanghai Mills	Shanghai Capital	Elsewhere Mills	Elsewhere Capital	Total Mills	Total Capital
Below 500,001			1	379,746	1	379,746
500,001–1,000,000	1	925,880			1	925,880
1,000,001–1,500,000	5	6,597,370			5	6,597,370
1,500,001–2,000,000	3	4,801,334			3	4,801,334
2,000,001–2,500,000	3	6,476,203	5	11,256,996	8	17,733,199
2,500,001–3,000,000	5	14,259,399	2	5,656,174	7	19,915,573
3,000,001–3,500,000	3	9,529,761			3	9,529,761
3,500,001–4,000,000			1	3,600,000	1	3,600,000
4,000,001–4,500,000	2	8,650,221			2	8,650,221
4,500,001–5,000,000	1	5,000,000	2	10,000,000	3	15,000,000
5,000,001–5,500,000	1	5,318,814			1	5,318,814
5,500,001–6,000,000			1	5,579,909	1	5,579,909
6,000,001–6,500,000	1	6,162,076	1	6,334,453	2	12,496,529
6,500,001–7,000,000	4	27,743,656			4	27,743,656
7,000,001 & above	1	10,647,924			1	10,647,924
Total	30	106,112,638	13	42,807,278	43	148,919,916

The capital investment for three British mills in China, which possess 153,320 spindles and 1,900 looms, is reported in one lump sum, namely, $12,500,000. In distributing the capital investment among the three mills, the average capital per loom of $880.425, which is obtained by averaging the mean capital per loom of $630.50 for the Chinese owned mill and the mean capital per loom of $1,157.35 for the Japanese owned mill, is employed in order to compute the average capital per spindle, which is $70.62. The capital investment for each mill is then obtained by multiplying the number of spindles or looms for the mill by the average capital per spindle or loom. The revision, in this way, gives a capital investment of $5,895,409 for mill 82, $2,068,462 for mill 83, and $4,536,129 for mill 84.[12]

12. The revision in capital statistics for 3 British mills, 1930, is given in detail below.

No. of mill	Original capital ($)	Revised capital ($) Spindle	Loom	Total	Spindles	Looms
82	12,500,000	5,106,548	788,861	5,895,409	72,312	896
83		1,792,009	276,453	2,068,462	25,376	314
84		3,928,636	607,493	4,536,129	55,632	690

Now that the size distribution of capital investment has been determined for the Chinese, Japanese and British mills respectively, it may be summed up for all these mills in Tables 89 and 90 in respect of the nationality of ownership as well as of geographical distribution. Tables 89 and 90 show that the greatest number of mills fall within the class of $2,000,001-2,500,000. 22 mills with a capital investment of $48,776,575 or 16.9 percent belong to this class, giving an average of $2,217,117 per mill. The mode, however, is lower than the mean ($2,402,-735), but higher than the median ($2,170,456). Tung Shing No. 1, a Japan-

Table 89. Cotton mills in China classified by size of capital investment and geographical distribution, 1930 (in dollars)

Capital	Shanghai			Elsewhere			Total		
per mill	Mills	Capital	%	Mills	Capital	%	Mills	Capital	%
Below 500,000	7	2,179,168	1.4	10	2,766,705	2.1	17	4,945,873	1.7
500,001 - 1,000,000	3	2,571,713	1.6	12	9,788,026	7.6	15	12,359,739	4.3
1,000,001 - 1,500,000	7	8,908,481	5.6	6	7,311,011	5.7	13	16,219,492	5.6
1,500,001 - 2,000,000	4	6,731,890	4.2	4	7,211,251	5.6	8	13,943,141	4.8
2,000,001 - 2,500,000	11	23,436,885	14.7	11	25,339,690	19.6	22	48,776,575	16.9
2,500,001 - 3,000,000	8	22,802,660	14.3	9	25,139,122	19.5	17	47,941,782	16.6
3,000,001 - 3,500,000	4	12,815,013	8.1	1	3,420,500	2.7	5	16,235,513	5.6
3,500,001 - 4,000,000				2	7,469,500	5.8	2	7,469,500	2.6
4,000,001 - 4,500,000	2	8,650,221	5.4	3	12,538,667	9.7	5	21,188,888	7.4
4,50,0001 - 5,000,000	2	9,536,129	6.0	2	10,000,000	7.8	4	19,536,129	6.8
5,000,001 - 5,500,000	1	5,318,814	3.2				1	5,318,814	1.8
5,500,001 - 6,000,000	2	11,844,674	7.4	1	5,579,909	4.3	3	17,424,583	6.1
6,000,001 - 6,500,000	1	6,162,076	3.9	2	12,414,453	9.6	3	18,576,529	6.5
6,500,001 - 7,000,000	4	27,743,656	17.4				4	27,743,656	9.6
7,000,001 & above	1	10,647,924	6.7				1	10,647,924	3.7
Total	57	159,349,304	100	63	128,978,834	100	120	288,328,138	100

Table 90. Cotton mills in China classified by size and nationality of capital investment, 1930 (in dollars)

Capital	Chinese			Japanese			British			Total		
per mill	Mills	Capital	%	Mills	Capital	%	Mills	Capital	%	Mills	Capital	%
Below 500,001	16	4,566,127	3.6	1	379,746	0.3				17	4,945,873	1.7
500,001 - 1,000,000	14	11,433,859	9.0	1	925,880	0.6				15	12,359,739	4.3
1,000,001 - 1,500,000	8	9,622,122	7.6	5	6,597,370	4.4				13	16,219,492	5.6
1,500,001 - 2,000,000	5	9,141,807	7.2	3	4,801,334	3.2				8	13,943,141	4.8
2,000,001 - 2,500,000	13	28,974,914	22.8	8	17,733,199	11.9	1	2,068,462	16.5	22	48,776,575	16.9
2,500,001 - 3,000,000	10	28,026,209	22.1	7	19,915,573	13.4				17	47,941,782	16.6
3,000,001 - 3,500,000	2	6,705,752	5.3	3	9,529,761	6.4				5	16,235,513	5.6
3,500,001 - 4,000,000	1	3,869,500	3.0	1	3,600,000	2.4				2	7,469,500	2.6
4,000,001 - 4,500,000	3	12,538,667	9.9	2	8,650,221	5.8				5	21,188,888	7.4
4,500,001 - 5,000,000				3	15,000,000	10.1	1	4,536,129	36.3	4	19,536,129	6.8
5,000,001 - 5,500,000				1	5,318,814	3.6				1	5,318,814	1.8
5,500,001 - 6,000,000	1	5,949,265	4.7	1	5,579,909	3.7	1	5,895,409	47.2	3	17,424,583	6.0
6,000,001 - 6,500,000	1	6,080,000	4.8	2	12,496,520	8.4				3	18,576,520	6.4
6,500,001 - 7,000,000				4	27,743,656	18.6				4	27,743,656	9.6
7,000,001 & above				1	10,647,924	7.2				1	10,647,924	3.7
Total	74	126,908,222	100	43	148,919,916	100	3	12,500,000	100	120	288,328,138	100

ese owned mill in Shanghai, has the largest capital investment, namely, $10,647,924. On the other hand, Cheng Shing, a Chinese owned mill in Wuchih, Honan, has the smallest capital investment, namely, $60,000. In respect of the nationality of ownership, whereas the commonest size for the Chinese mill falls within the class of below $500,001, that for the Japanese mill is higher, varying from $2,000,001 to $2,500,000. In exact figures, the mode is $285,387 for the former but $2,216,650 for the latter. The same is true with the median or the mean, being $2,750,001 or $3,463,-254 for the Japanese mill but $1,437,501 or $1,714,976 for the Chinese mill. In respect of the geographical distribution, whereas the commonest size for the Shanghai mills varies from $2,000,001 to $2,500,000, that for the mills elsewhere is lower, varying from $500,001 to $1,000,000. In exact figures, the mode is $2,130,626 for the former but $815,669 for the latter. The same is true with the median or the mean average, being $2,340,910 or $2,795,602 for Shanghai mills but $1,937,501 or $2,047,283 for the mills elsewhere.

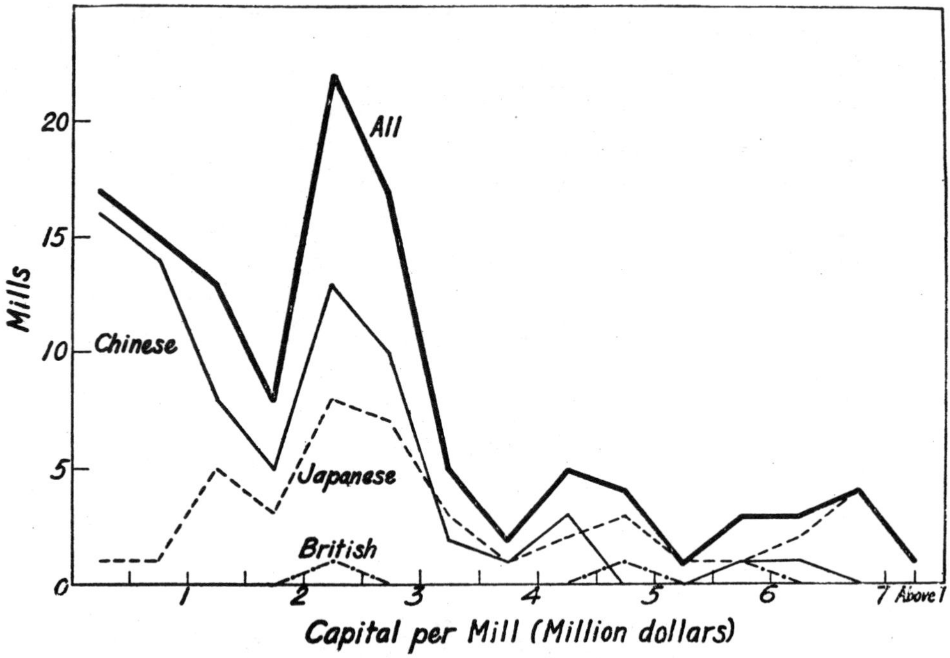

Fig. 35. Distribution of cotton mills in China by capital investment per mill, 1930 (*See* Table 90)

In Table 91 the mean, median and mode size of capital investment of the cotton mills in China is summed up in respect of the nationality of ownership as well as of geographical distribution.

No. §§§	Na
1	Naigai '
2	Shen Hs
3	China-Ja
4	Wing Or
5	Shangha
6	Ta Shen;
7	Ewo
8	Dai Nipp
9	Hua Hsi
10	Kung Ta
11	Hupeh
12	Tung Sh:
13	P'u I
14	Chin Hu:
Total for 6	
Total for 6	
Grand total	

Table 91. The mean, median and mode size of capital investment of cotton mills in China, 1930

Nationality of ownership	Mean	Median	Mode
Chinese	1,714,976	1,437,501	285,387
Shanghai	1,697,361	2,000,001	2,127,460
Elsewhere	1,723,431	1,333,334	815,669
Japanese	3,463,254	2,750,001	2,216,650
Shanghai	3,537,088	2,800,001	2,851,880
Elsewhere	3,292,868	2,625,001	2,251,399
All	2,402,735	2,170,456	2,217,117
Shanghai	2,795,602	2,340,910	2,130,626
Elsewhere	2,047,283	1,937,501	815,669

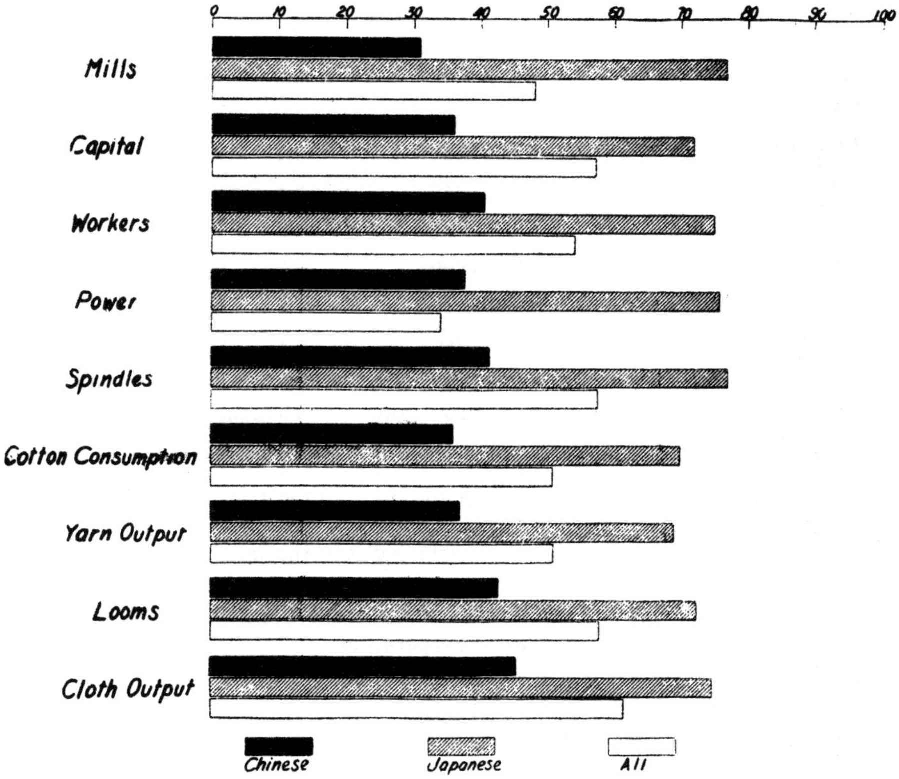

Fig. 36. Percentage of mills already integrated in China's cotton industry, 1930 (*See* Table 92b)

Tendency towards integration

The cotton mills in China, especially those of Japanese ownership, have shown a strong tendency towards integration during the post-war period, partly due to the revival of competition from the imported yarn and fabrics, and partly due to the desire for greater control of the industry.

As a result of this integration, mainly horizontal, 61 of the 127 cotton mills in China are in the hands of 14 companies, each of which possesses two or more mills that are either concentrated in one locality or scattered in different parts of the country. These 14 companies, of which seven are Chinese, six Japanese and one British, possess a capital of $165,108,885 (57.3%), 2,434,280 spindles (57.7%), 17,058 looms (58.3%), and 82,664 kilowatts of power capacity (34%), while employing 136,538 workers (54.2%), consuming 4,448,907 piculs of raw cotton (50.9%), spinning 1,255,654 bales of yarn (51.2%), and weaving 9,178,238 pieces of cloth (62.1%). In other words, about one half of the cotton mills in China, with more than one half of the capital and surplus, machinery, labor, raw materials, and output, have been integrated (Fig. 36). In Table 92a the statistics on these 14 companies are given in detail.

A further analysis of Table 92b shows that in respect of the nationality of ownership the Japanese mills are integrated to a much higher degree than the Chinese mills. Whereas only 25 of the 81 Chinese mills are integrated, as many as 33 of the 43 Japanese mills have come under the influence of integration. Again, whereas integration among Chinese mills applies only to 41.3 percent of the spindles, 43 percent of the looms, 37.5 percent of the power capacity, 40.6 percent of the working force, 36 percent of the raw cotton consumption, 36.9 percent of the yarn output, and 45.8 percent of the cloth output; such percentage

Table 92b. Statistics on 14 cotton mills in China having two or more plants each, 1930

Item	Chinese Amount	%*	Japanese Amount	%*	British Amount	%*	All Amount	%*
No. mills	25	30.9	33	76.7	3	100	61	48.0
Capital and surplus($),	45,743,468	36.0	106,865,425	71.8	12,500,000	100	165,108,893	57.3
Spindles	988,760	41.3	1,292,200	77.1	153,320	100	2,434,280	57.7
Spinning	959,472	41.2	1,118,696	75.1	153,320	100	2,231,488	56.2
Doubling	29,288	42.5	173,504	93.5	——	—	202,792	79.7
Looms	6,875	43.0	8,283	72.9	1,900	100	17,058	58.3
Motive power (K.W.)	34,358	37.5	48,306	75.7	——	—	82,664	34.0
K. W.	26,183	38.3	42,688	71.6	——	—	68,871	54.4
H. P.	10,900	35.1	7,490	100.0	——	—	18,390	11.8
Workers	65,809	40.6	57,729	74.9	13,000	100	136,538	54.2
Raw cotton consumed (piculs)	1,914,863	36.0	2,080,717	69.9	453,327	100	4,448,907	50.9
Yarn spun (bales)	553,394	36.9	572,738	69.4	129,522	100	1,255,654	51.2
Cloth woven (pieces)	3,037,244	45.8	6,140,994	75.3	——	—	9,178,238	62.1

* The percentage refers to the proportion that the integrated mills occupy in all mills in respect of the item concerned.

is much higher among the Japanese mills, being 77.1 percent for spindles, 72.9 percent for looms, 75.7 percent for power capacity, 74.9 percent for working force, 69.9 percent for raw cotton consumption, 69.4 percent for yarn output and 75.3 percent for cloth output. It may be noted, however, that integration has not led to an increase in efficiency. Among the integrated mills of Chinese ownership, for instance, 41.3 percent of the spindles produced but 36.9 percent of the yarn output. Similarly, among the integrated mills of Japanese ownership, 77.1 percent of the spindles produced but 69.4 percent of the yarn output. Even if the operating spindles with output statistics be taken as the basis for comparison, the conclusion is not much changed, for the percentage of spindles in integrated mills of Chinese ownership is only reduced from 41.3 to 40.4, and the percentage of spindles in integrated mills of Japanese ownership from 77.1 to 76.8.

Nationality of ownership	Total spindles	Spindles not operating	Spindles with no output statistics	Operating spindles with output statistics	%
Chinese mills					
All	2,395,792	180,720	46,024	2,169,048	100.0
Integrated	988,760	111,600	——	877,160	40.4
Japanese mills					
All	1,674,844	27,200	——	1,647,644	100.0
Integrated	1,292,200	27,200	——	1,265,000	76.8

Financial statements analyzed

As a rule, the financial statements of Chinese cotton mills are printed yearly for presentation at the meeting of the Board of Directors, but such statements, including the Profit and Loss Statement and the Balance Sheet, are seldom compiled according to modern accounting practice. In the Balance Sheet, no subdivision of the assets or of the liabilities is given. Similarly, the Profit and Loss statement is divided into two columns, namely, income and outgo, and it is only after detailed analysis that such items as sales, cost of goods sold, gross profit, selling expense, administrative expense, financial management income and outgo, operating profit and non-operating profit can be determined, although rather arbitrarily. Such determination is arbitrary because in many cases the data for different items are merged together in the same account which is vague and indefinite. Even when the account is more or less definite, in such items as insurance, it is hard to apportion it between the plant and the office. Again, certain items in both statements oftentimes disagree, such as depreciation and inventory. Depreciation may be provided for in the Profit and Loss Statement, but does not appear separately in the Balance Sheet. In such cases, the depreciation is merged with the item for which it is set aside (e.g. building). Finally, the statements of one mill differ considerably from those of another, and it would be difficult indeed to reduce the different items in these statements to a comparable basis. In our investigation of the six mills in Tientsin, the financial statements are secured for four mills, covering the ten year period from 1919 to 1928. These statements are re-arranged, as far as possible, according to modern accounting practices, and are given in *Appendix IV*.

Before we proceed to examine the financial statements in greater detail, the distinction between "nominal profit" and "net profit" must be made clearly. In Chinese mills it is a common practice to compute the former rather than the latter, and frequently the mill may have made a nominal profit, but actually it may have suffered a net loss. For in the computation of nominal profit in Chinese mills, many expense items, such as organization expense, depreciation, repair, '*bonus*'[13], loss from cotton purchase or exchange fluctuations, and tax are not set aside, but are defrayed from the nominal profit. On the other hand, the nominal loss may be actually smaller than the net loss, as in a losing year these expense items, especially depreciation, are neglected. Besides, the surplus and undivided profits of the previous years are used to cut down the nominal losses of the current year, or to swell the nominal profit. Whereas in almost all cases dividends are counted as a part of the nominal profit, in one case such dividends are, contrary to the new Company Act of China, section 171, excluded, and considered as an expense. In our analysis of the financial statements the nominal profit is given in the Balance Sheet, but in the Profit and Loss Statement both the nominal profit and the net profit are given.[14] Nominal profit, however, is different from either gross profit or operating profit. The gross profit is obtained by deducting the cost of goods sold from the sales, while the operating profit is the net profit minus the non-operating profit.

In Table 93 statistics on the paid-up capital, nominal profit, net profit, dividends, profit, surplus, and undivided profit are given. An

13. In Chinese mills the salary for the staff members is customarily low, but it is understood that the low salary will be compensated by the grant of a year-end 'bonus', which in prosperous years may be twice or triple the amount of the salary for the year. That was the case with many mills during the World War when huge profits were made easily because of the absence of competition from the imported goods. But beginning with 1923 or thereabouts, the tide turned and some mills were inflicted with serious losses. The year-end distribution of 'bonus' was still continued by some mills, but where such practice was discontinued an increase in the salary for the staff members generally took place. For these reasons I have considered 'bonus' as a part of the salary,—an expense item.

14. Even the net profit which we have calculated is over-stated; similarly, the net loss is under-stated. The reason is plain enough. Almost all of the mills studied make, in profit-making years, inadequate provision for depreciation reserve and other similar items, and no provision at all in losing years! Such failure to make adequate provision or no provision has a cumulative effect which cannot but weaken the financial position of the mill.

examination of the table confirms what we have said above with regard to the nominal and net profit. The nominal profit is usually larger than the net profit, while the nominal loss is usually smaller than the net loss. During some years in some mill where the nominal loss is larger than the net loss, such as in Mill D during 1927-1929, the explanation lies in the unsound financial practice of the mill. Whereas dividends as a rule are paid only after the mill has reaped a net profit, Mill D during the losing years of 1927-29 enlarged its nominal loss by the payment of a five percent dividend, which amounted to a total of $134,490 for each year. Consequently, the mill had, in 1929 for instance, a net loss of $49,859 but a nominal loss $184,080.

On the whole, the financial position of the Tientsin mills is highly unsound (Fig. 37). Except Mill C which has one losing year during the period 1919-1928, Mill A has five losing years out of ten, Mill B four losing years out of nine, and Mill D three losing years out of nine. These losing years started in 1923 for Mill A and Mill B, and have continued since then more or less for Tientsin mills. In 1926 even Mill C joined hand with Mill A in suffering a net loss of 5.18 percent. The highest percentage of loss, however, is that of Mill A in 1923, namely, 13.38%.

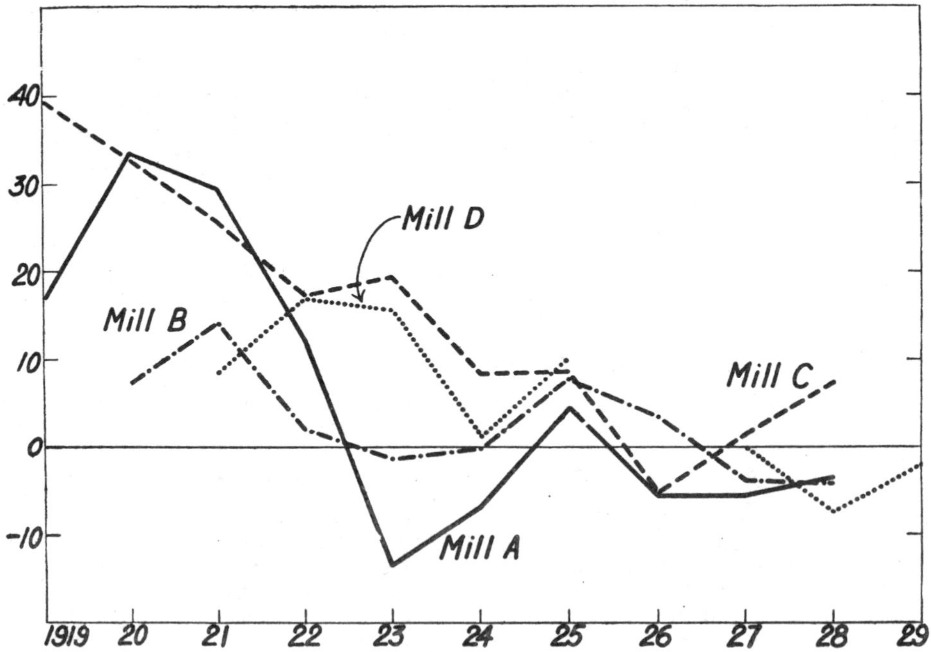

Fig. 37. Rates of net profit for Tientsin cotton mills compared, 1919-1928 (*See* Table 93)

Table 93. Capital, surplus, dividends and profits in Tientsin cotton mills, 1919-1929

	Capital	Nominal Profit††		Net Profit		Dividends		Profit		Surplus††		Undivided Profit†	
Mill A	$	$	%	$	%	$	%§	$	%§	$	%	$	%
1919	3,439,000	1,207,258	35.10	576,093	16.75	160,000	4.65	340,000	9.89			76,093	2.21
1920	3,600,000	1,811,742	50.33	1,204,748	33.46	288,000	8.00	720,000	20.00	80,917	2.25	115,831	3.22
1921	4,400,000	2,149,132	48.84	1,305,762	29.68	352,000	8.00	748,000	17.00	154,605	3.51	40,157	0.91
1922	5,100,000	913,765	17.92	619,041	12.14	393,271	7.71	196,635	3.86	172,326	3.38	–143,193	– 2.81
1923	5,560,350	– 257,801	– 4.64	–743,937	–13.38							–743,937	–13.38
1924	5,560,350	– 383,065	– 6.89	–383,065	– 6.89							–383,065	– 6.89
1925	5,560,350	272,061	4.89	258,972	4.66							258,972	4.66
1926	5,560,350	– 245,011	– 4.41	–301,084	– 5.41							–301,084	– 5.41
1927	5,560,350	365,531	6.57	–293,709	– 5.28					18,805	0.34	–312,514	– 5.62
1928	5,560,350	345,885	6.22	–187,165	– 3.37							–187,165	– 3.37
Mill B													
1920	3,465,500	423,100	12.21	249,930	7.21			207,930				42,000	1.21
1921	3,884,000	906,843	23.35	552,941	14.24	277,088	7.13	271,880	7.00	42,000	1.08	– 38,027	– 0.98
1922	4,000,000	329,463	8.24	76,462	1.91					50,000	1.25	26,462	0.66
1923	4,000,000	3,073	0.08	– 47,363	– 1.19					30,000	0.75	– 77,363	– 1.93
1924	4,000,000			– 3,073	– 0.08							– 3,073	– 0.08
1925	4,000,000	502,226	12.56	315,000	7.88	240,000	6.00	40,000	1.00			35,000	0.88
1926	4,000,000	256,256	6.41	135,000	3.38	120,000	3.00			35,000	0.88	– 20,000	– 0.50
1927	4,000,000	– 140,932	– 3.52	–140,932	– 3.52					15,000	0.38	–155,932	– 3.90
1928	4,000,000	– 152,174	– 3.80	–152,174	– 3.80							–152,174	– 3.80
Mill C													
1919§§	2,010,800	104,828	31.26	69,292	20.70	26,811	8.00	32,173	9.60			10,308	0.51
1919	2,010,800	1,378,518	68.56	793,060	39.44	160,864	8.00	522,808	26.00	4,591	0.23	104,797	5.21
1920	2,010,800	1,066,795	53.05	658,707	32.76	160,864	8.00	402,160	20.00	58,076	2.89	– 37,607	– 1.87
1921	2,010,800	907,920	45.15	519,624	25.84	160,864	8.00	321,728	16.00	47,088	2.34	– 10,056	– 0.50
1922	2,420,900	682,011	28.17	424,834	17.55	172,241	7.11	215,302	8.89	39,346	1.63	– 2,055	– 0.08
1923	2,421,900	763,813	31.54	470,848	19.45	193,709	8.00	227,383	9.39	30,233	1.25	19,523	0.81
1924	2,421,900	276,165	11.40	211,740	8.74	193,752	8.00			48,666	2.01	– 30,678	– 1.27
1925	2,421,900	231,941	9.58	211,229	8.72	193,752	8.00			13,021	0.54	4,456	0.18
1926	2,421,900	– 88,312	– 3.65	–125,482	– 5.18	121,095	5.00			10,561	0.44	–257,138	–10.62
1927	2,421,900	33,809	1.40	33,809	1.40	48,438	2.00					– 14,629	– 0.60
1928	2,421,900	181,376	7.49	181,376	7.49	169,533	7.00			–88,312	– 3.65	100,155	4.14
Mill D													
1921	1,935,000	140,471	7.26	165,322	8.54	144,850	7.49					20,472	1.06
1922	2,000,000	563,700	28.19	345,723	17.29	99,398	4.97	216,000	10.80	14,047	0.70	16,278	0.81
1923	2,478,300	608,638	24.56	395,103	15.94	116,374	4.70	225,000	9.08	51,046	2.06	2,683	0.11
1924	2,776,700	167,243	6.02	34,991	1.26	150,000	5.40			54,707	1.97	–169,716	– 6.11
1925	2,689,800	378,519	14.07	269,891	10.03	150,000	5.58	90,000	3.35	16,724	0.62	13,167	0.49
1926	2,689,800	– 526,281	–19.56	*	*	*	*			32,987	1.23		
1927	2,689,800	– 134,433	– 5.00	57		134,490	5.00						
1928	2,689,800	– 329,035	–12.23	–194,758	– 7.23	134,490	5.00					–329,249	–12.24
1929	2,689,800	– 184,080	– 6.84	– 49,895	– 1.84	134,490	5.00					–184,349	– 6.85

† After deducting dividends, profit and surplus from the net profit.
†† As given in the Balance Sheet.
§ % of the capital.
§§ Covers only two months of January and February. The fiscal year is from March 1 to Feb. 28.
* Data not available.

Before 1923 every one of the four mills studied was making profit. In 1919 Mill C made a profit as high as 39.44%, next to which was 33.46% for Mill A in 1920. The disposal of net profit during these years, nevertheless, is poorly done, with little consideration for the mill's future. For all of the four mills studied the provision for surplus has never exceeded four percent, the highest being 3.51% for Mill A in 1921. Mill C, which made a net profit of 39.44% in 1919, set aside a surplus of but 0.23 percent, the rest being distributed as dividend and profit. On the other hand, whenever any surplus has been accumulated, it is quickly diminished in losing years. In 1923 for instance, Mill A had an accumulated surplus of $407,849, or 9.27% of the paid-up capital, which was completely withdrawn in order to reduce the net loss from 13.38% to 4.64% Another unsound practice of Tientsin mills, which has been briefly referred to above, is the declaration of an annual dividend even in losing years. Of the four mills studied, two mills, namely, C and D, have made it a practice to declare an annual dividend. In 1926 when Mill C was already handicapped by a net loss of $125,482 it increased the loss by the payment of a five percent dividend.[15] Similarly, in 1928 when the net loss for Mill D amounted already to $194,758, or 7.23%, it was raised to $329,035 or 12.23% by the payment of a five percent dividend.

A third unsound practice of the Tientsin mills is the failure to provide the reserve for depreciation. Such a reserve is usually provided for only in profit-making years. As shown in Table 94, Mill A provides the reserve for depreciation during eight of the ten years, Mill B during five of the nine years, Mill C during nine of the eleven years, and Mill D during four of the nine years. Such a reserve for depreciation, covering fixed assets like building, machinery, furniture and fixture, is however highly inadequate in amount. Except Mill C the provision of reserve for depreciation never exceeds five percent of the total value of the fixed assets. In Mill D the percentage is as low as 0.26% for 1924 and 0.66% for 1925, while in 1923 the highest percentage is no higher than 1.08%. In Mill A the percentage varies from the lowest of 1.14% for 1925 to the highest of 2.25% for 1919. In Mill B the lowest percentage is that of 0.64% for 1920, while the highest is that of 4.80% for 1922. Mill C, which provided reserve for depreciation annually during the period 1919-1925, had the highest percentage of 14.09% in 1921, but the lowest of 1.06% in 1925. The total value of the fixed assets for each of the four mills, therefore, must have been cumulatively inflated above the market value because of the mill's failure to provide adequate reserve for depreciation from year to year.

15. The nominal loss is only 3.65%, but the undivided loss reaches as high as 10.62%.

A fourth unsound practice of the cotton mills in Tientsin is the heavy investment in fixed assets. As shown in Table 95, with the exception of Mill C the investment in fixed assets alone exceeds the paid-up capital. In 1921 Mill A, with a paid-up capital of $4,400,000, had an investment in fixed assets of $7,002,569. In other words, the latter is 1.59 times larger than the former. It is for this reason that Mill A is the most unfavorably situated financially among all the mills in Tientsin. Since 1921 the ratio that the investment in fixed assets bears to the paid-up capital has fluctuated between 1.45 and 1.59. That is to say, about one third of the investment in fixed assets has to be derived from loans instead

Table 94. Fixed assets (Including Building, Machinery, Furniture and Fixture) and reserve for depreciation* in Tientsin cotton mills, 1919-1929 (in dollars)

Year	Mill A			Mill B			Mill C			Mill D		
	Fixed assets	Reserve for depreciation	%	Fixed assets	Reserve for depreciation	%	Fixed assets††	Reserve for depreciation	%	Fixed assets	Reserve for depreciation	%
1919†							1,574,804	13,015†	4.98†			
1919	2,988,283	67,240	1.25				1,781,636	133,510	7.49			
1920	4,188,753	73,470	1.75	3,086,916	19,724	0.64	1,728,773	144,188	8.34			
1921	7,050,769	142,435	2.02	4,280,601	117,000	2.73	1,804,070	254,236	14.09	2,543,001		
1922	8,148,398	142,435	1.75	4,374,324	210,000	4.80	1,982,311	125,717	6.34	2,641,656	28,506	1.08
1923	8,543,288			4,411,207			1,924,778	111,633	5.80	2,825,398	30,433	1.08
1924	8,804,466			4,415,460			1,771,491	52,661	2.97	2,807,605	7,179	0.26
1925	8,763,029	100,000	1.14	4,584,354	103,801	2.26	1,739,532	18,473	1.06	2,874,657	19,001	0.66
1926	8,782,195	150,000	1.71	4,702,837	85,494	1.82	1,897,072			3,039,073		
1927	8,812,220	150,000	1.70	4,904,243			1,928,983			3,122,570		
1928	8,860,043	150,000	1.69	4,911,326			1,957,471	22,726	1.16	3,022,909		
1929										3,038,094		

* As provided for in the Profit and Loss Statement.
† Covers only Jan.-Feb., 1919. The fiscal year for Mill C extends from March to February.
†† Since in the Balance Sheet "Reserve for depreciation" is not separately provided for, such reserve as set aside in the Profit and Loss Statement must have been deducted already from the "Fixed assets" in the Balance Sheet. For this reason the amount of fixed assets as given here is the sum of the "Fixed assets" and "Reserve for depreciation."

Table 95. Fixed assets* and paid-up capital for Tientsin cotton mills, 1919-1929 (in dollars)

Year	Mill A Paid-up capital	Mill A Fixed assets	Mill A %	Mill B Paid-up capital	Mill B Fixed assets	Mill B %	Mill C Paid-up capital	Mill C Fixed assets	Mill C %	Mill D Pair-up capital	Mill D Fixed assets	Mill D %
1919†							2,010,800	1,691,850	84.14			
1919	3,439,000	3,081,213	89.60				2,010,800	1,781,075	88.58			
1920	3,600,000	4,214,443	117.07	3,465,500	3,320,231	95.81	2,010,800	1,718,067	85.44			
1921	4,400,000	7,002,569	159.15	3,884,000	4,494,192	115.71	2,010,800	1,683,316	83.71	1,935,000	2,587,478	133.72
1922	5,100,000	7,974,228	156.36	4,000,000	4,470,915	111.77	2,420,900	1,990,166	82.21	2,000,000	2,689,510	134.48
1923	5,560,350	8,247,436	148.33	4,000,000	4,297,798	107.44	2,421,900	1,946,641	80.38	2,478,300	2,873,251	115.94
1924	5,560,350	8,508,340	153.02	4,000,000	4,302,051	107.55	2,421,900	1,852,326	76.48	2,776,700	2,855,458	102.84
1925	5,560,350	3,366,146	150.46	4,000,000	4,470,945	111.77	2,421,900	1,854,555	76.57	2,689,800	2,922,510	108.65
1926	5,560,350	8,221,108	147.85	4,000,000	4,485,627	112.14	2,421,900	2,048,722	84.59	2,689,800	3,001,807	111.60
1927	5,560,350	8,169,829	146.93	4,000,000	4,601,539	115.04	2,421,900	2,080,633	85.91	2,689,800	3,026,598	112.52
1928	5,560,350	8,068,497	145.11	4,000,000	4,622,089	115.55	2,421,900	2,086,395	86.15	2,689,800	2,926,938	108.82
1929										2,689,800	2,942,122	109.38

† Covers only Jan.-Feb., 1919.
* Includes the total value of land, building, machinery, furniture and fixture, with reserve for depreciation for the same already deducted.

Table 96. Ratio of current assets to current liabilities for Tientsin cotton mills, 1919-1929 (in dollars)

Year	Mill A Current assets	Mill A Current liabilities	Mill A Ratio	Mill B Current assets	Mill B Current liabilities	Mill B Ratio	Mill C Current assets	Mill C Current liabilities	Mill C Ratio	Mill D Current assets	Mill D Current liabilities	Mill D Ratio
1918	1,120,888	1,073,029	1.04				1,077,567†	833,266†	1.29			
1919	1,967,039	322,692	6.10				1,691,855	191,500	8.84			
1920	2,313,790	980,092	2.36	1,271,123	1,183,496	1.07	1,806,428	409,501	4.41			
1921	2,510,709	695,042	3.61	1,544,402	1,608,763	0.96	1,843,589	522,625	3.53	363,647	374,146	0.97
1922	4,595,661	1,310,432	3.51	2,479,292	2,671,895	.93	2,278,382	1,055,513	2.16	1,445,019	511,595	2.82
1923	3,383,599	1,881,001	1.80	779,090	1,113,977	.70	2,506,759	1,114,073	2.25	2,098,830	955,132	2.20
1924	2,094,412	1,898,126	1.10	535,746	897,575	.60	2,309,690	1,235,951	1.87	1,708,894	708,799	2.41
1925	2,884,160	1,981,399	1.46	2,344,712	1,293,401	1.81	2,610,521	1,586,394	1.65	2,188,242	852,312	2.57
1926	2,259,422	1,973,305	1.14	2,568,770	1,518,063	1.69	1,640,078	1,034,816	1.58	989,460	1,119,359	0.88
1927	2,962,825	2,891,942	1.02	2,157,514	1,303,235	1.66	1,351,414	838,794	1.61	798,622	955,342	0.84
1928	3,359,772	3,261,497	1.03	2,935,062	2,176,659	1.35	1,653,396	981,570	1.68	873,466	1,253,004	0.70
1929												

† Covers only Jan.-Feb. 1919.

of from paid-up capital. For Mill D the ratio is smaller, varying from 1.03 to 1.34; for Mill B it varies from 0.96 to 1.16. Mill C is the only mill which devotes on the average about four fifths of the paid-up capital to the investment in fixed assets, leaving the other fifth as the circulating capital. Mill C, it may be reiterated, has had a fairly successful career since its establishment in 1919. Except 1926 it has made a varying rate of profit annually.

As a result of the heavy investment in fixed assets, the working capital in Tientsin mills is deplorably small. The working capital, which is the excess of current assets over current liabilities, is, according to the standard rule-of-thumb, equivalent to the amount of current liabilities. In other words, the standard ratio of current assets to current liabilities is two to one. [16] As shown in Table 96, this ratio has not been maintained, especially since 1923. Indeed, for Mill B the current liabilities alone exceeded the current assets in four years, from 1921 to 1924, the ratio being 0.96 in 1921, 0.86 in 1922, 0.62 in 1923 and 0.52 in 1924. The same is true for mill D, the ratio being 0.97 in 1921, 0.88 in 1926, 0.84 in 1927 and 0.70 in 1928. For the other years, the ratio is more favorable, even for Mills B and D. The highest ratio is 8.84 for Mill C in 1919, next to which may be mentioned 6.10 for Mill A in 1919, 4.41 for Mill C in 1920, 3.61 for Mill A in 1921, 3.53 for Mill C in 1921, 3.51 for Mill A in 1922, 2.82 for Mill D in 1922, and 2.36 for Mill A in 1920.

Employers' Associations

The Employers' Association was first started among the Chinese owned mills in 1918, on a nation-wide scale, but the Japanese owned mills have also their own organization, the Japanese Cotton Mill Owners' Association in China. Both organizations are located in Shanghai, where a small committee, representing the Chinese, Japanese and British millowners of Shanghai, meets to discuss matters of common interest once a month.[17] In other cities cotton millowners' association was also formed among the Chinese owned mills. The Hupeh Cotton Millowners' Association was formed at Hankow in 1921, the Wusih Cotton Millowners' Association in 1922, and the Tientsin Cotton Millowners' Association at about the same time. The Wusih Association, which was composed of only six mills, was

16. "In present-day practice, however, the rule is seldom strictly adhered to, probably because of the recognition of differences in types of business, location, date of issue of the statment, and other similar factors the effect of which is to vary somewhat the proportions involved. Whereas some lines of trade require a 2-to-1 ratio, others may necessitate a proportion of as high as 10 to 1, and still others will prove satisfactory risks even though their ratio is only 1 to 1. To extend credit accommodations to a merchant whose current liabilities exceed the current assets, representing a "floating debt", is equivalent to purchasing a lawsuit, since there is no likelihood that the current obligations will be met at maturity."—Beckman, Theodore N.: *Credits and Collections in Theory and Practice*, 2nd. edition, McGraw-Hill, 1930, p. 282.

17. Pearse, *Cotton Industry of Japan and China*, Manchester, 1929, p. 159.

reorganized into the Interior Cotton Millowners' Association in the province of Kiangsu in 1930, in order to raise its membership to seven or more and thereby to secure the approval of the Ministry of Industries which, under the New Industrial and Commercial Association Act of 1929, sec. 3, requires every association to be composed of a minimum of seven members. In the same year, the Tientsin Association was also re-organized, with a membership of six mills however, [18]

The Chinese Cotton Millowners' Association had its origin in an attempt to prevent the Japanese demand for the abolition of export tax on raw cotton in March, 1917. On the fifteenth of that month a meeting of the leading millowners was called by Mr. Lieu Pa-Sheng, (劉伯森), and a resolution was passed to request the government not to accept the Japanese demand. The request was granted, but the Association, having realized its object, relapsed into inactivity. Another meeting was therefore called on the fifteenth of September, with a view to deciding upon the necessity for a permanent organization. An affirmative resolution was passed, and a preliminary meeting for the approval of the draft constitution was called on the 27th of October. The first formal gathering for the Association was held on the 1st of December, with the presence of representatives from 15 mills. But it was not until the second meeting on the 14th of March, 1918 that, with the presence of representatives from 13 mills, the officials of the Association were elected. Chang Chieh, formerly Minister of Agriculture and Commerce and then owner of a series of mills in Nantung under the name of Ta Sheng, was elected the president, while C. C. Nieh, a cotton magnate in Shanghai, was elected the vice-president.[19]

The objects of the Association, as stated in the revised constitution of 1929, are of two categories, namely, the immediate and the basic. The immediate objects of the Association are, (1) to suggest means for government protection, and (2) to mediate disputes as well as to promote common welfare. The basic objects are (1) to improve the cotton culture and to extend the area for cotton cultivation, (2) to train up technicians and to initiate research in manufacturing technique, (3) to investigate the market conditions and to report on the status of supply and demand, (4) to compile statistics and to publish textile journals. Out of these four objects the Association has concentrated its past activities on the last two. It has undertaken annual field investigation on cotton production, the results of which are embodied in its annual booklet on the *Statistics of Cotton Production in China*, since 1918. It has, by means of correspondence, collected mill statistics more or less regularly every year. Thus far nine annual lists of cotton mills in China have been published, for the

18. *Textile News*, Feb. 13, 1930; Jan. 19, 1931; *China Cotton Journal*, Sep., 1921, pp. 271-2; Oct., 1922, pp. 221-2; *Tientsin Cotton*, Nov., 1930.
19. Kiangsu Industrial Bureau, *The Cotton Spinning and Weaving Industry of Kiangsu*, 1918, Part I, Chap. IV.

nine years including 1920-5, 1927-8, and 1930. It has published a technical quarterly, the *China Cotton Journal,* since October, 1919, and has maintained a semi-weekly publication, the *Textile News,* since April, 1923. The latter is a clearing house of information for the textile world at large, and for the cotton industry in particular. The Association, however, has done little in the improvement of cotton culture or in the extension of the area for cotton cultivation. The latter, like the second object of training up technicians and of initiating research in manufacturing technique, is costly, time-consuming, and difficult to realize. It is true that the Association organized the Cotton Improvement Committee in 1919, which succeeded in establishing the cotton experiment stations in Paoshan, Tangshan and Nanking, and was considerably enlarged when an annual appropriation of $35,000 was subscribed by the various Chinese mills during the following year. But in 1921 the Committee's work was amalgamated with that of the Department of Agriculture of the Southeastern University, with the understanding that the Association would turn over its appropriation for cotton improvement to the said institution. The fund, however, was soon discontinued, and so far as the Association was concerned, no further attempt was made to promote cotton improvement.[20]

The realization of the immediate objects is more evident. Among the past efforts may be mentioned the request to the government for the prohibition of cotton export and the abolition of likin, the attempt to settle industrial disputes between the members and their workers, the campaign against cotton adulteration, etc.

The members of the Association are of two classes, namely, Class A and Class B. Class A includes the local Chinese owned mills in Shanghai, while class B includes Chinese owned mills in other localities whose local association has already been affiliated with the association at Shanghai. The annual membership fee for Class A mills is fixed at 1.8 candareens per spinning spindle, 0.9 candareen per doubling spindle and 21.6 candareens per loom; while that for Class B is one half the amount for Class A mills. Under this arrangement, a mill with a spindle of 25,000, for instance, has to pay an annual membership fee of Tls. 200.00. Under the original arrangement, however, the membership fee is lower. It is fixed at a lump sum of 50 taels for any mill with more than 10,000 spindles, 100 taels for that with more than 20,000 spindles, 150 taels for that with more than 30,000 spindles, 200 taels for that with more than 40,000 spindles and 250 taels for that with more than 50,000 to 100,000 spindles. The membership fee is payable quarterly. Any member mill failing to pay the membership fee for longer than one year is expelled from the Association. Besides, there is an admission fee of 100 taels.[21]

20. See *Supra,* p. 28.
21. *Textile News,* April 15, 1929.

CHAPTER VIII. HANDLOOM WEAVING

Extent and distribution:—Among the leading Oriental countries where cotton handlooms are still employed, China, the most densely populated and probably no less backward in industrial development than India, is the only nation where handloom weaving still predominates over power loom weaving. In 1925 there were in Japan 238,999 cotton power looms as against 126,360 cotton handlooms, while in India in 1926 the cotton cloth production amounted to 1,950 million yards from power looms as against 1,160 million yards from handlooms.[1] In China the proportion of power weaving to hand weaving, in terms of yarn consumption, is only one to four. As shown in Table 97 below, of a total yarn consumption of 961 million pounds for China in 1930, the power looms consumed 207 million pounds, leaving the rest 754 million pounds or four fifths to the handlooms.

Table 97. Yarn and thread statistics for China, 1913 and 1930 (in pounds)

	1913		1930	
	Quantity[2]	%	Quantity[3]	%
Home production	200,000,000	35.84	982,070,800	102.22
Import	358,000,000	64.16	22,616,000	2.35
Minus export			43,987,064	4.57
Total consumption	558,000,000	100.00	960,699,736	100.00
For power looms	15,000,000	2.69	206,913,532	21.54
For handlooms	543,000,000	97.31	753,786,204	78.46

The above table also shows that although the yarn consumption by handlooms has shown an increase of 39% from 1913 to 1930, due chiefly to the rapidly increasing output of machine spun yarn, yet that by power looms during the same interval has increased almost 13 times. Power loom weaving is thus progressing at an amazing rate, but handloom weaving will undoubtedly persist so long as the agricultural economy, coupled with an over-growth of population and a low standard of living, remains primarily unaffected by modern industrial changes. The comments from the China Mission of the *Blackburn Chamber of Commerce*, although made several decades ago in 1897, may still be applied to a

1. *Encyclopaedia Britannica*, 14th edition, VI, 549-550.
2. Odell, *Cotton goods in China*, Washington, 1916, p. 185.
3. The production for 1930 is estimated at 2,455,177 bales by the Chinese Cotton Millowners' Association, which, if converted at 400 pounds per bale, amounts to 982,070,800 pounds. Similarly, the cloth production, estimated at 14,779,538 pieces, amounts to 206,913,532 pounds if converted at 14 pounds per piece. The import and export amount to 169,620 and 329,903 piculs, or 22,616,000 and 43,987,064 pounds respectively if converted at 133 1/3 pounds per picul. Of course, it is admitted that not all of the yarn and thread consumed is claimed by cloth weaving, but it is also clear that the yarn and thread consumption for other purposes than cloth weaving is small and may for our purpose be neglected.

land where medievaliam still prevails largely. In a visit to the great interior province of Szechuen, the Commissioners, struck by the prevalence of handloom weaving industry, remarked that "the lowly occupations of the people, the overwhelming abundance of cheap labor, ever seeking employment, and the desperate struggle for existence, compel every phase of household economy to be practiced. Hence the head of a family finds in his own house a power of productiveness equal to his family's requirements, whilst favorable conditions will give him, in many cases, an overplus beyond the needs of his own immediate circle, that enables him to supply the wants of others. It so comes about, then, that the textile industry is essentially a home one, and is pursued under economic conditions with which the foreigner, in spite of all mechanical advantages, cannot compete. The surplus of production is a source of spending power, which helps to maintain those who, at a cost of no wages, clothe the whole family. No sooner is a child capable of doing the smallest or slightest piece of work than its capacity is taken advantages of, and, in a land where the patriarchal system of family government is a religion, unrestricted by Board School regulations and Factory Act legislation, one finds young and old, child and adult, working side by side, to the utmost of their capacity and strength."[4]

Handlooms are scattered throughout China, and thousands of them are to be found in the homes of the farmers, where they are operated when the crops are gathered or during the idle days in winter. The principal centres are to be found in the leading port cities such as Shanghai, Hankow, Canton, Tientsin etc. As most of the hand woven cloths are consumed at home and not exported, the export statistics do not furnish us with a reliable guide in locating the hand weaving centres. But, in the absence of other statistics, the export statistics, reproduced below, may serve useful purposes.

Table 98. Original export of native cotton piece goods from Chinese ports, 1930 (in Hk. Tls.)

Port	Nankeens	Cloth, native, yarn dyed	Cloth, native, dyed in the piece	Cloth native, fancy	Total Value	%
Tientsin		4,321	32,830		37,151	0.24
Ichang	202,586				202,586	1.31
Shasi	91,680				91,680	0.59
Yochow	73,488				73,488	0.48
Hankow	219,398		2,442		221,840	1.44
Shanghai	12,289,060	1,005,032		20,769	13,314,861	86.34
Swatow	76,723	4,680		717	82,120	0.53
Canton	818,151	156,249			974,400	6.32
Kowloon	267,960				267,960	1.74
Samshui	19,514				19,514	0.12
Other	119,872	15,486	277		135,635	0.88
All ports	14,178,432	1,185,768	35,549	21,486	15,421,235	100.00

4. *Report*, 1896-7, by N. Neville and H. Bell, pp. 253-4.

Industrial organization:—Cotton handloom weaving in China is carried on in the country districts, but also in urban centres. The type of organization employed usually varies with the character of the districts, whether urban or rural. In the towns or cities, handlooms are found mostly in workshops. In Newchwang, for instance, there were in 1928 87 establishments, large and small, operating with 1,200 looms. Of this number 24 employed electric power and owned more than 500 iron looms.[5] In Mukden in 1924 there were 157 establishments, and by the end of 1927 over 300, but with the exception of two establishments, employing over 100 hands, all others had only half a dozen wooden looms each.[6] In Wusih in 1928 there were 17 establishments in cotton weaving, of which only one establishment, with 160 looms and a capital investment of half a million dollars silver, employed electric power. "Most of the mills are still in the family stage, having equipment of only a few wooden looms, and very limited capital, as low as $5,000".[7] In Anch'in in 1926 about 180 small cotton weaving establishments were operating with over 1,000 looms, all of the improved hand-power type, made of iron.[8] All these cities, Newchwang, Mukden, Wusih and Anch'in are fairly well urbanized, but handloom weaving there is carried on chiefly in workshops. In Tientsin, cotton handloom weaving, like rayon handloom weaving, is also carried on in small establishments, under the master craftsman system and the merchant employer system. These systems are rather typical of the small establishments elsewhere, and have been summed up in my previous report on the "Rayon and cotton weaving in Tientsin" in the following terms: "In this class of establishments, the master craftsman is the leading figure. He requires little capital for his business, whether fixed or circulating. His workshop can be rented; his looms, varying from a few to about a dozen, cost him but a few hundred dollars to install. The raw materials, whether rayon or cotton yarn, he can secure from the stores with a month's credit, while selling his fabrics for ready cash. It is true that he must provide room and board for his workers, as in China dormitory system has become an established rule in small industries, and occasionally in large ones. Such provision, however, is not costly, considering the fact that workshop is invariably converted into dormitory during night time, and that meals constitute the barest elements of food. Moreover, he can easily reduce his working force during slack period, and enlarge it when prosperity returns. His family, including wife and children, assists him in the preparatory processes of weaving, such as winding, spooling, reeling, etc. Its members live with him, and thus help to reduce his personal expenses and to eke out a living with his

5. *Chinese Economic Journal*, July, 1928, pp. 618-9.
6. *Ibid*, March, 1928, p. 256.
7. *Chinese Economic Bulletin*, July 21, 1928, p. 33.
8. *Ibid*, Feb. 6, 1926, p. 76.

petty earnings. This, in brief, is a picture of a great number of owners of small establishments, of those whom we designate as master craftsmen. Other owners, however, are only middlemen under the merchant employer system. They may provide the workshop and looms, and organize a small working force for weaving; but their raw materials, whether cotton or rayon yarn, are supplied by other establishments larger than their own. In other words, they do not weave on own account, but on that of other establishments." (p. 19)

In the country districts, cotton handloom weaving is a by-employment to agriculture in most cases. It is a dovetailing occupation, in which almost every member in the farmer's family is engaged in one way or the other during the off seasons. Wherever the cloth produced is barely sufficient for home consumption, the industry is *par excellence* in the household stage. But oftentimes the farmers work for market production in addition to meeting their own needs, in which case the type of organization is no less different from that existing elsewhere during the pre-industrial days. An excellent illustration is furnished by the farmers in the districts around Kaoyang. The cloth producing zone in this neighborhood includes a part of Paoting, Jenkiu (任邱), Anchow (安州), and Lihsien (蠡縣), but Kaoyang is the distributing centre for the total production in that part of the province. According to the former Bureau of Economic Information in 1926, "the cloth is woven chiefly in the farmers' cottages. Every farmer has at least one or two looms of the treadle type, and cloth weaving is pursued as a spare time occupation. The needy farmers who are not sufficiently capitalized to buy their own yarn generally weave cloth to the order of the city dealers. The latter supplies a certain quantity of yarn to each weaver, allowing him to take it back to his home, weave the fabric on his loom, and return the finished article within a specified period. The farmer himself generally does the weaving, while the women and children of the family help in such odd jobs as starching the yarn, etc. Wages are paid by the dealer to the farmer by the piece.... In addition to this wage payment, the farmer can always retain, with the full knowledge of the dealer, a small percentage of yarn as perquisite, if he is careful or skilful enough in economizing on waste". On the other hand, "the better financed farmers weave the cloth on their own account. They buy yarn from the city dealers, weave the cloth, and dispose of the finished articles in two ways: (1) to barter for yarn with some yarn dealers in the city, or (2) to sell the cloth at one of the fairs. Buying and selling cloth between the producer and the city dealer do not take place on any permanent site, but at periodical gatherings or fairs, which are held usually in some temples in the main channels of local trade."[9] This description is undoubtedly typical of conditions in many other cotton hand-

9. *Chinese Economic Journal*, June, 1927, pp. 555-6.

loom weaving districts, where the work is either dealt out to the farmers by the dealers under the commonly known 'putting out' system,[10] or undertaken by the farmers on own account. The fairs may be held at regular intervals of three or sometimes four days, while the dealers may perform a variety of services. In Tingchow, Hopei "the cloth dealers generally perform the functions of a broker, although sometimes they also buy and sell cloth on own account. Hundreds of Shansi cloth exporters come to Tingchow every year and make their purchases through the local dealers, who sometimes afford loan facilities to their clients."[11] Elsewhere, as in Nanchang, "the dealers collect cloth from the farmers and export the article to neighboring districts. These dealers usually have the cloth smoothed, dyed and sometimes printed before offering it for sale".[12] In still other cases, as in Hankow and Wuchang, "collectors usually establish buying offices in country villages to collect the product from farm houses and sell to the dealers in the city. They receive from wholesale dealers cash payment in tael or cash units. Transactions between wholesale dealers and buyers are conducted by brokers."[13]

Looms and cloths described:—The handloom employed is of several varieties, whether plain or figured, wooden or iron, old-fashioned or improved. The old-fashioned wooden loom, which one finds only in museums in America or Europe, is still the commonest type in China, especially in

10. In Siashih, Chekiang, native cotton cloths are turned out from the old style looms of the farmers' cottages in rural districts. "The latter kind is known locally as *kow pu* (扣布), which is woven by the women of the Siashih farmers to the order of the *kow pu* dealers in the town. The dealers usually issue a certain quantity of cotton yarn to each weaver, let her take the yarn back to her home, weave it on her own loom and return to the dealer the woven cloth. The cloth turned out by the old-fashioned wooden looms is generally very narrow, the width not being uniform, varying from 8 inches to 12 inches (Chinese measure). The pay for such work is ridiculously low, but the dealer generally allows the weaver to retain as perquisite any surplus amount of yarn left over after the required quantity of cloth has been woven. For each weaver, the dealer generally gives about 120 ounces of yarn at a time and requires her to bring back 80 per cent in weight of cloth, that is, 100 ounces of woven cloth, which amounts to about seven or eight pieces, each being about 20-30 feet by 8 to 12 inches, which take about 12 or 13 days for the weaver to finish. For such work, she is paid only from 30 to 60 cents, or at an average daily wage of hardly four cents. But if the weaver is skilful or careful enough, she can economise the yarn to such an extent as to enable her to obtain 10 percent of surplus from the yarn as perquisite, which will amply compensate her for the low wages. There are nine *kow pu* dealers in the town, who issue yarn to the farmers within a radius of over 60 *li* from the town. Not only those residing in the Siashih countryside but also those in the neighboring districts such as Kashing, Haiyen and Tunghsiang obtain orders from Siashih dealers to weave cloth. It is estimated that within this area about 20,000 looms are operating for the Siashih dealers and that the yearly output therefrom is in the neighborhood of 3,200,000 pieces."—*Chinese Economic Journal*, Aug., 1926, p. 336.

11. *Chinese Economic Bulletin*, Mar. 26, 1927, p. 163.

12. *Ibid.*, May 15, 1926, p. 258.

13. *Ibid.*, Sep. 5, 1925, p. 140.

rural districts. In urban communities, the improved handloom made of iron, or of iron and wood, was first introduced from Japan, and has now found favor with many establishments. The old figured loom of Chinese origin, designed mainly for silk weaving, is being replaced by the Jacquard loom, the famous French invention.[14] Here and there in port cities, one meets with machine shops producing these different types of looms. But they must be semi-modern in the eyes of western observers, as very few attempts to apply power to these looms have yet been made.[15]

In Mr. Odell's report on the "Cotton goods in China" published in 1916, a good description is given of the old-fashioned wooden handloom in China, which is undoubtedly the most prevalent as yet. According to Mr. Odell, these looms "are made almost entirely of wood, with the lay suspended from the ceiling in such a way as to permit it to be swung easily. The harness, made of twine, is hung from above by cord and springs. From the bottom of the harness, cords extend below to the foot pedals. Cords are tied to each of the pickers on the sides of the loom, run through a hook above, and extend down over the loom, moves the harness up and down by means of the pedals, pulls the lay back and forth with his right hand, and jerks the cord which throws the shuttle from one side to the other with his left hand. A stick extends across the cloth, in place of temples, to hold it out to the proper width and the cloth is wound on a roller by hand. On plain cloths a loom operated by a good weaver sometimes make 100 to 120 picks per minute."[16]

The preparatory processes, including winding, reeling, warping etc., are also simple. "In the establishments containing a number of looms the warps are prepared on a crude mill which follows in a general construction the plan of a modern warper. There is a V-shaped creel in which the spools containing the yarn are hung and the ends are run through a reed and wound on a beam by hand. All the yarn is wound by hand from skeins, on small bobbins for weft and on spools for warp. The skein is placed over a revolving frame; the empty bobbin or spool is on a spindle from which a cord belt extends to a large wheel. Small boys or women turn the wheels by hand and the spindle is thus made to revolve rapidly. With one hand the operative guides the yarn on the bobbin or spool, distributing it evenly."[17]

The Chinese are very skilful weavers in both silk and cotton and turn out a wide variety of fabrics, from plain, coarse, unbleached goods to fancy dobby and Jacquard fabrics. The variety is wider when we consider the great dispersion of handloom weaving in a country which is,

14. A beautiful illustration of the Chinese figured loom may be found in *Silk*, by Chinese Maritime Customs, 1917, Shanghai.
15. Fong, *Rayon and Cotton Weaving in Tientsin*, 1930, pp. 36-39.
16. Odell, *op. cit.*, p. 186.
17. *Ibid.*

in respect of area, larger than either Europe or the United States. These fabrics differ not only in name, but also in width, length, weight, color, design, the kind of yarn used, and the type of loom employed. In view of all these factors that enter into the production of a piece of hand woven cloth, it would have been impossible to give a complete enumeration of the cotton fabrics woven in China. A survey of the cloths woven in a few sample districts, however, may serve useful purposes.[18]

Siashih, Chekiang:—Native cotton cloth turned out from the old style looms in the rural districts is known locally as *kow up* (扣布), which varies in market value to a considerable extent. A piece of the highest grade fetches about $1.70 to $1.80 and of the lowest grade, hardly over ten cents. The latter is of course an exceptionally low grade cloth, used chiefly as mourning cloth. The yearly production of this class of cloth is, however, insignificant, as the market for it is limited. Cloth of medium quality is sold at $0.80 to $1.00 a piece on the local market. Siashih's total yearly export figure of *kow pu* of all grades is estimated at over $2,000,000. The *kow pu* is exported to districts north of Yangtze River, in Kiangsu and Anhwei provinces, to Southeastern Chekiang districts and even to Fukien province. Pucheng (浦城), a district in Fukien, consumes large quantities of Siashih *kow pu* yearly.

Nantung, Kiangsu:—The nankeen, the cloth produced at Nantung, is divided into two varieties, namely, *ta pu* (大布), which is white in color and of superior quality, and *siao pu* (小布), which is either white or blue in color, and inferior in quality as compared which *ta pu*. Both *ta pu* and *siao pu* are woven in special sizes and lengths to meet the requirements of different dealers. Generally, the goods demanded by *kwan chwang* dealers (from Manchuria) consist solely of *ta pu* variety, which is known on the market as *kwan chwang ta pu* (關莊大布), each piece measuring from 1.25 to 1.37 *chih* in width and 50 *chih* in length. *Kwan chwang ta pu* is further divided into three grades according to texture. The standard weight for first grade is 4 catties a piece, that of the second grade, 3½ catties, and that of the third grade, $3\frac{3}{16}$ catties. The product demanded by the *king chwang* dealers (from Kiangsu and Anhwei) is also of *ta pu* variety, and is known on the market as *king chwang ta pu* (京莊大布). The standard fixed for this variety is almost the same as that for *kwan chwang ta pu*, except that the weight is fixed at 3½ catties. As for the *hsien chwang* dealers (from Kiangsu, Auhwei, Chekiang and Kiangsui), both *ta pu* and *siao pu* are handled. In the case of *ta pu*, the standard weight and size is similar to that fixed by the *king chwang*

18. For references to Siashih, Kaoyang, Tingchow, Mukden and Newchwang see *Supra*, notes 5-6, 9, 10-11; but for Suning, Wuhan and Nantung, see *Chinese Economic Bulletin*, Feb., 1925, pp. 94-95; Sept. 5, 1925, p. 139; Aug. 29, 1931, p. 146.

dealers; but in regard to *siao pu*, the standard is fixed at from 0.81 to 0.82 *chih* in width and 25 *chih* in length, and the weight at $1\frac{1}{16}$ catties per piece.

As neither the weight nor the quality of nankeen is uniform, it is sold at a wide range of prices. Generally, *kwan chwang ta pu* is sold at Tls. 36, Tls. 34 and Tls. 32 per package of 40 pieces for the three different grades; *king chwang ta pu,* at Tls. 34 per package of 33 pieces; *hsien chwang ta pu,* at Tls. 32 per package of 30 or 40 pieces, and *hsien chwang siao pu,* at Tls. 30 per package of 50, 60, or 66 pieces.

Wuhan, Hupeh:—There are eight varieties of cloths woven in the two cities of Hankow and Wuchang, and named after the place of production. These include *Kinkow* (金口), *Yokow* (岳口), *Yanglo, Yanglow improved* (陽邏改機), *Sinchow* (新洲), *Kiufeng* (九峯), *Kotien* (葛店), and *Tsingshan* (青山). The width in *chih* units varies from 1.0 to 1.3, and the length from 30 to 40. The quality may be inferior or superior, coarse or fine; and the price per piece fluctuates from 0.5 to 1.4 taels. The annual production for different varieties runs from the lowest of 19,000 pieces to the highest 1,500,000 pieces. The market area extends from Hupeh, where the cloth is produced, to Shansi, Shensi, Hunan, Honan, Kiangsi, Kiangsu, Kwangtung, Kwangsi, Kweichow and Yunnan.

Kaoyang, Hopei:—Numerous varieties of cloth are produced by Kaoyang weavers. The most common kinds are *coarse cloth* (粗布), *fine drill* (細斜紋), *figured cloth* (提花布), and *patriotic cloth* (愛國布). A piece of *coarse cloth,* 104 *chih* by 24 to 26 *tsun,* is sold at from $5 to $9, a piece of *fine drill,* of the same length and width, at $8.40 to $8.50, a piece of *patriotic cloth,* 100 *chih* by 18 or 21 *tsun,* at $8 to $10, and a piece of *figured cloth,* of similar dimensions, at $7 to $15. The exact prices are determined by the quality or the weight of the cloth. The weight of a piece of *coarse cloth,* for instance, varies from seven to thirteen catties, and that of a piece of *fine drill,* from eight to nine catties. For weaving *coarse cloth* and *fine drill,* 16-counts yarn is used for both warp and woof, for *patriotic cloth* and *figured cloth,* 42-counts yarn is used for the warp and 32-counts yarn for the woof.

Tingchow, Hopei:—The length and width of a piece of cloth vary widely, but the *chwang pu* (莊布), made especially for the markets in Suiyuan, Mongolia etc., is of uniform dimensions, being about 1 *chih* wide by 30 *chih* long and sold locally at about a dollar per piece. The other varieties, including those for local consumption or for neighboring markets, are usually longer, each piece being 1.2 by 39 *chih* or thereabouts, and worth locally a little over $2. With the exception of the *chwang pu,* two pieces of cloth are rarely exactly equal in length and width. The cloth is usually packed in bundles of from 30 to 50 pieces each and exported to Kalgan, Fĕngchow, Kweihwa, Paotowchen, etc. About 1,600,000 pieces are exported from the district every year.

Suning, Hopei:—Native cloth produced in the district is divided into three kinds according to width and length. There is the 33 *chih* by 1 *chih* variety, of which about 150,000 pieces are produced yearly. This variety is consumed chiefly in Suiyuan and Paotowchen, on the Mongolian border. The 36 by 1.1 *chih* variety, with a yearly output of 200,000 pieces, is consumed largely at Weihsien and Kalgan. The 48 by 1.15 *chih* variety, with a total yearly output of 700,000 pieces, is exported chiefly to Shansi, Kalgan and Suanhwafu. The cloth is woven from a mixture of machine spun yarn and hand spun yarn. The warp generally consists of the former and the woof, of the latter. Cloth woven from such a mixture is claimed by Suning farmers to be better than that made entirely from machine spun yarn in that it is of better wearing quantity, warmer, and easier to dye. About 50,000 pieces of foreign style cloth woven by iron looms are also turned out yearly for the Paoting, Tientsin and Peking markets. The total yearly output of cotton cloth of the district, including both the native and foreign style variety, is valued at more than $2,500,000.

Mukden, Liaoning:—The native cloth falls into three classes: namely, *hwa chi pu* (花旗布), weighing 8¾ catties per piece of 104 *chih* in length and 2.6 *chih* in width; *ta chih pu* (大尺布), weighing 5⅜ catties per piece of 108 *chih* in length and 1.3 *chih* in width; and *hwa pu* (花布), weighing 6½ to 7¾ catties per piece of 104 *chih* in length and 1.8 to 2 *chih* in width. Of the three classes, the first two are products of coarse yarn of 10 to 16 counts, while the third is woven with various combinations of yarn from 20 up to 60 counts.

Newchwang, Liaoning:—The principal products here include *hwa chi pu*, a kind of coarse cloth, *ta chih pu*, checks, drills, etc. The length of a piece of *hwa chi pu* is 100 *chih*, that of *ta chih pu*, about 50 *chih*, and that of checks, about 56 *chih*. Checks are of several varieties, including stripes, cotton worsted twills, cretonnes, etc. A wooden loom can turn out one piece of *hwa chi pu*, more than one piece of *ta chih pu*, or one to one and a half pieces of checks daily, while an iron loom run by electric power can produce three pieces of *hwa chi pu* in a whole day.

Marketing methods:—Of the various kinds of native cloth woven, the commonest goes under the name of 'nankeen', or *tu pu*. In Nantung, Kiangsu province, an authentic estimate put the total quantity of its production at over 5,455,000 pieces a year, valued at about nine million dollars. These cloths are distributed by three groups of dealers, namely, *kwan chwang*, *king chwang*, and *hsien chwang*. The *kwan chwang* dealers, 16 in number, sell to Manchurian cities such as Newchwang, Dairen, Mukden and Harbin; and command the best financial resources as well as the largest turnover among the nankeen dealers in Nantung. Their transactions with buyers in Manchuria are conducted through brokers in Shanghai, who usually charge a commission of 0.7 percent, with a time-limit of ten days for payment. The *king chwang* dealers, 40 in number, sell to the buyers in the different cities of Kiangsu and Anhwei. Their business is done either by mail or through agents sent to Nantung by the buyers, on a cash basis. The *hsien chwang* dealers, 94 in number, are commission agents between local weavers and buyers from the different cities in Kiangsu, Anhwei, Chekiang and Kiangsi. Their profit is derived chiefly from the commission which varies from 1.6 cents to 5 cents per piece, but not infrequently from direct purchase and sale on own account. All three classes of dealers get their supplies directly from the weavers, who carry the goods to the city from their farmhouses. Upon arrival the size and weight of the cloth is first carefully tested, and if it measures up to the standard, the price is at once agreed upon. The deal being closed, the nankeen is then graded and wrapped into packages ready to be shipped to outside markets.

Nankeen is packed in several different ways, according to the trade custom ruling among each group of dealers. In the case of *kwan chwang* dealers, the cloth is packed into rolls of 40 pieces each, but in that of *king chwang* dealers it is made up into rectangular packages of 33 pieces each. The cloth for the *hsien chwang* dealers is also packed in rectangular form, but each package may contain from 36 to 66 pieces, depending upon the kind of cloth packed.

In shipping nankeen to outside markets, various means of transport are employed by the different groups of dealers. Goods handled by the *kwan chwang* dealers are first carried by junk to either of the two river ports near Nantung, and then shipped to Shanghai by junks or steam-launches. Upon arrival the cargo is again transferred to junks or steam launches for shipment to Newchang, where it is distributed to the various cities in Manchuria. No export duty is levied by the customs, but the freight is fixed at six to ten cents per package of 40 pieces from the city to the river port, twenty-five cents per package from the river port to Shanghai, and about three dollars per package from Shanghai to Newchwang,—a total charge of $3.35 per package. As *kwan chwang* cloth is sold at about 34 taels per package, the freight amounts to approximately eight percent of the selling price. The nankeen handled by the *king chwang* dealers is first taken by wheelbarrow to the river port, for shipment by steamer to Shanghai, and from Shanghai to Nanking by rail. The freight from Nantung to Shanghai is about 21 cents per package of 33 pieces, while that from Shanghai to Nanking is about 30 cents per package. The nankeen handled by the *hsien chwang* dealers is shipped directly from Nantung to the various consuming centres, either by junk or by steam-launch. But where these centres lie beyond the boundary of the province, in Anhwei, Kiangsi, or Chekiang, consignments are usually sent by means of parcel post.[19]

In Hankow there are nine nankeen wholesale dealers, engaged principally in the *Yokow* variety. Their capital varies between $10,000 and $20,000. In Wuchang there are sixteen wholesale dealers, ten dealing principally in the *Yanglo* variety and six in the *Kinkow* variety. All these dealers are licensed, and carry on transactions with the collectors—those who usually establish buying offices in country villages to collect product from farm houses—through brokers. The tael is used as the money unit with a 98% standard weight and an additional 2% discount. The time limit for payment is 15 days, but sometimes an advance payment for orders may be required. The likin tax for *Kiufeng* nankeen is 3.75 cash per piece. The cost of transport from the producing district to Wuchang or Hankow varies with the distance. To Wuchang 160 cash a picul, and to Hankow 200 to 300 cash a picul is generally charged. The ferrying charge across the river is 60 to 80 cash a picul.

Nankeen dealers in Hankow and Wuchang are all partnership companies, employing a manager ,a receipt assistant, a delivery assistant, a cashier and an accountant. The manager usually receives a monthly salary of $20, the assistant $15, the cashier $12, and the accountant $8. They are all entitled to share a bonus fixed at 20 percent of the net profit of the year.[20]

In Tientsin the method of marketing the cotton fabrics varies according to the territory covered. Most of the fabrics are exported to two groups of provinces, the eastern group including Manchuria and the western group including Shansi, Shensi and Kansu. Two methods are employed in marketing the fabrics in these provinces. According to the first method, the piece goods merchants, who are distinguished as eastern or western merchants according to their origin, may come to Tientsin and establish temporary headquarters in native hotels for the purchase of the fabrics. The practice is usually for the weaving establishments to dispatch own runners with samples of different fabrics, to the merchants at their respective hotels, for selection and purchase. The transaction is carried on in terms of credit, rarely in cash, to be settled at the middle or the end of the month, or during one of the three Chinese festivals,-the Dragon, the Moon and the Year-end festivals. According to the second method, the weaving establishment may start a sales office in some of

19. *Chinese Economic Bulletin*, Aug. 31, 1931, pp. 145-149.
20. *Ibid*, Sep. 5, 1925. p. 139.

the provinces mentioned above, such as Taiyuan or Harbin. In these places the office deals with the local piece goods merchants at wholesale. In marketing the fabrics in Tientsin itself, two methods are also employed. According to the first, the weaving establishment sends own runner with samples of different fabrics to piece goods firms, department stores or bazaars for selection and purchase. The client then places an order for a fixed quantity of certain fabrics, but is not obliged to purchase them unless actually sold. Here the transaction is also carried on in terms of credit, but occasionally in cash, the credit sales to be settled in the same way as that for the eastern or western merchants. A second method, resorted to by the small establishments, is for the peddlers (小行販), whether rural or urban, to purchase the fabrics directly at these establishments, on cash terms. Credit, however, may be granted, provided that the peddler secure some reputable guarantor. In such case the peddler must clear his account each time he makes a new purchase. These peddlers deal in native as well as imported fabrics. In busy seasons the rural peddlers have to come to and fro several times per month between Tientsin and their own territory, and establish temporary offices in small native hotels.[21]

In Kaoyang there are 157 cloth dealers, the biggest one being capitalized at $50,000 and employing over 70 men. About a score of others are also well-financed, their capital in each case being over $10,000. These shops maintain branches or sales agents at such centres as Peking, Kalgan, Loyang and Paotowchen. The rest are operating on a more limited scale. Some of the big dealers like *Fu Feng, Ho Kee, Yuan Hsin* and a score of others also maintain dyeing departments for both yarn and cloth. Of the ninety odd such establishments in the city, about thirty confine their operations to the dyeing of yarn, and the remaining sixty to the dyeing of cloth. In recent years, half a dozen big dyeworks equipped with up-to-date machinery for finishing and dyeing cloth have been opened in the city, mostly by graduates of technical colleges in Tientsin and other cities.

The local cloth dealers, after having collected cloth from the producers, either sell the cloth to a class of exporters from other provinces, or, in case of the well-financed dealers, export it on their own account. In the latter case, the dealer always has branches or sales agents, in other centres. The cloth is shipped in sack cloth packages of 20 pieces each either by the Peiping-Hankow or by the Tientsin-Pukow Railways. Shipments for the Peiping-Hankow Railway are carried to Paoting by mule carts and those for the Tientsin-Pukow line are sent to Potow (泊頭) in similar manner. Kaoyang cloth commands an extensive market in

21. Fong, *op. cit.*, pp. 45-46.

the country, often reaching such remote places as Harbin, Urga, Paotowchen, Taiyuan, Loyang, Tsinan, Hsuchow, and places in Shensi, Kansu and Chinese Turkestan. For the Shansi market the grey 'coarse cloth' is most in demand. The fabric is dyed usually in the Shansi local dyeworks after reaching the destination. Drills of the coarse variety are consumed in Kalgan. Those for Mongolia are dyed in primary colors such as red or yellow, in order to suit the taste of the inhabitants. The *piao pu* (標布) and the figured variety are popular on the Peiping market.

The production figure of Kaoyang cloth reached the high water mark between 1917 and 1919, when 5,000,000 pieces, it is estimated, were produced yearly. Since 1920, the industry has been on the decline owing to the civil war. In 1921 only 3,000,000 pieces were produced, and in 1927 the yearly output dwindled quickly to about 1,200,000 pieces.[22]

22. *Chinese Economic Journal*, June, 1927, pp. 554, 556-7.

CHAPTER IX. IMPORT AND EXPORT

Import

Early Import:—In the import of cotton manufactures the members of the East India Company were the pioneers. Even for them it was not until after forty years of persistent effort that a foothold was obtained in the China market—that is, in Canton. In 1786 Manchester tried the market for the first time, with its cottage weaving by handloom. According to the *Chronicles* of the Company, "The Patterns of Norwich, Manchester & Halifax Stuffs have been shewn to the Merchants (i. e. of the Cohongs), but it is not their opinion that any of them will answer for this Market; the Cotton Stuffs are too expensive, and the Chinese manufacture a variety of different kinds which tho' not so elegant are better adapted to their modes of dress".[1] Two years later the Court had sent out some samples of 'Norwich, Halifax, and Manchester Goods' to another merchant, Shy Kinqua, for inspection. The latter expressed the opinion that "they were unlike anything commonly made use of either for Dress or Furniture, that the Velvets and Velverets especially which are partly colored would never answer".[2] This opinion was also shared by Puanknequa, who remarked that they would never be brought into common use .....and at the same time that it would not be for the Interest of the Merchants to promote a Demand of such a Nature".[3] Shy Kinqua pointed out, nevertheless, "some Pieces of Manchester Goods called Denims and Royal Ribs which perhaps might be made something of, and he would have no objection to indent for a few Pieces for a Trial, the Colors however ought to be the same as those of the Woollens, viz. Blue, Black, Green, Ash and Brown, but no Yellow or Scarlet".[4] The trial was carried out in 1790, when the experimental shipment of Manchester cottons, including 50 pieces of Denims and 50 pieces of Royal Ribs, was invoiced at £612, and was sold for Tls. 2,000, about prime cost. But they were 'not approved of; they are thought much too costly and not held in such Estimation as many of their own manufactures'.[5] Since then no further attempt was made until the elapse of a long period of 22 years, in 1812. In that year another experimental consignment of printed cottons, invoiced at £4,774, was sent to Canton, but was not approved of. The designs were not adapted to the market, and the quality was considered unworthy of the Company.[6] Curiously enough, printed cottons to the value of £5,487 or Tls. 8,700 were included among the Company's import for the following year. Seven years later a third attempt also resulted in failure: In 1820 the British calicoes (4,509 pieces) and the velvets and velveteens (416 pieces), invoiced at £5,328, were sold by auction at Can-

1. Morse, H. B.: *The Chronicles of the East India Company Trading to China, 1635-1834*, Cambridge, 1926, 4 vols., Vol. II, p. 120. However, in the fifth volume published in 1929, the author recorded an import to Canton of cotton piece goods with a value of Tls. 188,424 or £62,808 for 1771. (Vol. V, p. 159)
2. *Ibid*, II: 152
3. *Ibid.*
4. *Ibid*, II: 152.
5. *Ibid*, II: 179-80.
6. *Ibid*, III: 180.

ton, realizing Tls. 6,500 and showing a loss of over 60 percent.[7] In the following year, a fourth attempt was again unsuccessful, but resulted in a smaller financial loss. At that year the English cotton goods, including 1,744 pieces of printed calico, 1,372 pieces of white cotton cloth, 860 pieces of black cotton cloth, 720 pieces of imitation Canton cloth, 1,132 dozens of handkerchiefs, and 5,000 pounds of cotton twist (yarn), were invoiced at £5,042, but sold at a loss of 35 percent, returning only ₮9,807.[8] Further losses were incurred by the Company in 1824 when the British calicoes were sold at nine dollars a piece to the value of Tls. 17,321, and in 1826, when a total worth of $50,200 of cotton piece goods was imported at "a smaller proportion of loss than in previous years".[9] In 1827, however, the Company had at last made good its footing, and British calicoes had for the first time been sold at a profit. "The importation on Company's account during the season was 15,300 pieces, invoiced free on board at £21,261, and cost, insurance, and freight at £23,241, and they were sold (not including duty) at an average price of seven dollars a piece, a total of 107,100 dollars". In the same year under the 'private' account was imported for the first time a total worth of $66,487 of cotton piece goods.[10] Indeed, the trade had then become so profitable that the import on private amount during the following year was trebled to a total value of $185,022, while the Company, although able to give a good account of British calicoes, which were 'held in general estimation in the market,' and were 'likely to continue in steady and regular demand', had to reduce its import to $69,614 because overstocked by importations on private account.[11] In 1829 the Company's import of cotton piece goods, valued at $243,800, showed a great increase over that for the previous year, but since then had remained rather stationary, being $231,000 for 1830, $273,681 for 1831, $214,020 for 1832 and $275,217 for 1833. On the other hand, the import of cotton piece goods on private account decreased considerably in 1829, from $185,022 in 1828 to $55,329, but after 1829, showed consistent increase, being $110,929 for 1830, $227,043 for 1831, $254,933 for 1832 and $351,957 for 1833. The combined import of cotton piece goods from England, both on Company's and on private account, showed a rather striking increase except in 1832. Such import amounted, in terms of silver dollars, to $173,587 in 1827, $254,636 in 1828, $299,129 in 1829, $341,929 in 1830, $500,724 in 1831, $468,953 in 1832, and $627,174 in 1833.[12]

The American ships, it seems, were more successful than the British in introducing cotton piece goods into China. Before the latter

7. *Ibid*, IV: 1.
8. *Ibid*, IV: 2.
9. *Ibid*, IV: 87-88, 124-5, 139.
10. *Ibid*, IV: 146, 158.
11. *Ibid*, IV: 178, 181. Beginning with 1828, the value of import was given for cotton manufactures, including cotton yarn.
12. *Ibid*, IV: 146, 158, 181, 195, 223, 248, 271, 339, 369.

succeeded in bringing in any cotton goods into Canton, the former had, as early as 1821, shipped a total worth of $179,410 of piece goods to Canton. With a few exceptions, the import by American ships showed an increase almost every year, being $161,918 for 1823, $154,388 for 1824, $240,736 for 1825, $261,700 for 1826, $357,386 for 1827, $174,413 for 1828, $414,420 for 1829, $359,179 for 1830, $483,382 for 1831 and $591,468 for 1832. The imports by American vessels, however, were "all of English manufacture, shipped from England to Canton in contravention of the East India Company's monopoly—at least the English manufacturers sold the goods to the Americans, who then transported them to Canton, as they were entitled to do, while the English were not".[13]

In this connection, it may be noted that whether the cotton manufactures were imported under English or under American flag, the total after 1827 included cotton yarn in addition to cotton piece goods. Inasmuch as this remained the case, the figures quoted above were inflated to the extent of the cotton yarn import. The cotton yarn import, however, did not assume large proportions until much later. It was first recorded on the Company's account in 1821, to the extent of 5,000 lbs. Six years elapsed until another import of cotton yarn, valued at $14,000, was recorded in favor of the private account, in 1827. In 1828 the Company imported 300 bales, or approximately 120,000 lbs., while in 1829 it imported 2,250 piculs, or approximately 300,000 lbs., valued at Tls. 56,700 or $78,750—about one third of the Company's import of cotton manufactures ($243,800). In the latter year the Americans for the first time imported 211 piculs or 28,000 lbs., valued at $8,840. In 1830 the cotton yarn import for the Company amounted to ₮58,320 or $81,000, which was also equivalent to about one third of the Company's import of cotton manufactures ($231,000).[14] The three years of continuous import of cotton yarn gave promise of a bright future, altho the Company was rather pessimistic with its first shipment of 300 bales in 1828. In that year the Company recorded that,

> We cannot at present hold out any hope that this will prove an advantageous article of Consignment to this country. The Dealers are all agreed as to the following—viz. that the quality of Twist from the number of 8 Hanks to the pound to that of 26 Hanks to the pound inclusive and which constitute the three prices of 10d., 10½., 11½d., are of a quality too coarse for the Chinese Market and for which little or no sale would be found, that again the numbers from 40 Hanks to 140 Hanks of the prices 18½d., 22½d., 2s. 4d., 2s. 9d., 3s. 2d., 3s. 11d., 4s. 5d., & 6s. 4d., are still more unsaleable, being of so fine a quality that the machinery in use among the Chinese is not capable of manufacturing it, and also that cloth of so fine a texture is in little use among the natives of this country; that the intermediate numbers viz. from 28 Hanks to 38 Hanks to the pound including the prices of 14d., 16d., 16½d., and 17½d., are those mostly in request and for which the best price will be obtained. Mowqua has now made an offer of 34 dollars per Pecul for the whole Consignment of 300 Bales.

13. *Iibd,* IV: 330.
14. *Ibid,* IV: 2, 158, 178, 186, 195, 223.

These comments were made on the trade in its cradle; but after the experience of a hundred years it is found that, in an importation which in some years has reached almost a million bales, the Chinese market demands for the greater part, almost entirely it may be said, counts of yarn from 12 to 24.[15]

Table 99. China's Import of cotton manufactures by ships of different flags, 1790-1833 (in silver dollars)**

Year	East India Company	British Private	Total	American	Total
1790	2,778		2,778		2,778
1812	15,000		15,000		15,000
1813	12,083		12,083		12,083
1820	9,028		9,028		9,028
1821	13,621		13,621	179,410	193,031
1823	21,600†		21,600†	161,918	183,518
1824	24,057		24,057	154,388	178,445
1825	2,632		2,632	240,736	243,368
1826	50,200		50,200	261,700	311,900
1827	107,100	66,487	173,587	357,386	530,973
1828	69,614	185,022	254,636	174,413	429,049
1829	243,800	55,329	299,129	414,420	713,549
1830	231,000	110,929	341,929	359,179	701,108
1831	273,681	227,043	500,724	483,382	984,106
1832	214,020	254,933	468,953	591,468	1,061,356††
1833	275,217	351,957	627,174	——	627,174

† Estimated at 8 dollars per piece for 2,700 pieces.
†† Including $935 for other flags.
** Since 1828 the figures refer to cotton manufactures, including yarns and piece goods. For source see Morse, *op. cit.*, II: 179; III: 174, 189; IV: 1, 2, 20, 84, 87-8, 99, 102, 118, 124-5, 139, 146, 158, 181, 195, 223, 248, 271, 339, 369.

Import since 1867 :—The import of cotton manufactures,[16] which amounted to Tls. 1,061, 356 in 1832, increased greatly during the following thirty-five years. In 1867 when the Customs returns were for the first time published with some degree of uniformity, the import of cotton manufactures reached the huge total of Tls. 14,617,268, which was equivalent to 21 percent of the total import of all commodities into China. This fourteen-fold increase from 1832 to 1867 can be explained by several factors, of which the most important must be assigned to the abolition in 1834 of the trade monopoly of the East India Company and the establishment of regular trade with foreign nations through the opening up of the five ports in 1842. Canton, the chief entreport for foreign commerce before the days of the First Opium War in 1840, was then officially opened

15. *Ibid*, IV: 178; *Supra*, p. 2.
16. The term 'cotton manufacture' or 'cotton goods' includes the following 3 classes: piece goods, yarn and thread, and other.

to foreign trade along with the other four ports, namely, Tientsin, Shanghai, Ningpo and Amoy. Like the East India Company, the cohongs in Canton were no longer given the exclusive privilege of trading with the foreign nationals, as monopoly had to give way to competition.

In 1868 the import of cotton manufactures was increased from Tls. 14,617,268 in 1867 to Tls. 22,373,056—an increase of 57 percent. Judging by the fact that in later years from 1869 to 1884 the value of import flutuated around that for 1868, the increase in 1868 might have been the result of an improvement in the collection of statistics by the Customs. Taking, for instance, 1913 as the base of 100, the index for 1868 amounts to 12.26, and that for the period 1869 to 1884 fluctuates from 8.80 for 1878 to 16.34 for 1871, but caters generally around 12. After 1884 there was a tendency for the import to increase. The index

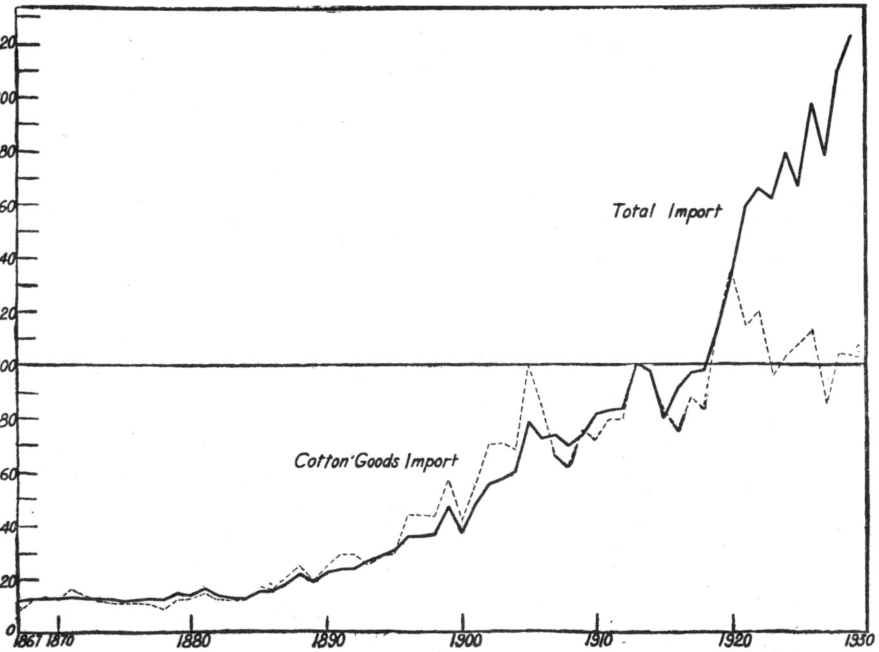

Fig. 38. Value of China's cotton goods import and total import compared, 1867-1930 (1913=100) (*See* Table 100)

consequently, rose to 17.26 in 1885, 24.68 in 1890 and 29.09 in 1895. The last year, however, marked a turning point, for with the conclusion of the Sino-Japanese War in that year, the import began to increase by leaps and bounds. The index rose from 29.09 in 1895 to 43.44 in 1896 and 56.72 in 1899. It fell to 41.45 in 1900, because of the Boxer Uprising, but recovered rapidly afterwards. In 1901 the index was increased to 54.63, from which it went up still further to 69.91 in 1902, 70.51 in 1903 and 99.47 in 1905—the year of the Russo-Japanese War. Since 1905 another

Table 100. Net import of cotton manufactures into China, 1867-1930

Year	Cotton manufactures (Hk. Tls.)	Index 1913=100	All commodities (Hk. Tls.)	Index 1913=100	% of cotton manufactures
1867	14,617,258	8.01	69,329,741	12.16	21.08
1868	22,373,056	12.26	71,121,213	12.47	31.46
1869	25,208,918	13.82	74,923,201	13.14	33.65
1870	22,037,717	12.08	69,290,722	12.15	31.80
1871	29,803,783	16.34	78,190,093	13.71	38.00
1872	25,407,069	13.93	74,826,130	13.12	33.95
1873	21,535,879	11.81	73,992,903	12.98	29.11
1874	20,334,470	11.15	71,395,801	12.52	28.49
1875	20,061,143	10.94	67,803,247	11.89	29.59
1876	20,216,246	11.08	70,269,574	12.32	28.79
1877	18,955,795	10.39	73,497,360	12.89	25.79
1878	16,029,231	8.80	70,804,027	12.42	22.64
1879	22,599,679	12.39	82,227,424	14.41	27.48
1880	23,382,957	12.81	79,293,452	13.91	30.54
1881	26,045,836	14.28	91,910,877	16.12	28.34
1882	22,706,784	12.45	77,715,228	13.63	29.21
1883	22,046,785	12.09	73,567,702	12.90	30.00
1884	22,141,222	12.14	72,760,758	12.76	30.43
1885	31,493,823	17.26	88,200,018	15.47	35.70
1886	29,114,622	15.96	87,479,323	15.34	33.28
1887	37,047,931	20.31	102,263,669	17.94	36.23
1888	44,437,525	24.36	124,782,893	21.88	35.61
1889	36,135,596	19.81	110,884,355	19.45	32.60
1890	45,020,302	24.68	127,093,481	22.29	35.41
1891	53,290,200	29.21	134,003,863	23.50	39.76
1892	52,707,432	28.89	135,101,198	23.69	39.71
1893	45,137,970	24.75	151,362,819	26.55	29.82
1894	52,105,448	28.56	162,102,911	28.43	32.14
1895	53,074,164	29.09	171,696,715	30.11	30.91
1896	79,243,431	43.44	202,589,994	35.53	39.12
1897	78,663,280	43.12	202,828,625	35.57	38.78
1898	77,618,824	42.55	209,579,334	36.76	37.04
1899	103,463,048	56.72	264,748,456	46.43	39.07
1900	75,603,360	41.45	211,070,422	37.02	35.82
1901	99,651,999	54.63	268,302,918	47.06	37.14
1902	127,524,120	69.91	315,363,905	55.31	40.43
1903	128,625,604	70.51	326,739,133	57.31	39.36
1904	124,048,311	68.00	344,060,608	60.34	36.05
1905	181,452,953	99.47	447,100,791	78.42	40.58
1906	152,727,845	83.72	410,270,082	71.96	37.23
1907	118,915,923	65.19	416,401,369	73.03	28.56
1908	110,898,379	60.79	394,505,478	69.19	28.11
1909	137,291,430	75.26	418,158,067	73.34	32.83
1910	130,682,634	71.64	462,964,894	81.20	28.23
1911	143,802,025	78.83	471,503,943	82.70	30.50
1912	144,088,874	78.99	473,097,031	82.98	30.46
1913	182,419,023	100.00	570,162,557	100.00	31.99
1914	178,259,045	97.72	557,109,048	97.71	32.00
1915	150,004,210	82.23	454,475,719	79.71	33.01
1916	136,679,386	74.93	516,406,995	90.57	26.47
1917	158,950,267	87.13	549,518,774	96.38	28.93
1918	151,380,423	82.98	554,893,082	97.32	27.28
1919	209,786,337	115.00	646,997,681	113.48	32.42
1920	246,813,429	135.30	762,250,230	133.69	32.38
1921	208,662,426	114.39	906,122,439	158.92	23.03
1922	218,523,170	119.79	945,049,650	165.75	23.12
1923	173,520,111	95.12	923,402,887	161.95	18.79
1924	188,500,998	103.33	1,018,210,677	178.58	18.51
1925	196,101,546	107.50	947,864,944	166.24	20.69
1926	205,466,537	112.63	1,124,221,253	197.17	18.28
1927	154,590,410	84.74	1,012,931,624	177.66	15.26
1928	190,029,938	104.17	1,195,969,271	209.76	15.89
1929	188,389,253	103.27	1,265,778,821	222.00	14.88
1930	149,838,808	82.14	1,309,755,742	229.72	11.44

Note: Since 1875 the value of *net* import alone has been recorded in the *Customs Returns*. In 1874 the only year for which both net and gross imports were recorded, the value was Hk. Tls. 18,270,196 for net import but Hk. Tls. 20,334,470 for gross import, in respect of cotton manufactures. In respect of all commodities, the value was Hk. Tls. 64,360,864 for net import but Hk. Tls. 71,395,801 for gross import. The haikwan tael was first used in 1875, before which only the tael was quoted.

Table 101. Distribution of China's import of cotton goods according to origin, 1905, 1913, and 1929

	Great Britain		Japan (incl. Formosa)		Hongkong		U. S. A. (incl. Hawaii)		British India		Other		All (direct gross imports)
	Hk. Tls.	%	Hk. Tls.	%	Hk. Tls.	%	Hk. Tls.	%	Hk. Tls.	%	Hk. Tls.	%	Hk. Tls.
Yarn and Thread													
1905	1,177,356	1.73	17,956,923	26.39	24,662,150	36.25			22,801,368	33.51	1,437,263	2.11	68,035,060
1913	644,603	0.88	32,431,586	44.46	18,909,754	25.92			18,446,558	25.29	2,514,404	3.45	72,946,905
1929	1,285,317	7.73	5,913,684	35.58	7,065,934	42.52	96,382	0.58	1,631,785	9.82	626,016	3.77	16,619,118
Piece goods													
1905	57,592,801	49.47	2,464,955	2.12	8,302,060	7.13	42,109,234	36.17	972,099	0.84	2,969,835	2.55	116,410,984
1913	58,244,032	56.30	18,753,919	18.10	9,808,217	9.50	8,090,447	7.80	446,772	0.40	8,058,584	7.79	103,401,971
1929	36,294,869	21.80	110,500,253	66.50	11,254,801	6.80	450,349	0.30	419,269	0.30	7,319,230	4.40	166,238,771
Other													
1905	706,866	34.87	544,564	26.87	447,166	22.06	291	0.01	12,981	0.64	315,105	15.54	2,026,973
1913	1,348,140	16.32	3,837,661	46.45	1,554,540	18.82	10,131	0.12	13,642	0.16	1,497,028	18.12	8,261,142
1929	468,175	6.39	5,025,359	68.57	1,249,446	17.05	56,456	0.77	17,274	0.23	512,523	6.99	7,329,233
All cotton goods													
1905	59,477,023	31.90	20,966,442	11.24	33,411,376	17.92	42,109,525	22.58	23,786,448	12.76	6,722,203	3.60	186,473,017
1913	60,236,775	32.63	55,023,166	29.81	30,272,511	16.40	8,100,578	4.39	18,906,972	10.24	12,070,016	6.54	184,610,018
1929	38,048,361	20.01	121,439,296	63.85	19,570,181	10.29	603,187	0.33	2,068,328	1.09	8,457,769	4.45	190,187,122

fall in the index had been registered until the last pre-war year, when a rise from 78.99 in 1912 to 100 took place. The course of change after 1913 is rather stationary, despite the rise in the price index of imports from 100.00 (1913) to 186.8 (1930) during the same period (Fig. 38).[17] The explanation, as given in Chapter I, lies in the rapid rise of the native cotton industry (Fig. 38). As a consequence of this rise, the proportion that the value of cotton manufactures import bears to the value of import for all commodities tends to decline. Such a proportion, expressed in terms of percentages, fluctuates between 35 and 40 from 1896 to 1905, but from 1907 onwards it falls below 30 except during a few years including 1909, 1911-15, and 1919-20. The percentage, as shown in Table 100, is 28.56 for 1907, 26.47 for 1916, 23.03 for 1921, 18.79 for 1923, and 11.44 for 1930.

Origin and destination of import, 1905-1929:—Not only has the import of cotton manufactures declined since 1905, but the origin and destination of such import have also changed, resulting in the rapid rise of Japan among the exporting nations, and the equally rapid rise of Antung and Dairen among the importing ports (Fig. 39). Taking the three years 1905, 1913 and 1929 for the purpose of comparison, we may first of all analyze the origin of import. As shown in Table 101, more than nine-tenths of the cotton manufactures were imported in each of the three years from five countries, namely, Great Britain, Japan, Hongkong, the United States and British India. The relative importance of these countries, however, has changed a great deal during the 25 years from 1905 to 1929. The rapid rise of Japan is phenomenal, so also is the equally rapid decline of Great Britain, Hongkong, the United States and British India. Japan, which occupied only 11.24 percent of the import in 1905, claimed 29.81 percent in 1913, and 63.85 percent in 1929. The percentage for the United States, which amounted to 22.58 in 1905—a percentage which was twice that for Japan in the same year, fell to 4.39 in 1913 and 0.33 in 1929. The percentage for British India, which amounted to 12.76 in 1905, fell to 10.24 in 1913 and 1.09 in 1929. Great Britain (and Hongkong),[18] occupying 49.82 percent in 1905, had about the same percentage in 1913, namely, 49.03. But like the United States and British India, her percentage was greatly reduced to 30.30 in 1929. In other words, the steady rise of Japan in the import of cotton manufactures into China was brought about at the expense first of the United States, then of British India, and finally of Great Britain—the mistress of the world's cotton textile industry. For the United States and Great Britain the decline would have been greater if cotton piece goods alone were taken into consideration.

17. *Journal of Economics and Statistics*, February, 1932, Nankai Institute of Economics, Tientsin, p. 147.

18. All imports from Hongkong into China are here taken as British. This is generally correct, as Hongkong is a port for tran-shipment and has no cotton manufacture of its own at all. Cf. Ellinger, Barnard: *Lancashire's Declining Trade with China*, Manchester Statistical Society, 1927, p. 22.

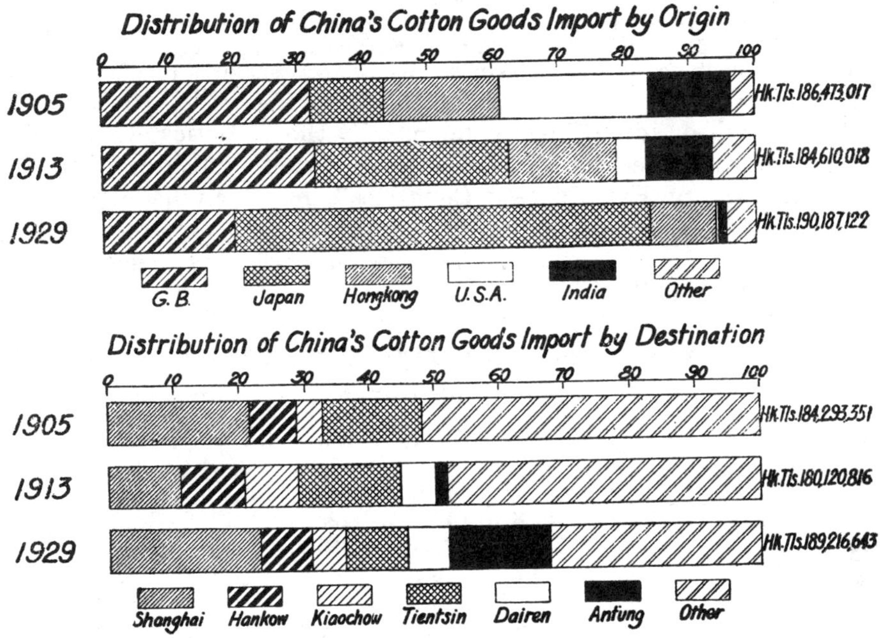

Fig. 39. Distribution of China's import of cotton goods by origin and destination, 1905, 1913 and 1929 (*See* Tables 101 and 104)

The percentage that Great Britain (and Hongkong) claimed in the value import of cotton piece goods was as high as 56.60 in 1905 and 65.80 in 1913, but in 1929 it was more than halved, to 28.60. For the United States the same percentage was 36.17 in 1905, but shrank considerably to 7.8 in 1913 and 0.3 in 1929. This loss of American trade in China's cotton piece goods market was saliently set forth in a report on the *Cotton Goods in China* by Mr. Ralph M. Odell, commercial agent for the U. S. Bureau of Foreign and Domestic Commerce, as early as 1915. In transmitting the report to the Secretary of Commerce, the Chief of the Bureau remarked that,[19]

> Ten years ago (i.e. 1905) American cotton goods had a large sale in China and the market occupied the first rank in our cotton-goods export trade. During the last few years, however, we have been losing ground rapidly and our shipments to China have radically declined. The loss of our trade has been primarily due to the competition of Japanese and, more recently, Chinese cotton mills, which secured an advantage in the use of cheaper raw material from China and India and in the lower cost of production. This competition has affected the trade of the United States more than that of any other country because our cotton-goods trade has been largely confined to coarse sheetings and drills, lines to which the Japanese and Chinese mills have given particular attention and in which they have been most successful owing to the fact that the cost of the raw material is an important factor in the total cost of the goods. After a careful study of

19. U.S. Bureau of Foreign & Domestic Commerce, *Special Agents Series*, *No.* 107, Washington, 1916, p. 5.

> the situation and interviews with leading importers and dealers in many parts of the coutry, Mr. Odell has reached the conclusion that American manufacturers can *never* hope to meet successfully this competition and regain the trade in sheetings and drills which they once held.

The above prophecy in 1915 was confirmed by the statistics already quoted. It is further confirmed by Mr. Moser in a recent study on "The Cotton Textile Industry of Far Eastern Countries", in which he expressed the opinion that "there is no volume trade in China for the American manufacturer.......His old trade in flannels and grey piece goods is gone, *never* to be restored."[20]

Table 102. Exports of cotton piece goods from Great Britain to China (including Hongkong), 1909-1930

Year	Grey	Bleached	Printed	Piece dyed	Yarn dyed	Total	Index
			Million linear yards				
1909-13 (av.)	217.5	205.8	28.7	129.9	5.4	587.3	100.0
1924	38.9	144.3	28.4	105.5	3.5	320.6	54.6
1925	22.6	90.7	16.7	58.2	3.1	191.3	32.6
1926	22.6	92.5	9.8	66.4	2.6	193.9	33.0
1927	8.8	55.0	7.6	42.3	3.2	116.9	19.9
1928	23.6	93.4	10.6	73.5	4.0	205.1	34.9
1929	23.6	96.8	11.4	71.8	6.3	209.9	35.7
1930	7.7	29.0	4.9	24.0	3.8	69.4	11.8

The decline in the cotton piece goods trade of Great Britain in China can be well illustrated by the statistics recently furnished by the *Report of the Cotton Mission*, of the British Economic Mission to the Far East, in 1931, and reproduced here in Table 102.[21] These statistics show that in terms of million linear yards the import of cotton piece goods from Great Britain to China (including Hongkong) has declined from the annual average of 587.3 in 1909-1913 to 209.9 in 1929 and 69.4 in 1930. In other words, the 1929 and 1930 imports amount respectively to but 35.7 and 11.8 percent of that for any of the five years from 1909 to 1913. Even these figures, however, are not sufficient to indicate the significance of the phenomenal decline in the British share of China'a cotton piece goods trade. The Mission adds that[22]

> The situation is all the more alarming because it is not certain whether a considerable portion of the trade still being done on behalf of Lancashire is not on account of old established "chops". China is one of the most conservative markets in the world, and though it cannot be doubted, in the light of what the Mission discovered, that with the present depleted buying power of the people and the low standard of living, aggravated as they are by an un-precedented fall in exchange, price often prevails against quality, yet it is questionable that a great deal of business is still done on "chops".

20. Published by the Pepperel Manufacturing Co., Boston, 1931, p. 74.
21. *Report*, Stationery Office, London, 1931, Sec. 1.
22. *Ibid*, Sec. 3.

The decline in British export of cotton piece goods to China cannot but bring depression and consequent unemployment to the British cotton industry which is characterized all along by its dependence upon foreign markets. As the Mission stated, "the British cotton industry is much more dependent on export trade than that of any other country. Probably not more than about one-fourth of the world production of cotton piece-goods passes into international trade, but the *Census of Production of 1924* indicated that in that year something like eighty percent of the British production was exported. Lancashire depends on foreign markets rather than on the home market, and in the past China has been one of her most important markets".[23] Indeed, whereas the volume of cotton piece goods export to China occupied as high as 9.1 percent during the period 1909-13, it was reduced to only 2.8 percent in 1930.[24]

Table 103. United Kingdom Exports of Cotton Piece goods, 1909-1930

Year	Total (Million linear yards)	To China (including Hongkong) (Million linear yards)	China's % in total export
1909-13 (average)*	6,483	587	9.1
1924	4,585	321	7.0
1925	4,637	191	4.1
1926	3,923	194	4.9
1927	4,189	117	2.8
1928	3,968	205	5.2
1929	3,765	210	5.6
1930	2,490	69**	2.8

* Converted into linear yards on the basis of the relation holding between square yardage and linear yardage in 1929.

** Including Flags, Handkerchiefs and Shawls, printed, not in the piece.

The destination of import for the cotton manufactures is shown in Table 104 (Fig. 39). In this table only those ports are included which in 1929 claim five percent or more of the import. Taking first of all the manufactures, it may be seen that six ports occupied 49.10% of the total import in 1905, 51.62% in 1913 and 67.71% in 1929. In order of relative importance in 1929 the ports include Shanghai (23.29%), Antung (15.65%), Tientsin (9.37%), Hankow (7.91%), Dairen (6.42%), and Kiaochow (5.07%). The relative position of the six ports in 1929, however, has changed greatly from that in 1905 or 1913. Among these ports the notable changes include the rapid rise of Antung from 1.86% in 1913 to 15.65% in 1929, and the equally rapid fall of Tientsin from 15.66% in 1913 to 9.37% in 1929. Shanghai, the largest port in 1905 as well as in 1929, maintained her stationary status rather precariously. The percentage that Shanghai occupied in China's import of cotton manufactures reached 21.75 in 1905, fell to 10.94 in 1913, but recovered again to 23.29 in 1929.

23. *Ibid*, Sec. 196.
24. *Ibid*, Appendix E.

Table 104. Distribution of China's import of cotton goods according to destination, 1905, 1913 and 1929

	Shanghai		Hankow		Kiaochow		Tientsin		Dairen		Antung		Other		Total (direct gross imports)
	Hk. Tls.	%	Hk. Tls.	%	Hk. Tls.	%	Hk. Tls.	%	Hk. Tls.	%	Hk. Tls.	%	Hk. Tls.	%	Hk. Tls.
Yarn and thread															
1905	6,806,086	10.18	6,005,826	8.98	3,282,777	4.91	6,795,748	10.17					43,965,656	65.76	66,856,093
1913	4,967,872	6.94	7,244,825	10.12	7,171,148	10.01	9,872,870	13.79	1,350,714	1.88	177,688	0.25	40,835,691	57.01	71,620,808
1929	2,845,481	17.18	73,041	0.44	263,802	1.59	687,048	4.15	681,213	4.11	2,463,682	14.88	9,545,636	57.65	16,559,903
Piece goods															
1905	32,715,675	28.46	7,115,060	6.19	3,922,790	3.41	21,073,375	18.34					50,101,484	43.60	114,928,384
1913	13,422,329	13.42	10,656,149	10.65	7,241,576	7.24	17,972,289	17.97	4,668,000	4.67	3,023,352	3.02	43,028,972	43.03	100,012,667
1929	40,049,455	24.22	14,667,107	8.87	9,144,054	5.53	15,243,562	9.22	10,020,205	6.06	26,547,279	16,06	49,654,362	30.04	165,326,024
Other															
1905	548,131	21.85	82,363	3.28	28,553	1.14	251,615	10.03					1,598,212	63.70	2,508,874
1913	1,317,689	15.53	205,499	2.42	106,942	1.26	367,132	4.33	3,081,968	36.31	140,601	1.66	3,267,510	38.49	8,487,341
1929	1,171,875	15.98	232,817	3.18	182,407	2.49	1,810,108	24.69	1,456,861	19.87	594,140	8.11	1,882,508	25.68	7,330,716
All cotton goods															
1905	40,069,892	21.75	13,203,249	7.16	7,234,120	3.93	28,120,738	15.26					95,665,352	51.90	184,293,351
1913	19,707,890	10.94	18,106,473	10.05	14,519,666	8.06	28,212,291	15.66	9,100,682	5.05	3,341,641	1.86	87,132,173	48.38	180,120,816
1929	44,066,811	23.29	14,972,965	7.91	9,590,263	5.07	17,740,718	9.37	12,158,279	6.42	29,605,101	15.65	61,082,506	32.29	189,216,643

The geographical distribution of cotton piece goods import differs, however, slightly from that of cotton yarn and thread import. Taking 1929 for instance, Shanghai claimed 24.22 percent of piece goods import, but 17.18 percent of yarn and thread import. Similarly, Dairen claimed 6.06 percent of piece goods import, but 4.11% of yarn and thread import; Tientsin claimed 9.22 percent of piece goods import, but 4.15 percent of yarn and thread import; Kiaochow claimed 5.53 percent of piece goods import, but 1.59 percent of yarn and thread import; Hankow claimed 8.87 percent of piece goods import, but 0.44 percent of yarn and thread import. It may, therefore, be safely concluded that the import of cotton yarn and thread is declining greatly in China's leading port cities such as Shanghai, Hankow, Tientsin, Kiaochow and Dairen, where the development of machine yarn spinning by local manufacturers has supplied the needs which were formerly met by foreign import.

Effects of Anti-Japanese Boycotts:—Before we attempt to analyze the effects of the Anti-Japanese boycotts on cotton goods trade between China and Japan, a brief resume of the boycott movement may serve as a useful background. The first anti-Japanese boycott occurred in 1908 when the Japanese steamer *Tatsu Maru* bound for Macao, a Portuguese colony on the China coast, was seized by Chinese officials on the charge of attempting to smuggling arms and ammunition into the hands of Chinese revolutionists. There was no mistake about the cargo and apparently none about the intent, but the Japanese government claimed that the steamer had been overhauled in Portuguese, not Chinese waters. As a result, Tokyo forced Peking to apologize, to pay an indemnity, to salute the Japanese flag when it was rehoisted over the *Tatsu Maru*, and to punish the Chinese customs officials who captured the vessel. The second anti-Japanese boycott occurred in September and October of 1909, as a protest against Japanese aggression in Manchuria. The immediate cause was Japan's insistence upon China's agreement to the extension of the Kirin-Horyeng Railway and the reconstruction of the Antung-Mukden Railway. Peking's capitulation to Japan's demands were bitterly opposed by the Chinese not only in Kirin and Antung, but also in Hongkong, Shanghai, Tientsin, Peiping and other parts of China. The agreement was made, however, and the agitation died down in the face of the inevitable. The next great boycott against Japan was staged in 1915, as a result of the Twenty-one Demands which have seriously disrupted Sino-Japanese relations from that day to this. Although the boycott was suspended, under pressure from Japan, by an official mandate from Peking in July, the humuliation and resentment of the Twenty-one Demands continued to rankle and resumed with redoubled force in 1919 when the Peace Conference at Versailles accepted Japan's claims on Shantung and incorporated them into the terms of the Peace Treaty. The 1919 boycott began in May of that year and continued into the next boycott in 1921. In that year Japan's insistence on direct negotiations with China of the Shantung question and China's desire to have it settled under the auspices of the Washington Conference on Limitation of Armament rekindled the boycott movement. The refusal of Japan to return Kwantung in 1923 when the original lease had expired and her insistence that the term should, under the Twenty-one Demands, be extended to 99 years, constituted the occasion for another boycott. In 1927 a boycott was started on account of the killing of Chinese citizens by Japanese troops in Tsingtao. In the following year the Japanese bombardment and occupation of Tsinan caused another boycott, which, however, came to an end with the withdrawal of Japanese troops. Finally, Japan's wilful disregard of the Wanpaoshan affair and the Korean massacres were responsible for the boycott in the Spring and Summer of 1931, which was re-enforced by the military occupation of Manchuria on the 18th of September, and the open conflict between China and Japan in Shanghai on the night of January 28, 1932.

In short, in the brief period from 1908 to 1932, a period of but one quarter of a century, nine anti-Japanese boycotts have taken place. Each boycott exerts an unfavorable influence upon the Sino-Japanese trade relation, especially upon China's import of Japanese goods. Although Japan's trade with China in terms of value has pursued an upward trend on the whole during this period, due partly to the rapid rise of price but largely to the substitution of Japanese goods for western products during the War period from 1914 to 1918, yet the boycott has been responsible, largely if not completely, either for a reduction in the volume of Japanese import or in the arrested rate of increase for such an import. As shown in Table 105, the first boycott in 1908 resulted in a fall in the index of China's import from Japan from 48.15 to 43.99, taking 1913 as the base of 100. During the other boycotts except in 1909, 1919 and 1928 similar effects were felt, the decline of China's import from Japan being, as compared with 1913 total, 5.75% in 1915, 15.73% in 1921, 17.09% in 1923 and 36.13% in 1927. The 1919 boycott, which brought about an increase rather than a decrease in China's import from Japan during the year, produced however a decrease in the following two years. Taking 1913 as the base of 100, the index of China's import from Japan rose from 200.13 in 1918 to 206.91 in 1919, but fell to 191.99 in 1920 and 176.26 in 1921 (Fig. 40).

The anti-Japanese boycott has, therefore, an immediate effect upon China's import from Japan, but in respect of cotton piece goods, such effect is less notable. In 1921, 1923 and 1927 the boycott brought about a reduction in the volume of cotton piece goods import from Japan, but in 1915 the volume of import showed a slight increase, although the rate of increase as compared with the preceding year was greatly reduced. In

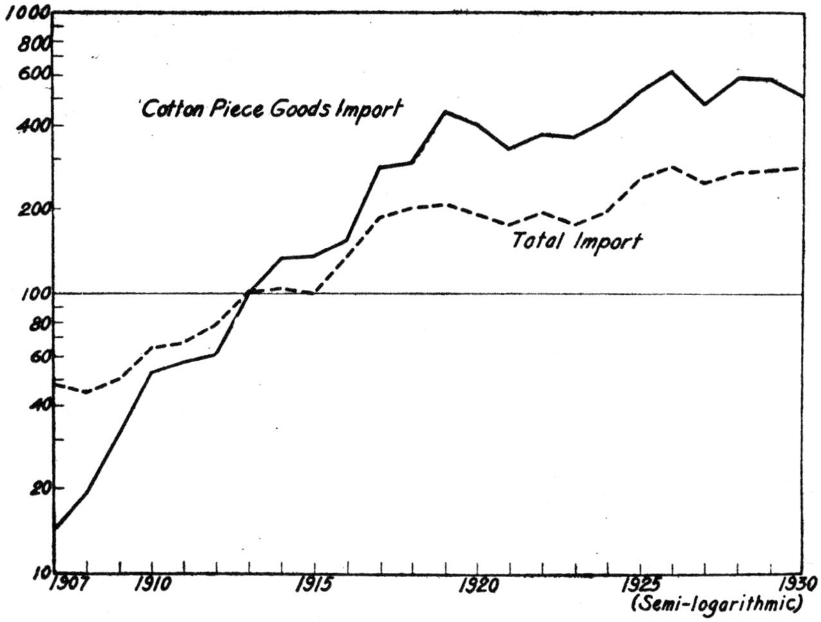

Fig. 40. China's import of cotton piece goods from Japan compared with China's total import from Japan, 1907-1930 (1913=100) (*See* Table 105)

1919 there was an increase of import in cotton piece goods, but in the following two years the decrease took place like in the import of all commodities (Fig. 40). That the effect of anti-Japanese boycott upon cotton piece goods import should have been less notable than that upon total import confirms the commanding position of the former in the China market. Japan alone of all the exporting nations can furnish the type of fabric which is both attractive in appearance and reasonable in cost, to a country which is fundamentally a price market, not a quality market. It is the failure of the British manufacturers to grasp fully the significance of this fact and to supply a type of fabric within the reach of the purchasing power of the Chinese mass that has brought about their tragic retreat in the China market. The decline of British share in China's cotton piece goods import from 65.8% in 1913 to 28.6% in 1929 is fatally counter-acted by the rapid rise of Japanese share from 18.1% to 66.5% during the same period.

Classification of cotton piece goods imported:—The classification for the cotton piece goods imported from abroad, as recorded in the Customs Returns, has gone through several revisions, in 1914, 1916 and 1925 respectively. With each revision there is an increase in the number of cotton piece goods enumerated. Whereas before 1914 the number of cotton piece goods enumerated amounted to 30 (Nos. 5-34), it was raised to 33 in 1914 (nos. 5-37), 42 in 1916 (nos. 5-46) and 56 in 1925 (nos. 1-56).

Table 105. China's import of cotton piece goods and all commodities from Japan compared, 1907-1930

	Cotton piece goods		All commodities	
Year	Hk. Tls.	1913=100	Hk. Tls.	1913=100
1907	2,627,245	14.01	57,461,410	48.15
8	3,620,417	19.30	52,500,960	43.99
9	5,926,448	31.60	59,975,187	50.25
1910	9,805,122	52.29	76,755,559	64.31
1	10,675,069	56.92	79,506,276	66.62
2	11,429,023	60.94	91,016,652	76.26
3	18,753,919	100.00	119,346,662	100.00
4	24,860,007	132.56	127,119,992	106.51
5	24,879,460	132.66	120,249,514	100.76
6	28,576,795	152.38	160,490,720	134.47
7	51,334,676	273.73	221,666,891	185.73
8	54,031,727	288.11	238,858,578	200.13
9	83,585,324	445.69	246,940,997	206.91
1920	75,350,093	401.78	229,135,866	191.99
1	60,250,008	321.27	210,359,237	176.26
2	68,752,920	366.61	231,428,885	193.91
3	67,668,256	360.82	211,024,297	176.82
4	78,557,520	418.89	234,761,863	196.71
5	99,095,397	528.39	299,755,611	251.16
6	115,059,215	613.52	336,909,441	282.29
7	90,385,398	481.95	293,793,760	246.16
8	110,837,526	591.00	319,293,439	267.53
9	110,500,253	589.21	323,141,662	270.76
1930	96,369,736	513.86	327,164,867	274.13

The 1925 revision. being the most recent, is also the most complete. The 56 items enumerated are further classified into four groups, namely, (1) grey, (2) white or dyed (irrespective of finish), (3) printed, and (4) miscellaneous. Since the 1925 revision is also applied to the cotton piece goods imported during the previous two years of 1923 and 1924 in the Customs Returns, we may well begin our analysis with 1923. As shown in Table 106, for the eight year period from 1923 to 1930 three-fourths of the total value of the 56 items of cotton piece goods imported belong to the 17 items . These 17 items are selected because either at the beginning or at the end of the period studied, each item counts for two percent or more of the total value of the cotton piece goods imported. For the period as a whole, however, 5 of the 17 items included have an average share of below two percent of the total value. The respective percentages for each of the 17 items may be arranged, in order of importance, as follows: 13.85, 12.56, 9.17, 6.18, 5.79, 4.48, 3.31, 3.21, 3.19, 3.03, 2.63, 2.16, 1.70, 1.68, 1.54, 1.33 and 0.63. The 17 items together occupy 76.43% of the total value of the cotton piece goods imported, the rest 23.57% being distributed among the remaining 39 items.

106. China's gross import of cotton piece goods classified by items, 19

		1928		1927		1926		1
	%	Hk. Tls.	%	Hk. Tls.	%	Hk. Tls.	%	Hk.
2	15.76	30,164,920	18.30	27,827,918	21.32	42,747,707	25.00	44,06
1	8.33	16,004,714	9.71	13,198,182	10.11	22,596,305	13.21	22,77
1	2.87	6,393,580	3.88	8,018,682	6.14	11,364,829	6.65	12,23
7	3.02	5,158,465	3.13	3,990,719	3.06	5,678,072	3.32	6,19
3	1.53	5,608,161	1.58	2,620,335	2.01	3,108,501	1.82	2,85
6	64.32	100,576,402	61.02	76,216,241	58.38	102,265,879	59.80	88,24
2	14.20	22,735,242	13.79	13,504,900	10.34	22,930,503	13.41	22,39
9	1.64	3,249,711	1.97	2,667,334	2.04	2,522,085	1.48	1,26
6	3.21	5,617,790	3.41	5,231,060	4.01	7,223,339	4.22	9,00
3	2.41	3,098,091	1.88	1,887,681	1.45	5,969,663	3.49	6,79
0	0.21	1,077,320	0.65	407,950	0.31	911,663	0.53	47
2	5.63	4,627,932	2.81	2,084,699	1.60	1,889,398	1.11	1,49
3	11.82	17,232,565	10.46	16,598,102	12.71	19,720,257	11.53	14,23
7	3.12	5,635,875	3.42	4,636,686	3.55	5,011,405	2.93	1,62
4	1.18	2,178,872	1.32	1,536,158	1.18	2,279,273	1.33	1,74
0	1.16	2,478,636	1.50	961,528	0.74	3,174,405	1.86	2,16
0	5.33	5,494,183	3.33	4,293,775	3.29	3,339,743	1.95	2,64
0	14.42	27,150,185	16.47	22,406,368	17.16	27,294,145	15.96	24,40
3	15.85	29,172,667	17.70	21,779,771	16.68	22,367,767	13.08	15,22
1	6.14	11,389,831	6.91	8,989,455	6.89	10,584,574	6.19	8,16
5	4.34	8,737,300	5.30	5,593,915	4.28	4,383,132	2.56	2,22
0	3.64	6,036,805	3.66	——		2,225		3
5	1.73	3,008,731	1.83	7,196,401	5.51	7,397,836	4.33	4,79
0	4.07	4,918,160	2.98	4,722,469	3.62	3,623,257	2.12	3,67
1	100.00	164,832,149	100.00	130,546,399	100.00	171,004,610	100.00	151,20
	77.72		77.14		71.70		75.77	
	22.28		22.86		28.30		24.23	

3-1930

925		1924		1923		1923-1930	
ls.	%	Hk. Tls.	%	Hk. Tls.	%	Hk. Tls.	%
),161	29.14	43,164,242	28.18	44,282,486	33.86	279,899,352	23.35
,524	15.06	25,565,768	16.69	25,990,571	19.87	150,538,327	12.56
,185	8.09	10,602,441	6.92	11,749,130	8.98	69,437,319	5.79
,043	4.10	3,039,743	1.98	3,051,667	2.33	36,358,644	3.03
,409	1.89	3,956,290	2.58	3,491,118	2.67	23,565,062	1.97
,573	58.36	94,488,727	61.69	75,292,344	57.57	722,654,682	60.28
,145	14.81	29,125,505	19.02	15,690,032	12.00	165,999,152	13.85
,992	0.84	2,886,522	1.88	2,405,714	1.84	20,398,653	1.70
,296	5.95	8,110,291	5.29	9,443,457	7.22	53,721,712	4.48
,774	4.49	8,445,767	5.51	7,731,212	5.91	39,718,172	3.31
,770	0.31	1,374,974	0.90	2,794,580	2.14	7,543,890	0.63
,932	0.99	1,393,684	0.91	737,734	0.56	31,564,609	2.63
,381	9.41	8,994,431	5.87	5,133,682	3.93	109,901,695	9.17
,925	1.07	——	—	——	—	25,951,239	2.16
,467	1.16	2,645,994	1.73	4,651,772	3.56	18,435,488	1.54
,008	1.43	3,647,085	2.38	5,506,914	4.21	20,120,292	1.68
,104	1.75	2,085,917	1.36	1,912,543	1.46	38,469,472	3.21
,779	16.15	25,778,557	16.83	19,284,704	14.74	190,830,308	15.92
,179	10.07	12,707,866	8.30	8,613,691	6.59	161,141,139	13.44
,175	5.40	9,493,972	6.20	6,682,722	5.11	74,086,755	6.18
,830	1.47	664,013	0.43	207,971	0.16	38,250,330	3.19
,080	0.02	35,608	0.02	——	—	15,894,881	1.33
,094	3.17	2,514,273	1.64	1,722,998	1.32	32,909,173	2.74
,269	2.43	2,818,005	1.84	2,599,376	1.99	35,208,226	2.94
,182	100.00	153,178,840	100.00	130,787,897	100.00	1,198,903,399	100.00
	76.36		77.12		79.28		76.43
	23.64		22.88		20.72		23.57

	Grey	White or dyed	Printed	Miscellaneous	Total
No. items	5	37	12	2	56
1923	33.86	57.57	6.59	1.99	100
1924	27.25	62.80	8.18	1.78	100
1925	29.14	58.36	10.07	2.43	100
1926	25.00	59.80	13.08	2.12	100
1927	21.32	58.38	16.68	3.62	100
1928	18.30	61.02	17.70	2.98	100
1929	15.76	64.32	15.85	4.07	100
1930	16.37	59.98	19.02	4.64	100
Average	23.24	60.43	13.40	2.92	100

Methods of distribution:—In describing the methods of distribution, we may confine our attention chiefly to the cotton piece goods for obvious reasons. In the first place, it is the cotton piece goods that cover practically the whole of the cotton goods now imported into China. The cotton piece goods, which occupied but 62.4 percent of the total import of cotton goods in 1905, claimed as much as 87.4 percent in 1929. On the other hand, the cotton yarn and thread, which occupied 36.5 percent of the total import of cotton goods in 1905, claimed but 8.7 percent in 1929. Secondly, the method of distributing yarn and thread does not differ much from that of distributing piece goods, and the same importer or dealer may distribute both yarns and piece goods at the same time.

Table 107. China's import of cotton goods, 1905, 1913 and 1929

	1905		1913		1929	
	Hk. Tls.	%	Hk. Tls.	%	Hk. Tls.	%
Yarn and thread	68,035,060	36.5	72,946,905	39.5	16,619,118	8.7
Piece goods	116,410,984	62.4	103,401,971	56.0	166,238,771	87.4
Other	2,026,973	1.1	8,261,142	4.5	7,329,233	3.9
Total	186,473,017	100.00	184,610,018	100.00	190,187,122	100.00

The methods of distributing cotton piece goods in China differ not only among different ports, but also among the importers of different nationalities. In Hongkong, the chief port of distribution for South China, sales are transacted in terms of local currency, whereas in Shanghai, the centre of distributing activities for Central and North China, sterling is commonly quoted. In the former the compradore system is still in full swing, with full financial guarantee, while in the latter it is being gradually given up by foreign firms. Instead, able Chinese merchants who would formerly make ideal compradores are invited to serve on the Board of Directors of the different firms. In Japanese firms the compradore system has seldom been resorted to even from the very beginning. In Tientsin and Manchuria where Japanese cotton piece goods largely predominate, and even in Shanghai, the system of distribution is either for the agents of the Japanese exporters to trade directly with the Chinese dealers, or for the Chinese dealers to maintain agents in Osaka or Kobe.[25]

25. *Ibid.* passim; Ellinger, *op. cit.*

The British method of distribution, which has the longest history in China, has undergone considerable changes during the last few decades. The system of marketing through a home shipping or merchant house and a local importing firm, which used to prevail in former years, "appears to have become obsolete, and through over-keen competition has resulted in the margin of profit, or commission, being reduced to a bare minimum. Thirty or more years ago the system worked fairly satisfactorily as certain importers confined their dealings to one or two particular shippers; the trade was then almost entirely in staple articles such as greys, whites, and black Italians which were well protected by established marks or chops, usually the property of the importing house, though in some instances owned by the Manchester firm. This trade was usually done by the importers on a merchant basis. The goods were bought for their own account and sold *ex-godown* (duty paid) on a silver basis. The importer used his best judgment as to when to buy and had full control over the question of covering exchange; he also had a more or less free market for his goods in China, and was not obliged to carry goods from season to season for the account of dealers who might eventually fail to fulfil their engagements". About twenty-five years ago, according to this importer, "Manchester shippers began to send their own representatives to China, and this led to the older importing houses, who had confined their operations to one or two shippers at home, finding it necessary to open their doors to representatives, and to place their orders on the spot. Instead, therefore, of buying for own account, the importers began to take indents from dealers to be placed with Manchester firms. One consequence was that importers were no longer able to command merchanting profit, but had to work solely on commission. Another consequence was that, as the indent system can be worked with a minimum of capital and staff, this state of affairs encouraged many people of small means to enter the trade, and it resulted in some cases in a certain perfunctoriness in the attention given to the piece goods side for, of course, these firms could not live on piece goods profits alone and had to deal in many different articles. Firms of this kind would content themselves by sending on to Lancashire, as indications of what was wanted, samples of what their neighbours were importing, or samples which were to ascertain the real requirements of the market." On the other hand, "the productions of a mill are broadcasted through several Manchester shipping houses to a still greater number of importers on this side, and ultimately same samples find their way to a comparatively small group of dealers at the port of entry. These dealers are often known to each other and are in a position to compare notes. When the dealers decide to place their orders they will start by offering through two or more importers, who in turn may try two or more shippers, and so for every inquiry many telegrams are sent and for the basing of the inquiry many samples of the same quality are collected and compared both as regards quality and price".[26]

The rise of small importers is accompanied by the growth of mushroom dealers. "Whereas there used to be from fifty to a hundred reputable dealers in former days, there are probably now not more than a dozen, or perhaps even fewer; a great many having gone out of the business owing to trade difficulties. There have sprung up, however, unfortunately both for the importer and the reputable dealer, a large number of mushroom dealers whose ideals of business morality are best summed up in the phrase 'Heads I win, tails you lose.' It was quite common to hear of this kind of dealer, significantly referred to as ricksha coolie dealer, scrapping together a nominal capital and being entrusted with goods to the value of tens of thousands of taels. So long as the market remains favorable he will honor his obligations, but not always even then, for if he considers the time is opportune he does not stand on the order of his going but simply disappears; sometimes to turn up again in a fresh spot with a new name, but more often he will clear off completely with his ill-gotten proceeds."[27] Because of this cut-throat competition from the mushroom dealers the reputable dealers have to handle Japanese goods in addition to British in order to maintain their margin of profit. "Until quite recently it was an invariable practice that the better dealers handling goods from British importers did not handle Japanese goods and *vice versa*. There is some danger of the few who are left, if they wish to remain in the piece goods trade, being driven to handle Japanese goods, which apart from the initial advantage they usually have in price even though this is the result of 'taking a view,' very often yield a higher margin of profit to the dealer."[28]

In distributing the piece goods from the foreign importer to the native dealer, the compradore generally serves as the connecting link. This system has its origin in the early days of Chinese trade when "the foreign merchant had not the means of judging the buying capacity or financial standing of the native dealers, and had to employ Chinese, who took the responsibility of guaranteeing and enforcing payment from the Chinese buyers and enforcing delivery of goods on contracts for the sale of native produce to the foreigner or acceptance of goods purchased by the Chinese. For his services he was paid a fixed salary and was under bond or guaranty for the faithful performance of his duties and for the money which he handled. With the growth of trade the importance and influence of the compradore has increased until today (1915) he occupies a unique and powerful position in the commercial life of China. Sometimes he is a partner in the firm and sometimes he buys goods on his

26. Report of the Cotton Mission, *op. cit.*, Sec. 156-7.
27. *Ibid*, Sec. 146.
28. *Ibid*, Sec. 147.

own account. He has his own organization, which often extends to distant cities and trading centers. In addition to his salary, he frequently receives a commission of not more than one half percent on all goods purchased or sold for the firm which employs him. He engages and pays the Chinese staff and handles the native customers, who seldom have direct dealings with the foreign members of the firm. He keeps in close touch with market conditions and is able to determine what goods can be sold, while his knowledge of the financial standing of native dealers enables him to protect the foreign firm from loss". The system, as here described, is not without its abuses and drawbacks. "Sometimes too much dependence is placed in the compradore and the foreign firm is in ingorance of actual conditions in trading circles. It is also claimed that the compradore takes too much squeeze, both from his employers and from the dealers for whom be acts as a middleman, and that he demands payment from the native staff for employing them and then retains a part of their wages as his commission".[29] Besides, the foreign firms claim that "it is quite common for a Chinese to act as compradore to one firm, and as dealer customer to others; that, in fact, such a one will not hesitate to exploit his intimate knowledge of his firm's business secrets."[30]

The compradore system has declined in importance as foreign merchants in China become more familiar with the Chinese trading practices. Formerly the compradore guaranteed the financial integrity of customers with whom he recommended business, and would make good a default; but in recent years the tendency has been for that guarantee to become more nominal, or, at best, partial. In Shanghai except in the case of the auction where circumstances are different and where the compradore guarantees the full purchase money, the usual percentage that a compradore "stands" today is 25 percent. In Hongkong it is still the case that most compradores guarantee the full amount. The Japanese manage as a rule to do business without compradores, and so do an increasingly large number of other foreign firms. There is today a tendency with some of the best firms to appoint on to their board of directors the type of able Chinese who formerly made the ideal compradore.[31]

The method of distributing cotton piece goods from the foreign importer to the Chinese dealer, sometimes through the medium of a compradore, is supplemented from the very beginning by the auction method. This method, which was started as early as 1873 by Maitland & Co. in Shanghai, has been growing in importance until recently. It was greatly stimulated in 1907 when many of the cotton piece-goods firms held large stocks of goods which the Chinese dealers, many of whom had ordered

29. Odell, *op. cit.*, pp. 102-3.
30. Report of Cotton Mission, *op. cit.*, Sec. 172.
31. *Ibid*, Sec. 171-2.

them, were unable to take off their hands. In 1915 when Mr. Odell of the U. S. Bureau of Foreign and Domestic Commerce made an investigation into the system in Shanghai, it was found that the principal firms engaged in the business included Maitland & Co. (Ltd.), Probst Hanbury & Co. (Ltd.), Jardine, Matheson & Co. (Ltd.), Noel Murray & Co. (Ltd.), and L. Moore & Co., all English firms. Their aggregate annual sales, according to Mr. Odell, "approximate 30 percent of the total imports of cotton goods imported into Shanghai. Some of them sell goods for other firms charging a commission that varies from one-fourth of 1 percent to 1 percent, according to private arrangement, the quantity sold etc., and some of them do an indent business in addition to selling at auction. Maitland & Co., the largest auction firm in Shanghai, is a Manchester firm (formerly Thorne & Co.) which buys goods outright in England and sells them at auction at the best prices obtainable. Because they buy in large lots, they often secure goods at low prices."[32] Fifteen years later in 1930, the British Economic Mission reported a considerable decline in the system. According to that Mission, "it is impossible to judge how far the auction method of distributing piece goods has outlived its utility. It may be that there is still room for one auction once a week, but we gathered that the business even of this one had fallen to less than a quarter of what it was formerly. Also we came accross many people in the piece goods business in Shanghai, not only British, but of other nationalities, who considered that in existing market conditions, it was easier to 'bear' the auction prices than it used to be; and as auction prices have a direct bearing on all selling prices, they are an important factor in times of stagnation in depressing the tone of the market generally."[33]

The auction system, as described by the British Economic Mission, works as follows: "Particulars of each week's auction and the prices and quantities of the various "chops" sold are known throughout China; partly through the weekly reports in the Press, and for the rest through the firm broadcasting information by circulars to dealers all over the country. The cloths sold through the auction are all well-known brands. Buyers bid for the goods on known quality, and take delivery out of stock. It is very rare that there is occasion for them to inspect samples. Dealers attend the auction from as far as Tientsin, but often up-country buyers will send an order to a dealer on the spot who puts through transactions of this kind on a low rate of commission. All goods are offered for sale without a reserve, and they open for inspection at the godown on the day before the auction. After the auction, purchasers are allowed 14 days within which to examine the goods, and if they are found damaged, an

32. Odell, *op. cit.*, pp. 116-7.
33. British Economic Mission Report, *op. cit.*, Sec. 168.

allowance has to be agreed upon between the company and the purchaser, but in no circumstances can goods once bought be returned."[34]

Although the auction system is gradually giving way, yet it is not without its advantages. As Mr. Odell has well pointed out, the auction sales "provide a means for quick sale, and thus obviate the necessity of carrying goods a long time at a heavy expense for storage, insurance, and interest; they make it possible to distribute goods over a wide extent of territory; and they bring the seller closer to the ultimate consumer. The dealers who attend the auctions in Shanghai constitute a distinct and separate class, and because they sell more directly to the retail merchants they can often afford to pay a higher price for the goods than if they made their purchases through importers who sell in the open market. The auctions also afford an opportunity to dealers who require a small lot of goods for immediate delivery. In introducing a new brand of goods the English manufacturer often finds it advantageous to use the auctions, because under this method the goods may be distributed in small quantities in several districts. It is better for the manufacturer who is endeavoring to introduce his goods to 'sell 50 bales in 10-bale lots to five dealers than to sell the entire lot to one dealer".[35]

The method of distributing the cotton piece goods from Lancashire, as described above, is succinctly summed up in the following terms by the British Economic Mission: "Speaking very generally, it may be stated that lately there have been only two main centres for the distribution of cotton piece goods in China—Hongkong for the South, and Shanghai for all the rest of the country, including Manchuria. A little direct business has been effected at Tientsin, Hankow, and other ports, but on the whole attempts to go outside the two markets mentioned have not of recent years met with much success. At the ports of entry, the bulk of this trade has been conducted through importing houses, mainly British and European, who have sold the goods to Chinese wholesale dealers, frequently on an indent basis, and have thereafter had no further concern with their distribution—all arrangements for the conveyance of the cargo to its ultimate destination and its sale to the retailer being left entirely in Chinese hands. From time to time experiments have been made by a few British importing houses to carry their interest in the goods up to a further point by seeking orders, and even maintaining stocks, at some of the outports, but the results of these efforts have not been encouraging —in fact except during a boom period when customers were clamoring for goods they were failures, and the firms concerned, in most if not all cases, have reverted to the general practice of leaving the Chinese dealers to make their own distributing arrangements. Apart from the attempts at direct up-country trading mentioned above, another important

34. *Ibid*, Sec. 169.
35. Odell, *op. cit.*, p. 117.

variation from the general practice has been that of the Shanghai auctions, which were at one time being held by three firms on three separate days each week, but which are now only operated by a single firm once a week".[36]

The method of distributing Lancashire cotton piece goods, as it now stands, is subject to several criticisms, and is partly responsible for the decline in British share of the cotton piece goods trade in China. Apart from the fundamental fact that the British goods stress more on quality than on price, and can thus hardly compete with Japanese goods that stress more on price than on quality, in a market where the purchasing power of the people has been reduced to an extremely low level by war, famine, flood, and recently, by the great depreciation in silver, the British methods of distribution in certain respects bear poor comparison with the Japanese. In the first place, the British sales are transacted in sterling, not in local currency, in the largest distributing centre—Shanghai. At a time of falling exchange like the present, such arrangement presses heavily upon the Chinese dealers. Secondly, the system of indent sales does not privide for the maintenance of stocks in the ports. The failure to maintain stocks would have been a lesser handicap but for the fact that Japan, in addition to her geographical propinquity, possesses the advantage of maintaining stocks in China ports. This is especially true of British prints, which are essentially an indent business, as the time that elapses between the choosing of designs and the arrival of the goods in China, makes dealers hesitate very much to place orders with Lancashire in view of the much shorter time in which their indents could be supplied from Japan. British importers, moreover, expressed themselves at a further disadvantage in that in order to get business in prints they had to send out patterns to prospective customers, and they were certain that often these got into the hands of dealers who picked out the best, have them copied, usually on a lower quality cloth, and placed their orders in Japan, if only to secure earlier delivery.[37] Thirdly, the severe competition among importers which arises from the system of Manchester shippers sending out their own representatives to China, results in a low margin of profit for the importers. The latter have to handle in addition to the British goods the Japanese goods, and cannot afford to concentrate on the British goods as much as would have been expected of them. Such competition encourages the "Chinese dealers playing one firm off against another, while anxiety to obtain the business has frequently resulted in less care being exercised in accepting business (from doubtful Chinese dealers) than should have been the case."[38]

36. Report of the Cotton Mission, *op. cit.*, Sec. 141.
37. *Ibid*, Sec. 150.
38. *Ibid*, Sec. 155.

On the basis of the above criticisms, the British Economic Mission has come to the conclusion that "Lancashire goods for China should be handled so far as export is concerned on a joint production and marketing basis, with the maintenance of selected stocks in suitable centres, and with a capable supervisory control of the release of the stocks in China, but utilizing existing Chinese channels of distribution. It was generally agreed (among the importers) that such a scheme, if it were practicable, would enable economics of production to be effected. Further, it would get over the difficulty of delay in delivery of selected lines; it would enable its supervisory staff in China to do something in the way of propaganda, advertisement, inspection, etc., up-country(but without making sales); thus maintaining a check on changes in fashion, on the adjustment of supplies to actual demand, and avoiding the present weakness of false ideas as to the capacity of the market, which arises from a great many importers receiving inquiries from a number of dealers about business which in bulk appears to be considerable but may actually refer to the same restricted demand."[39] In such a scheme it is presumed that "goods would be sold in local currency, and that exchange would have to be covered by the importer,"[40] thus obviating the exchange risk of the Chinese dealers.

The methods of distribution for the importers of piece goods from other nations except Japan do not differ greatly from those applying to British piece goods, according to the British Economic Mission. To this statement, however, may be added the result of an earlier investigation in 1915 by Mr. Odell, on the American selling methods in China. According to Mr. Odell, "American cotton goods reach China through export houses in New York with branches in China. Most of these are American firms, but a few large English firms and one Japanese firm with New York offices handle some of the business...... The export houses in New York purchase goods from the agents of the mills, and in two important particulars the methods employed are radically different from the methods used by the English. In the first place, the goods are usually sold under the mill brand and not the brand of the importer as in the case of Eng-

39. *Ibid*, Sec. 162. It may be mentioned that Mr. Ellinger, in an earlier report published in 1927 for the Manchester Statistical Society, has also voiced the necessity of closer co-operation. "I am confident," says Mr. Ellinger, "that in order to compete with the Japanese for the main lines of our export trade to China, we must look in the future to close collaboration with a view to an ultimate concentration of the production of certain articles in one unit (not necessarily under one roof), which will care for the spinning, weaving, bleaching, dyeing or printing, making-up, packing and merchanting. I do not mean one enormous amalgamation which will control the major part of the export of cotton goods, but rather to the formation of many units, each one of which will concentrate on one particular quality given, always, of course, that the demand for such quality is sufficient to warrant the formation of such a unit" (pp. 40-41). Mr. Ellinger's proposal is unique, and may help to supplement that sponsored by the Cotton Mission.

40. *Ibid*, Sec. 167.

lish goods. Secondly, except in a few rare instances, no one export house has exclusive control of a mill brand in the China market. It is not to be doubted that the American methods have their advantages. If the mill brand is used and it becomes firmly established on the market, the mill secures the benefit of the increased demand. If the importer has his own brand put on the goods the mill loses its identity, and it is always possible in standard cloths, such as sheetings and drills, for the importer to secure his supply of goods from another source if any differences regarding price, quality, shipments, etc., arise with the original mill. This works a hardship on the mill which may have made special preparations for producing the particular kinds of goods in demand...... From the importer's standpoint," however, "there are two great disadvantages in this system. In the first place, if an importer selects a certain brand American cloth and succeeds, after considerable work and expense, in establishing it in the market, he soon finds that competing firms can purchase the idential goods and secure some of the benefits which he has made possible in making the cloth popular in the market. In the second place, this practice, in the opinion of many, often results in that great demoralizing and depressing influence in the Chinese cotton-goods trade, the overflooding of the market."[41]

The Japanese method of distribution, as has been mentioned above, is different from the British method in at least two aspects, namely, the maintenance of stocks in the ports and direct trading without the medium of compradore. Because of Japan's geographical propinquity to the China market, the first aspect may not always hold true, but it is sufficiently representative in practice as to prevent forward sale by the Japanese merchants for lines which are handled in bulk, except under strict requirements. The Japanese merchants, as Mr. Ellinger stated in 1927, "will only sell forward against deposit of 10 percent to 15 percent with the order, and the importing merchant is very loathe to buy forward, because he fears that in the event of a rise in the market the goods destined for him will be resold at higher prices, and he will only get delivery at a later period ... According to the Japanese custom, May/June shipment, for instance, does not mean half May and half June, but May or June, and that in the event of a rising market the importer will get his goods at the end of June, whereas, in a falling market he would probably get them in the beginning of May." Consequently, "the Japanese exporter is in a position to resell goods much more freely than would be the case with English goods, and if the market goes down he will allow the dealers (importing merchants) to cancel on payment of the difference, and if the market goes up will often resell for the dealer, paying him the difference in the market value."[42] In the third place, the principal Japanese exporting

41. Odell, *op. cit.*, pp. 109-10.
42. Ellinger, *op. cit.*, pp. 25-6.

firms have their own houses in Shanghai and some of the other ports, and this practice is steadily increasing. They are said to keep a "black list" of shady dealers and to exchange information of a useful character in a more methodical manner than operates with British firms. Fourthly, apart also from the difference in price, Japanese goods are said to be more popular with Chinese dealers because they yield quicker sale results and a larger margin of profit than Lancashire goods, especially in Shanghai. It was also stated that their terms of payment are more elastic.[43] The last statement, which the British Economic Mission considers as "doubtful except in rare cases", was however stated positively in an earlier investigation in 1915. According to that investigation, Japanese firms in North China and Manchuria "offer every possible inducement to the leading Chinese wholesale dealers to handle Japanese goods. These inducements sometimes take the form of extending credit, and sometimes of an agreement to take native produce, such as beans, in exchange for cotton goods. They quote all prices *ex godown* at Mukden, Newchwang, Harbin, Tientsin, or other cities in which the sale is made, eliminating all questions of freights, duties, commissions, exchange, etc. In fact, as a representative of an American cotton-goods firm who spent some time in Manchuria expressed it, "the Japanese have practically reduced their piece-goods business to the basis of buying groceries at home at the corner store with a charge account to the good customer. This method appeals very strongly to the Chinese. Not infrequently Chinese dealers purchase goods on 30, 60, or 90 days' credit, make a quick sale for cash, and use the proceeds to speculate in exchange, or to lend at a high rate of interest, thus using their credit to make a turnover for themselves."[44] The same investigation also credits the Japanese with special advantages in Manchuria. "They secure reduced rates on railways and steamship lines running from Japan on shipments in quantity under general provisions that practically only Japanese avail themselves of; they virtually control the banking, railway, and postal facilities; and they have a large population of Japanese in the country through whom they can distribute their goods . It is also claimed that their goods escape local Chinese taxes, because they are shipped to the railway areas or concessions of the Japanese South Manchuria Railway. When leaving these areas for the interior the goods become subject to Chinese taxes, but the Chinese are adepts at evading taxation and undoubtedly many of the Japanese goods sold in the railway concessions are not taxed. Since June, 1913, all goods entering China via Antung, the border town between Manchuria and the Japanese possession, Chosen, are entitled to a one-third reduction in the customs tariff. This reduction applies to the goods of all nations, but the Japanese alone appear to have taken advantage of it, owing to the fact that English

43. Report of the Cotton Mission, *op. cit.*, sec. 145.
44. Odell, *op. cit.*, p. 107.

and American cotton goods for Manchuria are handled through Shanghai and Tientsin, from which ports the easiest and cheapest route to Manchuria is via Newchwang or Dalny; to ship via Japan or Chosen and thence by rail via Antung would doubtless cost, in additional freight and transhipment charges, so much as to offset the advantages to be gained from the reduction in duty. Unquestionably the systematic and aggressive methods employed by the Japanese, combined with the natural advantages which they enjoy with regard to the market, have exercised a strong influence in the phenomenal growth of their trade; but of equal importance is the fact that they have succeeded in producing goods suitable to the requirements of the Chinese at a lower cost f. o. b. the mill than their competitors. They also cater especially to the Chinese market and regulate their prices not always according to the actual cost of goods but according to market conditions. When prices are high and goods are not moving freely they will quote a little under the market to get business and keep their machinery going. China, with its enormous capacity for consuming cotton goods, is a market in itself, subject to its own conditions and peculiarities, and the Japanese have been quick to realize this and to adjust their methods to suit it."[45]

Export

Early export:—The first kind of cotton goods to be exported from China was the nankeens—handloom cotton cloths woven at Nanking. In 1734 the Court of the East India Company made the first trial order for 100 pieces of nankeen from Nanking, one yard wide and 20 yards long, at Tls. 3.50 per piece, and to be delivered in 90 days; but the cloth was not received in time.[46] Two years later, another effort was made to procure the nankeens, which proved successful. In all the *Richmond* secured 10,374 pieces, of which "some have more substance than others, but they are in general much better than what are made here in Canton, which will not hold their color in washing, as we are assured the true nankeen will."[47] The *Normanton*, another ship of the Company, also secured 11,930 pieces—2,560 pieces from Canton and 9,370 pieces from Ningpo. The cost for the 2,560 pieces from Canton amounted to Tls. 896, which was equivalent to Tl. 0.35 per piece.[48] In comparing this price with that given by the Company in its trial order in 1734, namely, Tls. 3.50, it seemed indeed very low. But we must remember that the size for the trial order was unusually large, and might be considered even fanciful. For generally a piece of nankeen has only a width of 13½ inches and a length of 6 yards, with a total area which is but one ninth of that specified in the trial order.[49]

45. *Ibid*, pp. 107-8.
46. Morse, *op. cit.*, I: 224.
47. *Ibid*, I: 254.
48. *Ibid*, I: 254, 255, 257.
49. *Ibid*, II: 61.

Since 1736 the export of nankeens from China, chiefly from Canton, became a regular feature of the Company's trading operations. From 1737 to 1741 the diary of the Company recorded a total export of 39,742 pieces, distributed annually as follows: 10,000 in 1737, 9,530 in 1738, 513 in 1739, 4,000 in 1740 and 15,699 in 1741. From 1742 to 1749 there was a hiatus of eight years in the collection of the supercargoes' diaries preserved in the India Office, and consequently no figures were available. However, it is evident that judging from the activities of the subsequent years, the export of nankeens became no longer a recurring feature every year. In 1750 5,740 pieces were exported; in 1753, 1,500 pieces; and in 1754, 7,200 pieces. Seven years elapsed before another export of 3,000 pieces took place in 1761. Then followed 18,000 pieces in 1765, 20,000 pieces in 1768, 30,000 pieces in 1769, 12,500 pieces in 1772, 10,000 pieces in 1775.[50] Beginning with 1781 the export apparently became more regular. The diary for that year stated that "at this period the Company was regularly sending each year to England 20,000 pieces of nankeen, 6 yards long, 13½ inches wide, costing Tl. 0.400 a piece".[51] This statement was confirmed by another export of 20,000 pieces as recorded in the diary for 1782, but subsquent to that year no record of export was founded until 1784 when 19,500 pieces were exported. In 1786 40,000 pieces were purchased on the Company's account and another 2,000 pieces on the private account. In 1790 the purchase amounted to 96,500 pieces, of which 40,000 pieces were for the Company's account and 56,500 pieces for the private account.[52]

Although the East India Company led in the export of nankeens in 1736, yet other nations must have followed suit rather closely. In 1764 statistics on the export of foreign ships showed that four Dutch ships exported 15,000 pieces, four French ships exported 11,510 pieces, two Danish ships exported 26,400 pieces, and one Swedish ship exported 8,000 pieces—a total of 60,910 pieces. In 1784 the first American ship, the *Empress of China,* carried away 864 pieces, with a weight of 24 piculs and at a cost of Tls. 362. In 1786 when the English ships were loaded with 42,000 pieces of nankeens, as stated above, the American share reached 33,920 pieces. The ships of other flags, meantime, were carrying even larger quantity, being 98,200 pieces for the Dutch, 78,000 pieces

50. *Ibid,* I: 259, 264, 271, 275, 282, 285, 291, 292; II: 3; V: 19, 101, 124, 138, 146, 168.
51. *Ibid,* II: 61.
52. *Ibid,* II: 74, 95, 119, 180.

Year
1786
1790
2
3
4
5
6
7
8
9
1800
1
2
3
4
5
6
7
8
9
1810
1
2
3
4
5
6
7
8
9
1820
1
2
3
4
5
6
7
8
9
1830
1
2
3
1817-1833
1786-1833
1786-1833

for the Danish, and 72,000 pieces for the French. Besides, the Swedish ships carried 10,900 pieces and the Spanish 37,000 pieces.[53]

In Tables 108a and 108b the export of nankeens from Canton was classified according to the nationality of the exporting ships (Fig. 42). Table 108a shows that during the 48 year period from 1786 to 1833 Canton exported a total of 40,274,164 pieces of nankeens. The American ships led with 22,776,943 pieces or 56.55 percent, after which followed the English with 15,169, 553 pieces or 37.67 percent. The ships of other nationalities, including Netherland, Denmark, Sweden, France, Spain, etc., exported altogether 2,327,668 pieces or 5.78 percent.[54] Of this total export of 40,274,164 pieces, 19,232,919 pieces or 47.76 percent were valued at $13,254,142, giving an average price of 68.91 cents per piece. Table 108a also shows that the nankeens carried by the English ships were of a more expensive kind than those carried by the American ships, the average price per piece being 80.79 cents for the former but 57.47 cents for the latter.

The nankeens exported from Canton in English ships were mostly for the Company's or for private account, while those exported in American ships were largely destined for the United States. Available statistics, as given in Table 109,[55] show that of the 7,219,809 pieces exported during the 11 years between 1819 and 1832 (1820-21, 1823 excepted) in American ships, 5,878,109 pieces or 81.42 percent went to the United States, while only 1,056,000 pieces or 14.63 percent went to Europe. The other 285,700 pieces or 3.95 percent were exported to South America and elsewhere.

53. *Ibid,* V: 121-2; II: 95, 119, 180. Ping Chia Kuo, in an article on *Canton and Salem* (being Part III of *Some Oriental Influences on Western Culture,* American Council, Institute of Pacific Relations, 1931), stated that "If the name of China was made familiar to the American people by the introduction of tea and other edibles, her influence was felt even more strikingly in clothing. Along with large chests of teas and peppers, nankeens were among the favorite objects the early sailors to China brought back to their country. What were at first carried home as curios to please their wives and friends soon assumed the importance of a regular commodity. By the brig *Hope,* which entered Salem in early February, 1790, George Dodge ordered $198.89 worth of nankeens, while it was to the wealthy Benjamin Hodges that $1,352.40 of the cloth was consigned. But a few months later, on the ship *Astrea* which entered the port on June 5, the total amount of nankeens carried was estimated at as much as $16,104. This influx of nankeens opened a new epoch in the history of American clothing. With its unique yellow, at once bright and serene, nankeen lent no little charm to the apparel of New England women. The most fashionable jackets and trousers were made of this cloth named from Nanking. Not only could a lady find in John Scobie's store, at the corner of Elm and Newberry Streets, a great variety of striped, clouded, and yellow nankeens, but shopping at the frequent auctions at William Lang's office, on Essex Street, she could pick up as much of it as she wanted at much lower prices out of the heaps of 'Indian' clothes".

54. For references to Tables, 108a and 108b see *Ibid,* V: 121-2; II: 119, 180, 193, 205, 256, 266, 278, 294, 311, 322, 348, 358, 389, 401, 416; III: 2, 27, 55, 77, 101, 131, 158, 175, 190, 206, 228, 243, 308, 329, 331, 345, 347, 366, 369, 384; IV: 4, 22, 53, 68, 71, 86, 89, 100, 103, 119, 123, 140, 159, 162, 182, 185, 196, 223, 249, 253, 272, 325, 340, 343, 370.

55. *Ibid,* III: 367; IV: 69, 101, 120, 141, 160, 183, 197, 250, 273, 341.

Table 108b. Canton's export of nankeens by ships of other than English and American flags, 1764-1832 (in pieces)

Year	Dutch	Danish	Swedish	French	Spanish	Other	Total	% of Grand Total
1764	15,000	26,400	800	11,510			60,910	100.0
1786	98,200	78,000	10,900	72,000	37,000		296,100	79.6
1790	22,200	70,000		154,500			246,700	48.4
2	11,400	41,000	35,000	143,600	17,100	10,000	258,100	64.2
3	25,000		30,000			21,000	76,000	17.8
4	13,500					157,500	171,000	28.6
5			45,000		150,000		195,000	19.4
6		50,000			151,000		201,000	24.5
7		100,000	25,000				125,000	21.8
8		226,000	36,700				262,700	12.4
9		75,000					75,000	6.5
1800		481	385			59	925	6.3
2	500	28,500	13,500	34,000		19,000	95,500	9.1
3		40,000			27,000	9,000	76,000	8.0
4		62,000	23,000				85,000	4.9
5		57,000				6,500	63,500	3.8
6		75,000					75,000	8.7
1809					15,000		15,000	12.0
1815	128		15				143	2.1
1832	10,000						10,000	5.9

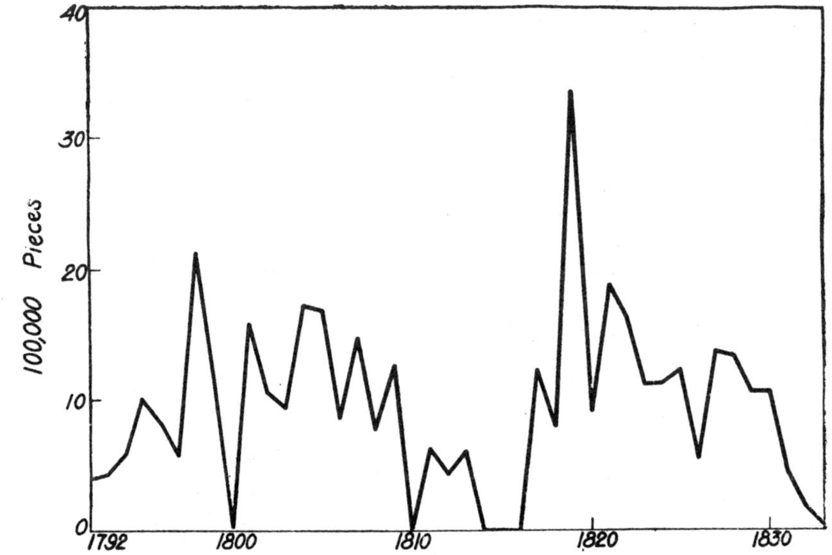

Fig. 42. Export of nankeens from Canton, 1786-1833 (*See* Table 108a)

Table 109. Destination of nankeens exported from Canton by American ships, 1819-1832 (in pieces)

Year	U. S.	Europe	S. America etc.	Total
1819	1,841,000	958,000	133,000	2,932,000
1822	1,070,706	12,000	25,000*	1,107,706
4	532,000	4,000		536,000
5	664,000	15,000	42,000	721,000
6	267,400		41,300	308,700
7	524,500			524,500**
8	392,900	60,000		452,900**
9	305,568		44,400	349,968**
1830	118,750	7,000		125,750
1	122,285			122,285
2	39,000			39,000
Total	5,878,109	1,056,000	285,700	7,219,809
	81.42%	14.63%	3.95%	100.00%

* To Manila and Batavia.

** The quantities for each of the three years 1827-29 disagree with those given in Table 108a, but the total quantities for the three years together, 1,327,368 pieces, are not far apart from those given in Table 108a, namely, 1,322,000 pieces.

Export since 1867:—The nankeen cloth, which was first exported to England in 1736, remained the only kind of China's cotton goods exported to foreign countries for almost two centuries. In the preceding paragraph statistics on nankeen export were given up to 1833, from which year a gap occurred in the trade statistics until 1867. During this interval from 1833 to 1867 the export of nankeens must have decreased considerably. Whereas in 1830 China exported 1,051,000 pieces, in 1867 the export from China, as shown in Table 110a, was reduced to 441 piculs or 15,876 pieces.[56] Except 1869 China's annual export from 1867 to 1874 never exceeded one thousand piculs or 36,000 pieces. Beginning with 1875 a slow but interrupted increase was witnessed, reaching 2,687 piculs in 1886. Since 1886 the increase had become more rapid. The export was raised to 6,617 piculs in 1887, 8,112 piculs in 1891, 17,086 piculs in 1893, and 36,663 piculs in 1895. From 1896 to 1910 there were ups and downs, catering always around the total for 1895. After 1910 another increase was witnessed, reaching the highest figure of 75,848 piculs in 1921. A fall again occurred after the latter year, resulting in a total export for 1930 (37,798 piculs) which was slightly above that for 1895 (36,663 piculs) (Fig. 43). In short, the export of nankeens had definitely lost its prominent place

56. *Ibid.*

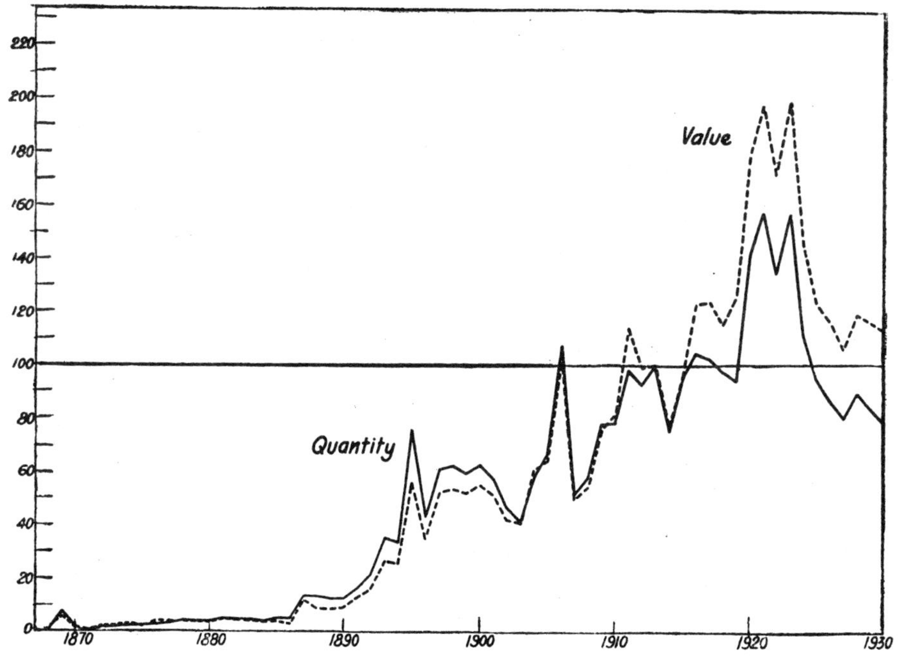

Fig. 43. Value and quantity of China's export of nankeens, 1867-1930 (1913=100) (*See* Table 110a)

in China's foreign trade which it enjoyed in the early part of the nineteenth century. The recovery, which it secured during the beginning of the present century, had but slightly held its own. It became insignificant in view of the fact that the exclusive position which the nankeens held in China's cotton trade has since the beginning of the present century been seized by newer and finer products. As shown in Table 110b, up to the five year period 1896-1900, nankeens constituted fully one hundred percent of the value of China's export of cotton goods. But the percentage began to decline progressively after that period, being reduced to 98 during 1901-1905, 90.49 during 1906-1910, 77.78 during 1911-1915, 49.12 during 1916-1920, 27.45 during 1921-1925, and finally to 7.88 during 1926-1930. The rapid decline, of course, was chiefly accounted for by the equally rapid growth of China's machine spinning and weaving industry, and it would not be too much to forecast its entire disappearance in the course of the next few decades. The days of the handloom industry have long been a historical fact in western nations, and even in China where industrialization has been introduced but recently these days can easily be counted.

Table 110a. China's export of nankeens to foreign countries, 1867-1930

Year	Piculs	Hk. Tls.*	Year	Piculs	Hk. Tls.
1867	441	21,160	1899	28,745	1,231,015
8	238	13,791	1900	30,180	1,301,283
9	3,631	154,302	1	27,586	1,221,471
1870	728	29,322	2	22,487	983,631
1	192	7,657	3	19,759	961,405
2	669	35,901	4	27,984	1,433,428
3	828	42,163	5	32,116	1,523,588
4	969	53,665	6	51,233	2,362,628
5	1,245	53,146	7	24,709	1,179,552
6	1,447	105,488	8	27,545	1,282,313
7	1,788	88,907	9	37,188	1,793,386
8	2,091	100,319	1910	37,671	1,929,925
9	2,027	98,904	1	47,184	2,683,042
1880	1,975	92,971	2	44,412	2,328,099
1	2,763	133,349	3	48,056	2,358,551
2	2,602	110,213	4	36,523	1,814,013
3	2,531	98,291	5	45,742	2,270,460
4	2,224	88,867	6	50,015	2,888,454
5	2,797	95,433	7	48,887	2,912,371
6	2,687	80,759	8	46,826	2,714,705
7	6,617	292,684	9	45,132	2,965,372
8	6,483	222,403	1920	67,736	4,217,146
9	6,112	210,829	1	75,848	4,670,884
1890	6,185	229,827	2	64,664	4,034,020
1	8,112	302,392	3	75,605	4,704,041
2	10,343	383,280	4	53,656	3,408,965
3	17,086	645,304	5	45,743	2,918,992
4	16,324	613,896	6	41,722	2,749,601
5	36,663	1,343,801	7	38,761	2,507,510
6	21,016	828,290	8	43,237	2,816,626
7	29,378	1,240,197	9	39,968	2,742,758
8	29,869	1,254,198	1930	37,798	2,677,644

* The Haikwan Tael was introduced in 1875, before which only the tael was used.

Table 110b. China's export of nankeens to foreign countries, 1867-1930 (by quinquennial periods)

Period	Nankeens Piculs	%	Hk. Tls.	%	Cotton goods Hk. Tls.	% of nankeens in all cotton goods
1867-1870	5,038	0.32	218,575	0.25	218,575	100.00
1871-1875	3,903	0.24	192,532	0.22	192,532	100.00
1876-1880	9,328	0.59	486,589	0.56	486,589	100.00
1881-1885	12,917	0.81	526,153	0.61	526,153	100.00
1886-1890	28,086	1.76	1,036,502	1.20	1,036,502	100.00
1891-1895	88,528	5.56	3,288,673	3.79	3,288,673	100.00
1896-1900	139,188	8.74	5,854,983	6.76	5,854,983	100.00
1901 1905	129,932	8.16	6,123,523	7.07	6,247,380	98.00
1906-1910	178,346	11.20	8,547,804	9.86	9,446,729	90.49
1911-1915	221,917	13.93	11,454,165	13.22	14,725,367	77.78
1916-1920	258,596	16.23	15,698,048	18.11	31,960,419	49.12
1921-1925	315,516	19.81	19,736,902	22.78	71,903,775	27.45
1926-1930	201,486	12.65	13,494,139	15.57	171,229,532	7.88
Total	1,592,781	100.00	86,658,588	100.00	317,117,209	27.33

China's export of cotton goods after 1905 may be divided into three categories, namely, piece goods, yarn and thread, and others. As shown in Table 111, during the 26 year period from 1905 to 1930, China's export of cotton goods has grown from the small amount of Hk. Tls. 1,647,445 to the huge sum of Hk. Tls. 31,968,629—an increase of 19.4 times (Fig. 44). This increase, however, is unequally distributed among the three groups of cotton goods. In 1905 when the total export amounted to Hk. Tls. 1,647,445, piece goods occupied Hk. Tls. 1,523,588 or 92.48 percent, and other goods which referred to cotton waste occupied Hk. Tls. 123,857 or 7.52 percent. In 1913 when the total export amounted to Hk. Tls. 2,945,327, the proportion for the piece goods showed a decline to 87.51 percent, with a simultaneous increase of the other goods to 11.92 percent. The export of yarn and thread, which began in 1912, occupied not even one percent in 1913 (0.57 percent). In 1920 the total export had increased to Hk. Tls. 8,209,732. The percentage for the piece goods showed a further decline to 60.29, while that for yarn and thread increased rapidly to 35.35. This trend of development persisted until 1930, when the percentage for

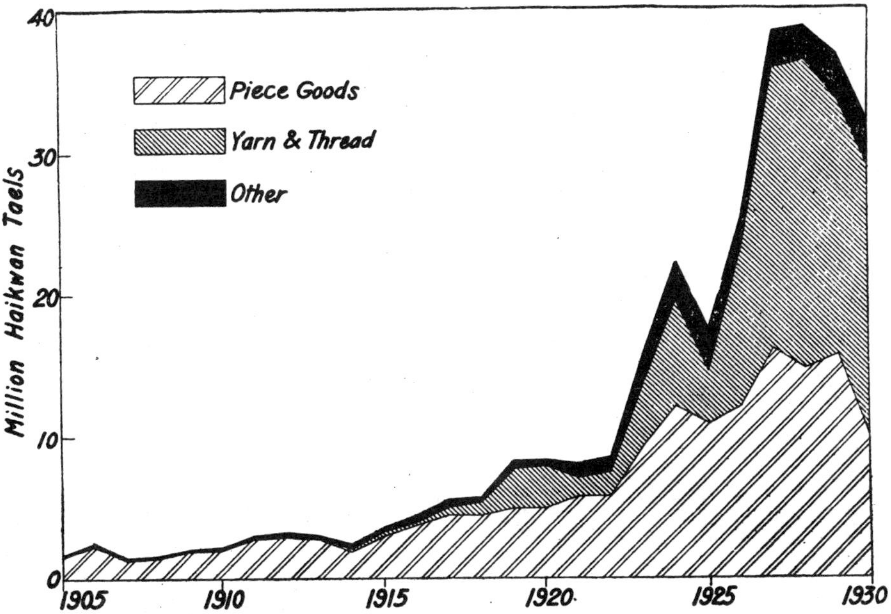

Fig. 44. China's export of cotton goods classified by groups, 1905-1930 (*See* Table 111)

piece goods had declined from the highest of 92.48 in 1905 to the lowest of 30.64 in 1930. On the other hand, the percentage for yarn and thread had increased from the lowest of 0.57 in 1913 to the highest of 59.33 in 1930. An examination of the destination of these exports in the following paragraph explains partly if not wholly the developments here described.

Table 111. China's export of cotton goods to foreign countries classified by groups, 1905-1930

Year	Piece goods				Yarn and thread		Other		All cotton goods	
	Nankeens		All							
	Hk. Tls.	%	Hk. Tls.	%	Hk. Tls.	%	Hk. Tls.	%	Hk. Tls.	%
1905	1,523,588	92.48	1,523,588	92.48			123,857	7.52	1,647,445	100.0
6	2,362,628	92.21	2,362,628	92.21			199,600	7.79	2,562,228	100.0
7	1,179,552	88.21	1,179,552	88.21			157,636	11.79	1,337,188	100.0
8	1,282,313	88.27	1,282,313	88.27			170,332	11.73	1,452,645	100.0
9	1,793,386	91.77	1,793,386	91.77			160,778	8.23	1,954,164	100.0
1910	1,929,925	90.16	1,929,925	90.16			210,579	9.84	2,140,504	100.0
1	2,683,042	92.94	2,683,042	92.94			203,823	7.06	2,886,865	100.0
2	2,328,099	75.30	2,826,229	91.41	35,141	1.14	230,536	7.45	3,091,906	100.0
3	2,358,551	80.08	2,577,579	87.51	16,721	0.57	351,027	11.92	2,945,327	100.0
4	1,814,013	78.82	1,965,149	85.39	46,979	2.04	289,321	12.57	2,301,449	100.0
5	2,270,460	64.87	2,955,043	84.44	203,993	5.83	340,784	9.74	3,499,820	100.0
6	2,888,454	66.03	3,657,528	83.61	181,016	4.14	536,007	12.25	4,374,551	100.0
7	2,912,371	52.23	4,465,946	80.09	450,204	8.07	660,242	11.84	5,576,392	100.0
8	2,714,705	48.43	4,384,942	78.23	1,000,497	17.85	219,625	3.92	5,605,064	100.0
9	2,965,372	36.19	4,962,446	60.56	2,695,863	32.90	536,281	6.54	8,194,590	100.0
1920	4,217,146	51.37	4,949,734	60.29	2,901,876	35.35	358,122	4.36	8,209,732	100.0
1	4,670,884	58.18	5,872,617	73.15	1,175,796	14.65	979,529	12.20	8,027,942	100.0
2	4,034,020	47.22	5,756,869	67.39	1,668,794	19.53	1,116,948	13.08	8,542,611	100.0
3	4,704,041	30.21	9,153,556	58.79	4,369,860	28.06	2,047,371	13.15	15,570,787	100.0
4	3,408,965	15.32	12,081,198	54.28	7,523,511	33.80	2,651,965	11.92	22,256,674	100.0
5	2,918,992	16.67	10,894,951	62.75	3,774,477	21.56	2,746,333	15.69	17,415,761	100.0
6	2,749,601	10.95	12,062,894	48.03	10,816,252	43.06	2,238,215	8.91	25,117,361	100.0
7	2,507,510	6.51	16,094,858	41.82	19,770,469	51.37	2,622,261	6.81	38,487,588	100.0
8	2,816,626	7.26	14,706,261	37.89	21,591,699	55.64	2,510,203	6.47	38,808,163	100.0
9	2,742,758	7.44	15,639,957	42.44	18,348,131	49.79	2,859,703	7.77	36,847,791	100.0
1930	2,677,644	8.38	9,793,910	30.64	18,968,419	59.33	3,206,300	10.03	31,968,629	100.0

Origin and destination of export, 1913-1929:—In an analysis of the origin and destination of the export of native goods from Chinese ports, either to foreign countries or to other Chinese ports, a few words may be said on the method of compiling the export statistics. Theoretically speaking, what is exported from Chinese ports under the category 'original export' should be equivalent to the sum of what is imported into foreign countries and what is imported into other Chinese ports as 'net import'. Actually, however, the former may be larger or smaller than the latter, in the Customs Returns. Take, for instance, the export of native cotton goods. As shown in Table 112, the original export of cotton goods from Chinese ports is larger than the sum of the export to foreign countries and the net import into Chinese ports by Hk. Tls. 1,680,874 in 1913 and Hk. Tls. 8,758,980 in 1920, while in 1929 the former is smaller than the latter by Hk. Tls. 12,445,113. Taking the original export as 100%, the sum of the export to foreign countries and the net import amounts to 83.64% in 1913, 88.56% in 1920 and 117.36% in 1929. The difference is, therefore, 16.36% in 1913, 11.44% in 1920 and 17.36% in 1929. Since no explanation is given in the Customs Returns for the difference, it may better serve our purpose of determining the destination of the export of native goods, whether to foreign countries or to Chinese ports, by taking the sum of the export to foreign countries and the net import into Chinese ports, but not the original export, as 100%. In this way, Hk. Tls. 22,879,263

Table 112. Statistics on the export of cotton goods from China, 1913, 1920 and 1929

	Export to foreign countries		Net import into Chinese ports		Total	Original export from Chinese ports
	Hk. Tls.	%	Hk. Tls.	%	Hk. Tls.	Hk. Tls.
Yarn and thread						
1913	16,721	0.11	14,632,541	99.89	14,649,262	17,304,402
1920	2,901,876	4.31	64,445,712	95.69	67,347,588	72,055,010
1929	18,348,131	12.98	123,034,610	87.02	141,382,741	134,317,226
Piece goods						
1913	2,577,579	23.94	8,187,002	76.06	10,764,581	9,843,611
1920	4,949,734	21.02	18,593,427	78.98	23,543,161	27,408,768
1929	15,639,957	19.75	63,560,880	80.25	79,200,837	74,572,876
Other						
1913	351,027	85.46	59,720	14.54	410,747	357,451
1920	358,122	65.37	189,685	34.63	547,807	733,758
1929	2,859,703	36.02	5,080,036	63.98	7,939,739	7,188,102
All cotton goods						
1913	2,945,327	11.41	22,879,263	88.59	25,824,590	27,505,464
1920	8,209,732	8.98	83,228,824	91.02	91,438,556	100,197,536
1929	36,847,791	16.12	191,675,526	83.88	228,523,317	216,078,204

or 88.59% in 1913, Hk. Tls. 83,228,824 or 91.02% in 1920, and Hk. Tls. 191,675,526 or 83.88% of the total export of native cotton goods in 1929 were 'net imports into Chinese ports'; while Hk. Tls. 2,945,327 or 11.41% in 1913, Hk. Tls. 8,209,732 or 8.98% in 1920, and Hk. Tls. 36,847,791 or 16.12% of the same in 1929 were exported to foreign countries. In other words, the foreign export amounts to but ten to fifteen percent of the total export, the other eighty-five to ninety percent being 'net import into the Chinese ports'.

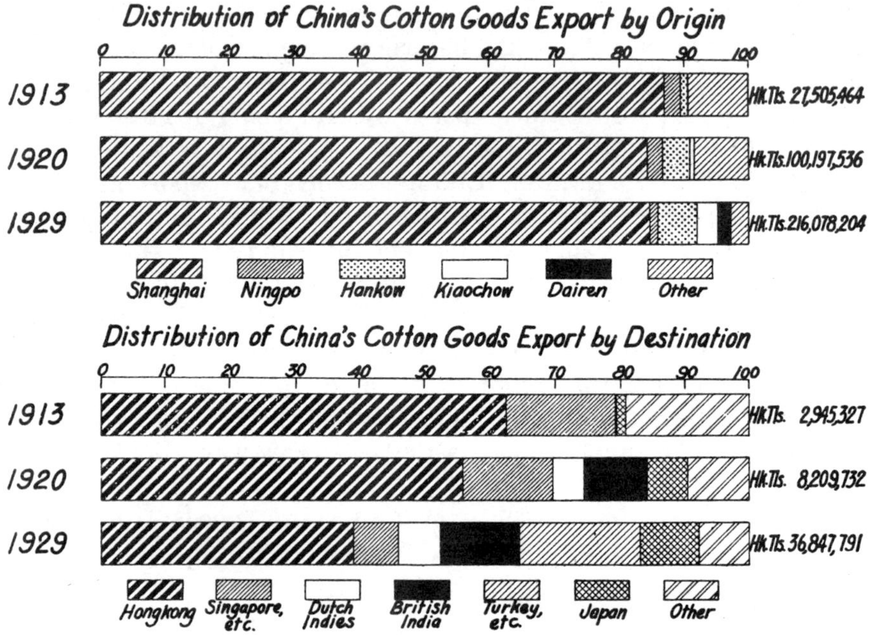

Fig. 45. Distribution of China's export of cotton goods by origin and destination, 1913, 1920 and 1929 (*See* Tables 113 and 115)

Table 113 classifies the original export of native cotton goods according to origin, i.e. according to the port of export (Fig. 45). Shanghai, in which about two-thirds of China's cotton industry is located, occupied as much as 86.93% of the total original export of native cotton goods in 1913, 84.30% in 1920 and 84.55% in 1929. The other four ports, including Hankow, Kiaochow, Ningpo and Dairen, occupied 3.68% in 1913, 7.26% in 1920, and 12.47% in 1929. Of the total original export of native cotton goods, the yarn and thread group occupied about two thirds, namely, 62.91% in 1913, 71.91% in 1920 and 62.16% in 1929. It is exported from Shanghai and other ports chiefly to meet the needs in other Chinese ports where machine spinning is as yet undeveloped and where handloom weaving is carried on with machine spun yarn, no longer with homespun yarn

Table 113. Original export of cotton goods from China classified by origin, 1913,1920 and 1929

	Shanghai		Ningpo		Hankow		Kiaochow		Dairen		Other		Total
	Hk. Tls.	%	Hk. Tls.	%	Hk. Tls.	%	Hk. Tls.	%	Hk. Tls.	%	Hk. Tls.	%	Hk. Tls.
Yarn and thread													
1913	16,529,623	95.52	673,368	3.89							101,411	0.59	17,304,402
1920	61,523,519	85.39	2,351,844	3.26	2,838,706	3.94	607,666	0.84	9,139	0.01	4,724,136	6.56	72,055,010
1929	111,814,102	83.25	2,557,720	1.91	7,914,899	5.89	4,208,614	3.13	4,231,366	3.15	3,590,525	2.67	134,317,226
Piece goods													
1913	7,055,313	71.67	4,579	0.05	297,483	3.02			16,974	0.17	2,469,262	25.09	9,843,611
1920	22,286,296	81.31	7,650	0.03	1,373,626	5.01	9,979	0.04	2,784	0.01	3,728,433	13.60	27,408,768
1929	64,355,799	86.30			4,916,340	6.59	2,834,064	3.80	80,648	0.11	2,386,025	3.20	74,572,876
Other													
1913	325,354	91.02	17,414	4.87	1,623	0.45					13,060	3.66	357,451
1920	656,659	89.49	51,241	6.98	10,569	1.44	5,001	0.68			10,288	1.41	733,758
1929	6,514,260	90.63	21,279	0.30	150,784	2.10	22,742	0.32	7,398	0.10	471,639	6.55	7,188,102
All cotton goods													
1913	23,910,290	86.93	695,361	2.53	299,106	1.09			16,974	0.06	2,583,733	9.39	27,505,464
1920	84,466,474	84.30	2,410,735	2.41	4,222,901	4.22	622,646	0.62	11,923	0.01	8,462,857	8.44	100,197,536
1929	182,684,161	84.55	2,578,999	1.19	12,982,023	6.01	7,065,420	3.27	4,319,412	2.00	6,448,189	2.98	216,078,204

from the spinning-wheels. The other third of the total original export is taken up by cotton piece goods, the percentage being 35.79 in 1913, 27.35 in 1920 and 34.51 in 1929. The 'other' group, including cotton waste in 1913 and 1920, but cotton waste, blankets and counterpanes, socks and stockings, towels, wadding, etc. in 1929, is rather insignificant, occupying only 1.3% in 1913, 0.74% in 1920 and 3.33% in 1929.

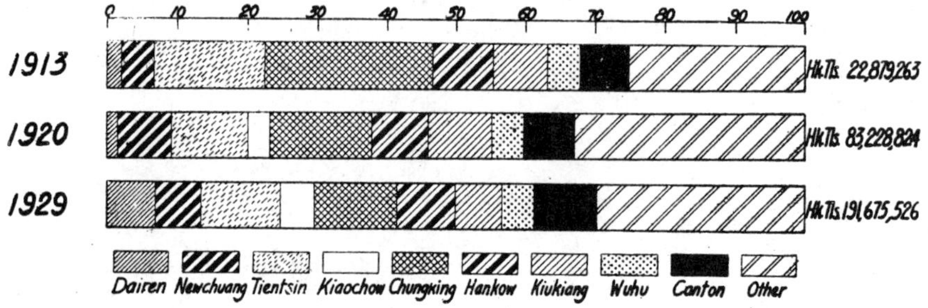

Fig. 46. Distribution of China's import of native cotton goods by ports, 1913, 1920 and 1929 (*See* Table 114)

Whereas about four fifths of the original export comes from the single port of Shanghai, it is imported into a large number of other ports (Fig. 46). As shown in Table 114, the nine chief ports in 1929 have a percentage of net import ranging respectively from the lowest of 4.63 (for Wuhu) to the highest of 11.95 (for Chunging). These nine ports occupied 75.06% of the total net import of native cotton goods in 1913, 67.04% in 1920, and 70.47% in 1929. In other words, they occupied as much as two thirds of the total net import. In 1929 the percentage of net import is, in order of importance, 11.95 for Chungking, 11.33 for Tientsin, 9.05 for Canton, 8.43 for Hankow, 7.12 for Dairen, 6.71 for Kiukiang, 6.40 for Newchuang, 4.85 for Kiaochow, and 4.63 for Wuhu,—a total of 70.47% for the nine ports. A comparison between 1913 and 1929 statistics shows that the percentage for Chungking, Tientsin, Hankow, Kiukiang and Wuhu has fallen and that the percentage for Canton, Dairen, Newchuang, and

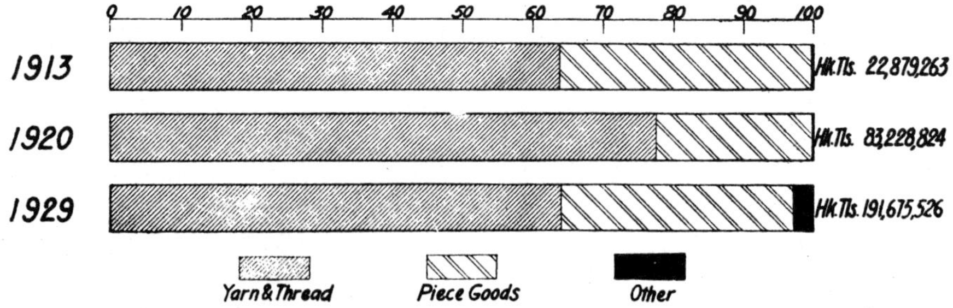

Fig. 47. Distribution of China's import of native cotton goods by groups, 1913, 1920 and 1929 (*See* Table 114)

Yarn and thread
1913
1920
1929
Piece goods
1913
1920
1929
Other
1913
1920
1929
All cotton goods
1913
1920
1929

Kiaochow has risen. Chungking has fallen rapidly from 24.07% in 1913 to 11.95% in 1929, so has Tientsin from 15.70% to 11.33% during the same period. On the other hand, the percentage for Dairen has risen from 2.06 in 1913 to 7.12 in 1929, and that for Canton from 6.84 to 9.05 during the same period.

The export to foreign countries is distributed chiefly among six regions, namely, Hongkong; Singapore, Straits, etc.; Dutch Indies; British India; Turkey, Persia, Egypt, Aden, etc.; and Japan (including Formosa). These six regions claimed 81.02% of the total foreign export of native cotton goods in 1913, 90.22% in 1920, and 92.20% in 1929 (Fig. 45). With the exception of Hongkong which is a port for trans-shipment to Canton or to foreign countries, and of Japan which is more industrialized than China, the regions to which China exports her cotton goods are poorly developed from an industrial viewpoint. Among the six regions Hongkong led with 62.51% of the total export of native cotton goods in 1913, 55.76% in 1920 and 39.16% in 1929, after which followed the region of Singapore, Straits, etc. with 16.78% in 1913, 13.84% in 1920 and 6.77% in 1929. During the period from 1913 to 1929, however, these different regions have changed in relative importance. The percentage for Hongkong has declined repidly from 62.51 in 1913 to 39.16 in 1929; so has that for Singapore, Straits, etc. from 16.78 to 6.77 during the same period. The percentage for the other four regions has risen uniformly, from 1913 to 1929. The percentage for Dutch Indies has risen from 0.04 to 6.41; that for British Indies from 0.25 to 12.09; that for Turkey, Persia, Egypt, Aden etc. from zero to 18.57; and that for Japan from 1.44 to 9.20.

CHAPTER X. PROSPECT AND RETROSPECT

Summary of China's cotton industry and trade

History and localization:—Hand spinning and weaving of cotton constituted one of the earliest industries in China, but power spinning and weaving had a recent origin. Li Hung-chang, one of the most far-sighted statesmen of the Manchu dynasty, was responsible for the organization of the first Machine Weaving Mill, the Yang-pu-chü (洋布局), in 1890, in Shanghai. Since then four periods of development may be distinguished, namely, the formative period from 1890 to 1904, the period of slow growth from 1905 to 1913, the period of rapid development from 1914 to 1925, and the period of recession since 1925. Taking the total spindles in 1930 as equivalent to 100%, the first period is credited with 12.21%, the second with 10.61%, the third with 62.50%, and the fourth with 14.68%. The Sino-Japanese War in 1894-95 and the Russo-Japanese War in 1904-5 mark the turning points for the first and the second periods respectively, while the third period follows with the occurrence of the World War. The third period, which is the most important, witnesses not only a remarkable growth in the number of Chinese owned spindles, but also a sudden and even more rapid increase in that of Japanese owned spindles. Taking 1913 as the base of 100, Japanese owned spindles increased to 700.87 during the last year of the third period (1925), while Chinese owned spindles increased only to 346.28 during the same year. With the termination of the World War and with the return of foreign cotton goods to the China market, the effect of competition was immediately felt by the poorly financed Chinese mills that had grown up during the third period. A reduced rate of growth in the number of spindles became but an expected development, despite the immense possibilities for further expansion offered by a native population of over 400 million. During the period the total number of spindles increased by only 4.40%, from 411.67 in 1925 to 429.78 in 1930 (relative to 1913 as 100). In the latter year there were 4,223,956 spindles, of which 2,395,792 spindles or 56.72% were owned by the Chinese, 1,674,844 spindles or 39.65% by the Japanese, and 153,320 spindles or 3.63% by the British. A similar distribution in respect of the nationality of ownership obtains for the looms. In 1930 there were 29,272 looms in China, of which 16,005 looms or 54.68% were owned by the Chinese, 11,367 looms or 38.83% by the Japanese, and 1,900 looms or 6.49% by the British.

The cotton industry in China is a highly localized business, and the province of Kiangsu is comparable to Lancashire in this respect. In 1918 this province claimed as much as 80.32% of the total spindleage in China, and even after other provinces have begun to develop their mills, Kiangsu's leadership in China's cotton industry has not been challenged.

Briefly, its percentage since 1918 has been as follows: 66.11 in 1924, 66.30 in 1927 and 66.42 in 1930. Hupeh, with 7.80% of China's total spindleage in 1918, used to rank after Kiangsu. As its percentage since 1918 has remained stationary, being 6.69 in 1924, 7.82 in 1927 and 7.33 in 1930, its position as the second cotton spinning province is now yielded to Shantung. The latter, with only 1.73% of China's total spindleage in 1918, increased its share to 8.58% in 1930. Hopei, the fourth cotton spinning province, had only 2.60% of China's total spindleage in 1918, but 7.26% in 1930. In these four provinces of Kiangsu, Shantung, Hupeh and Hopei are to be found six cotton centres with 85% of China's total spindleage, namely, Shanghai, Wusih and Tungtsunghai in Kiangsu, Tsingtao in Shantung, Wuhan in Hupeh and Tientsin in Hopei. In 1930 the percentage was 55.79 for Shanghai, 7.88 for Tsingtao, 7.33 for Wuhan, 5.70 for Tientsin, 4.42 for Tungtsunghai, and 3.36 for Wusih—a total of 84.48%. The factors for localization are not far to seek. The abundance of raw cotton, the availability of coal and electric power, the facility of transport, the presence of a great market, the possession of commercial and financial facilities, and the early development of mills,—all these help in one way or the other to bring about the localization of China's cotton industry in a few favored centres.

Industrial organization:—As the largest factory industry of China today, cotton manufacturing is carried on in large mills with considerable outlay of capital and a great number of workers. A statistical measurement of the scale on which the industry is organized, on the basis of the data contained in the *Revised List of Cotton Mills in China for 1930*, a list which is compiled by an organization no less authoritative than the *Chinese Cotton Millowners' Association*, is perhaps the best approach to the subject. The statistics given, however, are incomplete and inconsistent, and it is only after critical revision that they may be used to determine the size distribution of the cotton mills in China.

In an analysis of the size distribution, three types of averages, the mode, the median and the mean, have been computed for the Chinese owned mills, the Japanese owned mills and all mills in China. The British owned mills, of which there are only three in China, are not separately analyzed. Among the three types of averages, the mode is the lowest and the mean the highest, with the median standing between the two extremes. The median sized mill, in this way, has a capital investment of $2,170,456, with 28,588 spindles, 501 looms, 1,030 kilowatts of motive power, and 1,711 workers. Such a mill consumes annually 63,531 piculs of raw cotton, but produces 17,263 bales of yarn and 262,501 pieces of cloth. The Japanese owned mill, however, has a heavier capital investment than the Chinese owned mill ($2,750,001 versus $1,437,501), with a greater number of spindles (34,168 versus 25,334), looms (751 versus 401), and kilowatts of motive power (1,230 versus 921). The Chinese owned mill, on the other hand, employs more workers (1,769 versus 1,615), consumes more raw cotton (64,168 versus 60,001 piculs) and spins a greater quantity of yarn (17,501 versus 15,626 bales) than the Japanese owned mill. The Japanese owned mill, having a far greater number of looms (mostly up-to-date ones) than the Chinese owned mill (751 versus 401), weaves a far greater quantity of cloth with its own yarn (583,335 versus 177,778 pieces).

The cotton mills in China, especially those of Japanese ownership, have shown a strong tendency towards integration during the post-war period, partly due to the revival of competition from the imported yarn and fabrics, and partly due to the desire for greater control of the industry. As a result of this integration, mainly horizontal, 61 of the 127 cotton mills in China are in the hands of 14 campanies, each of which possesses two or more mills that are concentrated in one locality or scattered in different parts of the country. These 14 companies, of which seven are Chinese, six Japanese and one British, possess a capital investment of $165,108,885 (57.3%), and an equipment 2,434,280 spindles (57.7%), 17,058 looms (58.3%) and 82,664 kilowatts of power capacity (34%), while employing 136,538 workers (54.2%), consuming 4,448,907 piculs of raw cotton (50.9%), spinning 1,255,654 bales of yarn (51.2%) and weaving 9,178,238 pieces of cloth (62.1%). In other words, about one half of the cotton mills in China, with more than one half of the capital and surplus, machinery, labor, raw materials, and output, have been integrated. Again, the Japanese owned mills in China are integrated to a much higher degree than the Chinese owned mills. Whereas only 25 of the 81 Chinese mills are integrated, as many as 33 of the 43 Japanese owned mills have come under the influence of integration. In other respects the percentage of integration is also higher for the Japanese owned mills, being 71.8 for capital and surplus (versus 36.0), 77.1 for spindles (versus 41.3), 72.9 for looms (versus 43.0), 75.7 for motive power (versus 37.5), 74.9 for workers (versus 40.6), 69.9 for cotton consumption (versus 36.0), 69.4 for yarn output (versus 36.9) and 75.3 for cloth output (versus 45.8).

The financial position of a Chinese owned mill, as indicated above, is weaker than that of a Japanese owned mill, having a much smaller capital investment but a quicker turnover of output. Such a weakness is further aggravated by the unsound financial practices in many mills. In an analysis of the financial statements for four mills in Tientsin, it is found that Mill A has five losing years out of ten; Mill B, four losing years out of nine; Mill C, one losing year out of ten; and Mill D, three losing years out of nine. Before 1923 every one of the four mills was making profit, but the disposal of the profit made was poorly done, with little consideration for the mill's future. For all of the four mills the provision for surplus has never exceeded four percent, the highest being 3.51% for Mill A in 1921. On the other hand, whenever any surplus has been accumulated, it is quickly diminished in losing years. A second unsound practice is the declaration of an annual dividend even in losing years, which, for two of the four mills studied, has become an established policy. A third unsound practice is the failure to provide the reserve for depreciation. Such a reserve, which is usually provided for only in profit-making years, is however highly inadequate in amount, and seldom exceeds the minimum requirement of five percent of the total value of the fixed assets. A fourth unsound practice is the heavy investment in fixed assets, which, with the exception of Mill C, exceeds in every case the paid-up capital. Consequently, the working capital is deplorably small. The working capital, which is the excess of current assets over current liabilities, is, according to the standard rule-of-thumb, equivalent to the amount of current liabilities. That is to say, the standard ratio of current assets to current liabilities is two to one. In Tientsin mills this ratio has not been maintained, especially since 1923. Indeed, for Mill B the current liabilities alone exceeded the current assets in four years, from 1921 to 1924, the ratio being 0.96 in 1921, 0.86 in 1922, 0.62 in 1923 and 0.52 in 1924.

The Employers' Association was first started among the Chinese owned mills in 1918, on a nation-wide scale, but the Japanese owned mills have also their own organization, which is known as the Japanese Cotton Millowners' Association in China. Both organizations are located in Shanghai, where a small committee, representing the Chinese, Japanese and British millowners, meets to discuss matters of common interest once a month. In other cities the Cotton Millowners' Association was also formed among the Chinese owned mills. The Hupeh Cotton Millowners' Association was formed at Hankow in 1921, the Wusih Cotton Millowners' Association in 1922, and the Tientsin Cotton Millowners' Association at about the same time. The Wusih Association, composed of only six mills, was reorganized into the Interior Cotton Millowners' Association in the Province of Kiangsu in 1930, in order to raise its membership to seven or more and thereby to secure the approval of the Ministry of Industries which, under the New Industrial and Commercial Association Act of 1929, required every association to have a minimum of seven members. In the same year, the Tientsin Association was also re-organized, with, however, a membership of only six mills.

Raw cotton:—Cotton, the raw material for China's cotton industry, is partly produced at home and partly imported from abroad. In 1929, for instance, of the total mill consumption of 7,338,000 piculs, 2,515,000 piculs or 34.27% were imported from abroad, chiefly from India, the United States and Japan. The import, however, supplies a need which differs from that met by the home production. Imported cotton is used mostly for fine spinning, while native cotton is used for the spinning of coarser counts.

The region of cotton culture in China lies between 20° to 40° northern latitude, but east of 110° eastern longitude. Within this region three sub-regions can be further distinguished, namely, the Basin of the Yellow River in the north, the Basin of the Yangtze River at the centre, and the Basin of the Sikiang River in the South. Among these three sub-regions, two thirds of Chinese cotton are grown in the central sub-region and another third in the northern sub-region, while the southern sub-region, because of the competition of silk and tea, grows little cotton that enters into domestic or foreign trade. The cotton region, in other words, is confined chiefly to that portion of China lying between 28° and 40° in the northern latitude. In the central sub-region six provinces produced 4,816,000 piculs of lint cotton during the season 1929-30, or 68.5% of the total production, the other 2,211,000 piculs or 31.5% being produced by another five provinces in the northern sub-region.

China's cotton production, however, has actually shown a decline since 1918. In 1918 the total production amounted to 10,221,000 piculs—the record figure, but in 1929 it was reduced to 7,027,000 piculs, a reduction of about 30 percent. This decline in total output, largely due to the recurrence of civil war, famine and insect pest, is accompanied by a similar decline in the amount of yield per mow, from 27.3 catties in 1919-1920 to 21.3 in 1929-30. Both types of decline have naturally called forth attempts at improvement along the three directions of technique, seed and area. The planting of better seed under improved technique in a larger area will undoubtedly raise the quality as well as the quantity of Chinese cotton. These attempts, unfortunately, are more or less sporadic, and poorly supported by a weak and decentralized government. The only exception to this statement is the recent success in preventing adulteration—one of the gravest abuses in the marketing of all staple crops in China. The movement towards anti-adulteration was started by the foreign merchants as early as 1901 in Shanghai and 1911 in Tientsin, but a system of government control has been definitely established since 1929. In that year the Bureau of Testing and Inspection for Commercial Commodities was inaugurated under the Ministry of Industry, Commerce and Labor (now the Ministry of Industries) in the four cotton marketing centres of Shanghai, Hankow, Tsingtao and Tientsin respectively. In each Bureau a Cotton Testing House was organized, to which all export cotton must be submitted for certification, at the payment of a small testing fee of six cents per picul. The maximum percentage allowed for certification, 12% in Tientsin but 15% in Shanghai, Hankow and Tsingtao, is high as compared with the 'regain' of 7.83% prevalent in other countries, but it is hoped that further reduction of the moisture percentage may be enforced under more favorable circumstances. The same is true with the scope of testing which, except in Tientsin, is confined to the export cotton.

In bringing raw cotton from the producer to the consumer, whether intermediate or ultimate, it has to go through three types of markets, local, primary and terminal. The first two types of markets can be found practically all over the cotton regions, but the terminal markets are limited in number. Shanghai, Hankow and Tientsin are the chief terminal markets, next to which may be mentioned Shasi, Chenchow, Shihchiachuang, Tsingtao and Ningpo. Spot trading is carried on in all types of markets, but future trading is officially sanctioned on the Chinese Cotton Goods Exchange in Shanghai.

Local market, the original market at which cotton farmers sell their products, is usually established at country fairs, at which farmers, brokers, dealers and buying agents from larger markets meet to transact business. Because of their large volume of trade as well as their advantageous position, some of the local markets have developed into primary markets. Unlike the local market at which all kinds of farm products are sold, a primary market always specializes in one kind of produce. Again, in a primary market there are cotton inns which can seldom be found in a local market. These inns are frequently visited by large farmers who travel a long distance to sell their cotton at the primary market, as well as by buying agents of cotton merchants, exporters and mills from the terminal markets and elsewhere. In both local and primary markets, there are brokers and dealers. The farmer is invariably a seller, while the ginnery may buy or sell in the local market, but sells in the primary market. The buying agents of foreign exporters were active several years ago, but at present they have ceased to visit the primary market because of the recurrence of civil war, and the abolition of the exclusive privilege to the transit pass in 1925 and of the likin system in 1931.

In the terminal market there are three classes of persons engaged in the cotton trade, namely, buyers, sellers and brokers. In Tientsin, the sellers include the dealers and agents of cotton inns of different primary markets, through whom cotton is shipped from the primary markets to Tientsin for sale. Having no permanent establishment of their own in Tientsin, most of them live and transact their business in the cotton houses during the marketing season. These houses are of the same character as the cotton inns of the primary markets, but are run on a much larger scale. Their principal function is to sell cotton for the customers, although trading on own account is also resorted to. The buyers, on the other hand, include the exporters, mills and retailers.

Shanghai, the chief centre of cotton industry in China, is also the largest terminal market in raw cotton trade. In many respects the market in Shanghai differs from that elsewhere. Shanghai, in the first place, is the largest consuming centre in China, both of native and of foreign cotton. Of the total amount of cotton consumed by the cotton mills in

China in 1930, 8,750,019 piculs, Shanghai's share reached 4,439,857 piculs or 50.74%. It is for this reason that the largest amount of spot trade is centred in Shanghai, between the cotton mills on the one hand, and the cotton merchants on the other. Again, in Shanghai may be found the only cotton futures market in China,—the Chinese Cotton Goods Exchange. Elsewhere such as in Tientsin and Ningpo, futures were traded in at one time or the other, and even in Shanghai there used to be another exchange, the Shanghai Stock and Produce Exchange, in which some business was done in cotton futures. But all these markets have suspended operation in raw cotton. In view of the supreme position that Shanghai now occupies in China's cotton trade, it is unlikely that other markets will spring up to challenge its well-established lead.

Chinese cotton is packed in a number of different ways, and a great deal of confusion exists with respect to form, size, weight and the materials used. Every cotton district has its own method of packing, with own materials, which differs for the different kinds of cotton. Some cotton is pressed before packing, while others are simply packed in a loose state. Of these the former is preferred over long distance transport, both to facilitate cotton movement and to reduce freight charges. Besides, pressing reduces loss from dropping and petty theft, as well as the chance for deterioration due to contact with moisture. As to transport, both modern and primitive means are employed, the former referring to the railway and the steamer, and the latter to the junks, carts and wheelbarrows. The cart, driven by mules and other animals in North China, and the wheelbarrow, driven by coolie labor in South China, are employed for short distance transport, but where both railway and water transport are not available, as is generally true in the interior, the cart or the wheelbarrow becomes at once the sole means of transport. The railway has the advantage of speed, but in war-ridden China, its certainty is questionable. The steamer or junk transport is reasonable but slow, thereby reducing the rate of capital turnover and increasing the interest charges. In North China, however, it is not available during winter season when the river is blockaded by ice. Because of the diversity in the means of transport employed in each cotton district the cost differs considerably for the same unit of distance travelled, varying, for instance, from 0.25 cent per kilometre-picul from Shihchiachuang to Tientsin to 0.70 cent from Hantan to Tientsin. As to taxation, likin used to constitute the most irregular and burden-some levy on raw cotton. But with its official abolition in January, 1931 it has been done away with in most provinces where the authority of the National government is not challenged by local militarists. The only legal tax on raw cotton now is the export duty, which is fixed under the Revised Export Tariff of 1931 at Hk. Tls. 1.20 per picul. This represents a raise of about two and half times over the rate of Hk. Tl. 0.35

per picul under the preceding tariff, in order to discourage cotton export from China.

Labor:—According to the Chinese Cotton Millowners' Association the workers in cotton mills have grown from 195,691 in 1924 to 234,540 in 1927 and 252,031 in 1930. In 1930 the 252,031 workers were distributed among the 11 provinces as follows: 162,434 or 64.45% in Kiangsu, 26,084 or 10.35% in Hupeh, 20,948 or 8.31% in Hopei, 17,184 or 6.82% in Shantung, 7,750 or 3.08% in Honan, 6,849 or 2.72% in Liaoning, 4,610 or 1.83% in Chekiang, 2,350 or 0.93% in Hunan, 1,451 or 0.58% in Shansi, 1,300 or 0.52% in Anhwei, and 1,071 or 0.42% in Kiangsi. Cotton workers, however, can be more broadly defined as to include those in other branches. In a survey of the factory workers in nine provinces chiefly in central and south China, the cotton workers were found to be 327,842 in number, or 27.22% of the total factory workers (1,204,318). Of these, 206,532 were spinners or cotton mill workers proper, 109,809 weavers, and 11,501 ginners, doublers, mixture weavers and finishers. But the Ministry's survey on the number of cotton spinners is incomplete, as it fails to cover five provinces where cotton mills also exist, namely, Hopei, Honan, Hunan, Liaoning and Shansi. Besides, for the six provinces covered in the Ministry's survey, Kiangsu, Chekiang, Hupeh, Shantung, Kiangsi and Anhwei, the number of cotton mill workers (206,532) is smaller than that given by the Chinese Cotton Millowners' Association (212,683) by 6,151.

Most of the cotton mill workers, about 84%, are concentrated in the six centres in the four cotton provinces. In 1930, the percentage distribution of the 252,031 cotton mill workers among these centres was as follows: 50.63% in Shanghai, 10.35% in Wuhan, 6.87% in Tungtsunghai, 6.09% in Tientsin, 6.03% in Tsingtao and 3.71% in Wusih. Because of the prominent position in cotton industry occupied by Shanghai and Tientsin, the former representing central China and the latter north China, our analysis of labor conditions is primarily confined to these two cities. In both, the employment of cotton workers used to be entrusted to the foremen under the notorious contract system, especially among the foreign owned mills, but recently the practice has been for the mill to recruit new workers more directly. The applicant is customarily introduced to the mill through the medium of the foremen. Whenever new hands are needed, the news spreads out immediately among the foremen, who in turn undertakes to introduce them to the management. The latter usually lays down a set of guiding rules in selecting new hands; but the extent of their enforcement necessarily varies with different mills. A point of importance in this connection is the source of supply. Most of the workers are not natives of the city, but are recruited from the country districts in the province where the city is located. Of the 1,919 workers in a Japanese owned mill in Shanghai, only 231 workers or 12.04% are natives of Shanghai, the rest being born elsewhere in Kiangsu and other provinces. The percentage of workers from Kiangsu is as high as 82.96. In Tientsin, a sample survey of 3,898 workers in three mills points to a similar conclusion. It shows that 927 workers or 23.78% are natives of Tientsin, while Hopei, the province in which the city is located, supplies 79.06%.

Labor turnover is a term which has been commonly identified with three aspects of labor mobility, namely, (1) the number of employees hired (accessions), (2) the number leaving (separations), and (3) the number of replacements required to keep up the working force. The rate at which employees leave may be called the separation rate, and the rate at which they are hired, the accession rate. Whichever of these two rates is lower, may, for all practical purposes, be used as the replacement rate. In Tientsin the separation rate in 1929 is 42.1 in Mill C which is also the replacement rate, while the accession rate is 50.1. This rate is rather high among the cotton mills in Tientsin except Mill D, which has a separation rate of 76.8 in 1930 because of re-organization. In Mill A the separation rate is 35.5 in 1927, 20.8 in 1928 and 12.3 in 1929; while in Mill B it is 28.4 in 1927, 15.7 in 1928, 6.6 in 1929 and 5.8 in 1930. Generally speaking, the separation rate in Tientsin mills is rather low. Whereas in Tientsin the length of stay of over three years applies to 72.2% of the workers, in Shanghai it holds true for only 47.3% of the male spinners, 42.8% of the female spinners, 18.3% of the male weavers and 22% of the female weavers. Evidently, Shanghai, as the industrial and commercial metropolis of China, offers greater opportunity for work, which is one way or the other responsible for the higher mobility of labor.

Three systems of wage payment prevail in cotton mills, namely, time, piece and time-plus-piece. The first two systems are well known, while under the third system a time rate is fixed, in addition to which a standard is also set for the day's work. If a worker exceeds the standard in output, a piece rate is paid for the extra work. In Shanghai, the piece payment system is the more important. In a study of wages for 10,080 cotton weavers and 36,293 cotton spinners in Shanghai, it is found that 31,191 spinners and weavers or 67.26% are paid under the piece system. The percentage for the weaver, 77.77, is higher than that for the spinner, 64.50. This study also shows that the daily wage rates in Shanghai, 49.3 cents, are higher than those in Tientsin, 46.8 cents. But earnings, including besides wage rates several kinds of bonus such as the full attendance bonus, the reward for good work, the melon bonus in summer time, and the year-end bonus, are higher in Tientsin than in Shanghai. The average monthly earnings for cotton spinners and weavers in Tientsin, $14.69, are 1.2% higher than those in Shanghai, $14.51.

In Shanghai the average annual income per family for the cotton workers is $390.72, which is 34.1% higher than that in Tientsin, $291.37. This difference can be partly explained by the larger family size in Shanghai (3.75 versus 2.80 male adults), and partly by the greater employment of child and woman labor. In Tientsin the husband contributes 74.71%, and the wife and children 16.57%; while in Shanghai the percentage is only 43.5 for the former but 35.6% for the latter. In respect of the distribution of the average annual expenditure, the data at our disposal reveal a higher standard of living in Shanghai. The percentage for food, which is only 56.6% in Shanghai, reaches 63.8% in Tientsin. On the other hand, Shanghai workers spend more for clothing (9.2% versus 6.7%) and miscellaneous items (20% versus 12.7%). The cost for fuel and light is higher in Tientsin because of the climatic requirement (9.7% versus 7.6%), but that for rent is approximately the same (6.6% versus 7.1%). For all classes of families in both cities, the expenditure for food, rent, fuel and light tends to decrease as the income increases, but that for clothing and miscellaneous items tends to increase under similar conditions.

The hours of work are generally twelve in Chinese owned mills, but eleven in Japanese owned mills. Actually, however, the hours of work are about equal, as in Chinese owned mills more loafing and sitting about is allowed. During the noon time or midnight, from one half to one hour is allowed for meals. Rest days are arranged to suit individual cases. Some stop every Sunday, others every ten days, still others allow two days per month. Holidays run from ten to fifteen in number during the year, including the New Year, the Spring festival, the Dragon festival, the Moon festival, the National Independence day, and other holidays sanctioned by the National government.

The employment of child and woman labor is a common feature in the cotton industry. Indeed, of the 327,842 cotton workers in the 28 cities in central and south China in 1930, there were 202,738 woman workers or 61.84% and 20,633 child workers or 6.29%—a total of 223,371 woman and child workers or 68.13%. In the cotton spinning branch the percentage occupied by the woman labor, 69.61, is even higher, although that occupied by the child labor, 5.97, is lower. In that branch there were 206,532 workers, including 143,767 woman workers and 12,330 child workers. Generally speaking, woman labor is more prevalent in central and south China than in north China. It predominates in the roving, spinning, reeling, waste cotton picking, warping and weaving departments, in Shanghai for instance, while in the blowing, carding, baling, mechanical and finishing departments man labor claims the majority. As is commonly expected, the average daily wage rates for male workers in Shanghai, 59.5 cents, are higher than those for female workers (47.1 cents) or child workers (31.4 cents).

In a study of 880 cases of cotton mill workers treated by the Industrial Hospital of Shanghai, it is found that the percentage of the injured is the highest among child patients (67), next to which are 41 among male patients and 26 among female patients. For all classes of workers 42% of the injuries occur in the upper extremity, 31% in the lower extremity, 16% in the head, 7% in the trunk, and 4% in other parts; while the nature of the injuries may be distributed as follows: lacerations, 59%; compound fracture, 18%; simple fracture, 5%; burns, 8%; and others, 10%. 25% of the accidents result in permanent disability, but only 1.8% in death. In Shanghai 49 mills with an average size of 2,069 workers per mill reported in 1930 an average of 2,667 times of sickness arising from employment and 132 times of injuries attributed to the self-same cause. Wages were paid by 36 mills for sickness, and by 44 mills for injury; while medical care was given by 47 mills for both sickness and injury. The average wage cost per mill is estimated at $134.84 for sickness, and $43.61 for injury; while the average medical cost per mill amounts to $5,454.60 for sickness and $274.67 for injury. In case of permanent injury wages were paid by 2 mills, but in case of death no wages were paid by any mill. In both cases medical care was given by only 13 mills.

Cotton workers are the pioneers of union movement. A strike in May, 1925 in Naigai Wata Kaisha, the largest Japanese owned mill in China, led to the famous May 30 incident—the incident that was mainly responsible for the rapid growth of unions during the following few years. On the 20th of August when the Shanghai Cotton Mill Workers' Union was organized as one of the 16 industrial unions under the Shanghai General Labor Union, it had 118,223 members—nearly all the workers in the cotton mills in Shanghai at that time. As the General Labor Union had altogether 217,804 members, the members from the cotton mills claimed about 54%. Meantime, unionization spread among the cotton mill workers in other cotton centres, in Wuhan in 1926 and in Tientsin in 1928. In the latter year, however, the Kuomingtang undertook to abolish or re-organize all peasant and labor unions of a questionable character ,and consequently, the Cotton Mill Workers' Union, like other unions, was considerably reduced in membership. In 1930, an investigation by the Ministry of Industries reported only 76,132 organized workers in the cotton industry in south and central China, with 70,226 workers in the cotton spinning branch. In that branch Wuhan led with 29,899 members, after which followed Tsingtao with 13,463, Wusih with 10,317, Nantung with 5,961, and Shanghai with 5,211. The 76,132 organized workers in the cotton industry were equally divided between males and females, there being 38,317 or 50.33% for the former and 37,815 or 49.67% for the latter. However, as female workers accounted for 61.84% and male workers for 31.87% of the workers in the cotton industry, we may conclude that male workers were organized to a much larger extent than female workers.

Partly due to unionization and partly due to other causes, the labor strikes in Shanghai cotton mills showed an abnormal increase during the three years from 1925 to 1927. During the twelve year period from 1918 to 1929 in Shanghai, there were altogether 209 strikes, of which 171 or 81.8% occurred within three years, namely, 38 in 1925, 78 in 1926 and 55 in 1927. The total number of workers involved in the 209 strikes was estimated at 577,239, giving an average of 2,762 workers per strike. For 155 of these strikes the number of man-days lost reached 6,721,957, giving an average loss of 43,367 man-days per strike. Calculating on the basis of an average daily wage of 49.3 cents for the cotton mill workers in Shanghai, the total loss per strike amounted to $21,380. Among the 209 strikes 151 or 72.25% were related to collective bargaining, the remaining 58 strikes or 27.75% being not so related. Among both groups of strikes the engagement or dismissal of workers resulted in 50 strikes, wages in 45 strikes, political causes in 35 strikes, factory regulations in 14 strikes, sympathetic causes in 13 strikes, hours of work in 10 strikes, systems of work in 8 strikes, and treatment in 6 strikes. The demands for 67 strikes were entirely accepted, those for 57 strikes partially accepted, and those for 61 strikes rejected. The results for 24 strikes were indeterminate or unknown.

Apart from the workers' attempt to organize for collective bargaining, and to enforce such bargaining through strike as the last resort, labor legislation offers another solution to the labor problems in Chinese industries. Recently, several labor laws have been passed by the National government, which, if effectively enforced, may have a significant bearing upon all industries, especially upon the cotton industry. The Factory Act, promulgated on December 30, 1929 and nominally enforced on the first of August 1931 by means of official proclamation, regulates the conditions of work in power driven plants employing 30 or more workers, of which cotton mills offer the best example. It provides for 8-hour work, prohibition of night work for child and woman labor, a minimum age limit of 16 for child labor, equal pay for equal work, annual rest days and holidays with pay, workers' representation, workmen's compensation, motherhood pension, continuation education, etc. The Labor Union Act, promulgated on October 21, 1929 and enforced on November 1, 1929, recognizes two types of unions, the trade or craft union with a minimum membership of 50 and the industrial union with one of 100. A worker is allowed to join only one type of union, and neither the union nor the employer is to interfere with his right to membership. Many functions, now performed in other countries by the government or the employer, are relegated to the union. This Act also provides that in case of dispute between the employer and the workers, no strike shall be declared unless attempts have first been made to settle it by means of conciliation and arbitration, and unless the case has subsequently been referred to a general meeting of the union, at which at least two-thirds of its members have voted by secret ballot in favor of the strike. On the other hand, an employer or his agent shall not dismiss any of his employees during the period of conciliation and arbitration. In the Labor Disputes Act promulgated on June 9, 1928 and amended on March 17, 1930, the machinery for conciliation and arbitration is provided for. It re-enforces the Labor Union Act by providing that during the course of conciliation and arbitration neither strike nor lockout shall be ordered by either of the parties concernad.

Manufacturing and marketing:—The fundamental processes of cotton manufacture are cleaning, carding, drawing, roving, spinning, and lastly weaving, which is usually termed manufacturing. Bleaching, dyeing, printing and finishing are known as the finishing processes. In China the preparatory processes including spinning are carried on in one mill, in which weaving may also be performed at the same time. In 1930 China had 127 mills, of which 77 were engaged in spinning, 48 in spinning and weaving, and 2 in weaving. Bleaching and dyeing are carried on in small works, where the products of both power and hand looms are received for treatment.

The costs in cotton manufacture include the cost for raw cotton and other costs, of which the former claims about four fifths in the spinning of yarn. The higher the counts spun, however, the lower the cost of raw cotton. In one cotton mill in Tientsin, for instance, the cost of raw cotton claims 87.92% of the total cost for ten counts, 84.87% for fourteen counts, 82.61% for sixteen counts, and 77.64% for twenty counts three ply. The other costs include labor, power, materials, depreciation, interest, tax and overhead (including insurance, office and sundries). The depreciation of machinery and building is thought of only after a dividend has been fixed and a surplus declared. As to tax, there are on every bale of yarn an excise varying from $8.25 to $11.25, and an export duty of Hk. Tls. 2.10. As to the other items an analysis of data for certain mills in Shanghai and Tientsin reveals a rather constant proportion despite the variation in the counts of yarn spun. The cost for labor claims from 30 to 35%, that for interest from 25 to 35%, and that for materials, power and overhead, from 10 to 15% respectively. However, for the spinning of different counts of yarn, especially of fourteen and sixteen counts, the cost is much higher in Tientsin than in Shanghai. In Tientsin the cost of spinning 14 counts excluding raw cotton amounts to $31.96, while in Shanghai it is only $27.08. Similarly, in spinning 16 counts the cost excluding raw cotton is $42.39 in Tientsin, but $31.78 in Shanghai.

The efficiency of cotton mills in China, especially of cotton labor, may be revealed after a critical analysis of the data contained in the *Revised List of Cotton Mills in China for 1930.* In respect of cotton labor, the analysis shows an average efficiency of 19.30 spindles per worker in all mills, irrespective of nationality of ownership. The worker in Japanese owned mills, however, operates a much higher number of spindles (24.14) than his comrade in Chinese owned mills (16.05). This is due primarily to better supervision and more up-to-date equipment. Consequently, the worker in Japanese owned mills consumes a greater quantity of raw cotton (43.00 versus 34.55 piculs per year), requires a larger amount of power capacity (0.8281 versus 0.5301 K.W.), and produces a greater quantity of yarn (11.95 versus 9.85 bales per year). Similarly, the worker in Japanese owned mills operates a larger number of looms (1.10 versus 0.58 loom) and weaves a far greater quantity of cloth (786.38 versus 261.73 pieces per year) than his comrade in Chinese mills, the average number of loom per worker in all mills irrespective of nationality of ownship being 0.73,[1] and the average cloth output per worker per year being 414.19 pieces.

The per worker efficiency for the cotton mills in China is further reflected in the per spindle efficiency. Since the worker in Chinese owned mills operates a far smaller number of spindles than his comrade in Japanese owned mills, the per spindle output of yarn for all counts is higher in Chinese than in Japanese owned mills (0.692 bale or 276.8 lbs. versus 0.501 bale or 200.4 lbs. per year). The same holds true with the per spindle consumption of raw cotton, which is 2.453 bales per year in Chinese owned mills as compared with 1.806 bales per year in Japanese owned mills.

The above analysis of mill efficiency may be supplemented by the statistics on spindle and loom output actually collected from the mills. The spindle output on a 24-hour working basis seems more favorable to the Japanese owned mills for 14's, 16's, 20's and 40's. In Shanghai the average output for 16's is 1.283 lbs. in Japanese owned mills, but 1.100 lbs. in Chinese owned mills. For 20's it is 1.026 lbs. in Japanese owned mills but 0.960 lb. in Chinese owned mills. Among the Chinese mills the spindle output in Shanghai is higher than that in Tientsin, which difference can be explained as much by the lower efficiency of northern workers as by the poorer climatic conditions. The average spindle output for 10's is 2.20 lbs. in Shanghai but 1.77 lbs. in Tientsin; that for 14's is 1.50 lbs. in Shanghai but 1.13 lbs. in Tientsin; that for 16's is 1.10 lbs. in Shanghai but 0.90 lb. in Tientsin; and that for 42's is 0.38 lb. in Shanghai but 0.26 lb. in Tientsin. In Shanghai, again, the spindle output seems to have increased in recent years. The investigation in 1918 gave an average

1. This statement must not be readin the light that every weaver operates only 0.73 loom in China. It implies rather that in order to operate 0.73 loom the service of one worker in weaving finishing etc. is required.

spindle output of 1.4 to 1.7 lbs. for 10's, but in 1929 it was raised to 2.2 lbs. Similarly, the spindle output for 14's was 1.06 to 1.30 lbs. in 1918 but 1.50 lbs. in 1929; that for 16's, 0.90 to 1.09 lbs. in 1918 but 1.10 lbs. in 1929; and that for 20's, 0.60 to 0.70 lb. in 1918 but 0.96 lb. in 1929.

The products of cotton industry embrace yarn and thread on the one hand, and cloth on the other. According to the Chinese Cotton Mill-owners' Association, the total output of yarn and thread has increased from 1,473,768 bales in 1924 to 2,102,829 bales in 1927, and 2,455,177 bales in 1930, while that of cloth has increased from 4,000,767 pieces in 1925 to 8,999,370 pieces in 1927 and 14,779,538 pieces in 1930. In 1930 1,500,248 bales of yarn and thread or 61.11% were spun by the Chinese owned mills, 825,407 bales or 33.62% by the Japanese owned mills, and 129,522 bales or 5.27% by the British owned mills. In respect of cotton cloth, 8,153,994 pieces or 55.17% were woven by the Japanese owned mills and 6,625,544 pieces or 44.83% by the Chinese owned mills. The yarns spun in China are mostly of low counts. An investigation of the products of 69 mills in China in 1928 showed that 16's was spun by 61 mills, 10's by 57 mills, 20's by 49 mills, 12's by 44 mills, 14's by 44 mills, 32's by 28 mills and 42's by 9 mills. All the other counts, running from 4's to 80's, were spun by no less than one but no more than nine mills. The cloth woven in China is of two types, grey and dyed. The grey cloth includes sheetings, shirtings, drills, jeans and T-cloth, while the dyed cloth includes a far greater number of varieties, each variety being determined primarily by the color scheme.

Yarn is packed in the usual manner with 40 bundles in a bale, each bundle containing 10 pounds 4 ounces, net; but cloth is put up in bales of 20 pieces each. The transport of both is mostly by means of steamships, but occasionally through railways, and the freight is calculated in terms of foot space. The taxes include the excise and the export duty. The former was introduced on the first of February 1931, as a substitute for likin abolished a month earlier. This tax, applicable to cigarettes, flour, cotton yarn, match and cement, divides the cotton yarn into two major groups, namely, (1) cotton yarn, grey, 23 counts or below, and (2) cotton yarn, grey, above 23 counts. For the first group the tax is fixed at $2.75 per picul; for the second, at $3.75. Any cloth woven of the taxed yarn is exempted from further levy. Under the Revised Export Tariff of 1931 the export duty is fixed at Hk. Tl. 0.037 per gross on "cotton thread, sewing, on spools or cops (or 50 yds. or less)"; while that for "cotton thread, not otherwise provided for", is, like that for cotton yarn, fixed at Hk. Tls. 1.10 per picul. The export duty on cotton cloths or piece goods is fixed at Hk. Tls. 1.50 per picul; and that on "cotton piece goods, not otherwise provided for", at 7½% *ad valorem*.

Trading in cotton goods is carried on by the dealers who distribute not only native, but also imported products. Indeed, the first dealers rose at a time when the import of foreign cotton goods had been put on a more or less permanent basis, after the seventies. In Shanghai a recent investigation estimates the number of yarn shops at 63, and that of cloth shops at 87. In Tientsin the number of yarn shops is estimated at 32, and that of cloth shops at 44. The number of cloth shops is, therefore, larger than that of yarn shops, indicating the preponderance of piece goods over yarns in both markets. But a yarn shop may also trade in cloth and a cloth shop in yarn, although a major portion of the trade for each type of shops is devoted to its own specialities.

The dealers may buy directly from the mills or indirectly through the Exchange, and may sell directly to the clients or indirectly through the 'runners'. They may also act as brokers, receiving a commission of from Tl. 0.25 to Tl. 0.50 for every bale of cotton yarn transacted. In all these transactions, trading may be carried on in spots or in futures. Both types of contracts, especially the futures, used to be transacted in the two exchanges in Shanghai, namely, the Chinese Cotton Goods Exchange and the Chinese Stock and Produce Exchange. The latter has suspended future contracts in cotton yarn since June, 1929, and at present, the former is the only future market for cotton yarn in China. Future contracts in cotton cloth are provided for in the regulations of the Chinese Cotton Goods Exchange, but due to the great variety of cloth on the market and the immense difficulty of grading, they have not yet been traded in.

Imports and exports:—China's foreign trade in raw cotton began over two centuries ago, under the leadership of the East India Company, in 1704. In that year, 1,116 piculs of raw cotton were despatched from Surat in Northern Bombay to Malacca, but sold at Amoy at a price of Tls. 5.50 per picul. The Amoy shipment was however incidental, and 32 years again elapsed before another import of 605 piculs, at a price of Tls. 8.50 per picul, was recorded in 1735. Then followed an intermittent import of various quantities until 1785, after which a rapid increase in the import of Indian cotton took place. During the whole period of 39 years from 1785 to 1833 for which records on raw cotton trade were kept by the Company, China imported altogether 13,404,659 piculs from India, almost entirely in English vessels (98.78%). The average annual import amounted to 343,709 piculs, but four peaks, each higher than the preceding, were reached in 1789 (226,789 piculs), 1805 (414,208 piculs), 1816 (463,867 piculs), and 1830 (501,920 piculs) respectively.

The statistics on raw cotton import from 1833 to 1867 are not available, but in comparing the figures between these two years the change during the period could not have been very great, the raw cotton import being 442,640 piculs in 1833 but 335,976 piculs in 1867. An export, meantime, was developing, which amounted to 29,391 piculs in 1867. In other words, there was in 1867 an unfavorable balance of 306,585 piculs for China's foreign trade in raw cotton. The unfavorable balance continued, with the exception of 1874, for a period of 21 years, up to 1887. After the latter year China exported more cotton than she imported, and thus acquired, with the exception of 1899, a favorable balance during a period of 32 years from 1888 to 1919. After 1919, however, another period of unfavorable balance was ushered in, which reached the climax in 1930. In the latter year China imported 3,456,494 piculs but exported 825,545 piculs, with an unfavorable balance reaching as high as 2,630,949 piculs. China's foreign trade in raw cotton from 1867 to 1930 can, therefore, be divided into three periods, namely, the period of unfavorable balance from 1867 to 1887, the period of favorable balance from 1888 to 1919, and the period of unfavorable balance from 1920 to 1930. The transition from the second to the third period is at least due to two sets of factors, the ocurrence of civil war and the growth in China's cotton industry. The first factor is responsible for the reduction in China's cotton production, while the second one gives rise to a greater demand for raw cotton in China.

During the period from 1867 to 1930, China had a total import of 30,752,063 piculs and a total export of 32,831,619 piculs, with a favorable balance of 2,079,556 piculs. Of the total import of 30,752,063 piculs during the period of 64 years, the ten year period from 1921 to 1930 claimed 21,152,168 piculs or 68.78%. On the other hand, of the total export of 32,831,619 piculs during the same period, the twenty-five year period from 1906 to 1930 claimed 21,997,108 piculs or 67%. The export, therefore, was more evenly distributed than the import. Indeed, the five year period from 1926 to 1930 claimed as much as 13,047,919 piculs or 42.43% of the total import. Another fact to be noted is the relatively lower price paid for the cotton exported from China. During the period from 1867 to 1930 the total import of 30,752,063 piculs of foreign cotton was valued at Hk. Tls. 865,604,848, giving an average price of Hk. Tls. 28.14 per picul, while the total export of 32,831,619 piculs of Chinese cotton during the same period was valued at Hk. Tls. 734,925,937, giving an average price of Hk. Tls. 22.44 per picul. As is generally expected, this discrepancy in the price paid for Chinese and foreign cotton proves indirectly the lower quality of the former.

China's foreign trade in raw cotton may be further examined in respect of origin and destination. During the 19 years from 1912 to 1930 China imported altogether 23,872,155 piculs of raw cotton, of which 13,128,154 piculs or 54.1% came from British India, 5,280,291 piculs or 21.8% from the United States, and 5,267,264 piculs or 21.7% from Japan.

As Japan is not a cotton producing country, much of the cotton imported from Japan is tran-shipped from other countries via Japan, especially India. Taking the three years 1913, 1920 and 1929 for the purpose of comparison, the share for British India in China's cotton import declined from 59.56% in 1913 and 60.85% in 1920 to 51.97% in 1929, while that for the United States, which fell from 18.84% in 1913 to 4.95% in 1920, rose to 32.18% in 1929. The increasing importance of American cotton is a hopeful sign, as it indirectly confirms that China is demanding a better quality of cotton for the spinning of finer counts of yarn. The share for Japan, which rose from 10.89% in 1913 to 23.53% in 1920, declined again to 14.30% in 1929.

During the period 1912-1930 more than nine-tenths of China's cotton import were absorbed by the three principal centres, Shanghai, Kiaochow and Tientsin. Of the total import of 23,946,751 piculs during the period, Shanghai claimed 19,289,342 piculs or 80.6%, Kiaochow 2,108,941 piculs or 8.8%, and Tientsin 1,013,597 piculs or 4.2%. The percentage for Shanghai is rather constant, being 80.84 in 1913 and 81.31 in 1920, but in 1929 it falls slightly to 75.54 For Kiaochow the cotton import is a recent development, beginning with the first import of 206 piculs in 1915. The amount rose to 7,871 piculs or 1.15% in 1920 and 225,803 piculs or 8.94% in 1929. The same may be said of Tientsin. The latter imported only 5 piculs in 1912, but increased suddenly to 1,067 piculs in 1916. Since then the amount of import has shown a considerable fluctuation, due chiefly to the fluctuation in Tientsin's cotton import from the interior. The highest import is that for 1929, namely, 179,156 piculs or 7.09%.

China's export of raw cotton during the period 1912 to 1930 amounted to 38,280,474 piculs, of which only 16,867,011 piculs or 44.06% were exported to foreign countries, the rest being imported into other Chinese ports for home consumption. A comparison of the percentage that the export to foreign countries occupied in China's total export during 1913, 1920 and 1929 confirms indirectly her growing demand for raw cotton arising from the rapid development of the cotton industry. Such percentage, which amounted to 77.71 in 1913, fell to 43.17 in 1920 and 33.92 in 1929.

Of the total export of 16,867,011 piculs of raw cotton from China during the period 1912 to 1930, 13,466,053 piculs or 79.84% went to Japan, and 1,934,968 piculs or 11.47% to U. S. A. The percentage that Japan occupied in China's cotton export has increased from 58.56 in 1920 to 80.04 in 1929, while that for the U.S.A. has fallen during the same period, from 31.80 to 12.24.

The chief ports of China's cotton export include Hankow and Shasi on the one hand and Tientsin on the other. During the whole period from 1912 to 1930 Hankow and Shasi exported 20,349,123 piculs or 53.16%

while Tientsin exported 9,266,451 piculs or 24.21%. That these three ports should have contributed altogether more than three-fourths of China's total cotton export is not unexpected, as Hankow and Shasi are located in the heart of the central producing region, while Tientsin is the collecting centre for the raw cotton from the northern producing region. However, whereas the percentage that Hankow and Shasi claims in China's cotton export has shown a consistent increase from 23.94 in 1913 to 49.74 in 1920 and 62.76 in 1929, such percentage for Tientsin has shown a consistent decrease from 35.29 in 1913 to 29.67 in 1920, and 22.58 in 1929. Another difference to be noted is that while Hankow cotton is exported to Shanghai and other cotton centres along the Yangtze Valley for home consumption, Tientsin cotton is exported to foreign countries, especially to Japan and the United States, for padding, medecinal cotton, gunpowder, and mixture with other fibres.

In the import of cotton goods the members of the East India Company were not so successful as in that of raw cotton, for it was not until after 42 years of persistent offort, from 1786 to 1827, that a foothold was finally obtained in the China market—that is, in Canton. In 1827 British calicoes were for the first time sold at a profit: "The importation on Company's account during the season was 15,300 pieces, invoiced free on board at £21,261, and cost, insurance, and freight at £23,241, and they were sold (not including duty) at an average price of seven dollars a piece, a total of 107,100 dollars". Meantime, Americans had, as early as 1821, shipped a total worth of $179,410 of piece goods to Canton, although the imports by American vessels were "all of English manufacture, shipped from England to Canton in contravention of the East India Company's monopoly."

The import of cotton goods, which amounted to Tls. 1,061,356 in 1832, increased greatly during the following thirty-five years. In 1867 the import of cotton goods reached the huge total of Tls. 14,617,258, which was equivalent to 21% of the total import into China. In the following year when the collection of customs statistics was further perfected, the import was increased by 57% to Tls. 22,373,056,—a total around which the imports for later years fluctuated until 1884. Taking the 1913 import of Hk. Tls. 182,419,023 as equivalent to 100, the ratio was only 12.26 in 1868, 17.26 in 1885, 24.68 in 1890, 29.09 in 1895, 54.63 in 1901, 99.47 in 1905, 135.30 in 1920, and 82.14 in 1930. 1920, the peak year during the whole period from 1867 to 1930, witnessed an import of Hk. Tls. 246,813,429, or 32.38% of the total import for China. In 1930 the total import of cotton goods was reduced to Hk. Tls. 149,838, 808, which amounted to only 11.44% of China's total import, the lowest percentage during the whole period from 1867 to 1930.

Not only has the import of cotton goods declined since the last few decades, but the origin and destination of such an import have also changed, resulting in the rapid rise of Japan among the exporting nations, and the equally rapid rise of Antung and Dairen among the importing ports. During the three years 1905, 1913, and 1929 more than nine-tenths of the cotton goods were imported from the four countries of Great Britain (including Hongkong), Japan, the United States, and British India. Japan, which supplied only 11.24% of the total import in 1905, contributed 29.81% in 1913 and 63.85% in 1929. The percentage for the United States, 22.58, was twice that for Japan in 1905, but fell to 4.39 in 1913 and 0.33 in 1929. Similarly, the percentage for British India, 12.76 in 1905, fell to 10.24 in 1913 and 1.09 in 1929. Great Britain, supplying 49.82% in 1905, had about the same percentage in 1913, 49.03%. But like the United States and British India, her percentage was greatly reduced to 30.30% in 1929. In other words, the steady rise of Japan in China's cotton goods import was brought about at the expense first of the United States, then of British India, and finally of Great Britain—the mistress of the world's cotton textile industry. Such a rise is easily explained by Japan's ability to supply a lower priced fabric, as well as other advantages inherent in goegraphical propinquity and cultural similarity.

The change in the origin of cotton goods import gives rise to a similar change in its destination—similar in the sense of the causes affecting it. Among the six ports that absorbed 49.10% of the total cotton goods import in 1905, 51.62% in 1913 and 67.71% in 1929, the most notable changes were the rapid rise of Antung's share from 1.86% in 1913 to 15.65% in 1929, and of Dairen's share from zero in 1905 to 6.42% in 1929, as well as the equally rapid fall of Tientsin's share from 15.66% in 1913 to 9.37% in 1929. Shanghai, the largest port of import in 1905 and 1929, maintained her status rather precariously, her share being 21.75% in 1905, 10.94% in 1913, and 23.29% in 1929. The percentage for Hankow, 7.16 in 1905, rose to 10.05 in 1913, but fell to 7.91 in 1929. Similarly, Kiaochow's percentage, 3.93 in 1905, rose to 8.06 in 1913, but fell to 5.07 in 1929.

The first kind of cotton goods to be exported from China was the "nankeens"—handloom cotton cloths woven at Nanking. In this as in other respects of China's foreign trade, the members of the East India Company were again the pioneers. Since the first trial order of the Company for 100 pieces in 1734, the "nankeens" had been exported more or less intermittently for almost half a century. Beginning with 1786 the export became a little more regular, while four years later it was recorded almost without interruption in the *Chronicles* of the Company until 1833. Most of the "nankeens", however, were carried by American ships and destined for the United States. Of a total export of 40,274,164 pieces from Canton during the 48 year period from 1786 to 1833, 22,776,943 pieces or 56.55% were exported through the American vessels, while the vessels of the Company carried only 15,169,553 pieces or 37.67%, thus leaving the other 2,327,668 pieces or 5.78% to the vessels of other flags.

The "nankeen" cloth, the only kind of cotton goods exported for a period of almost two centuries since 1734, became less and less important in China's export trade after 1833. Whereas in 1830 its export amounted to 1,051,000 pieces, in 1867 it was reduced to only 441 piculs or 15,876 pieces. Except 1869 its annual export from 1867 to 1874 never exceeded 1,000 piculs or 36,000 pieces. Beginning with 1875 a slow but intermittent increase took place, reaching 2,687 piculs (96,732 pieces) in 1886. Since 1886 the increase had become more rapid. The export was raised to 6,617 piculs in 1887, 8,112 piculs in 1891, 17,086 piculs in 1893, and 36,663 piculs (1,319,868 pieces) in 1895. From 1896 to 1910 there were ups and downs, catering always around the total for 1895. After 1910 another increase was witnessed, reaching the highest figure of 75,848 piculs (2,730,528 pieces) in 1921. A fall again occurred after the latter year, resulting in an export for 1930 of 37,798 piculs (1,360,728 pieces),—a total which was slightly higher than that for 1895, 36,663 piculs (1,319,868 pieces). It seems, therefore, that the export of "nankeens", which grew rapidly during the 18th century, had barely held its own during the 19th and the first part of the 20th. In terms of relative importance in China's export trade in cotton goods, however, it had declined rapidly. Up to the five year period 1896-1900, "nankeens" constituted fully 100% of the total value of China's export in cotton goods. But the percentage began to decline progressively after that period, being reduced to 98 during 1901-05, 77.78 during 1911-15, 27.45 during 1921-25, and finally to 7.88 during 1926-30. The rapid decline, of course, was chiefly accounted for by the equally rapid growth of China's machine spinning and weaving industry.

China's export of cotton goods to foreign countries after 1905 may be divided into three categories; piece goods, yarn and thread, and others. During the 26 year period from 1905 to 1930, China's export of cotton goods has grown from the small amount of Hk. Tls. 1,647,445 to the huge sum of Hk. Tls. 31,968,629—an increase of 19.4 times. This increase, however, is unequally distributed among the three groups of cotton goods. In 1905 when the total export amounted to Hk. Tls. 1,647,445, piece goods occupied Hk. Tls. 1,523,588 or 92.48%, and other goods which referred to cotton waste occupied Hk. Tls. 123,857 or 7.52%. In 1913 when the total export amounted to Hk. Tls. 2,945,327, the proportion for the piece goods showed a decline to 87.51%, with a simultaneous increase of that for the other goods to 11.92%. The export of yarn and thread, which began in 1912, occupied not even one percent in 1913 (0.57%). In 1920 the total export had increased to Hk. Tls. 8,209,732. The percentage for piece goods showed a further decline to 60.29%, while that for yarn and thread increased rapidly to 35.35. This trend of development persisted until 1930, when the percentage for piece goods had declined from the highest of 92.48 in 1905 to the lowest of 30.64. On the other hand, the percentage for yarn and thread had increased from the lowest of 0.57 in 1913 to the highest of 59.33.

China's export of cotton goods flows in two directions, one to the foreign countries and the other to the Chinese ports. The export to foreign countries, however, is much less important than that to Chinese ports, being only 11.41% in 1913, 8.98% in 1920, and 16.12% in 1929; it is distributed chiefly among six regions: Hongkong; Singapore, Straits, etc.; Dutch Indies; British India; Turkey, Persia, Egypt, Aden, etc.; and Japan (including Formosa). These six regions claimed 81.02% of the total foreign export of native cotton goods in 1913, 90.22% in 1920, and 92.20% in 1929. With the exception of Hongkong which is a port for trans-shipment, and of Japan which is more industrialized than China, the regions to which China exports her cotton goods are poorly developed from an industrial viewpoint. Among the six regions Hongkong absorbed 39.16% in 1929, after which followed Turkey, Persia, Egypt, Aden, etc. with 18.57%, British India with 12.09%, Japan with 9.20%, Singapore, Straits, etc. with 6.77%, and Dutch Indies with 6.41%. During the period from 1913 to 1929, however, these different regions have changed in relative importance. The percentage for Hongkong has declined rapidly from 62.51 in 1913 to 39.16 in 1929; so has that for Singapore, Straits, etc. from 16.78 to 6.77 during the same period. The percentage for the other four regions has risen uniformly, from 1913 to 1929. The percentage for Dutch Indies has risen from 0.04 to 6.41; that for British India from 0.25 to 12.09; that for Turkey, Persia, Egypt, Aden etc. from zero to 18.57; and that for Japan from 1.44 to 9.20.

The original export of China's cotton goods, embracing under this category both the "foreign" and the "inter-port" export, is derived chiefly from Shanghai. Shanghai, whereat about two-thirds of China's cotton industry are located, supplied as much as 86.93% of the total original export of native cotton goods in 1913, 84.30% in 1920, and 84.55% in 1929. The other four ports, including Hankow, Kiaochow, Ningpo and Dairen, supplied 3.68% in 1913, 7.26% in 1920, and 12.47% in 1929. Of the total original export of native cotton goods, the yarn and thread group occupies about two-thirds: 62.91% in 1913, 71.91% in 1920, and 62.16% in 1929. It is exported from Shanghai and other ports chiefly to meet the needs in other Chinese ports where machine spinning is as yet undeveloped and where handloom weaving is carried on with machine spun yarn and no longer with home spun yarn from the spinning wheels. The other third of the total original export is taken up by cotton piece goods, the percentage being 35.79 in 1913, 27.35 in 1920 and 34.51 in 1929. The 'other' group, including cotton waste in 1913 and 1920, but cotton waste, blankets and counterpanes, socks and stockings, towels, wadding, etc. in 1929, is rather insignificant, occupying only 1.3% in 1913, 0.74% in 1920 and 3.33% in 1929.

Comparative position of China's cotton industry

China's cotton industry has grown very rapidly since the outbreak of the world war in 1914. Indeed, among the leading cotton manufacturing nations in the world, the rate of growth in terms of spindleage is the most rapid in China. Taking the number of spindles in 1913 as the base of 100, the index for China has increased to the highest figure of 397.25 in 1931, while during the same year it was but 312.65 for Japan, 149.98 for India, 138.57 for France, 116.22 for Italy, and 105.84 for the United States. For other nations the index has instead shown a decline, being 99.27 for Russia, 98.71 for Great Britain and 96.89 for Germany. If the world at large is taken into consideration, the increase from 1913 to 1931 amounts to 14.03%, while for China it has reached as high as 297.25% or over twenty times the total increase for the world (Fig 48).

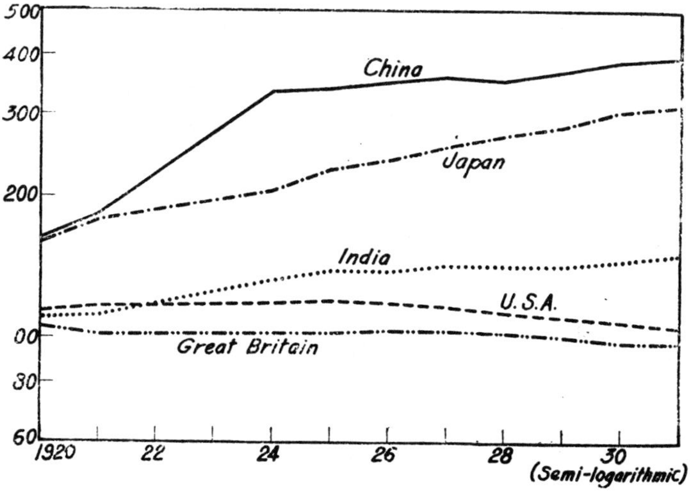

Fig. 48. Growth of cotton spindles in leading countries of the world, 1920-1931 (1913=100) (*See* Table 116)

Despite the almost spectacular increase in China's spindleage since the World War, the number of spindles in proportion to her population is still the lowest among the cotton spinning nations of the world. Great Britain, the mistress of the world's cotton textile industry, has the highest figure of 1,199 spindles per 1,000 population, while China has but 9 spindles per 1,000 population, a figure which is only ¾ of one percent of that for Great Britain. Indeed, China, with only 9 spindles

Table 116. Distribution of raw cotton spinning spindles in the world, 1913-1931*

	1913	1920	1921	1924	1925	1926	1927	1928	1929	1930	1931
						In thousand spindles					
Great Britain	55,652	58,692	56,140	56,750	57,116	57,286	57,325	57,136	55,917	55,207	54,933
U. S. A.	31,505	35,834	36,618	37,786	37,937	37,585	36,728	35,542	34,829	34,031	33,345
Germany	11,186	9,400	9,400	9,464	9,500	10,480	10,800	11,153	11,250	11,070	10,838
France	7,400	9,400	9,600	9,600	9,428	9,511	9,567	9,770	9,880	10,250	10,254
India	6,084	6,689	6,763	7,928	8,500	8,510	8,714	8,703	8,704	8,907	9,125
Russia	7,668	7,200	7,200	7,246	7,246	7,246	6,945	7,311	7,465	7,612	7,612
Japan	2,300	3,690	4,126	4,825	5,292	5,573	5,952	6,272	6,530	7,072	7,191
Italy	4,600	4,515	4,507	4,570	4,771	4,833	5,086	5,189	5,210	5,342	5,346
China	983	1,600	1,800	3,300	3,350	3,436	3,568	3,504	3,602	3,829	3,905
Other	16,071	17,457	16,902	17,350	18,223	19,263	19,912	20,253	20,824	20,788	21,022
Total	143,449	154,477	153,056	158,819	161,363	163,723	164,597	165,103	164,211	164,108	163,571
					Index (1913=100)						
Great Britain	100.00	105.46	100.88	101.97	102.63	102.94	103.01	102.67	100.48	99.20	98.71
U. S. A.	100.00	113.74	116.23	119.94	120.42	119.30	116.58	112.81	110.55	108.02	105.84
Germany	100.00	84.03	84.03	84.61	84.93	93.69	96.55	99.70	100.57	98.96	96.89
France	100.00	127.03	129.73	129.73	127.41	128.53	129.28	132.03	133.51	138.51	138.57
India	100.00	109.94	111.16	130.31	139.71	139.88	143.23	143.05	143.06	146.40	149.98
Russia	100.00	93.90	93.90	94.50	94.50	94.50	90.57	95.34	97.35	99.27	99.27
Japan	100.00	160.43	179.39	209.78	230.09	242.30	258.78	272.70	283.91	307.48	312.65
Italy	100.00	98.15	97.98	99.35	103.72	105.07	110.57	112.80	113.26	116.13	116.22
China	100.00	162.77	183.11	335.71	340.79	349.54	362.97	356.46	370.19	389.52	397.25
Other	100.00	108.62	105.17	107.96	113.39	119.86	123.90	127.70	129.58	129.35	130.81
Total	100.00	107.69	106.70	110.72	112.49	114.13	114.74	115.10	114.47	114.40	114.03

* League of Nations, *Statistical Yearbook, 1930-31*, Table 92; Id., *Memorandum on Cotton*, 1927, p. 7.

per 1,000 population, bears poor comparison even with two of the world's largest agricultural nations, i.e. India with 26 and Russia with 48 spindles per 1,000 population (Fig. 49).

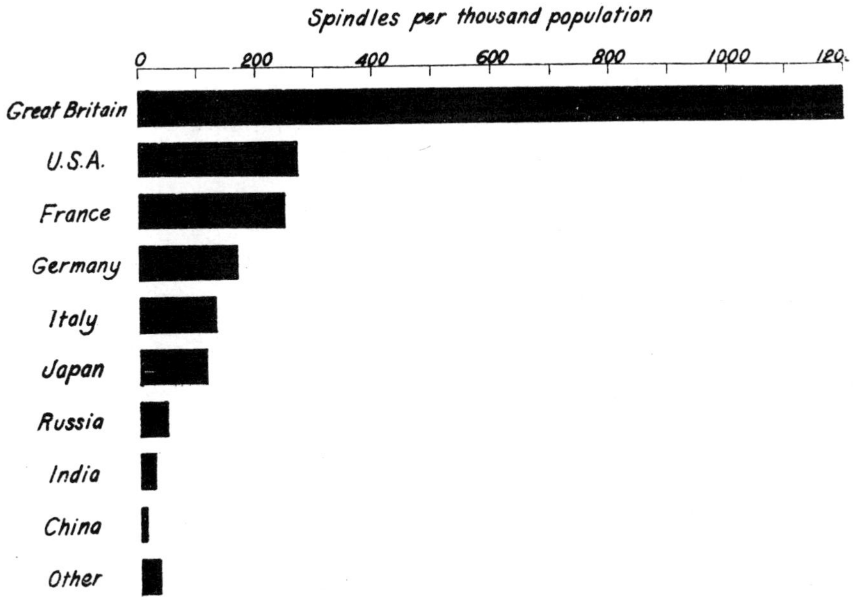

Fig. 49. Cotton spindles per 1,000 population in leading countries of the world, 1931 (*See* Table 117)

The number of spindles, however, does not serve as the good index of a country's producing capacity. The producing capacity is doubled under two shift than under one shift system, provided each shift be composed of the same number of working hours. Again, even if one shift system prevails, as is true with most of the industrialized countries in Europe and America, the producing capacity varies according to the length of the shift, the efficiency of labor and management, the character of the machinery employed and the number of counts spun. For these and other reasons the producing capacity per spindle in China is necessarily higher than that in many other countries, not excepting India and Japan. In China the two shift system of 12 hours each still prevails despite the provisions in the new Factory Act prohibiting night labor; while lower counts, mostly 10, 16, 20, are as yet the commonest varieties spun by less efficient labor. Under such circumstance a better index of her relative position in the world's cotton industry, therefore, is the mill consumption of raw cotton per spindle. As shown in Table 118, the mill consumption of raw cotton per thousand spindles in China is, with the exception of Japan in 1924, the highest in the world for the three years 1924, 1926 and 1927. In 1927 China's mill consumption of cotton per thousand spindles reaches 558.2 running bales, as compared with 455.8 for Japan, 298.2 for India, 192.5 for U.S.A., 185.9 for Italy, 136.2 for Germany, 123.8 for France and 51.6 for Great Britain. The figure for Great Britain is especially low, because of working on short time and of spinning on finer counts.

Table 117. Distribution of raw cotton spinning spindles per 1,000 population in the world, 1931*

Country	Raw cotton spinning spindles, 1931 (000's omitted)	%	Estimated population, 1929 (000's omitted)	Population per spindle, 1931	Spindle per 1,000 population
Canada	1,277	0.78	9,860	7.72	130
U. S. A.	33,345	20.39	122,285	3.67	273
Mexico	799	0.49	16,350	20.46	49
Brazil	2,775	1.70	40,273	14.51	69
China	3,905	2.39	444,000	113.70	9
India	9,125	5.58	348,000	38.14	26
Japan	7,191	4.40	63,740	8.86	113
Germany	10,838	6.63	64,104	5.91	169
Austria	742	0.45	6,704	9.04	111
Belgium	2,154	1.32	8,060	3.74	267
Denmark	96	0.06	3,525	36.72	27
Spain	2,070	1.27	22,761	11.00	91
Finland	263	0.16	3,370	12.81	78
France	10,254	6.27	41,190	4.02	249
Hungary	211	0.13	8,640	40.95	24
Italy	5,346	3.27	41,506	7.76	129
Norway	52	0.03	2,803	53.90	19
Netherlands	1,204	0.74	7,833	6.51	154
Poland	1,547	0.95	30,737	19.87	50
Portugal	503	0.31	5,809	11.55	87
Great Britain	54,933	33.58	45,833	0.83	1,199
Sweden	592	0.36	6,120	10.34	97
Switzerland	1,387	0.85	4,060	2.93	342
Czechoslovakia	3,648	2.23	14,657	4.02	249
Russia	7,612	4.65	157,500	20.69	48
Other	1,702	1.04	473,050	277.93	4
Total	163,571	100.00	1,992,500	12.18	82

* League of Nations, *Statistical Yearbook, 1930-31*, Table 92.

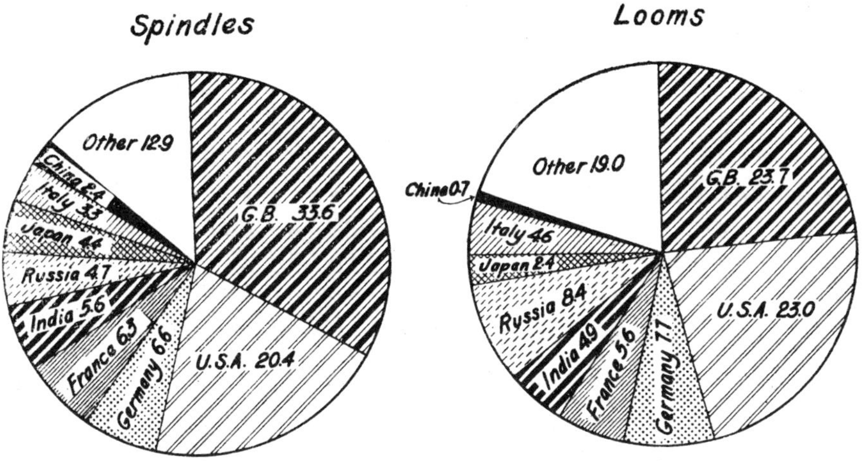

Fig. 50. Percentage distribution of cotton spindles and power looms in the world by countries (*See* Tables 117 and 121)

Table 118. Consumption of cotton, per thousand spindles, by countries, 1922-1927* (in running bales)

Country	1922	1923	1924	1925	1926	1927
World	137.3	141.2	128.0	144.3	151.0	157.2
Great Britain	50.6	48.9	47.8	56.6	53.2	51.6
France	110.8	126.0	113.5	119.0	124.3	123.8
Germany	126.2	111.9	81.9	127.4	110.4	136.2
Italy	175.6	195.9	206.1	210.0	216.4	185.9
Czechoslovakia	104.0	71.2	120.5	139.4	134.5	139.4
Spain	200.5	194.0	201.8	194.1	166.3	207.1
Belgium	151.2	161.9	170.0	170.5	191.7	193.4
Switzerland	57.5	48.7	66.6	71.1	74.5	71.0
Poland	184.9	189.6	162.5	178.3	147.0	229.1
Holland	175.5	165.5	81.6	166.4	147.8	162.3
Sweden	133.4	148.0	151.4	149.6	161.0	156.2
Portugal	156.0	177.1	180.9	149.1	168.9	143.1
Finland	142.2	133.6	119.5	110.6	154.1	150.1
Denmark	188.2	296.0	262.5	236.7	223.4	218.7
Norway	111.9	112.6	90.9	172.6	109.0	100.0
India	336.7	307.0	260.4	287.0	242.5	298.2
Japan	519.2	535.0	484.3	464.6	511.2	455.8
U. S. A.	159.8	177.4	148.5	161.6	176.5	192.5
Canada	149.6	163.9	130.2	122.0	180.4	174.3
Mexico	179.8	177.4	185.7	237.1	268.1	220.0
Brazil	300.7	328.6	222.9	273.3	322.6	172.6
China**			406.1		525.5	558.2

* *International Federation of Master Cotton Spinners' and Manufacturers' Associations'* statistics quoted in the *Yearbook of the National Association of Cotton Manufacturers*, Boston, 1928, p. 78.

** Calculated by the present writer on the basis of data contained in *Supra*, p. 8. One bale of 500 lbs. is equivalent to 3.76 piculs.

The higher consumption of raw cotton per 1,000 spindles may be expressed in still other ways. As shown in Table 119, whereas in 1924 China possessed but 2.08% of the raw cotton spinning spindles in the world, the raw cotton consumption of these spindles amounted to 7.64% of the world's total. In 1926 almost the same proportion was maintained, the former being 2.10% and the latter 7.11%. In other words, China's percentage in the world's spindle consumption of raw cotton is three to four times her percentage in the world's raw cotton spinning spindles.

Table 119. Raw cotton spinning spindles and their consumption of raw cotton in China and the world compared, 1924-1926*

Year	China				World			
	Spindles		Cotton consumption		Spindles		Cotton consumption	
	No.	%	No.§	%	No.	%	No.§	%
1924	3,300	2.08	1,571	7.64	158,819	100.00	20,430	100.00
1925	3,350	2.08	1,610	6.91	161,363	100.00	23,294	100.00
1926	3,436	2.10	1,755	7.11	163,723	100.00	24,681	100.00

* League of Nations, *Memorandum on Cotton*, 1927, p. 7; Annex III.

§ In 1,000 running bales.

Table 120. Estimated number of looms in India, Japan, Great Britain and the United States, 1900-1926* (1913=100)

Year	China**	India	Japan	United States	Great Britain
1900	87	43	–	67	81
1905	87	53	34	83	85
1909	100	82	57	98	92
1910	100	88	73	–	92
1911	100	91	84	–	94
1912	100	95	90	–	98
1913	100	100	100	100	100
1920	181	127	209	–	98
1921	220	132	227	–	99
1922	252	143	251	–	99
1923	275	154	254	116	98
1924	311	161	265	–	98
1925	312	164	281	–	98
1926	312	–	–	–	95

* Source: *Encyclopaedia Britannica*, 14th edition, VI: 549.

** *Supra*, p. 8.

Since the outbreak of the World War in 1914 the number of cotton power looms in China, like that of cotton spinning spindles, has also increased at an amazing if not equally rapid rate. Taking China's cotton power looms in 1913, 9,389, as the base of 100, the index has increased to 312 in 1925, with 29,272 looms. Such a rapid rate of increase is unsurpassed by any other nation in the world, not excepting Japan and India. As shown in Table 120, the index for Japan has risen only to 281 in 1925, 164 in India, and 116 in the United States. For Great Britain, the index has instead shown a decline to 98 in 1925 and to 95 in 1926.

In spite of the rapid increase in the number of China's cotton power looms since 1914, the relative position of China's cotton power weaving industry in the world is even lower than that of her cotton power spinning industry. Whereas China claimed 2.1% of the world's total spindleage and 7.11% of the world's total spindle consumption of raw cotton in 1926, her share in the world's cotton power looms amounted to but 0.74% in 1927 (Fig. 50). In terms of cotton power looms per million population, China's rank is naturally the lowest. China, with only 54 looms per million population, compares most unfavorably with Great Britain having 16,746 looms per million population,—a figure which is 310 times larger than China's. Similarly, the number of looms per million population for other important cotton weaving nations exceeds China's by many times: U. S. with 6,097 looms, France with 4,438 looms, Germany with 3,900 looms, Italy with 3,614 looms, Russia with 1,719 looms, Japan with 1,209 looms, and finally, India with 458 looms. (Fig. 51)

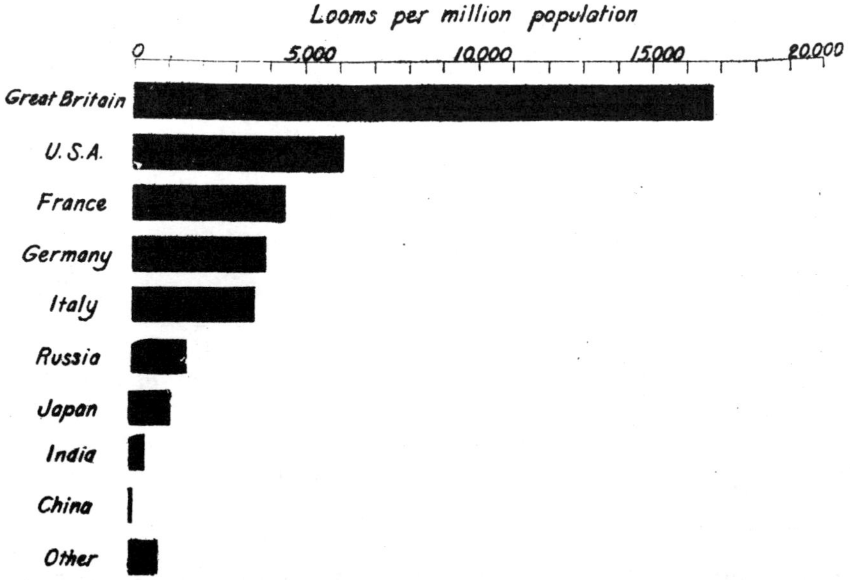

Fig. 51. Cotton power looms per 1,000,000 population in leading countries of the world, 1927 (*See* Table 121)

Table 121. Distribution of cotton power looms per million population in the world, 1927*

Country		No. of looms, 1927		Estimated population, 1929	Population per loom, 1927	Looms per million population
		No.	%	(000's omitted)		
Great Britain	1927	767,524	23.66	45,833	59.71	16,746.10
U. S. A.		745,520	22.99	122,285	164.03	6,096.58
Canada	1926	35,712	1.10	9,860	276.10	3,621.91
Germany	1927	250,000	7.71	64,104	256.42	3,899.91
Russia	1926	270,712	8.35	157,500	581.80	1,718.80
Poland	1927	42,561	1.31	30,737	722.19	1,384.68
Finland	1927	6,700	0.21	3,370	502.99	1,988.13
France	1927	182,800	5.64	41,190	225.33	4,437.97
Hungary	1927	9,800	0.29	8,640	881.63	1,134.26
Austria	1927	14,942	0.46	6,704	448.67	2,228.82
Czechoslovakia	1927	110,000	3.39	14,657	133.25	7,504.95
Switzerland	1927	27,057	0.83	4,060	150.05	6,664.29
Italy	1927	150,000	4.62	41,506	276.70	3,613.94
Spain	1927	71,000	2.19	22,761	320.58	3,119.37
Portugal	1927	22,000	0.68	5,809	264.05	3,787.23
Belgium	1927	54,000	1.66	8,060	149.26	6,699.75
Sweden	1927	16,000	0.49	6,120	382.50	2,614.38
Norway	1927	2,853	0.09	2,803	982.47	1,017.84
Denmark	1927	5,891	0.18	3,525	598.37	1,671.21
India	1926	159,464	4.92	348,000	2,182.31	458.23
China	1927	24,047	0.74	444,000	18,463.84	54.16
Japan	1927	77,043	2.38	63,740	827.33	1,208.71
Brazil	1927	75,631	2.33	40,273	532.49	1,877.96
Mexico	1927	31,296	0.96	16,350	522.43	1,914.13
Other		90,832	2.80	480,613	5,291.23	188.89
Total		3,243,385	100.00	1,992,500	614.33	1,627.80

* Data from *Comtelburo's Cotton Handbook*, quoted in *Yearbook of the National Association of the Cotton Manufacturers*, Boston, 1928, p. 179.

Factors affecting development

An examination of China's relative position in the world's cotton spinning and weaving industry in the preceding section reveals at once her immense possibilities for further development. Were China to equip her population with the same number of *spinning spindles* as India or Japan, she would have to increase her spindles in 1931, 3,905,000, by roughly 3 or 13 times respectively. Similarly, were China to equip her population with the same number of looms as India or Japan, she would have to increase her cotton power looms in 1927, 24,047, by roughly 9 or 22 times. The prospect for the immediate development of China's cotton manufacturing industry is indeed great, but the rate of its increase since

1925, as compared with that obtaining during the war and post-war period (from 1914 to 1925), is not all too rapid. Taking the number of spindles in China in 1913 as the base of 100, the index has increased to 340.79 in 1925 but 397.25 in 1931. The annual increase, which amounts to 20% from 1913 to 1925, is reduced to but 10% from 1925 to 1931. The renewal of competition from imported goods offers a partial explanation, but more fundamental factors that account for the retarded growth must be sought elsewhere. This is especially true with the Chinese owned mills.

Among the factors retarding the development of China's cotton industry, the most important is undoubtedly the chaotic political conditions that prevail today. The recurrence of civil war entails an inreasing burden of taxation, gives rise to the uncertainty of transport, reduces the area of cotton production, and shuts off the market within the war area. It interrupts with the normal operation, and saps the vitality of almost every industry. Capital, instead of being invested in profitable channels, is concentrated in a few port cities and deposited in the vaults of a few reliable banks, sometimes actually at a negative rate of interest. Under such circumstances, new mills can be erected only in a few exceptionally favored spots, while old ones are hard pressed from all sides by the increasing burden of taxation, the growing uncertainty of transport, the declining supply of raw cotton, the decreasing size of market, and above all, the higher rate of interest for the running capital.

Other factors, mainly economic, are more or less inherent in the transition of China from a medieval to a modern economic order. In such a transition, much can be drawn from the experience of the west; but a great deal will have to be acquired by the painful process of trial and error. In China's cotton industry, the largest factory industry today, the economic factors are at work everywhere. The textile machinery can be imported wholesale from foreign countries, but its efficient operation demands a managing and working staff which is impossible to train up overnight. The large scale organization on a share basis can be copied from the writings of the West, but its application as an instrument of prudent investment requires the necessary capitalistic traits which are as yet absent in the Chinese manufacturers. As a result, the native owned mills in China, unlike the foreign owned ones, have not proven to be profit-making enterprises except during the abnormal period of World War. The lack of capital, the corruption of management, and the inefficiency of labor,—all these become at once fundamental factors retarding the development of Chinese owned mills.

The lack of capital, applying chiefly to the Chinese owned mills, is the most important of the economic factors. A Chinese owned mill is handicapped at the very beginning by the insufficiency of capital. The mill, after having its plan for a certain size in respect of building and machinery made out on the basis of the subscribed capital and approved by the board of directors, starts to place orders with the building contractors and foreign importers of textile machinery. But before the arrival of machinery or the completion of building, it is confronted with the practical difficulty of having to collect the full share of the subscribed capital, because in cotton as in many other industries, the subscribed capital is seldom paid up to the full amount. This difficulty is enhanced by a second practice, that of heavy investment in fixed assets. In Tientsin, for instance, for three of the four mills studied the investment in fixed assets is so heavy as to exceed, in some cases, the paid-up capital. The explanation lies in the fact that when these mills were making huge profits, at a rate as high as 50 to fully 100 percent around 1920, they were rapidly acquiring new machinery. "The big sums of money they made during such golden times," according to a leading millowner in Shanghai who has himself been the victim of insufficient capital, "were used up in extending existing plants. Only a very small percentage was set aside for reserve. So when the hard time comes, their financial conditions are just as tight as ever, although their assets may be larger, i.e. they may have more spindles than before. But this fact, as can be readily seen, makes it still harder for them to finance". For the old mills, old in the sense of age, a further handicap is the failure to provide adequate reserve for depreciation. Generally speaking, the depreciation of machinery and buildings is thought of only after a dividend has been fixed and a surplus declared. No reserve for depreciation is usually provided for in losing years, while in profit-making years such a reserve is highly inadequate in amount—exceeding in no case the minimum requirement of five percent among three of the four mills studied in Tientsin. As a consequence, the total value of the fixed assets is cumulatively inflated above the market value, and an old mill is thus disabled to renew a part if not all of its machinery when out of repair or requiring replacement.

The lack of capital leads to another consequence. The lack of capital, stated the same millowner referred to above,

> puts most of the mills into such a position that they cannot buy their raw materials and sell their products most advantageously. Because of the tightness of money, mills in Shanghai usually purchase their cotton from and sell their yarn to brokers. It is not infrequent to find that a single bale of cotton may pass through several brokers, each reaping some profit, before it actually reaches the hands of the manufacturer.

On the other hand,

> If a mill has enough running capital at its disposal, purchasing agencies may be sent out to the different cotton growing centres to buy their own supply. Some mills have done so and have found it most profitable. Taking Chenchow (shipping point of Shensi cotton) as an instance, the experience with the writer is that on every picul of cotton bought at Chenchow, press packed

> there, and finally sent to Shanghai with all expenses paid, a saving of one to two taels can be easily made. Besides, there is always a difference of Tls. 2.00 in quality between the cotton bought in Chenchow and that purchased locally ,for when the cotton is pressed in Chenchow, a good percentage of short staple is mixed.

As much can be cited in the sale of cotton yarn. The above writer continues that,

> If a mill has enough capital and establishes distributing agencies in internal shipping points, such as Hankow, Chungking, Tientsin, etc., unquestionably a great saving can be attained. The difference in price of one bale of yarn between Shanghai and Hankow, it has been found out, is more than Tls. 15.00, while freignt, insurance and all kinds of charges amount to less than Tls. 5.00. Between Shanghai and Chengtu, chief city in the province of Szechuen, the difference drifts still further apart.

Poor management is another economic factor retarding the development of China's cotton industry. The whole system of management among Chinese owned mills is usually polluted by ignorance, facoritism and squeeze. In particular, the mills established by inexperienced men who were attracted solely by the magnetism of huge profits during the war period are utterly inefficient. The whole plant, worth millions of dollars, may be entrusted to a manager who knows nothing about spinning. The latter, usually the trusted appointee of the most influential stockholder, has frequently neither a grasp of the technical complexity of spinning and weaving, nor a knowledge of cost accounting, financing and marketing. Instead, he delegates his duties to the subordinates, and relies upon the good turn of luck for the mill's profits. In such a mill, the head of the spinning or weaving department, oftentimes a close friend or relative of the manager or the stockholder, considers his job as the source of squeeze, but delegates in turn his duties to one of the foremen, who, although skilled in mechanics, lacks scientific training. Consequently, machinery is not well kept, and is not running in an efficient order. Laborers are not well selected and trained, but recruited under the notorious contract system. The finished products deteriorate in quality, while their cost mounts higher and higher. In time of short supply like during the war, profits are easily made, and these decifiencies ignored. But once 'normalcy' returns with the end of the war, these mills are immediately confronted with foreign competitors who have not only a superior command of capital and technique, but also a better marketing organization.

Labor inefficiency constitutes a third economic factor retarding the rapid development of Chinese mills. In the past too much has been written on the cheapness of Chinese labor because of wretchedly low wages. But labor is not cheap because wages are low. On the contrary, low wages in China are partly if not wholly responsible for the high cost of labor. That this is the case can be confirmed by a comparison of labor efficiency in Japanese owned mills paying relatively higher wages and Chinese owned mills paying relatively lower wages. The annual yarn output per worker in Chinese owned mills, 9.85 bales, is lower than that in Japanese owned mills, 11.95 bales, by 21.3%. Similarly, the annual cloth output per worker in Chinese owned mills, 261.73 pieces, is lower than that in Japanese owned mills, 786.38 pieces, by 200.4%. The vastly greater quantity of cloth output per worker in Japanese owned mills may be attributed, in addition to the difference in wage level, to the employment of automatic looms.

The labor efficiency in China, as compared with that in Japan, stands at a low ebb. The number of operatives employed per 1,000 spindles in all mills in China, 52, is almost three times that in Japan, 18.6. The former, however, is lower for Japanese owned mills, 42, but higher for Chinese owned mills, 62. The comparison is less unfavorable to the mills in China in respect of looms, due perhaps to the weaving of finer cloth in Japan. The number of operatives employed per 100 looms in all mills in China, 137, is about two times that in Japan, 62.2 The former is again lower for the Japanese owned mills in China, 91, but higher for the Chinese owned mills, 172.[2]

The factors mentioned above, both political and economic, are responsible for the retarded development of China's cotton industry under circumstances which, otherwise, would have been considered as highly favorable. The Chinese owned mills are heavy sufferers from the political factor, while the foreign owned mills, partly immune from the political factor, are almost wholly free from the economic. The former, therefore, are placed under a twofold competition, one from the imported goods and the other from the native products manufactured under foreign supervision and control. The removal of the political factor, which can be realized only with the cessation of recurrent civil strife, may hasten to improve the economic factors such as the lack of capital, the corruption of management, and the inefficiency of labor. But with the prospect for civil war still luring, the cotton mills in China, especially the native owned, will always be in a precarious position, although the recent rapid rise of gold, almost doubling the cost for most of the imported goods in terms of silver, may promise some relief by the substitution of the native for the foreign cotton goods.

2. For the Japanese figures, referring to those in 1925, see *Encyclopaedia Brittania*, 14th edition, VI: 569; for the Chinese figures, see *Supra*, p. 94.

Bibliography

CONTENT

Bibliography

I. In foreign languages*

A. Books and pamphlets

Anderson, George E.: *Cotton Goods Trade in China,* U.S. Bureau of Manufactures, Department of Commerce and Labor, Washington, 1911, 32pp.

*Bank of China, Research Department: *Statistics of China's Foreign Trade 1912-1930,* Shanghai, Bank of China, 1931, 133pp.

Tabulates import and export statistics on raw cotton and cotton yarn for the period covered, with graphs; and incorporates China's import tariffs of 1843, 1858, 1902, 1918, 1922, 1928, 1930 and export tariffs of 1843, 1858 and 1931.

Blackburn Chamber of Commerce: *Report of the Mission to China, 1896-97,* Blackburn, 1898, F.S.A. Bourne's Section, 152pp.; H. Neville and H. Bell's Section, 386pp.

Blanco, A. E.: *Piece Goods Manual,* Shanghai, Statistical Department of the Inspectorate General of Customs, 1917, 181pp.

British Economic Mission to the Far East, 1930-31: *Report of the Cotton Mission,* London, Stationery Office, 1931, 96pp.

*Chen, Ta: *Study of the Applicability of the Factory Act of the Chinese Government,* Institute of Scientific Management, Shanghai, 1931, 91pp.

Among the 228 factories surveyed there are 49 cotton spinning and 13 cloth weaving mills.

China. Maritime Customs:

Piece goods duty index, Second edition revised, Shanghai, 1929, 116pp.
Handbook of Customs Procedure in Shanghai, 1926.

*Chu, T. S. & Chin, T.: *Marketing of Cotton in Hopei Province,* Institute of Social Research, Bulletin III, Peiping, 1929, 54pp.

Decker, H. W.: Industrial Hospital, a Review of 880 Cases from the Cotton Mills, Reprint from the *China Medical Journal,* March, 1924.

Ellinger, Barnard: *Lancashire's declining trade with China: causes and remedies,* Manchester Statistical Society, Manchester, 1927, 55pp.

Fang, Fu-an: *Chinese labor, an economic and statistical survey,* Shanghai, Kelly and Walsh, 1931, 185pp.

Contains useful secondary statistics on cotton labor and English versions of various labor laws recently promulgated.

*An asterick preceding each reference indicates that Chinese notation or version is also given or available, in the same volume or separately.

Fong, H. D.: New cotton futures market in China, Reprint from the *China Weekly Review*, Sep. 29, 1928.

*Fong, H. D.: *Rayon and cotton weaving in Tientsin*, Nankai University Committee on Social and Economic Research, Industries series No. 2, Tientsin, 1930, 79pp.

Great Britain Foreign Office: *Hankow native cotton manufacture*, London, 1886.

Griffing, J. B.: *Report of three years' cotton improvement work*, Nanking, 1923.

*Ho, Franklin L.: *Wholesale prices and price index numbers in North China, 1913-1929*, Nankai University Committee on Social and Economic Research, Tientsin, 1929, 145pp.

Contains price quotations for raw cotton, cotton yarn and piece goods from pages 70 to 86.

Jamieson, James William: *Report on the cotton mills of China*, London, Harrison and Sons, 1905.

King, Miss S. T. & Lieu, D. K.: *China's cotton industry, a statistical study of ownership of capital, output and labor conditions*, Shanghai, 1929, 51pp. Also reprinted in Condliffe, J. B. (ed.): *Problems of the Pacific 1929*, Chicago University Press, 1930, pp. 262-299.

League of Nations, Economic and Financial Section: *Memorandum on cotton*, Geneva, 1927, 78pp.

Lyon, Chambre de Commerce de: *La Mission Lyonnaise de'Exploration Commerciale en Chine, 1895-1897*, Lyon, 1898, xxxvi, 386, 473pp.

Contains *Rapport sur le cotton et les cotonnades*, par MM. Riault, A. Waeles et A. Vial, in Part II, pp. 349-74.

Morse, H. B.: *The Chronicles of the East India Company Trading to China, 1635-1834*, Oxford, Clarendon Press, Vols, I, II, III & IV, 1926; Vol. V, 1929.

Contains original data on the early cotton trade between China and foreign nations, with interesting descriptive references.

Moser, Charles K.: *The Cotton Textile Industry of the Far Eastern Countries*, Pepperell Manufacturing Company, Boston, 1930, 144pp.

Has a section on China, pp. 65-96.

North-China Daily News and Herald: *Cotton cultivation in China and something about the spinning and weaving mills*, Shanghai, 1917, 55pp.

A short summary of this work may be found in *Appendix E* to *The New Atlas and Commercial Gazatteer of China*, edited by Edwin G. Dingle and published by the Far Eastern Georgraphical Establishment, Shanghai, 2nd ed., 1918 (?)

Odell, Ralph M.: *Cotton Goods in China*, U.S. Bureau of Foreign and Domestic Commerce, Special Agents Series No. 107, Washington, 1916, 241pp.

Orchard, John E.: *Japan's Economic Position,* New York, McGraw-Hill, 1930, xvi, 504pp.

Chapter XXIV analyses the effects of Anti-Japanese boycotts on Japan's export trade to China, especially cotton goods.

Pearse, Arno S.: *The Cotton Industry of Japan and China, being the Report of the Journey to Japan and China,* Feb.-April, 1929, Manchester, 222pp.

The section on China covers pages 153 to 222.

*Sheng, T.: *The cost of living index number of Shanghai,* Shanghai, National Tariff Commission, Statistical Series No. 4, 1930, 28pp.

The index is based upon a family budget inquiry of 230 cotton mill workers' families in Jessfield Village, Shanghai.

Shanghai Bureau of Social Affairs:

**Report on wages and hours of labor in Greater Shanghai, 1929,* Shanghai, 1930.

**Annual Report on Labor Strikes in Greater Shanghai, 1928,* Shanghai, 1929. The subsequent two reports for 1929 and 1930 are published under the new title *Strikes and lockouts in Greater Shanghai.*

Utley, Freda: *Lancashire and the Far East,* London, George Allen and Unwin, 1931, 395pp.

Chapter IX deals with "Chinese market and Chinese production", pp. 230-249.

*Yang, C. and others: *Statistics of China's foreign trade during the last sixty-five years,* National Research Institute of Social Sciences, Academia Sinica, Shanghai, 1931, xiv, 189pp.

Contains statistics on import and export of raw cotton and cotton yarn from 1868 to 1928.

*Yang, Simon: *A study of the standard of living of working families in Shanghai,* Institute of Social Research, Peiping, 1931, 86, lviipp.

A family budget study of 230 cotton mill workers in Jessfield village.

B. Periodicals and annuals

China. Maritime Customs:

**Report and Abstract of Statistics,* 1867-date (Annual).

**Analysis of foreign trade of China (Import and Export),* 1905 to date (Annual).

Monthly Returns of the Foreign Trade of China, December, 1931 to date.

**Shanghai Monthly Returns of Foreign Trade*, January, 1932 to date.

**Tientsin Monthly Returns of Foreign Trade*, March, 1932 to date.

China Weekly Review (Formerly *Millard's Review*), 1915 to date, Shanghai.

Chinese Economic Bulletin (Weekly), 1921-date, Bureau of Foreign Trade, Ministry of Industries, Shanghai (Formerly Chinese Government Bureau of Economic Information, Peking; Bureau of Industrial and Commercial Information, Shanghai).

Chinese Economic Journal (Formerly *Chinese Economic Monthly*), 1923-date, Bureau of Foreign Trade, Ministry of Industries, Shanghai.

Commerce Reports (Weekly), U. S. Bureau of Foreign and Domestic Commerce, Washington.

Cotton Facts (Annual), New York, Shepperson Publishing Co.

International Cotton Bulletin (Quarterly), International Federation of Master Cotton Spinners' and Manufacturers' Association, Manchester.

League of Nations Statistical Yearbook, League of Nations, Geneva.

Nankai Weekly Statistical Service, 1928 to date, Tientsin, Nankai Institute of Economics.

National Tariff Commission (Formerly Shanghai Bureau of Markets):

**Shanghai Market Prices Report* (Quarterly), 1923-date.

**Monthly Report of Prices and Price Indexes in Shanghai*, 1925-date.

II. In Chinese and Japanese languages

A. Books and pamphlets

Chen, T. C.: *A proposal for the classification of Tientsin cotton*, Tientsin Bureau for Testing and Inspection of Commercial Commodities, Ministry of Industries, Tientsin, 1930, 50pp.

陳天敬：擬定天津棉花品質檢驗意見書，工商部天津商品檢驗局，民一九

Ch'ien, Kwan I: *Outline of China's Cotton Spinning and Weaving Industry*, Shanghai, 1930, 8pp.

錢貫一：中國棉紡織工業全誌(目錄初稿)，上海，民一九

China Textile Institute: *Bye-laws*, Shanghai, 1931, 21pp.

中國紡織學會章程，上海，民二〇

Chinese Cotton Goods Exchange **上海華商紗布交易所：**

Constitution, Shanghai, 1924, 10pp.

上海華商紗布交易所股份有限公司章程

Bye-laws and Regulations, Shanghai, 1925, 58pp.

上海華商紗布交易所股份有限公司營業細則

Brokers' Association: Bye-laws and Regulations, Shanghai, 12pp.

上海華商紗布交易所股份有限公司經紀人公會規約

Chinese Cotton Millowners' Association 華商紗廠聯合會：

Complete List of Cotton Mills in China for 1920, 1921, 1922, 1923, 1924, 1925, 1927, 1928, 1930, Shanghai.

中國紗廠一覽表，民九，十，十一，十二，十三，十四，十六，十七，十九

Handbook of the Trade-marks of Chinese Cotton Yarn and Cloth, Shanghai, 1928, 9pp.

中國紗布商標一覽，民一七

List of the Trade-marks of Chinese Cotton Yarn and Cloth, 1931, Shanghai.

中國紗廠紗布商標一覽表，上海，民二〇

Feng, Tzu Hsin: *Chinese Cotton*, Shanghai, Peihsin Book Company, 1929, 193pp.

馮次行：中國棉業論，上海，北新，民一八

Hamata, Hotaro: The Textile Industry in China, Shanghai, 1923.

濱田峯太郎：支那ニ於ケル紡織業，上海，日本堂書店，大正十二

Imura, Kunyo: *Chinese cotton textile industry and products* tr. into Chinese by Chow Pei Lan, Shanghai, Commercial Press, 1928, 319pp.

井村薰雄：中國之紡織業及其出品（周培蘭譯），上海，商務，民一七

Kasamoto, Ryomei: *China's cotton industry*, Tokyo, East Asia Economic Investigation Bureau, 1920, 69, 31pp.

笠本良明：生產機關の發達より觀たる支那綿業，經濟資料第十五卷第三號，東亞經濟調查局，昭和四

Kiangsu Cotton Experiment Station 江蘇省立棉作試驗場：

A brief survey, Nantung, 1930, 36pp.

江蘇省立棉作試驗場一覽，南通，民一九

Report of the breaking strength and spinning test of the Chicken-Foot cotton, Nantung, 1930, 28pp.

改良鷄脚棉成紗强力試驗報告，南通，民一九

Kiangsu Industrial Bureau: *The cotton spinning and weaving industry of Kiangsu,* Shanghai, Commercial Press, 1920, 89, 94pp.
江蘇實業廳第三科：江蘇省紡織業狀況，上海，商務，民九

Kuo, Tan Sien: *Cotton Culture,* Shanghai, Commercial Press, 1928, 79, 5pp.
過探先：種棉法，上海，商務，民一八

Matsushima, Kan: *Manchuria cotton* (in Japanese), revised edition, South Manchuria Railway, Dairen, 1929, 199pp.
松島鑑：滿洲の棉花，產業資料其十九，南滿洲鐵道株式會社興業部農務課，大連，昭和三，再版

Ministry of Industries: *A National Survey of the Workers' Livelihood and Industrial Production,* Bulletin Nos. 1,2,3,4, Nanking, 1930.
工商部：全國工人生活及工業生產調查統計報告書，第一至四號，民一九

Ojima, Joji: *Marketing of Tientsin Cotton,* Tientsin, 1931, 278pp.
大島讓次：天津棉花と物資集散事情，天津，昭和五

Shanghai Bureau for Testing and Inspection of Commercial Commodities, Ministry of Industries: *Cotton Production in China,* Shanghai, 1930, 77pp.
工商部上海商品檢驗局：中國棉產狀況，叢刊第二期，民一九

Shanghai Bureau of Social Affairs: *Shanghai Industries,* Shanghai, Chung Hua Book Company, 1930.
上海特別市社會局：上海工業，上海，中華，民一九

Shanghai Commercial and Savings Bank, Research Department: *Cotton,* in Commodity Series No. 2, Shanghai, 1931, 184pp.
上海商業儲蓄銀行調查部：棉，商品調查叢刊第二編，上海，民二〇

Woo, C. L.: *Modern Chinese Industries,* 2 vols., Shanghai, Commercial Press, 1929.
吳承洛：今世中國實業通志，上下册，上海，商務，民一八

Yang, Yin P'u: *Stock and produce exchange in China,* Shanghai, Commercial Press, 1930.
楊蔭溥：中國交易所論，上海，商務，民一九

B. Periodicals and annuals

Bankers' Weekly, 1917-date, Shanghai.
銀 行 週 報，上 海 銀 行 週 報 社

China Cotton Journal (Quarterly up to 1931, Semi-annual since 1932), October 1919 to date, Shanghai, Chinese Cotton Millowners' Association.

華商紗廠聯合會季刊，上海

China Textile Institute Annual, 1931, Shanghai, China Textile Institute.

紡織年刊，紡織學會，上海

China Weekly Economic Bulletin, 1923-1927, Peking, Chinese Government Bureau of Economic Information (Now Bureau of Foreign Trade, Ministry of Industries).

中外經濟週刊，經濟討論處，北京

Economic Weekly, Nos. 1-52, Mar. 3, 1930 to Feb. 23, 1931, published in *Ta Kung Pao*, Tientsin, for the Nankai University Committee on Social and Economic Research, Tientsin.

大公報經濟研究週刊，一至五十二期，民一九，三，三至二〇，二，二三，天津南開大學社會經濟研究委員會編

Foreign Trade Guide, April, 1930 to date, Shanghai, Bureau for Testing and Inspection of Commercial Commodities, Ministry of Industries.

國際貿易導報，實業部上海商品檢驗局

Human Arts, February, 1930 to date, Shanghai

This is the only current magazine in China which contains a comprehensive "Guide to Periodical Literature".

人文：最近雜誌要目索引，人文編輯所，上海

Journal of National Commerce, (formerly *Journal of the General Chamber of Commerce of Shanghai*) (Monthly) July 1921 to date, Shanghai, General Chamber of Commerce of Shanghai (Chinese).

商業月報（前上海總商會月報），上海總商會

Journal of the Ministry of Agriculture and Commerce (Monthly), 1914-1924, Peking.

農商公報，農商部，北京

Semi-monthly Economic Journal, November 1, 1927 to date, Shanghai, Bureau of Foreign Trade, Ministry of Industries.

工商半月刊（前經濟半月刊），實業部國際貿易局，上海

Social Monthly, July, 1929 to date, Shanghai, Bureau of Social Affairs, City Government of Greater Shanghai.

社會月刊（上海），上海特別市社會局

Statistical Annual of the Ministry of Agriculture and Commerce, 1912-1921, Peking.

中國農商統計，農商部，北京

Statistics of Cotton Production in China, 1918 to date, an annual booklet by the Chinese Cotton Millowners' Association, Shanghai.

中國棉產統計，華商紗廠聯合會，上海

Textile Industry, April, 1931, Nantung, Nantung Textile Institute.

紡織之友，南通學院紡織科學友會

Textile News (Weekly), April, 1923 to date, Shanghai, Chinese Cotton Millowners' Association.

紡織時報，華商紗廠聯合會，上海

Textile Weekly, April 17, 1931 to date, Shanghai, Textile Weekly Society.

紡織週刊，紡織週刊社，上海

Tientsin Cotton (Monthly), June 1930 to date, Tientsin Bureau for Testing and Inspection of Commercial Commodities, Ministry of Industries.

天津棉鑑，實業部天津商品檢驗局

Tientsin Trade Annual (in Japanese), Japanese Chamber of Commerce, Tientsin.

天津貿易年報，天津日本人商業會議所

Index

ERRATA

Page	Paragraph	Line or 1st word in line	Table	Column	Footnote	Error	Correction
3	1	2				1967	1867
11	2	18				Table 2 Table 3	Table 3 Table 2
16		Honan	5a	4		95,240	85,240
16		Wuchih	5a	10		2,800[26]	2,880[26]
16			5a	13		Kiangsu 107,120 Shanghai 30,000 Wusih 107,120 Tungtsunghai 30,000	Kiangsu 107,102 30,000* Shanghai 107,120 Wusih 30,000*
18	2	5				Shanghai - Hankow - Ningpo	Shanghai - Hangchow - Ningpo
23	2	15				southern region	central region
26		1923-4	6a	7		931	231
42		1874	11a	7		—738,269	+738,269
42		1897	11a	7		+5,132,265	+5,133,265
42		1901	11a	4		+37,010	+36,010
42		1911	11a	2		39,171	39,676
48		Other countries	13	8		1,002,966	1,003,222
48		Total	13	8		16,867,011	16,867,267
52	2	1				exporter procedure	export procedure
67	3	1				Shanghai	Chinese
76		Nov.	15			40.45	40.91
80		1895	17	11		21.89	22.89
81	1	7				69 cents	62 cents
84		1930	18	7		14,033,224	14,038,224
86		1917	19	2		75.81	75.00
86		1919	19	3		9.93	9.63
88			20	14-6		.63 7.75	.64 7.86 37.21 8.72 25.00 25.00 — — 10.46 18.61
106		1930	27	3-4		114.3 –7.1	115.1 –6.0
106		Jan.	27	4,7		–0.6 –2.1	–7.7 –8.1
113		Other	32	2			11,501
118	1	1				height	weight
123		Average	37	4		90.05	91.05
141	4	2				Sunday afternoon	Sunday
147		Hangchow	50b	5		64.20	89.68
154	1	18				workness	workers
175	2	12				other districts	other cotton districts
193		Spindle	77	11		116	119
210		Total		4	10	172,820,277	172,920,277
227	2	9				0.86..0.62..0.52	0.93..0.70..0.60
236	3	18				Kiangsui	Kiangsi
244	1	20				amount	account
247	1	1				Tientsin	Foochow
249		1905	101	12-3		2,969,835 2.55	4,969,835 4.26
273		1811	108a	2		292,200	295,200
273		1821	108a	2		147,999	147,000
296	3	15-16				47.1 cents .. 31.4 cents	51.9 cents .. 25.0 cents
298	3	11				minimum	maximum
310		Other	116	9		20,253	20,523
312		Other	117	4-5		473,050 277.93	472,780 277.77

Afterword

This book's original English version published in 1932 contains two volumes. Because the main idea of the book has been fully expressed in volume one, this book only includes volume one.

Editorial Department of the Commercial Press
April 2014

图书在版编目(CIP)数据

中国之棉纺织业＝Cotton industry and trade in China:英文/方显廷著. —北京:商务印书馆,2014
(中华现代学术名著丛书. 英文本)
ISBN 978-7-100-08958-6

Ⅰ. ①中… Ⅱ. ①方… Ⅲ. ①棉纺织工业—研究—中国—民国—英文 Ⅳ. ①F426.81

中国版本图书馆 CIP 数据核字(2014)第 058816 号

中华现代学术名著丛书
中国之棉纺织业
(英文本)
方显廷 著

商 务 印 书 馆 出 版
(北京王府井大街36号 邮政编码 100710)
商 务 印 书 馆 发 行
北 京 瑞 古 冠 中 印 刷 厂 印 刷
ISBN 978-7-100-08958-6

2014 年 7 月第 1 版　　开本 700×1000 1/16
2014 年 7 月北京第 1 次印刷　　印张 23¼ 插页 6
定价: 79.00 元